Economic Imperialism

Economic Imperialism

A Book of Readings

edited by
Kenneth E. Boulding
and
Tapan Mukerjee

Ann Arbor
The University of Michigan Press

Copyright © by The University of Michigan 1972
All rights reserved
ISBN 0–472–16830–4 (clothbound)
ISBN 0–472–08170–5 (paperbound)
Library of Congress Catalog Card No. 74–146490
Published in the United States of America by
The University of Michigan Press and simultaneously
in Don Mills, Canada, by Longman Canada Limited
Manufactured in the United States of America

Acknowledgments

Grateful acknowledgment is made to the following individuals and publishers for kind permission to reprint materials:

George Allen & Unwin Ltd. for "The Economic Taproot of Imperialism," from *Imperialism* by J. A. Hobson. Reprinted by permission of the publishers.

The Macmillan Company for "Dynamics of Imperialism." Reprinted with permission of The Macmillan Company from *Imperialism and World Politics* by Parker T. Moon. Copyright 1926 by The Macmillan Company.

Harvard University Press for "On Imperialism." Excerpted by permission of the President and Fellows of Harvard College from pp. 3-8, 83-96 of Joseph A. Schumpeter, *Imperialism and Social Classes*, New York: Augustus M. Kelley, Inc. Copyright 1951 by Elizabeth Boody Schumpeter.

The Economic History Review and Mrs. Gertrude Koebner for "The Concept of Economic Imperialism," by Richard Koebner. Reprinted by permission of the publisher and Mrs. Gertrude Koebner from *The Economic History Review*, Vol. II, No. 2, 1949.

The Economic History Review for "'Imperialism': An Historiographical Revision," by D. K. Fieldhouse. Reprinted by permission of the author and publisher from *The Economic History Review*, Vol. XIV, No. 2, 1961.

The Journal of Economic History for "Some Thoughts on the Nature of Economic Imperialism," by David S. Landes. Reprinted by permission of the author and publisher from *The Journal of Economic History*, Vol. XXI, No. 4, 1961.

Yale University Press for "Economic Imperialism Revisited," by Mark Blaug. Reprinted by permission of the author and publisher from *The Yale Review*, Vol. 50, March 1961. Copyright 1961 by Yale University Press.

Monthly Review Inc. for "Notes on the Theory of Imperialism," by Paul A. Baran and Paul M. Sweezy. Reprinted by permission of Monthly Review Inc. from *Monthly Review*, Vol. 17, No. 10, March 1966. Copyright © 1966 by Monthly Review Inc.

The Journal of Economic History for "A Quantitative Approach to the Study of the Effects of British Imperial Policy upon Colonial Welfare: Some Preliminary Findings," by Robert Paul Thomas. Reprinted by permission of the author and publisher from *The Journal of Economic History*, Vol. XXV, No. 4, 1965.

Princeton University Press for "The Dilemma of Rising Demands and Insufficient Resources," by Harold and Margaret Sprout from *World Politics*, Vol. XX, No. 4. Copyright © 1968 by Princeton University Press. Reprinted by permission of Princeton University Press.

The Peace Research Society (Int'l) for "War as an Investment: The Strange Case of Japan," by Kenneth E. Boulding and Alan H. Gleason. Reprinted by permission of the authors from *Peace Research Society (Int'l) Papers*, Vol. III, 1965.

Chatham College for "Russian Imperialism Today," by Thomas P. Whitney. Reprinted by permission of the author and Chatham College from *The Legacy of Imperialism*, Essays by Barbara Ward, Thomas P. Whitney, Robert Strausz-Hupé, and Charles Malik. Pittsburgh: 1960.

The Institute of Economics and Statistics, Oxford University, for "The Mechanism of Neo-Imperialism: The Economic Impact of Monetary and Commercial Institutions in Africa," by Thomas Balogh. Reprinted by permission of the author and publisher from *Bulletin, Institute of Economics and Statistics*, Vol. 24, No. 3, August 1962.

Richard D. Irwin, Inc. for "Burdens and Benefits of Empire: American Style," by Martin Bronfenbrenner. Reprinted by permission of the author and publisher from *Empire Revisited*, edited by Leland Hazard. Homewood, Illinois: 1965.

We would like to thank Mrs. Vivian Wilson for her invaluable assistance throughout the preparation of this manuscript. Without her help it would have been almost impossible to complete this volume.

TAPAN MUKERJEE
KENNETH E. BOULDING

Contents

Introduction

Kenneth E. Boulding

The word "imperialism" is one of those linguistic casualties which has been drained of much of its intellectual content by its use as an arouser of emotion in propaganda battles. Economic imperialism, by which we presumably mean that aspect of imperialism which is particularly concerned with the production, consumption, and transfer of exchangeables, has been even more drained of content by the intense emotions associated with socialist criticism and the cold war. It is an enterprise verging on rashness therefore to try to put together a collection of writings on the economics of imperialism which will bring together in convenient form the literature of controversy as well as some attempt to achieve an intellectual resolution. Still, no matter how muddied the waters, the literature of the economics of imperialism is an important stream of thought and refers to a significant subset of the total social system. It is a stream, however, with a large amount of inaccessible watershed. The main purpose of this volume is to increase its accessibility and to show the reader perhaps that the many diverse tributaries do in fact converge towards a single stream of thought.

A volume of this sort is inevitably a sample—actually a very small sample—of the total amount of worthwhile literature. We have excluded a number of contributions to the subject on the sole grounds that they are easily accessible. Of these, the most important omission is undoubtedly Adam Smith's great discussion of colonies in *The Wealth of Nations* (Book IV, Chapter 7) which should be read by every serious student of the subject.[1] No modern work begins to approach Adam Smith in depth of insight, and reading him is both delightful in itself and depressing, because one realizes not only that this is a very ancient problem, but also that not very much has been contributed towards its understanding in the last two hundred years.

In this brief introduction we cannot do more than outline the questions which any inquiry into the subject must try to answer. The first is what are the useful boundaries and subdivisions of

[1] Adam Smith, *The Wealth of Nations,* New York: Random House, Modern Library Edition, pp. 523-606.

the concept. A word like "imperialism," which can be used to describe almost anything which the author does not like, tends also to become imperialistic and to claim areas of the social system far beyond its original meaning. This is easy to do in so far as the intellectual domain which we are considering does not have clear natural boundaries, but is surrounded by a large penumbra of related phenomena. If we ask ourselves therefore, "Is the relationship between A and B imperialistic or not?" we have to look for a number of different elements in the relationship. In the first place the imperial relationship is between groups rather than between individuals. The problem of what groups are affected by this relationship is indeed an important but largely unacknowledged source of the long-continuing dispute. In the second place, the relationship implies inequality of status, the imperialist, of course, having the higher or more dominant status, and the subject the lower or dominated status. This inequality of status usually arises out of the exercise of superior threat. It is indeed an example of what I have elsewhere called a "threat-submission" system.

Threat, however, in the imperial relationship must be legitimated and regularized in some way and hence must be made part of a political system. We do not generally regard the bandit or the Mafia as imperialist, even though they exercise threat and may exact tribute. Imperialism is related to the degree of legitimation of the dominance relationship. Thus, the dominance which a capital city and a political elite exert over the provinces of a single country is not usually regarded as imperialistic because of the high degree of legitimacy which the relationship draws from the fact that the people of a single country regard themselves as part of a single integrative system. But wherever one group within a political unit denies legitimacy to the relationship then the word imperialist probably applies. Thus, W. S. Gilbert refers to "that glorious country called Great Britain—to which some add—and others do not—Ireland."[2] It should be observed that it is legitimacy and not legality which really defines the relationship. Even after the union of Parliaments the relationship between Great Britain and Ireland could only be described as imperialistic. Likewise, the relationship between France and Algeria, in spite of a similar union, also became defined by the parties as imperialistic, and the relationship between Portugal and its overseas colonies is defined by most people outside the Portuguese elite as imperialistic, in spite of Portugal's assertion that

[2]W. S. Gilbert, *Utopia, Limited.*

they are all one single uniform country. It may actually be easier
to legitimate an imperialist relationship when it is acknowledged and
organized quite frankly, as was frequently the case in the nineteenth-
century British Empire, outside of Ireland.

In all cases, however, there seems to be an almost irresistible
tendency for the legitimacy of an imperial relationship to be eroded,
though the reasons for this are not always clear. This loss of legitimacy
can come on both sides—from a "loss of nerve" on the part of the
imperial power which comes to feel that its dominance is no longer
justifiable, and also from a loss of submission on the part of the
subjects, who come to refuse to acknowledge the legitimacy of an
inferior status.

The economic aspects of imperialism relate to inputs, outputs,
and transfers of goods, "good" being defined simply as anything which
somebody wants. Goods therefore include what are usually known
as services. Transfers of goods are of two kinds, one-way transfers
which constitute what is coming to be called the "grants economy,"
and two-way transfers, that is, exchange, in which A transfers goods
of some sort to B and B transfers other kinds of goods to A. Goods
here include not only such things as food, clothing, furniture, houses,
domestic animals, slaves, labor, and so on, but as society develops,
include such things as money, securities, contracts of all sorts and
so on.

In what might be called "classical imperialism" the one-way
transfer predominates, creating what John Hicks has termed a "revenue economy."[3] The transfer of goods here is tribute as a result
of a threat system, the threatener saying to the threatened, "You
give me things that I want or I will do things to you that you don't
want." This often turns out to be a system of considerable stability,
for with the goods which the threatener receives he can organize
his threat capability and therefore his threat credibility. For this
system to be possible, of course, there must be some kind of surplus
of goods from the producer, but this is usually the almost automatic
result of the development of agriculture. Indeed, this is why agriculture
seems to produce empire with an almost unfailing regularity. We
should perhaps reserve the word empire for cases in which the
subjects differ from the rulers in race, culture, language, or other
significant characteristics. The phenomenon, however, is not very
different even when the rulers and the ruled are of the same speech
and culture, for even if they start off in this way, class differentiation

[3]John Hicks, *A Theory of Economic History*. New York: Clarendon Press,
1969.

soon insures that the rulers are imperial, at least in the sense that they have superior status to the ruled.

The development of exchange as a social organizer—that is, of the market—introduces a very different set of relationships from that of the tribute or revenue economy. Even so, the revenue economy does permit a good deal of division of labor, as the kings, for instance, use the food which they extract from the food producer in order to feed artisans, builders, potters, and other craftsmen who make specialized goods for the need of the ruling class. Exchange, however, is a very different kind of relationship from tribute. As economists have continually pointed out, in uncoerced exchange both parties benefit or the exchange will not take place. The trader is a very different sort of person from the soldier. He persuades and entreats rather than threatens, even though a legitimate threat system in the case of the legal enforcement of contracts may be necessary for any very elaborate system of exchange to develop. Indeed, exchange in its pure form is almost the antithesis of imperialism. It implies equality of status rather than inequality, for if A gives B something and B gives A something, they both stand at that moment on an equal footing. Where there is inequality of status, exchange must frequently be legitimated by what might almost be called a "ritual of inequality." The unctuous servility, for instance, of the merchant or the shop keeper in the face of the king or aristocrat serves only to disguise and to make palatable the fundamental equality of the relationship. It is not surprising therefore that as exchange develops as a social organizer and begins to replace the threat system and the economics of tribute, it tends to destroy the legitimacy of inequality and to foster political institutions, such as political democracy, which are based on the myth of political equality.

Industrialization, in the sense of the development of highly productive nonagricultural specializations, extends the boundaries of the market and still further undermines the tribute economy of classical imperialism. A city like Birmingham, Manchester, or Chicago is very different from the cities of classical imperialism such as Babylon, Rome, or even Venice. These manufacturing cities gain their inputs of food not by establishing a politicized threat system which exacts food as tribute from the farmer, but by producing something in the way of manufactured articles which the farmer wants and which he is willing to exchange freely for food. It is the cloth of Manchester, the metal goods of Birmingham, and the innumerable diverse manufactures of Chicago, not a political power based on armies, which enables these cities to feed themselves. It is striking in the modern world that what might be called "pure political cities," like Washington and many of the state capitals—Springfield, Illinois; Salem, Oregon; Jefferson City, Missouri—and national capitals such as Ottawa, Canberra, even Bonn, tend to be relatively small cities, quite overshadowed by the great commercial and manufacturing centers over which they supposedly rule. Even the old political capitals, like London and Paris, have had to transform themselves into centers for the production of goods and services in order to maintain their viability. Even in London the political and imperial city of Westminster is quite overshadowed by the service-providing City of London and the manufacturing suburbs. It is only as the state in the twentieth century has returned to something like a tribute economy in the interest of social justice, that is, the welfare state, that the capital city has once again begun to grow at the expense of the manufacturing and commercial centers.

The plain historic fact for which there is now an abundance of evidence, both documentary and statistical, is that with the coming of industrialization empire in the classical sense simply ceased to pay. As I have put it elsewhere, with the development of science-based productivity it became possible to squeeze ten dollars out of nature by production and exchange for every dollar that could be squeezed out of subject, class, people, or colony by the use of imperial power and the exaction of tribute. As the historical evidence accumulates, the contention of Schumpeter that imperialism in the nineteenth century was a kind of social lag, which did not pay, and which represented as it were leftovers from a previous age of threat and tribute, becomes abundantly more justified. Certainly from the middle of the nineteenth century and perhaps even earlier, it was countries like Sweden which had abandoned any external imperialism and stayed home and minded their own business well which developed at the fastest rate, whereas the economic development of the imperial countries, such as Britain and France, lagged noticeably. Portugal after four hundred years of empire now has the lowest per capita income in Europe.

The historical evidence of the unprofitability of empire to the imperialist is now so clear that it creates two very real puzzles. The first is a puzzle in the history of thought. Why did the view become so widely accepted that imperialism, especially in the nineteenth and twentieth centuries, had any sort of economic base or rationale? This view prevailed among the left, and is reflected especially in the writings of Hobson and Lenin and indeed of the whole "Marxist-Leninist" school. The second puzzle is why it seemed to take the rulers and decision-makers of the imperial countries such a long time to find out that from an economic point of view at any rate imperialism was a fraud. The abandonment of empire by Britain, France, and Japan has produced not only a substantial increase in the rate of economic growth in these countries, but also—though this is harder to document—a substantial improvement in their internal problem-solving capacities. This seems to be true even of the smaller imperial countries, like Belgium and the Netherlands, which seem to have recovered economically from the loss of very large empires in a remarkably short time. The Netherlands is a particularly good case in point. The Dutch probably succeeded in squeezing tribute out of their empire for a longer time than any other imperial power, yet the loss of their empire seems to have made remarkably little difference to their economic growth and prosperity. Why then did it seem to take so long for these countries to realize that their empires acted as millstones around their necks? Why did a whole influential school of economic thought develop that placed the economic gains of empire at the heart of its interpretation of the dynamics of society? The essays collected in this volume will not answer these questions, but they will provide the student with some raw material with which he can pursue the matter further.

It is easier perhaps to explain the mistakes of practical man than the remarkable success of the theoretical fallacies. The governing class of the imperialist countries even in the nineteenth and twentieth centuries was deeply imbued with the aristocratic "threat and tribute"-oriented view of the world which it had inherited from the previous age. This was true even in France, where the Revolution exterminated the aristocrats physically, but somehow enshrined their view of the world in republican national forms. There is something heady about rising national power, even when it is based fundamentally on production and exchange, as in the case of the United States. Here those temporary kings which we elect as our chief executives turn into shadows of the ancient Caesars, as we see unfortunately even in the 1970's. The military apparatus of a democratic state, even though it may have been conceived originally merely as defense against external aggression, begins to think in imperial terms simply because it is a system of threat capability. It then starts to use its threat system aggressively, even though the returns in terms of tribute are minute and the cost of obtaining them both in resources withdrawn from civilian life and in terms of the loss of internal legitimacy and coherence may well be enormous. Any economic benefits, for instance, which the United States might hope to get out of the political domination of Vietnam would hardly be worth a day's cost of the war. It is quite impossible to explain modern imperialism in economic terms. The only possible exception to this, paradoxically enough, is the socialist imperialism exercised by the Soviet Union on Eastern Europe and especially on East Germany after the Second World War. The Soviet Union probably extracted more goods from East Germany in the ten years after the Second World War than Britain did in two hundred years from India, and this was pure tribute. Even here, however, the tribute turned out to be unstable and the socialist countries have been forced to rely increasingly on bilateral exchange, although the Soviet Union has not been above using its threat of military power to obtain favorable terms of trade.

In the light of the historical evidence, the astonishing and long-continued vogue of the doctrines of Hobson and Lenin and even their modern equivalents in the "new left" becomes all the more puzzling. Hobson himself we can perhaps explain because his prime interest was under-consumption. In many ways he was a forerunner of Keynes, as indeed was Malthus also. There is a kind of underworld tradition of under-consumption in nineteenth-century economics, especially in England, which only came to fruition in Keynes in the 1930's. Hobson was concerned with what today we should call an export multiplier. He saw that in conditions of underemployment an export surplus could generate employment and that export surpluses can be generated by foreign wars and by foreign investment. The historical fact was that foreign investment in the case of the developed countries went primarily to other developed countries, or to countries of like culture and language and more recent settlement, and not to the colonial empires. It was a fact that he simply glossed over in his anxiety to demonstrate his major thesis. We can at least say this for Hobson, that the Keynesian Revolution which he foreshadowed has made even this flimsy excuse for empire in terms of a full-employment policy completely unnecessary and obsolete.

Lenin is harder to excuse, except to say that he was writing not science, but revolutionary propaganda, and that he was concerned much more than Hobson with delegitimating capitalism in all its forms and works. We should remember that the First World War broke on the world of 1914 like an inexplicable social tornado, just as the depression of the 1930's was an inexplicable cancer, and any plausible explanation of the inexplicable is gratefully welcomed. The intellectual success of Marxist-Leninist doctrines therefore even in the West may perhaps partly be explained along these lines. We should remember also that the left represents a move towards the delegitimation of profit and non-labor income generally, which the left regards not as exchange but as tribute. In Marxist thought, profit plays much the same role that tribute does in the revenue economy of the classical empires. Socialism also to some extent represents a return to the more heroic and non-economic attitudes of classical imperialism. The merchant and the trader have always had a bad press. The poets, the philosophers, the prophets, even in our day the scientists, have tended to regard trade as in some sense a low-class, despicable occupation, not fit for heroes, revolutionaries, aristocrats, statesmen, scientists or saints. Schumpeter again was very perceptive of this point in his *Capitalism, Socialism and Democracy,* in which he pointed out that capitalism was undermined not so much by its failures as by its successes, in the sense that it required a moral base for its operations which was inherited from a previous age and which the institutions of capitalism themselves did not sustain. If, for instance, the institutions of the capital market—banking, insurance, foreign exchanges and so on—are to persist and to be legitimated, there must be a widespread ethic of trust, responsibility, fulfillment of promises and so on, an ethic which is not fostered in itself by the kind of wheeling and dealing which a life devoted to trade and speculation may involve. Thus, the ethic which sustains capitalism may come out of a religious and aristocratic tradition which preceded it, and if the acids of rationalism destroy these ethics-sustaining institutions, the rationalistic institutions of the market which depend on them will likewise fall. Schumpeter may have underestimated the capacity of capitalist institutions for moral adaptations, but the point that he makes is a very serious one. Whereas bourgeois economists see the expansion of trade and foreign investment and the growth of the international corporations simply as an example of the benevolence of exchange, producing a division of labor, making everybody richer, and exploiting nobody, the Marxist sees the capitalist and the corporation as the successor of the emperor and the czar extracting tribute in the form of profits from both an internal and an external proletariat. Statistical demonstrations, for instance, that profits in the undeveloped world are not particularly high relative to risk, or that foreign investment produces returns not only to the investor but to the whole society in which the investments are made, are likely to fall on deaf ears, for no quantity of fact can overcome a poem, and in a sense the Marxist vision of the world is a poetic vision of considerable power. The fact that revolutionaries are heroes enables them to justify the enormous amount of human misery which they cause, and the fact that bankers are not heroes prevents them from justifying even the inconspicuous but possibly quite large amounts of human betterment which they foster.

There is one point, however, at which the doctrines of economic imperialism promoted by the left have some validity. They do point to the fact that capitalism, simply because it is a current embodiment of scientific revolution, is an enormously expansive and aggressive force which often presents an almost insuperable challenge to precapitalist traditional societies, and which may disorganize them more than it benefits them. It is indeed only the very strong traditional societies, like Japan, which have been able to make the adaptation to the modern world. In most of the traditional and merely "civilized" societies of the tropics, modern technology, whether in the hands of European imperialists or of the international corporations, has frequently been so disruptive of traditional societies and traditional identities that these societies have been unable to generate an indigenous adaptation to the knowledge and the pressures of the modern world. We may see much the same thing happening in China under the socialist rather than the capitalist guise, for the reactions of the Chinese to Russian socialist intervention are strikingly reminiscent of the reactions of the old capitalist colonies. This is a grave and at the moment a seemingly almost insoluble problem which is going to take perhaps a hundred years or more to work out. It has very little to do with capitalism, however, or even with the socialist criticisms of capitalism; it is a problem of the impact of the iron hammer of scientific technological society, whether in its capitalist or in its socialist form, on the delicate earthen vessels of traditional and pre-scientific cultures. This impact can easily result in devastating human tragedies and the disorganization of once great societies. Nevertheless means can be found for moderating and mediating the impact. It may be that some traditional societies which are not ready for the mighty hurricane of the modern world should board up their windows and go into a period of withdrawal and retirement, as Japan did in the Tokugawa Period after 1618. Indeed, one might almost name this syndrome "Tokugawa shock." Burma is perhaps the best example at the moment. Such a temporary withdrawal—a kind of "chrysalis stage"—may be necessary, if society is to reorganize itself sufficiently to be able to participate in the modern world on an equal footing rather than as a disorganized inferior.

Imperialism, in many forms, is perhaps the greatest unanswered question of the future. Do we look forward to the reduction and ultimate abolition of imperialism, with a large number of states, societies, groups and organizations of more or less equal status using exchange or integrative relationships rather than threat as the major organizer of social organization and the division of labor? Or will we move into the super-imperialism of the world state with a centralized authority, dominated as it inevitably must be by a small elite, and imposing its will by ultimate sanctions of threat against its subject peoples? Of these two alternatives, the former looks much more attractive, and at the moment even more plausible. We have seen that imperialism does not pay and that its legitimacy erodes. Our political thought, however, has been so dominated by the image of an imperial elite organizing subject masses by means of threat that we have not really devoted much attention to this other kind of non-imperial political order. Socialist and anarchist criticisms perhaps hinted at it, but in practice socialism has fallen under the heavy hand of imperialism even more than capitalism, and anarchism never got much beyond the status of a dream or rather a nightmare. Nevertheless, the study of imperialism offers some hope that there are alternatives and as these alternatives begin to be realized, the literature of imperialism will take on even more significance.

The Economic Taproot of Imperialism[1]

J. A. Hobson

J. A. Hobson (1858-1940), the British economist, was born and bred in the Midlands and received his education at Oxford. Hobson's first major work (with A. F. Mummery), *The Physiology of Industry* (1889), deals with the concept of oversaving. His other major work, *Imperialism: A Study* (1902), was an extension of his oversaving theory and it derived most of its historical background from Hobson's experience as a correspondent for the *Manchester Guardian* in South Africa. His other notable works are: *The Evolution of Modern Capitalism: A Study of Machine Production* (1894); *The Industrial System: An Enquiry into Earned and Unearned Income* (1909); *Work and Wealth* (1914) and *Confessions of an Economic Heretic* (1938).

The major theme of Hobson's theory of imperialism may be traced back to the underconsumptionists—Malthus, Rodbertus, and Sismondi. Slumps and underemployment in developed capitalist economies were due to the fact that consumption failed to keep pace with production. What was the cause of this malady existing in capitalist economies? Hobson theorized that it was due to the maldistribution of wealth in a capitalist society. Hobson's solution to the problem was to achieve a more equitable distribution of income through state action in the way of regulation of monopolies and taxation of the surpluses that were accumulated over and above the level necessary for maintenance and growth.

Hobson's work had great impact on Lenin's *Imperialism: The Highest Stage of Capitalism* and on the work of Hilferding, Luxemburg, Bauer, and Bukharin.

Hobson's efforts, in his *Imperialism: A Study,* were directed towards explaining European expansionism in terms of underconsumptionist tendencies in capitalist economies and poliltical manipulations of the various interest groups.

No mere array of facts and figures adduced to illustrate the economic nature of the new Imperialism will suffice to dispel the popular delusion that the use of national force to secure new markets by

[1]Reprinted from *Imperialism: A Study*, Ann Arbor, University of Michigan Press, 1967, pages 71-93.

annexing fresh tracts of territory is a sound and a necessary policy
for an advanced industrial country like Great Britain.[2] It has indeed
been proved that recent annexations of tropical countries, procured
at great expense, have furnished poor and precarious markets, that
our aggregate trade with our colonial possessions is virtually stationary,
and that our most profitable and progressive trade is with rival
industrial nations, whose territories we have no desire to annex, whose
markets we cannot force, and whose active antagonism we are provok-
ing by our expansive policy.

But these arguments are not conclusive. It is open to Imperialists to argue thus: "We must have markets for our growing manufactures, we must have new outlets for the investment of our surplus
capital and for the energies of the adventurous surplus of our population: such expansion is a necessity of life to a nation with our great
and growing powers of production. An ever larger share of our
population is devoted to the manufactures and commerce of towns,
and is thus dependent for life and work upon food and raw materials
from foreign lands. In order to buy and pay for these things we
must sell our goods abroad. During the first three-quarters of the
nineteenth century we could do so without difficulty by a natural
expansion of commerce with continental nations and our colonies,
all of which were far behind us in the main arts of manufacture
and the carrying trades. So long as England held a virtual monopoly
of the world markets for certain important classes of manufactured
goods, Imperialism was unnecessary. After 1870 this manufacturing
and trading supremacy was greatly impaired: other nations, especially
Germany, the United States, and Belgium, advanced with great rapidity, and while they have not crushed or even stayed the increase
of our external trade, their competition made it more and more
difficult to dispose of the full surplus of our manufactures at a
profit. The encroachments made by these nations upon our old
markets, even in our own possessions, made it most urgent that
we should take energetic means to secure new markets. These new
markets had to lie in hitherto undeveloped countries, chiefly in the
tropics, where vast populations lived capable of growing economic
needs which our manufacturers and merchants could supply. Our
rivals were seizing and annexing territories for similar purposes, and
when they had annexed them closed them to our trade. The diplomacy
and the arms of Great Britain had to be used in order to compel
the owners of the new markets to deal with us: and experience showed

2Written in 1905.

that the safest means of securing and developing such markets is by establishing 'protectorates' or by annexation. The value in 1905 of these markets must not be taken as a final test of the economy of such a policy; the process of educating civilized needs which we can supply is of necessity a gradual one, and the cost of such Imperialism must be regarded as a capital outlay, the fruits of which posterity would reap. The new markets might not be large, but they formed serviceable outlets for the overflow of our great textile and metal industries, and, when the vast Asiatic and African populations of the interior were reached, a rapid expansion of trade was expected to result.

"Far larger and more important is the pressure of capital for external fields of investment. Moreover, while the manufacturer and trader are well content to trade with foreign nations, the tendency for investors to work towards the political annexation of countries which contain their more speculative investments is very powerful. Of the fact of this pressure of capital there can be no question. Large savings are made which cannot find any profitable investment in this country; they must find employment elsewhere, and it is to the advantage of the nation that they should be employed as largely as possible in lands where they can be utilized in opening up markets for British trade and employment for British enterprise.

"However costly, however perilous, this process of imperial expansion may be, it is necessary to the continued existence and progress of our nation;[3] if we abandoned it we must be content to leave the development of the world to other nations, who will everywhere cut into our trade, and even impair our means of securing the food and raw materials we require to support our population. Imperialism is thus seen to be, not a choice, but a necessity."

The practical force of this economic argument in politics is strikingly illustrated by the later history of the United States. Here is a country which suddenly broke through a conservative policy, strongly held by both political parties, bound up with every popular instinct and tradition, and flung itself into a rapid imperial career for which it possessed neither the material nor the moral equipment, risking the principles and practices of liberty and equality by the establishment of militarism and the forcible subjugation of peoples

---

[3]"And why, indeed, are wars undertaken, if not to conquer colonies which permit the employment of fresh capital, to acquire commercial monopolies, or to obtain the exclusive use of certain highways of commerce?" (Loria, *Economic Foundations of Society*, p. 267).

which it could not safely admit to the condition of American citizenship.

Was this a mere wild freak of spread-eagleism, a burst of political ambition on the part of a nation coming to a sudden realization of its destiny? Not at all. The spirit of adventure, the American "mission of civilization," were as forces making for Imperialism, clearly subordinate to the driving force of the economic factor. The dramatic character of the change is due to the unprecedented rapidity of the industrial revolution in the United States from the eighties onwards. During that period the United States, with her unrivaled natural resources, her immense resources of skilled and unskilled labor, and her genius for invention and organization, developed the best equipped and most productive manufacturing economy the world has yet seen. Fostered by rigid protective tariffs, her metal, textile, tool, clothing, furniture, and other manufactures shot up in a single generation from infancy to full maturity, and, having passed through a period of intense competition, attained, under the able control of great trust-makers, a power of production greater than has been attained in the most advanced industrial countries of Europe.

An era of cut-throat competition, followed by a rapid process of amalgamation, threw an enormous quantity of wealth into the hands of a small number of captains of industry. No luxury of living to which this class could attain kept pace with its rise of income, and a process of automatic saving set in upon an unprecedented scale. The investment of these savings in other industries helped to bring these under the same concentrative forces. Thus a great increase of savings seeking profitable investment is synchronous with a stricter economy of the use of existing capital. No doubt the rapid growth of a population, accustomed to a high and an always ascending standard of comfort, absorbs in the satisfaction of its wants a large quantity of new capital. But the actual rate of saving, conjoined with a more economical application of forms of existing capital, exceeded considerably the rise of the national consumption of manufactures. The power of production far outstripped the actual rate of consumption, and, contrary to the older economic theory, was unable to force a corresponding increase of consumption by lowering prices.

This is no mere theory. The history of any of the numerous trusts or combinations in the United States sets out the facts with complete distinctness. In the free competition of manufactures preceding combination the chronic condition is one of "over-production," in the sense that all the mills or factories can only be kept at work by cutting prices down towards a point where the weaker competitors are forced to close down, because they cannot sell their goods at a price which covers the true cost of production. The first result of the successful formation of a trust or combine is to close down the worse-equipped or worse-placed mills, and supply the entire market from the better-equipped and better-placed ones. This course may or may not be attended by a rise of price and some restriction of consumption: in some cases trusts take most of their profits by raising prices, in other cases by reducing the costs of production through employing only the best mills and stopping the waste of competition.

For the present argument it matters not which course is taken; the point is that this concentration of industry in "trusts," "combines," etc., at once limits the quantity of capital which can be effectively employed and increases the share of profits out of which fresh savings and fresh capital will spring. It is quite evident that a trust which is motivated by cut-throat competition, due to an excess of capital, cannot normally find inside the "trusted" industry employment for that portion of the profits which the trustmakers desire to save and to invest. New inventions and other economies of production or distribution within the trade may absorb some of the new capital, but there are rigid limits to this absorption. The trust-maker in oil or sugar must find other investments for his savings: if he is early in the application of the combination principles to his trade, he will naturally apply his surplus capital to establish similar combinations in other industries, economizing capital still further, and rendering it ever harder for ordinary saving men to find investments for their savings.

Indeed, the conditions alike of cut-throat competition and of combination attest the congestion of capital in the manufacturing industries which have entered the machine economy. We are not here concerned with any theoretic question as to the possibility of producing by modern machine methods more goods than can find a market. It is sufficient to point out that the manufacturing power of a country like the United States would grow so fast as to exceed the demands of the home market. No one acquainted with trade will deny a fact which all American economists assert, that this is the condition which the United States reached at the end of the century, so far as the more developed industries are concerned. Her manufactures were saturated with capital and could absorb no more. One after another they sought refuge from the waste of competition in "combines" which secure a measure of profitable peace by restricting the quantity of operative capital. Industrial and financial princes in oil, steel, sugar, railroads, banking, etc., were faced with the dilemma of either spending more than they knew how to spend, or forcing markets outside the home area. Two economic courses were open to them, both leading towards an abandonment of the political isolation of the past and the adoption of imperialist methods in the future. Instead of shutting down inferior mills and rigidly restricting output to correspond with profitable sales in the home markets, they might employ their full productive power, applying their savings to increase their business capital, and, while still regulating output and prices for the home market, might "hustle" for foreign markets, dumping down their surplus goods at prices which would not be possible save for the profitable nature of their home market. So likewise they might employ their savings in seeking investments outside their country, first repaying the capital borrowed from Great Britain and other countries for the early development of their railroads, mines, and manufactures, and afterwards becoming themselves a creditor class to foreign countries.

It was this sudden demand for foreign markets for manufactures and for investments which was avowedly responsible for the adoption of Imperialism as a political policy and practice by the Republican party to which the great industrial and financial chiefs belonged, and which belonged to them. The adventurous enthusiasm of President Theodore Roosevelt and his "manifest destiny" and "mission of civilization" party must not deceive us. It was Messrs. Rockefeller, Pierpont Morgan, and their associates who needed Imperialism and who fastened it upon the shoulders of the great Republic of the West. They needed Imperialism because they desired to use the public resources of their country to find profitable employment for their capital which otherwise would be superfluous.

It is not indeed necessary to own a country in order to do trade with it or to invest capital in it, and doubtless the United States could find some vent for their surplus goods and capital in European countries. But these countries were for the most part able to make provision for themselves: most of them erected tariffs against manufacturing imports, and even Great Britain was urged to defend herself by reverting to Protection. The big American manufacturers and financiers were compelled to look to China and the Pacific and to South America for their most profitable chances; Protectionists by principle and practice, they would insist upon getting as close a monopoly of these markets as they could secure, and the competition of Germany, England, and other trading nations would drive them to the establishment of special political relations with the markets they most prize. Cuba, the Philippines, and Hawaii were but the *hors d'oeuvre* to whet an appetite for an ampler banquet. Moreover, the powerful hold upon politics which these industrial and financial magnates possessed formed a separate stimulus, which, as we have shown, was operative in Great Britain and elsewhere; the public expenditure in pursuit of an imperial career would be a separate immense source of profit to these men, as financiers negotiating loans, shipbuilders and owners handling subsidies, contractors and manufacturers of armaments and other imperialist appliances.

The suddenness of this political revolution is due to the rapid manifestation of the need. In the last years of the nineteenth century the United States nearly trebled the value of its manufacturing export trade, and it was to be expected that, if the rate of progress of those years continued, within a decade it would overtake our more slowly advancing export trade, and stand first in the list of manufacture-exporting nations.[4]

This was the avowed ambition, and no idle one, of the keenest business men of America; and with the natural resources, the labor and the administrative talents at their disposal, it was quite likely they would achieve their object.[5] The stronger and more direct control over politics exercised in America by business men

Export Trade of United States, 1890-1900.

Year.	Agriculture. £	Manufactures. £	Miscellaneous. £
1890	125,756,000	31,435,000	13,019,000
1891	146,617,000	33,720,000	11,731,000
1892	142,508,000	30,479,000	11,660,000
1893	123,810,000	35,484,000	11,653,000
1894	114,737,000	35,557,000	11,168,000
1895	104,143,000	40,230,000	12,174,000
1896	132,992,000	50,738,000	13,639,000
1897	146,059,000	55,923,000	13,984,000
1898	170,383,000	61,585,000	14,743,000
1899	156,427,000	76,157,000	18,002,000
1900	180,931,000	88,281,000	21,389,000

[4]Post-war conditions, with the immense opportunities afforded for exports of American goods and capital brought a pause and a temporary withdrawal from imperialist policy.

[5]"We hold now three of the winning cards in the game for commercial greatness, to wit—iron, steel and coal. We have long been the granary of the world, we now aspire to be its workshop, then we want to be its clearing-house." (The President of the American Bankers' Association at Denver, 1898.)

enabled them to drive more quickly and more straightly along the line of their economic interests than in Great Britain. American Imperialism was the natural product of the economic pressure of a sudden advance of capitalism which could not find occupation at home and needed foreign markets for goods and for investments.

The same needs existed in European countries, and, as is admitted, drove Governments along the same path. Over-production in the sense of an excessive manufacturing plant, and surplus capital which could not find sound investments within the country, forced Great Britain, Germany, Holland, France to place larger and larger portions of their economic resources outside the area of their present political domain, and then stimulate a policy of political expansion so as to take in the new areas. The economic sources of this movement are laid bare by periodic trade-depressions due to an inability of producers to find adequate and profitable markets for what they can produce. The Majority Report of the Commission upon the Depression of Trade in 1885 put the matter in a nutshell. "That, owing to the nature of the times, the demand for our commodities does not increase at the same rate as formerly; that our capacity for production is consequently in excess of our requirements, and could be considerably increased at short notice; that this is due partly to the competition of the capital which is being steadily accumulated in the country." The Minority Report straightly imputed the condition of affairs to "over-production." Germany was in the early 1900's suffering severely from what is called a glut of capital and of manufacturing power: she had to have new markets; her Consuls all over the world were "hustling" for trade; trading settlements were forced upon Asia Minor; in East and West Africa, in China and elsewhere the German Empire was impelled to a policy of colonization and protectorates as outlets for German commercial energy.

Every improvement of methods of production, every concentration of ownership and control, seems to accentuate the tendency. As one nation after another enters the machine economy and adopts advanced industrial methods, it becomes more difficult for its manufacturers, merchants, and financiers to dispose profitably of their economic resources, and they are tempted more and more to use their Governments in order to secure for their particular use some distant undeveloped country by annexation and protection.

The process, we may be told, is inevitable, and so it seems upon a superficial inspection. Everywhere appear excessive powers of production, excessive capital in search of investment. It is admitted by all business men that the growth of the powers of production in their country exceeds the growth in consumption, that more goods can be produced than can be sold at a profit, and that more capital exists than can find remunerative investment.

It is this economic condition of affairs that forms the taproot of Imperialism. If the consuming public in this country raised its standard of consumption to keep pace with every rise of productive powers, there could be no excess of goods or capital clamorous to use Imperialism in order to find markets: foreign trade would indeed exist, but there would be no difficulty in exchanging a small surplus of our manufactures for the food and raw material we annually absorbed, and all the savings that we made could find employment, if we chose, in home industries.

There is nothing inherently irrational in such a supposition. Whatever is, or can be, produced, can be consumed, for a claim upon it, as rent, profit, or wages, forms part of the real income of some member of the community, and he can consume it, or else exchange it for some other consumable with some one else who will consume it. With everything that is produced a consuming power is born. If then there are goods which cannot get consumed, or which cannot even get produced because it is evident they cannot get consumed, and if there is a quantity of capital and labor which cannot get full employment because its products cannot get consumed, the only possible explanation of this paradox is the refusal of owners of consuming power to apply that power in effective demand for commodities.

It is, of course, possible that an excess of producing power might exist in particular industries by misdirection, being engaged in certain manufactures, whereas it ought to have been engaged in agriculture or some other use. But no one can seriously contend that such misdirection explains the recurrent gluts and consequent depressions of modern industry, or that, when over-production is manifest in the leading manufactures, ample avenues are open for the surplus capital and labor in other industries. The general character of the excess of producing power is proved by the existence at such times of large bank stocks of idle money seeking any sort of profitable investment and finding none.

The root questions underlying the phenomena are clearly these: "Why is it that consumption fails to keep pace automatically in a community with power of production?" "Why does under-consumption or over-saving occur?" For it is evident that the consuming power, which, if exercised, would keep tense the reins of production, is in part withheld, or in other words is "saved" and stored up for investment. All saving for investment does not imply slackness of production; quite the contrary. Saving is economically justified, from the social standpoint, when the capital in which it takes material shape finds full employment in helping to produce commodities which, when produced, will be consumed. It is saving in excess of this amount that causes mischief, taking shape in surplus capital which is not needed to assist current consumption, and which either lies idle, or tries to oust existing capital from its employment, or else seeks speculative use abroad under the protection of the Government.

But it may be asked, "Why should there be any tendency to over-saving? Why should the owners of consuming power withhold a larger quantity for savings than can be serviceably employed?" Another way of putting the same question is this, "Why should not the pressure of present wants keep pace with every possibility of satisfying them?" The answer to these pertinent questions carries us to the broadest issue of the distribution of wealth. If a tendency to distribute income or consuming power according to needs were operative, it is evident that consumption would rise with every rise of producing power, for human needs are illimitable, and there could be no excess of saving. But it is quite otherwise in a state of economic society where distribution has no fixed relation to needs, but is determined by other conditions which assign to some people a consuming power vastly in excess of needs or possible uses, while others are destitute of consuming power enough to satisfy even the full demands of physical efficiency. The following illustration may serve to make the issue clear. "The volume of production has been constantly rising owing to the development of modern machinery. There are two main channels to carry off these products—one channel carrying off the product destined to be consumed by the workers, and the other channel carrying off the remainder to the rich. The workers' channel is in rockbound banks that cannot enlarge, owing to the competitive wage system preventing wages rising *pro rata* with increased efficiency. Wages are based upon cost of living, and not upon efficiency of labor. The miner in the poor mine gets the same wages per day as the miner in the adjoining rich mine. The owner of the rich mine gets the advantage—not his laborer. The channel which conveys the goods destined to supply the rich is itself divided into two streams. One stream carries off what the rich 'spend' on themselves for the necessities and luxuries of life. The other is simply an 'overflow' stream carrying off their 'savings.' The channel for spending, i.e. the amount wasted by the rich in luxuries, may broaden somewhat, but owing to the small number

standard of consumption to correspond with every increased power of production, and can find full employment for an unlimited quantity of capital and labor within the limits of the country which it occupies. Where the distribution of incomes is such as to enable all classes of the nation to convert their felt wants into an effective demand for commodities, there can be no over-production, no under-employment of capital and labor, and no necessity to fight for foreign markets.

The most convincing condemnation of the current economy is conveyed in the difficulty which producers everwhere experience in finding consumers for their products: a fact attested by the prodigious growth of classes of agents and middlemen, the multiplication of every sort of advertising, and the general increase of the distributive classes. Under a sound economy the pressure would be reversed: the growing wants of progressive societies would be a constant stimulus to the inventive and operative energies of producers, and would form a constant strain upon the powers of production. The simultaneous excess of all the factors of production, attested by frequently recurring periods of trade depression, is a most dramatic exhibition of the false economy of distribution. It does not imply a mere miscalculation in the application of productive power, or a brief temporary excess of that power; it manifests in an acute form an economic waste which is chronic and general throughout the advanced industrial nations, a waste contained in the divorcement of the desire to consume and the power to consume.

If the apportionment of income were such as to evoke no excessive saving, full constant employment for capital and labor would be furnished at home. This, of course, does not imply that there would be no foreign trade. Goods that could not be produced at home, or produced as well or as cheaply, would still be purchased by ordinary process of international exchange, but here again the pressure would be the wholesome pressure of the consumer anxious to buy abroad what he could not buy at home, not the blind eagerness of the producer to use every force or trick of trade or politics to find markets for his "surplus" goods.

The struggle for markets, the greater eagerness of producers to sell than of consumers to buy, is the crowning proof of a false economy of distribution. Imperialism is the fruit of this false economy; "social reform" is its remedy. The primary purpose of "social reform," using the term in its economic signification, is to raise the wholesome standard of private and public consumption for a nation, so as to enable the nation to live up to its highest standard of production.

Even those social reformers who aim directly at abolishing or reducing some bad form of consumption, as in the Temperance movement, generally recognize the necessity of substituting some better form of current consumption which is more educative and stimulative of other tastes, and will assist to raise the general standard of consumption.

There is no necessity to open up new foreign markets; the home markets are capable of indefinite expansion. Whatever is produced in England can be consumed in England, provided that the "income" or power to demand commodities, is properly distributed. This only appears untrue because of the unnatural and unwholesome specialization to which this country has been subjected, based upon a bad distribution of economic resources, which has induced an overgrowth of certain manufacturing trades for the express purpose of effecting foreign sales. If the industrial revolution had taken place in an England founded upon equal access by all classes to land, education and legislation, specialization in manufactures would not have gone so far (though more intelligent progress would have been made, by reason of a widening of the area of selection of inventive and organizing talents) ; foreign trade would have been less important, though more steady; the standard of life for all portions of the population would have been high, and the present rate of national consumption would probably have given full, constant, remunerative employment to a far larger quantity of private and public capital than is now employed.[8] For the over-saving or wider consumption that is traced to excessive incomes of the rich is a suicidal economy, even from the exclusive standpoint of capital; for consumption alone vitalizes capital and makes it capable of yielding profits. An economy that assigns to the "possessing" classes an excess of consuming power which they cannot use, and cannot convert into really serviceable capital, is a dog-in-the-manger policy. The social reforms which deprive the possessing classes of their surplus will not, therefore, inflict upon them the real injury they dread; they can only use this surplus by forcing on their country a wrecking policy of Imperialism. The

---

[8]The classical economists of England, forbidden by their theories of parsimony and of the growth of capital to entertain the notion of an indefinite expansion of home markets by reason of a constantly rising standard of national comfort, were early driven to countenance a doctrine of the necessity of finding external markets for the investment of capital. So J. S. Mill: "The expansion of capital would soon reach its ultimate boundary if the boundary did not continually open and leave more space" (*Political Economy*). And before him Ricardo (in a letter to Malthus): "If with every accumulation of capital we could take a piece of fresh fertile land to our island, profits would never fall."

of those rich enough to indulge in whims it can never be greatly enlarged, and at any rate it bears such a small proportion to the other channel that in no event can much hope of avoiding a flood of capital be hoped for from this division. The rich will never be so ingenious as to spend enough to prevent over-production. The great safety overflow channel which has been continuously more and more widened and deepened to carry off the ever-increasing flood of new capital is that division of the stream which carried the savings of the rich, and this is not only suddenly found to be incapable of further enlargement, but actually seems to be in the process of being dammed up."[6]

Though this presentation over-accentuates the cleavage between rich and poor and over-states the weakness of the workers, it gives forcible and sound expression to a most important and ill-recognized economic truth. The "overflow" stream of savings is of course fed not exclusively from the surplus income of "the rich"; the professional and industrial middle classes, and to some slight extent the workers, contribute. But the "flooding" is distinctly due to the automatic saving of the surplus income of rich men. This is of course particularly true of America, where multi-millionaires rise quickly and find themselves in possession of incomes far exceeding the demands of any craving that is known to them. To make the metaphor complete, the overflow stream must be represented as reentering the stream of production and seeking to empty there all the "savings" that it carries. Where competition remains free, the result is a chronic congestion of productive power and of production, forcing down home prices, wasting large sums in advertising and in pushing for orders, and periodically causing a crisis followed by a collapse, during which quantities of capital and labor lie unemployed and unremunerated. The prime object of the trust or other combine is to remedy this waste and loss by substituting regulation of output for reckless over-production. In achieving this it actually narrows or even dams up the old channels of investment, limiting the overflow stream to the exact amount required to maintain the normal current of output. But this rigid limitation of trade, though required for the separate economy of each trust, does not suit the trust-maker, who is driven to compensate for strictly regulated industry at home by cutting new foreign channels as outlets for his productive power and his excessive savings. Thus we reach the conclusion that Imperialism is the endeavor of the great controllers of industry to broaden the channel for

[6]*The Significance of the Trust*, by H. G. Wilshire.

the flow of their surplus wealth by seeking foreign markets and foreign investments to take off the goods and capital they cannot sell or use at home.

The fallacy of the supposed inevitability of imperial expansion as a necessary outlet for progressive industry is now manifest. It is not industrial progress that demands the opening up of new markets and areas of investment, but maldistribution of consuming power which prevents the absorption of commodities and capital within the country. The over-saving which is the economic root of Imperialism is found by analysis to consist of rents, monopoly profits, and other unearned or excessive elements of income, which, not being earned by labor of head or hand, have no legitimate *raison d'être*. Having no natural relation to effort of production, they impel their recipients to no corresponding satisfaction of consumption: they form a surplus wealth, which, having no proper place in the normal economy of production and consumption, tends to accumulate as excessive savings. Let any turn in the tide of politico-economic forces divert from these owners their excess of income and make it flow, either to the workers in higher wages, or to the community in taxes, so that it will be spent instead of being saved, serving in either of these ways to swell the tide of consumption—there will be no need to fight for foreign markets or foreign areas of investment.

Many have carried their analysis so far as to realize the absurdity of spending half our financial resources in fighting to secure foreign markets at times when hungry mouths, ill-clad backs, ill-furnished houses indicate countless unsatisfied material wants among our own population. If we may take the careful statistics of Mr. Rowntree[7] for our guide, we shall be aware that more than one-fourth of the population of our towns is living at a standard which is below bare physical efficiency. If, by some economic readjustment, the products which flow from the surplus saving of the rich to swell the overflow streams could be diverted so as to raise the incomes and the standard of consumption of this inefficient fourth, there would be no need for pushful Imperialism, and the cause of social reform would have won its greatest victory.

It is not inherent in the nature of things that we should spend our natural resources on militarism, war, and risky, unscrupulous diplomacy, in order to find markets for our goods and surplus capital. An intelligent progressive community, based upon substantial equality of economic and educational opportunities, will raise its

[7] *Poverty: A Study of Town Life.*

only safety of nations lies in removing the unearned increments of income from the possessing classes, and adding them to the wage-income of the working classes or to the public income, in order that they may be spent in raising the standard of consumption.

Social reform bifurcates, according as reformers seek to achieve this end by raising wages or by increasing public taxation and expenditure. These courses are not essentially contradictory, but are rather complementary. Working-class movements aim, either by private co-operation or by political pressure on legislative and administrative government, at increasing the proportion of the national income which accrues to labor in the form of wages, pensions, compensation for injuries, etc. State Socialism aims at getting for the direct use of the whole society an increased share of the "social values" which arise from the closely and essentially co-operative work of an industrial society, taxing property and incomes so as to draw into the public exchequer for public expenditure the "unearned elements" of income, leaving to individual producers those incomes which are necessary to induce them to apply in the best way their economic energies, and to private enterprises those businesses which do not breed monopoly, and which the public need not or cannot undertake. These are not, indeed, the sole or perhaps the best avowed objects of social reform movements. But for the purposes of this analysis they form the kernel.

Trade Unionism and Socialism are thus the natural enemies of Imperialism, for they take away from the "imperialist" classes the surplus incomes which form the economic stimulus of Imperialism.

This does not pretend to be a final statement of the full relations of these forces. When we come to political analysis we shall perceive that the tendency of Imperialism is to crush Trade Unionism and to "nibble" at or parasitically exploit State Socialism. But, confining ourselves for the present to the narrowly economic setting, Trade Unionism and State Socialism may be regarded as complementary forces arrayed against Imperialism, in so far as, by diverting to working-class or public expenditure elements of income which would otherwise be surplus savings, they raise the general standard of home consumption and abate the pressure for foreign markets. Of course, if the increase of working-class income were wholly or chiefly "saved," not spent, or if the taxation of unearned incomes were utilized for the relief of other taxes borne by the possessing classes, no such result as we have described would follow. There is, however, no reason to anticipate this result from trade-union or socialistic measures. Though no sufficient natural stimulus exists to force the well-to-do classes to spend in further luxuries the surplus incomes which they save, every working-class family is subject to powerful stimuli of economic needs, and a reasonably governed State would regard as its prime duty the relief of the present poverty of public life by new forms of socially useful expenditure.

But we are not here concerned with what belongs to the practical issues of political and economic policy. It is the economic theory for which we claim acceptance—a theory which, if accurate, dispels the delusion that expansion of foreign trade, and therefore of empire, is a necessity of national life.

Regarded from the standpoint of economy of energy, the same "choice of life" confronts the nation as the individual. An individual may expend all his energy in acquiring external possessions, adding field to field, barn to barn, factory to factory—may "spread himself" over the widest area of property, amassing material wealth which is in some sense "himself" as containing the impress of his power and interest. He does this by specializing upon the lower acquisitive plane of interest at the cost of neglecting the cultivation of the higher qualities and interests of his nature. The antagonism is not indeed absolute. Aristotle has said, "We must first secure a livelihood and then practise virtue." Hence the pursuit of material property as a reasonable basis of physical comfort would be held true economy by the wisest men; but the absorption of time, energy, and interest upon such quantitative expansion at the necessary cost of starving the higher tastes and faculties is condemned as false economy. The same issue comes up in the business life of the individual: it is the question of intensive versus extensive cultivation. A rude or ignorant farmer, where land is plentiful, is apt to spread his capital and labor over a large area, taking in new tracts and cultivating them poorly. A skilled, scientific farmer will study a smaller patch of land, cultivate it thoroughly, and utilize its diverse properties, adapting it to the special needs of his most remunerative markets. The same is true of other businesses; even where the economy of large-scale production is greatest there exists some limit beyond which the wise businessman will not go, aware that in doing so he will risk by enfeebled management what he seems to gain by mechanical economies of production and market.

Everywhere the issue of quantitative versus qualitative growth comes up. This is the entire issue of empire. A people limited in number and energy and in the land they occupy have the choice of improving to the utmost the political and economic management of their own land, confining themselves to such accessions of territory as are justified by the most economical disposition of a growing population; or they may proceed, like the slovenly farmer, to spread their power and energy over the whole earth, tempted by the speculative value or the quick profits of some new market, or else by mere greed of territorial acquisition, and ignoring the political and economic wastes and risks involved by this imperial career. It must be clearly understood that this is essentially a choice of alternatives; a full simultaneous application of intensive and extensive cultivation is impossible. A nation may either, following the example of Denmark or Switzerland, put brains into agriculture, develop a finely varied system of public education, general and technical, apply the ripest science to its special manufacturing industries, and so support in progressive comfort and character a considerable population upon a strictly limited area; or it may, like Great Britain, neglect its agriculture, allowing its lands to go out of cultivation and its population to grow up in towns, fall behind other nations in its methods of education and in the capacity of adapting to its uses the latest scientific knowledge, in order that it may squander its pecuniary and military resources in forcing bad markets and finding speculative fields of investment in distant corners of the earth, adding millions of square miles and of unassimilable population to the area of the Empire.

The driving forces of class interest which stimulate and support this false economy we have explained. No remedy will serve which permits the future operation of these forces. It is idle to attack Imperialism or Militarism as political expedients or policies unless the axe is laid at the economic root of the tree, and the classes for whose interest Imperialism works are shorn of the surplus revenues which seek this outlet.

Dynamics of Imperialism[1]

Parker T. Moon

Parker T. Moon (1892-1936) was Professor of International Relations at Columbia University. The following piece has been taken from his book *Imperialism & World Politics,* published in 1927. According to the author, imperialism is a result of the alliance between the various interest groups and ideas such as altruism, national honor, surplus population, economic nationalism and self-protection. Empire building is not done by a nation as a whole but by individuals and groups. Moon examines the nature of the interest groups and the reasons why majorities pay for the expenses associated with imperialist expansion. Hobson's influence is quite noticeable in the author's writings. (For a review of the American writings on the economics of imperialism, see E. M. Winslow, "Marxian, Liberal, and Sociological Theories of Imperialism," *The Journal of Political Economy,* Vol. 39 (1931), p. 737. The reader should also consult *Empire and Commerce* by Leonard Woolf.)

Men and Motives

Language often obscures truth. More than is ordinarily realized, our eyes are blinded to the facts of international relations by tricks of the tongue. When one uses the simple monosyllable "France" one thinks of France as a unit, an entity. When to avoid awkward repetition we use a personal pronoun in referring to a country—when for example we say "France sent *her* troops to conquer Tunis"—we impute not only unity but personality to the country. The very words conceal the facts and make international relations a glamorous drama in which personalized nations are the actors, and all too easily we forget the flesh-and-blood men and women who are the true actors. How different it would be if we had no such word as "France," and had to say instead—thirty-eight million men, women and children of very diversified interests and beliefs, inhabiting 218,000 square miles of territory! Then we should more accurately describe the Tunis expedition in some such way as this: "A few of these thirty-eight million persons sent thirty thousand others to conquer

[1]Reprinted from *Imperialism and World Politics,* New York, The Macmillan Company, 1926, pages 58-74.

Tunis." This way of putting the fact immediately suggests a question, or rather a series of questions. Who were the "few"? Why did they send the thirty thousand to Tunis? And why did these obey?

Empire-building is done not by "nations" but by men. The problem before us is to discover the men, the active, interested minorities in each nation, who are directly interested in imperialism, and then to analyze the reasons why the majorities pay the expenses and fight the wars necessitated by imperialist expansion.

Business Interests

First and foremost among the active imperialist groups come certain business interests. Not the whole so-called "capitalist class," as many an earnest Socialist would have us believe, but only a minority of business interests are directly interested in imperialism. They are easily identified. To begin with, there are the exporters and manufacturers of certain goods used in colonies. The following figures of English exports to India tell the story.

English Exports to India (Average 1920-2)

Cotton goods and yarn	£53,577,000
Iron and steel, tools, machinery and locomotives	37,423,000
Wagons, trucks, and automobiles	4,274,000
Paper	1,858,000
Brass goods	1,813,000
Woolens	1,600,000
Tobacco	1,023,000

No other item over £1,000,000.

Obviously the cotton industry and the iron industry are the important factors. The imports of most other colonies and backward countries tell almost exactly the same story of cotton and iron, with minor variations. Many colonies provide a spongelike market for cheap alcoholic beverages. Cigarettes have fifth place in China's imports.

In some cases coal is important. Kerosene has also played a significant role. But cotton and iron have been dominant. In more human terms, the makers of cotton and iron goods have been very vitally interested in imperialism. Their business interests demand the opening-up and development of colonial markets, and, in many cases, the exclusion of foreign competitors. Such aims require political control—imperialism. One specific instance may show how important imperialistic control over colonies is to these business groups. India, if free, would long ago have established a tariff to protect Indian

spinners and weavers against British competition, but the cotton manufacturers of Lancashire, England, have used imperial England's authority to prevent any such blow to their business; when in 1896
a small import duty of 3½ per cent was established by the Indian
government, the London government, pressed by British cotton barons,
insisted that the effect of the duty be nullified by a countervailing
excise duty of 3½ per cent on Indian cottons.[2] As one Indian remarked,
"There are indeed sixty good reasons" for this British interference,
"for there are sixty Lancashire members who have votes in the
House of Commons."

Next in line come the import interests. The British merchants
who import tea from India, the Belgians who import rubber and
palm nuts from Congo, the Frenchmen who import wines from Algeria
are vital factors in imperialism. The development of such business
enterprises on a large scale requires at least a degree of orderly
government sufficient to protect investments in plantations, warehouses
and railways; often it demands expensive public works, such as dams,
irrigation systems, roads, and railways, which a backward native government cannot or will not undertake; occasionally, also, governmental
authority is considered necessary to compel natives to work. In short,
imperial control by a progressive nation is demanded. And the importers, together with planters and other allied interests, usually desire
that the imperial control shall be wielded by their own nation,
because from it they may hope to receive privileged treatment. There
is only one reason why 197 million francs' worth of rubber, palm
nuts and palm oil, copal, and copper from Belgian Congo are
exported to Belgium and handled by Belgian merchants, whereas only
13 millions go to England, 17 millions to all America, and only
two-fifths of a million to France. The reason is that Belgium owns
Congo. And the Belgian importers are aware of this fact, as are
their competitors in other imperialist countries.

Of late years this group of import interests has been enormously
strengthened by the demand of giant industries for colonial raw
materials—rubber, petroleum, iron and coal, cotton, cocoa. The oil
trusts of England and the United States have enlisted the aid
of naval and diplomatic officials in their worldwide rivalry. The cotton
industry of Germany hoped to obtain from Asiatic Turkey, under
German imperialist control, raw cotton for German spindles; the
cotton interests of England have been striving for a generation

---

[2]In 1917 the duty on imported cotton goods was raised to 7½%, without
a corresponding increase of the 3½% excise on Indian cottons, so that a net
protection of 4% was afforded. In 1925 the excise was abolished.

to develop plantations in British colonies; their French and Italian rivals have been hardly less interested in colonial potentialities. The European cotton industry, it may be remarked, as an export business and as an import business, is doubly imperialist.

Shipping magnates form a third powerful business group. The annals of empire-building bristle with the names of shipowners. It is no accident that the greatest shipping nation has the greatest of empires. Shipowners demand coaling stations for their vessels, and naval bases for protection; they desire development of colonial trade and of emigration. It was William (later Sir William) Mackinnon,—"a leetle, dapper, upright man, with an acquiline nose, side whiskers, a pouting mouth, and a strutting manner of walking"—chief owner of the British India Steam Navigation Company, who first proposed that the British should take Zanzibar, and who later organized a group of British capitalists to develop East Africa.

To these interest groups may be added the makers of armament and of uniforms, the producers of telegraph and railway material, and other supplies used by the government in its colonies. These have been aptly styled the "parasites of imperialism." They do not directly cause imperialism, but thrive on it.

Finally, the most influential of all business groups, the bankers, may be said not only to have a direct interest in imperialism, through colonial investments, but to represent indirectly all the above-mentioned interests, for banks have financial fingers in every industrial pie. The many billions of francs, pounds, and dollars invested in colonies have been invested through banks, for the most part. Banks underwrite the loans of colonies and backward countries, the capital issues of railways and steamship lines; they extend credit to colonial plantation-owners, to importers and exporters, to manufacturers and distributors. The six largest Berlin banks, in pre-war days, were represented, through interlocking directorates, in more than three hundred industrial corporations. The Deutsche Bank was the mainspring of German imperialism in the Near East. The Rothschilds, it will be recalled, lent Disraeli the money to buy shares in the Suez Canal, and, more than that, utilized their political influence to bring about the conquest of Egypt. The French conquest of Tunis has been called a piece of high finance—*un coup de Bourse*. The National City Bank has played an important role in the Caribbean policy of the United States.[3] British bankers have established literally thousands of colonial branches.

[3]The lists of financial interests given in Dunn, *American Foreign Investments*, offer impressive confirmation of the general thesis advanced in this paragraph.

All these business interests taken together may be much less important than the interests which have no direct concern in imperialism, since nothing like half of the world's commerce,[4] shipping, production, and finance, is accounted for by colonies. But the imperialist business interests are powerful, well-organized, and active. Through lobbies and campaign funds they influence political parties. For example, Mr. Doheny, being interested in Mexican oil, gave generous contributions to both of the major parties in the United States, in order to make sure that his Mexican interests would be favorably regarded in any case. Cecil Rhodes, the diamond king of South Africa, contributed to the Liberal Party on condition that it would not "scuttle out of Egypt," for he needed Egypt as the northern terminus for his projected Cape-to-Cairo Railway and telegraph line. But campaign contributions represent only one of innumerable methods of influencing the government. A Bismarck, a William II, a Nicholas II, or a lesser official may be induced to invest in colonial enterprises. The son-in-law of a president may be paid a handsome retainer, to use his influence at the White House in favor of American oil interests in Mexico. A Cecil Rhodes may purchase newspapers to praise his projects. The methods are legion.

Their Allies

Moreover, the imperialist business interests have influential allies. Military and naval officers are often predisposed in favor of imperialism. Rear Admiral Rodgers, retired, recently declared that "if our successors remain a virile people as the world fills up they will remain armed to take what they want at the expense of others"; the United States, he believed, would have to engage in imperialist conquests when its population passed the 200,000,000 mark. Admiral Dewey urged annexation of the Philippines. Lord Fisher, rugged British sea-dog, joined forces with the oil interests to secure Britain's navy an adequate supply of oil. Similar illustrations could be multiplied endlessly for every imperialist nation. Military and naval leaders who have helped to conquer colonies usually believe ardently in the desirability of extending the white man's dominion over the "inferior races." To think otherwise would be unnatural for an officer who has won his spurs in colonial wars; for one of the strongest of our

[4]In 1922-3 the total international commerce of the world was almost fifty billion dollars, of which the colonies and protectorates accounted for about ten billions, and other partially dependent countries (Cuba, Nicaragua, Panama, Dominican Republic, Haiti, Egypt and Liberia which are nominally independent accounted for another billion.

impulses is to find some justification for our own work. Furthermore, by mental processes more often subconscious than conscious, fighting men sometimes proceed from the premise that promotions are more rapid in expanding armies and navies, to the conclusion that in a world of greed and force each nation must "remain armed to take what they want at the expense of others." Rarely is the militarist's belief in armaments and expansion consciously based on class interest or personal advantage; but it would be difficult to find a clearer case of class psychology.

Quite similar is the interest of diplomatists, colonial officials and their families. Prestige and advancement are almost assured for the diplomatist who obtains something for his country. Colonial officials make careers and names for themselves not by prosaic administration, but by adding new provinces to old. As their profession is the governing of backward races, they feel certain of their country's mission to govern more, and ever more, of the colored peoples. An altruistic professional faith blends with personal ambition. One needs but mention the name of a Lord Milner, a Lord Curzon, a Lord Cromer, a Sir Harry Johnston, to support this statement; their deeds will appear in later pages. But the host of more obscure administrators should not be ignored in favor of a few celebrities. Thousands of families in England and France have provided recruits for the colonial administration, and take a kind of family pride in imperialism. Some of these families are very influential, particularly in England where so many a proud but impecunious nobleman finds in imperialism a solution of the problem of "younger sons"; for all except the eldest heir must be located in honorable professions such as Parliament, the Church, the Army, the Navy, or the Colonies.

To this motley company of business men, fighting men, and "younger sons" must be added another incongruous element—the missionary. The nineteenth century, following hard on the heels of an age of doubt, witnessed a remarkable religious revival in Europe, and one of the most notable manifestations of increased fervor was the sudden expansion of missionary effort. Going out to preach a kingdom not of this world, missionaries found themselves very often builders of very earthly empires. Sometimes they promoted imperialism quite unintentionally; being killed by savages, for example, was a very effective though not a deliberate, patriotic service, inasmuch as it might afford the home country a reason or a pretext for conquest. Thus the murder of two German missionaries in China gave Germany a pretext for seizing a Chinese port. But more important was the direct impetus intentionally given to imperialism by missionaries.

Livingstone, the famous Scottish missionary to Africa, desired with all his heart that British rule might be extended in the Dark Continent, to wipe out slavery, to spread civilization and Christianity. Fabri, whom we have mentioned as one of the leading advocates of colonial expansion in Bismarck's time, was inspector of a German missionary society active in South West Africa; he probably converted more Germans to imperialism than Africans to Christianity. Time and again missionaries in some savage land have called upon their mother-country to raise its protecting flag above them. Time and again British missionaries have persuaded a converted chieftain to offer his fealty to the British crown. Protestant missionaries representing national churches have doubtless been particularly predisposed to regard themselves as representatives, pioneers, of their own nation; but Catholic missionaries of France, though their creed was international, were hardly less nationalistic in aiding the expansion of French power in Africa. Often, too, missionaries by teaching natives to wear clothes and use tools have paved the way for the merchant, who in turn has brought the warship. And while missionaries toiled in heathen lands, enthusiastic missionary societies at home, and the leaders of the churches, learned to take a direct interest in Asia, Africa, and the South Sea Islands, and to urge upon statesmen the need of extending civilized Christian government over benighted pagans. In all this there is a note of tragic irony. Where grasping merchant and murderous machine-gun followed the missionaries' trail, the message of Christianity was not always appreciated, nor were Christian morals advanced by the gin and the venereal disease brought by trader and soldier. But the fact remains that the missionary organizations were among the active groups which promoted imperialism.

Explorers and adventurers—if we may couple them with prejudice to neither—were conspicuous in the early days of imperialism. Henry Morton Stanley was something of both, and a journalist to boot. By birth he was a Welshman, of the name Rowlands. Born in Wales, of a poor family, he ran away from school, to find work in the city of Liverpool, first in a haberdasher's shop, then with a butcher. When this grew tedious, he worked his way across the sea to New Orleans. There he was adopted by a merchant by the name of Henry Morton Stanley, whose name he accepted and later made illustrious. Young Stanley had begun a prosaic existence as a country storekeeper in Arkansas when the Civil War called him to a more stirring career. Enlisting in the Confederate army, he was captured by the enemy; with ready versatility he then joined the Union army to fight against his former comrades-in-arms. Toward the close of the war he discovered a latent talent for journalism, which, when peace returned, led him to Salt Lake City, to describe the extraordinary customs of the Mormons, then to Asia Minor in search of thrilling adventure; then with General Hancock against the Indians, with the British against Abyssinia, and to Crete, and Spain. When David Livingstone, the famous missionary-explorer, was lost in the heart of Africa, Stanley was selected by James Gordon Bennett, owner of the *Herald,* to find him. And Stanley did. This exploit, in 1871, converted Stanley into an African explorer. In succeeding years he made repeated trips into the interior of Africa. We are not concerned here with the details of his explorations, however, but with his influence on imperialism. After making his historic journey, in the years 1874-1877, across the hitherto unexplored Congo basin in Central Africa, Stanley became an apostle of imperialism. With eloquent pen and tongue he portrayed the marvelous economic potentialities of the region he had discovered; but, far from being sordidly materialistic, he urged the sending of missionaries, the abolition of the slave traffic, and the civilization of the natives.

How this extraordinary adventurer-explorer-journalist, failing to arouse the interest of cautious English capitalists, lent his services to Leopold of Belgium and established a huge empire for that monarch, a later chapter will tell. But a speech he delivered before a gathering of the Manchester Chamber of Commerce—chiefly cotton merchants—may perhaps be quoted in part. Assuming that civilization and Christianity would teach the naked negroes of Congo to wear decent cotton clothes, at least on Sundays, he estimated that one Sunday dress for each native would mean "320,000,000 yards of Manchester cotton cloth" (Cheers from the audience); and in time, when the natives had learned the importance of covering their nakedness on weekdays as well as Sundays, the amount of cloth required would amount to twenty-six million pounds sterling per annum. In his peroration he fused the mercantile and missionary motives in masterly style:

> There are forty millions of people beyond the gateway of the Congo, and the cotton spinners of Manchester are waiting to clothe them. Birmingham foundries are glowing with the red metal that will presently be made into ironwork for them and the trinkets that shall adorn those dusky bosoms, and the ministers of Christ are zealous to bring them, the poor benighted heathen, into the Christian fold.[5]

Stanley may have been unique in his versatility and his logic, but as an imperialist explorer he was in some measure typical of

[5]Pamphlet issued by the Manchester Chamber of Commerce, 1884.

scores. It was an explorer, Gustav Nachtigal, who declared the German protectorates in Kamerun and Togoland. Henry Hamilton Johnston (later Sir Harry), began his career as a scientific explorer, interested in architecture, and art, and languages, and biology, but became an empire-builder in Africa, annexing vast territories for England, and striving to complete the Cape-to-Cairo route of which he dreamed. There is no need to lengthen the list beyond the reader's patience.

Last, but by no means least, let us add a sprinkling of politicians to our already heterogeneous array of active empire-builders, with definite personal interests at stake. Some premiers and presidents have acted, more or less unwillingly, at the instigation of business and other interest-groups: Gladstone, for example, was compelled to seize Egypt though his heart may have been heavy; Bismarck yielded to the imperialist only after long resistance; Woodrow Wilson opposed imperialism with extraordinary courage, yet was driven to more than one imperialist enterprise. But others have deliberately promoted imperialism either because they believed in it, or because they felt that it would bring prestige and votes, or campaign contributions. Disraeli, apparently, believed in England's eastern empire, and at the same time was very much aware of the strength of the appeal he could make to voters on the issue of national pride. Roosevelt, with his "big stick" policy and his "Rough Rider" campaign parades, skillfully stimulated and utilized imperialist sentiment in America.

Interests and Ideas

But, a sceptical reader may object, imposing as the array of importers, exporters, shippers, financiers, admirals, generals, officials, diplomats, missionaries, explorers, and politicians may appear when reviewed in detail, still it remains true that these active imperialist interests are minority interests. The overwhelming majority of a nation has no direct business, or professional, or military interest in colonial empire. Not only is this true of the poorer classes, who of course have no colonial investments,[6] but it applies also to many, probably a majority, of capitalists and business men. Indeed, imperialism might appear to be directly contrary to the economic interests of many business men. For instance, American ownership of Hawaii injures the beet-sugar producers, by admitting Hawaiian cane sugar free of duty. French ownership of Algeria may injure French wine-producers by developing the production of Algerian wine, much of which is used to slake

---

[6]Although admittedly a considerable percentage of the working class is employed directly in the production of goods for export to colonies, or in industries utilizing colonial raw materials.

the thirst of Frenchmen, in substitution for domestic vintages. The issue is not between "capital" and "the masses"; capital is divided, one section against another, one industry against another. Why, then, does the majority so cheerfully follow the leadership of the imperialist minorities?

Not direct interests, but ideas, not property or profession, but principles, actuate the public at large. The theories spread broadcast by imperialist propaganda are the dynamic factors impelling nations to send out armies, defray expenditures, risk wars, for the conquest of distant colonies and protectorates. It requires ideas, attuned to instinctive emotions, to make modern nations fight. The ideas which have been particularly potent in imperialism are the idea of preventive self-defense, which awakens the primitive emotion of fear; the idea of surplus population, resting on the instinct of self-preservation; the ideas of economic nationalism, and national prestige, appealing to instincts of gregariousness and self-aggrandizement; and an aggressive sort of altruism, which gratifies our innate pride. These ideas require analysis.

Fear, so easily aroused in the human soul, and so powerful when once awakened, is a cardinal factor in imperialist world politics. The citizens of modern nations fear attack, defeat, conquest. To persuade them that such calamities may be prevented by preparedness for war, is a relatively easy task, as the universality of armies and navies all too convincingly testifies. But of what use is a navy without coaling stations and naval bases? Thus the argument proceeds. If hostile fleets are to be held off from a vulnerable coast, the nation must have outlying naval bases and defeat the enemy's squadrons before they approach. That Great Britain has secured naval bases in all the seven seas, every schoolboy knows. But Great Britain is not unique in this respect. The need of naval bases was one of the chief arguments used by Jules Ferry in the eighties to justify French annexations. It is one of the most popular justifications for American ownership of the Philippines, Hawaii, Samoa, Porto Rico, the Danish West Indies. It has given anxiety to the Japanese, the Germans, the Dutch, the Italians.

A kindred theory, springing from the same motive of self-protection, is that a nation must control raw material in time of war. It is all very well, imperialists argue, to purchase iron, and coal, and cotton, and rubber, and nitrate, and oil from neighbors in time of peace, but in war a nation must have its own supplies, else its cannon will lack shells, its arsenals will stand idle without coal, its warships, tanks, and airplanes will have no fuel, its laboratories will look in vain for ingredients of explosives. What argument could be more plausible, or more moving? The unimpassioned student may perhaps inquire whether ownership of oil wells in some distant colony will be of value, in war, to any except the supreme naval power, that is, England. But to the "man in the street" such doubt rarely occurs.

Even more influential has been the idea that the great civilized nations, being "overpopulated," need colonies as outlets for their "surplus population." To France, of course, no such argument could be applied, nor was it much used in England; but it has enjoyed an extraordinary vogue in Germany, Japan, and Italy, and it is not unfamiliar in the United States. In a densely populated country, where competition for employment is keen and the cost of living is rising, it is easy to believe that overcrowding is responsible for unemployment and poverty, and that additional breathing-room for the teeming millions is an absolute necessity. The case is all the more convincing, if thousands of emigrants are annually leaving their "overcrowded" mother-country, to find homes in more spacious lands.

Germany was in this situation, on the eve of the outburst of imperialism. In the decade from 1871 to 1880, no fewer than 625,968 Germans forsook the Fatherland, to become inhabitants of the United States, Brazil, and other foreign countries. And yet, the population in Germany increased, at the same time, from about forty-one to over forty-five millions. After 1880 the figures became even more startling. In the years 1881-1884, some 747,168 Germans emigrated—more in four years than in the previous decade. Such figures the imperialist propagandists in Germany used with telling effect. Germans became so profoundly convinced of their "surplus population," that the argument was still being mouthed long after the emigration figures had sunk—as they did in the 1890's and after—to an insignificant figure, and after the growth of population in Germany to fifty, then to sixty, then to sixty-five millions had demonstrated that the anxiety expressed in the eighties was quite unwarranted.[7]

[7]The following table computed from the *Statistisches Handbuch für das Deutsche Reich* (Berlin, 1907), shows the situation more plainly.

	Emigration in 5 Yrs.	Increase of Population in 5 Yrs.	Total Population at End of Period.
1871-75	394,814	1,668,558	42,729,360
1876-80	231,154	2,506,701	45,236,061
1881-85	857,287	1,621,643	46,857,704
1886-90	485,136	2,570,766	49,428,470
1891-95	402,567	2,651,431	52,279,901
1896-1900	127,398	4,087,277	56,367,178

The Italian public, likewise, was alarmed by emigration figures, which rose from 94,000 in 1881 to 118,000 in 1891, to 282,000 in 1901, and have continued to exceed two hundred thousand a year. Most of these emigrants, to be sure, have gone to European and American countries, and many have returned to Italy with their savings, but Italian imperialists have eloquently urged the necessity of African colonies as outlets for this tide, regardless of the fact that emigrants seem to prefer civilized countries where employment is easily found.

In Japan, an increase of population from thirty-three to fifty-six millions during the half-century after 1872, and the emigration of about 600,000 during the same period,[8] provided imperialists with plausible grounds for their thesis that Japan must be permitted to conquer colonies to relieve overcrowding. Curiously enough, this was one of the arguments popularly used to justify Japan's seizure of the Chinese province of Shantung, in 1915, although Shantung happens to be more densely populated than Japan.

A little reflection reveals the fallacy of using "surplus population" as an argument for imperialism. Development of industry and commerce enables supposedly overpopulated countries to support ever-increasing populations. For such development, a country needs increased investment of capital at home. Emigrants leave, not because there is no room for them, but because they believe they can earn more money, or enjoy greater freedom elsewhere, and they seek prosperity, regardless of flag or nationality, in the country that seems to offer the most attractive opportunities. The colonies that were to be had, and were taken, during the imperialist age from 1875 to the present, have been unsuitable for European colonization, and have failed to attract immigrants. We shall return to this problem later on, but for the present the point to be made is, that the idea of surplus population, fallacious as it may be, has been and still is a vital factor in popularizing imperialism.

The third popular belief, which we have called economic nationalism, has already been elucidated but needs practical application here. The teachings of economists and arguments of List and Fabri and Ferry and Chamberlain and their compeers have sunk so deeply into popular consciousness, that Europeans, except Socialists, and many Americans take it for granted that there is such a thing as "national

---

[8]The census of 1925 showed a population of 59,736,704, not including Chosen (Korea), Taiwan (Formosa), and Karafuto (Sakhalin). In June, 1922, the Japanese Foreign Office estimated the number of Japanese residing abroad as 590,000 including 134,000 in South Manchuria.

wealth," and that this thing is increased if a rich colony or a profitable concession is secured overseas. The diamond and gold mines of South Africa are regarded as an addition to Britain's store of wealth; the resources of North Africa are added to those of France; the profits to be made by an oil concession in the Near East or in Mexico are added to the income of the American nation. Germany, it has been generally assumed, was made poorer by the loss of her colonies in 1919.

There might be other ways of looking at such matters. Norman Angell and other persuasive pacifists have endeavored to prove that conquests do not profit a nation. A sceptic may ask whether "national wealth" is more than a phrase; certainly the profits of Cecil Rhodes were not shared by the denizens of the London slums, nor have the dividends from Mexican oil been distributed equally throughout the American nation. One might even go further, and inquire whether the Boer War, while profitable to mine-owners, did not prove an actual loss, in money, to the bulk of English taxpayers. But national sentiment stills all such doubts, and perhaps even a pauper may have some share in the glorious consciousness that "we" own rich mines here and fertile fields there; that "we" have billions invested in tropical lands. And certainly national sentiment responds with instant thrill when one's fellow-countrymen clash with foreigners in rivalry for a railway concession in some backward country, or for the commerce of a colony. So strong is this sentiment, that applause rather than surprise greets the action of the foreign minister or secretary of state who officially takes up diplomatic cudgels to defend against foreign competitors the business interests of certain citizens belonging to his nation, albeit he would not think of giving the same governmental support to a private business interest at home.

Quite as subtle, and as potent, is the complex of imperialist ideas clustering around the notion that a nation's honor and prestige must be zealously cherished. The fundamental impulse is primitive enough to be easily comprehended. Each of us naturally desires any group or organization with which he is identified to be better than rival groups. Our own egotism, or vanity, may perhaps be at the bottom of the desire, for we enjoy the prestige reflected upon us by our group. We enjoy this prestige, whether it is reflected by our family, our fraternity, our college, our club, our team, our city, our state, or our nation. Most of all our nation. We are willing to die for that, but not for club or college. The impulse may be simple, but the applications in imperialism are subtle. For example, the desire for prestige, for greatness, impels Italian taxpayers to pour out hundreds of millions of lire on a relatively barren African empire. Possessing unprofitable and rebellious but impressively extensive colonies, enables Italians to feel that they belong to a Great Power; that theirs is one of the imperial races. The hearts of true Britons beat faster at the thought of England's world empire and world mission, at the sight of world-maps showing Britain's vast possessions all colored in conspicuous red. Germans—before the great defeat—demanded their "place in the sun," meaning a large share of tropical Africa and Asia, as the rightful heritage of a great nation, and eagerly published maps showing Germany's ambitious claims. Frenchmen, learning the phrases of Ferry, repeated the prophecy that unless France built up a great African empire she would become a second or third-rate power. And what patriot desires his nation to be third-rate?

The same solicitude for prestige is responsible for the belief that a nation, a great nation, must punish atrocities or insults to the flag, and protect its citizens and their property in other countries. To refuse protection, most of us feel, is to sacrifice national honor. No proud nation can tolerate affronts. The blowing-up of the United States battleship *Maine* had to be avenged in blood. If German missionaries are murdered in China, Germany must maintain her honor by seizing a Chinese port, and by exacting reparation and apologies. If British fortune-hunters surge into the South African Republic, attracted by the gold mines, and are denied the vote, British statesmen indignantly protest that Englishmen are not to be treated as "helots," and British armies are sent to conquer the country. If an Italian girl is kidnapped by a Moslem, Italy is justified in seizing Tripoli. If Mexicans refuse a salute to the Stars and Stripes, American marines occupy Vera Cruz.[9] If Chinese officials arrest murderers on a ship flying the British flag, Britain has reason to make war on China, and to demand Chinese territory. National honor must be maintained.[10]

National honor is at stake also when two imperialist nations contend for the dubious privilege of conquering a backward nation. When, for example, Germany questions the right of France to subject the unruly and bankrupt African empire of Morocco, it would be humiliating for France to yield, and no less humiliating for Germany: national honor is involved. Even though a compromise may be affected,

[9]They did not actually refuse.
[10]See the interesting collection of interpretations of this concept in L. Perla, *What Is National Honor?* (N. Y., 1918.)

there will be widespread resentment in both countries, for national honor admits of no compromise.

Finally, some attention must be given to what may be called, for lack of a better name, aggressive altruism. Kipling styled it "The White Man's Burden." His celebrated poem, written in 1899, urges us to—

> Take up the White Man's Burden—
>   Send forth the best ye breed—
> Go bind your sons to exile
>   To serve your captives' need;
> To wait in heavy harness,
>   On fluttered fold and wild—
> Your new-caught, sullen peoples,
>   Half-devil and half-child.

The white man's burden, in plain prose, is to govern and civilize the Asiatics and Africans, the backward peoples who are half devil and half child, sullen and wild. Jules Ferry made it plainer; the "superior races" (including France, naturally) have "the duty of civilizing the inferior races." France has a *mission civilisatrice* in Africa. Germans devoutly believe in their call to give German Kultur to the hapless negroes of Africa,—or, more accurately, to impose it upon them by force. Americans, to a lesser degree, take pride in the sanitary, educational, and other reforms which they have achieved in conquered islands of the Caribbean and Pacific. President Mc-Kinley declared, as a reason for annexing the Philippine Islands, that "there was nothing left for us to do but to take them all, and to educate the Filipinos, and uplift and civilize and christianize them as our fellow-men for whom Christ also died." Wilson's Mexican policy was, as Ambassador Page told the British government, "shooting men into self-government." The British foreign secretary found this phrase difficult to grasp, but he had no difficulty in appreciating England's beneficent task of keeping order in India and other disorderly countries.

This is altruism, and aggressive altruism, because it means using force, brutal force, to impose on unwilling native peoples the blessings of French, or German, or British, or American civilization. Indeed, this altruism goes to such lengths that the civilizing nations are willing not only to shoot Hindus, or Zulus, or Filipinos, or Mexicans, into culture, but even to undergo the hardships of war with equally zealous civilizing nations, and to call upon savages from Africa, as they did in 1914, to join in the battle in behalf of the superior variety of European civilization. An altruism so earnest as this is a very important factor in the popular support for imperialism.

Altruism, national honor, economic nationalism, surplus population, self-protection—such are the principles or ideas which nerve nations to valiant feats of empire-building. The initiative, to be sure, is taken by interests; but the support is given by ideas. When a colony or a protectorate is acquired, the first steps are taken, as a rule, by the business or naval or missionary interests described in the first part of this chapter; not infrequently the public, ignorant not only of what has been going_on, but even of the geographical location of the region about to be annexed, is confronted with an accomplished deed, a *fait accompli,* which needs only to be officially solemnified, popularly applauded, and, perchance, defended. Then the ideas function. The public rallies to the support of importer, exporter, banker, or shipper, missionary, administrator, admiral, or explorer. Imperialism, nay, all history, is made by the dynamic alliance of interests and ideas.

On Imperialism[1]

Joseph A. Schumpeter

Joseph A. Schumpeter (1883-1950) was born in Moravia and educated in Vienna. Although he studied in several scholarly fields, his major contributions were in economics. During his lifetime, most of which was spent in universities, he taught in Austria, Germany, Japan and the United States. From 1932 till his death he was at Harvard as a professor of economics. He was elected to the presidency of the American Economic Association and was a founding member of the Economic Society. Schumpeter's impressive list of scholorly works includes: *The Theory of Economic Development: An Inquiry into Profits, Capital, Credit, Interest and the Business Cycle* (1912); *Economic Doctrine and Method; an Historical Sketch* (1914); *Imeprialism and Social Classes* (1919-1927); *Business Cycles: A Theoretical, Historical, and Statistical Analysis of the Capitalist Process* (1939); *Capitalism, Socialism and Democracy* (1942); *History of Economic Analysis* (1954—published posthumously).

Schumpeter in the following piece from his *Imperialism and Social Classes* rejects the view that economic explanations can adequately explain the phenomenon of imperialism. According to him imperialism was not a necessary stage in the development of capitalism, but capitalism was inherently anti-imperialist. Modern imperialism was not a result of economic factors but a product of pre-capitalist ideas. It was an alliance between a small group of highly selfish capitalists and the members of a small group of people who retained a feudal outlook.

The reader is advised to examine the following articles in connection with Schumpeter's work:

M. Green, "Schumpeter's Imperialism: A Critical Note," *Social Research*, XIX, December 1952, p. 453-63.

E. Heimann, "Schumpeter and the Problem of Imperialism," *Social Research*, XIX, June 1952, p. 177-97.

Our problem arises from the fact that aggressive attitudes on the part of states—or of such earlier organizational structures as history may record—can be explained, directly and unequivocally, only in part by the real and concrete interests of the people. Examples will

[1]Reprinted from *Imperialism and Social Classes* (translated by Heinz Norden), New York, Augustus M. Kelley Publishers, 1951, pages 3-8, 83-101, 108-118, 125-130.

best illustrate what we mean. When two tribes come into conflict over essential salt deposits or hunting grounds; or when a state, hemmed in on all sides by customs and communication barriers, resorts to aggression in order to gain access to the sea, we have a case in which aggression is explained by interests. It is true that there are many methodological difficulties in speaking of the interests of a people as such. Here, however, reference to "concrete" interests explains everything that would seem to stand in need of explanation. A concrete interest need not be economic in character. When a state resorts to aggression in order to unite its citizens politically, as was the case with Piedmont in 1848 and 1859, this likewise betokens a real, concrete interest, explaining its conduct. The interest, moreover, need not necessarily extend to the *entire* population of the state. When a planter aristocracy prevails upon its government to seize some foreign base of operations for the slave trade, this too is explained by a real, concrete interest. The interest that actually explains a warlike act need not, finally, be openly admitted—or of the kind that *can* be openly admitted; it need not, to use our own term, be an *avowed* interest. Such cases nevertheless come under the present heading, if the concrete interests of a sufficiently powerful class are accessible to scientific consideration. There are, on the other hand, certain cases that do *not* belong here, such as that of a group of people who contrive to have a declaration of war issued because they gain financially from the waging of war, or because they need a war as a diversion from domestic political difficulties. Here there is no concrete interest, in the sense that applies to the aforementioned cases. True, there must be *some* concrete interest. There must be a reason for the declaration of war. But that *reason* is not the *cause*. The true cause, of course, must also lie in an interest. But that interest is not in the concrete war aims. It is not a question of the advantages offered by the attainment of those aims, but of an interest in the waging of war as such. The questions that then arise are how the people came to acquire such a generally belligerent disposition and why they happened to choose this particular occasion for war. Thus mere reference to a concrete interest is satisfactory under only three conditions: In the first place, such a concrete interest *must be present,* in the sense that has now been made clear—an interest which the observer can grasp as such, of course taking into account the social structure, mentality, and situation of the people in question. In the second place, the conduct of the state which is under study must be calculated to *promote* this interest, with the sum total of predictable sacrifices and risks in some proportion to the anticipated gains. In the third place, it must be possible to *prove* that this interest, whether avowed or not, is actually the *political driving force* behind the action.

In the individual case it may often become difficult to establish whether these conditions obtain. The fabric of social interests is so closely woven that scarcely ever can there be any action on the part of a state that is not in keeping with the concrete interest of someone,, an interest to which that action can be reduced without manifest absurdity. To this must be added the belief, inculcated into the people, especially in the present age, that concrete interest of the people dictate the behavior of the state and that concrete advantages for all classes are to be expected. Government policies are always officially justified in this way, and often, without the slightest doubt, in perfect good faith. Finally, current fallacies, especially of an economic character, may serve to create the semblance of an adequate, concrete interest in the mind of the people—and occasionally even in the mind of the scientific observer, especially the historian. In such cases the true background is laid bare only by an inquiry into the manner in which the people came to their belief. But the individual case does not concern us. We are concerned only with the fact, which is beyond doubt, that the three above-mentioned conditions are frequently not fulfilled. Whenever such is the case, a problem arises. And among the problems of this nature is the problem of imperialism.

No one calls it imperialism when a state, no matter how brutally and vigorously, pursues concrete interests of its own; and when it can be expected to abandon its aggressive attitude as soon as it has attained what it was after. The word "imperialism" has been abused as a slogan to the point where it threatens to lose all meaning, but up to this point our definition is quite in keeping with common usage, even in the press. For whenever the word imperialism is used, there is always the implication—whether sincere or not—of an aggressiveness, the true reasons for which do not lie in the aims which are temporarily being pursued; of an aggressiveness that is only kindled anew by each success; of an aggressiveness for its own sake, as reflected in such terms as "hegemony," "world dominion," and so forth. And history, in truth, shows us nations and classes—most nations furnish an example at some time or other—that seek expansion for the sake of expanding, war for the sake of fighting, victory for the sake of winning, dominion for the sake of ruling. This determination cannot be explained by any of the pretexts that bring it into action, by any of the aims for which it seems to be struggling at the time. It confronts us, independent of all concrete purpose or occasion, as an enduring disposition, seizing upon one opportunity as eagerly as the next. It shines through all the arguments put forward on behalf of present aims. It values conquest not so much on account of the immediate advantages—advantages that more often than not are more than dubious, or that are heedlessly cast away with the same frequency—as because it *is* conquest, success, action. Here the theory of concrete interest in our sense fails. What needs to be explained is how the will to victory itself came into being.

Expansion for its own sake always requires, among other things, concrete objects if it is to reach the action stage and maintain itself, but this does not constitute its meaning. Such expansion is in a sense its own "object," and the truth is that it has no adequate object beyond itself. Let us therefore, in the absence of a better term, call it "objectless." It follows for that very reason that, just as such expansion cannot be explained by concrete interest, so too it is never satisfied by the fulfillment of a concrete interest, as would be the case if fulfillment were the motive, and the struggle for it merely a necessary evil—a counterargument, in fact. Hence the tendency of such expansion to transcend all bounds and tangible limits, to the point of utter exhaustion. This, then, is our definition: imperialism is the objectless disposition on the part of a state to unlimited forcible expansion.

Now it may be possible, in the final analysis, to give an "economic explanation" for this phenomenon, to end up with economic factors. Two different points present themselves in this connection: First, an attempt can be made, following the basic idea of the economic interpretation of history, to derive imperialist tendencies from the economic-structural influences that shape life in general and from the relations of production. I should like to emphasize that I do not doubt in the least that this powerful instrument of analysis will stand up here in the same sense that it has with other, similar phenomena—if only it is kept in mind that customary modes of political thought and feeling in a given age can never be mere "reflexes" of, or counterparts to, the production situation of that age. Because of the persistence of such habits, they will always, to a considerable degree, be dominated by the production context of past ages. Again, the attempt may be made to reduce imperialist phenomena to economic class *interests* of the age in question. This is precisely what neo-Marxist theory does. Briefly, it views imperialism simply as the reflex of the interests of the capitalist upper stratum, at a given stage of capitalist development. Beyond doubt this is by far the most serious contribution toward a solution of our problem. Certainly there is much truth in it. We shall deal with this theory later. But let us emphasize even here that it does not, of logical necessity, follow from the economic interpretation of history. It may be discarded without coming into conflict with that interpretation; indeed, without even departing from its premises. It is the treatment of this factor that constitutes the contribution of the present inquiry into the sociology of the *Zeitgeist*. Our analysis of the historical evidence has shown, first, the unquestionable fact that "objectless" tendencies toward forcible expansion, without definite, utilitarian limits—that is, non-rational and irrational, purely instinctual inclinations toward war and conquest—play a very large role in the history of mankind. It may sound paradoxical, but numberless wars—perhaps the majority of all wars—have been waged without adequate "reason"— not so much from the moral viewpoint as from that of reasoned and reasonable interest. The most herculean efforts of the nations, in other words, have faded into the empty air.[2] Our analysis, in the second place, provides an explanation for this drive to action, this will to war—a theory by no means exhausted by mere references to an "urge" or an "instinct." The explanation lies, instead, in the vital needs of situations that molded peoples and classes into warriors—if they wanted to avoid extinction—and in the fact that psychological dispositions and social structures acquired in the dim past in such situations, once firmly established, tend to maintain themselves and to continue in effect long after they have lost their meaning and their life-preserving function. Our analysis, in the third place, has shown the existence of subsidiary factors that facilitate the survival of such dispositions and structures—factors that may be divided into two groups. The orientation toward war is mainly fostered by the domestic interests of ruling classes, but also by the influence of all those who stand to gain individually from a war policy, whether economically or socially. Both groups of factors are generally overgrown by elements of an altogether different character, not only in terms of political phraseology, but also of psychological motivation. Imperialisms differ greatly in detail, but they all have at least these

2This is not meant to prejudice the question of whether such efforts, in the final reckoning, achieved objective cultural gains or not, a subject falling outside our present province. Personally, I take a predominantly negative view of their significance. But my arguments along these lines are again beyond the present study.

traits in common, turning them into a single phenomenon in the field of sociology, as we noted in the introduction.

Imperialism thus is atavistic in character. It falls into that large group of surviving features from earlier ages that play such an important part in every concrete social situation. In other words, it is an element that stems from the living conditions, not of the present, but of the past—or, put in terms of the economic interpretation of history, from past rather than present relations of production.[3] It is an atavism in the social structure, in individual, psychological habits of emotional reaction. Since the vital needs that created it have passed away for good, it too must gradually disappear, even though every warlike involvement, no matter how non-imperialist in character, tends to revive it. It tends to disappear as a structural element because the structure that brought it to the fore goes into a decline, giving way, in the course of social development, to other structures that have no room for it and eliminate the power factors that supported it. It tends to disappear as an element of habitual emotional reaction, because of the progressive rationalization of life and mind, a process in which old functional needs are absorbed by new tasks, in which heretofore military energies are functionally modified. If our theory is correct, cases of imperialism should decline in intensity the later they occur in the history of a people and of a culture. Our most recent examples of unmistakable, clear-cut imperialism are the absolute monarchies of the eighteenth century. They are unmistakably "more civilized" than their predecessors.

It is from absolute autocracy that the present age has taken over what imperialist tendencies it displays. And the imperialism of

[3]Imperialism is one of many examples of the important fact, already alluded to in the beginning, that the application of the economic interpretation of history holds out no hope of reducing the cultural data of a given period to the relations of production of that same period. This always serves to support objections to the basic economic approach, particularly since one of the consequences of the cited fact is that relations of production in a given period may often be reduced to existing economic sentiments that are independent of those relations. For example, the constitutional and political order of the Normans in southern Italy cannot be explained by the relations of production prevailing in that country. The very economy of the Normans in southern Italy becomes comprehensible only by reference to their capacity and wishes. But this does not actually refute the economic interpretation, for the mentality of the Normans was not something that existed outside the economic sphere. Its sources are found in the economic background from which the Normans came to southern Italy.

absolute autocracy flourished before the Industrial Revolution that created the modern world, or rather, before the consequences of that revolution began to be felt in all their aspects. These two statements are primarily meant in a historical sense, and as such they are no more than self-evident. We shall nevertheless try, within the framework of our theory, to define the significance of capitalism for our phenomenon and to examine the relationship between present-day imperialist tendencies and the autocratic imperialism of the eighteenth century.

The floodtide that burst the dams in the Industrial Revolution had its sources, of course, back in the Middle Ages. But capitalism began to shape society and impress its stamp on every page of social history only with the second half of the eighteenth century. Before that time there had been only islands of capitalist economy imbedded in an ocean of village and urban economy. True, certain political influences emanated from these islands, but they were able to assert themselves only indirectly. Not until the process we term the Industrial Revolution did the working masses, led by the entrepreneur, overcome the bonds of older lifeforms—the environment of peasantry, guild, and aristocracy. The causal connection was this: A transformation in the basic economic factors (which need not detain us here) created the objective opportunity for the production of commodities, for large-scale industry, working for a market of customers whose individual identities were unknown, operating solely with a view to maximum financial profit. It was this opportunity that created an economically oriented leadership—personalities whose field of achievement was the organization of such commodity production in the form of capitalist enterprise. Successful enterprises in large numbers represented something new in the economic and social sense. They fought for and won freedom of action. They compelled state policy to adapt itself to their needs. More and more they attracted the most vigorous leaders from other spheres, as well as the manpower of those spheres, causing them and the social strata they represented to languish. Capitalist entrepreneurs fought the former ruling circles for a share in state control, for leadership in the state. The very fact of their success, their position, their resources, their power, raised them in the political and social scale. Their mode of life, their cast of mind became increasingly important elements on the social scene. Their actions, desires, needs, and beliefs emerged more and more sharply within the total picture of the social community. In a historical sense, this applied primarily to the industrial and financial leaders of the movement—the bourgeoisie. But soon it applied also to the working masses which this movement created and placed in an altogether new class situation. This situation was governed by new forms of the working day, of family life, of interests—and these, in turn, corresponded to new orientations toward the social structure as a whole. More and more, in the course of the nineteenth century, the typical modern worker came to determine the overall aspect of society; for competitive capitalism, by its inherent logic, kept on raising the demand for labor and thus the economic level and social power of the workers,[4] until this class too was able to assert itself in a political sense. The working class and its mode of life provided the type from which the intellectual developed. Capitalism did not create the intellectuals—the "new middle class." But in earlier times only the legal scholar, the cleric, and the physician had formed a special intellectual class, and even they had enjoyed but little scope for playing an independent role. Such opportunities were provided only by capitalist society, which created the industrial and financial bureaucrat, the journalist, and so on, and which opened up new vistas to the jurist and physician. The "professional" of capitalist society arose as a class type. Finally, as a class type, the rentier, the beneficiary of industrial loan capital, is also a creature of capitalism. All these types are shaped by the capitalist mode of production, and they tend for this reason to bring other types—even the peasant—into conformity with themselves.

These new types were now cast adrift from the fixed order of earlier times, from the environment that had shackled and protected people for centuries, from the old associations of village, manor house, clan fellowship, often even from families in the broader sense. They were severed from the things that had been constant year after year, from cradle to grave—tools, homes, the countryside, especially the soil. They were on their own, enmeshed in the pitiless logic of gainful employment, mere drops in the vast ocean of industrial life, exposed to the inexorable pressures of competition. They were freed from the control of ancient patterns of thought, of the grip of institutions and organs that taught and represented these outlooks in village, manor, and guild. They were removed from the old world, engaged in building a new one for themselves—a specialized, mechaniz-

---

[4]There is here a conflict (not elaborated in the present study) with Marxism, primarily with the theories of increasing misery and the reserve army, but indirectly also with the basic conception of the whole process of capitalist production and accumulation.

ed world. Thus they were all inevitably democratized, individualized, and rationalized.[5] They were democratized, because the picture of time-honored power and privilege gave way to one of continual change, set in motion by industrial life. They were individualized, because subjective opportunities to shape their lives took the place of immutable objective factors. They were rationalized, because the instability of economic position made their survival hinge on continual, deliberately rationalistic decisions—a dependence that emerged with great sharpness. Trained to economic rationalism, these people left no sphere of life unrationalized, questioning everything about themselves, the social structure, the state, the ruling class. The marks of this process are engraved on every aspect of modern culture. It is this process that explains the basic features of that culture.

These are things that are well known today, recognized in their full significance—indeed, often exaggerated. Their application to our subject is plain. Everything that is purely instinctual, everything insofar as it is purely instinctual, is driven into the background by this development. It creates a social and psychological atmosphere in keeping with modern economic forms, where traditional habits, merely because they were traditional, could no more survive than obsolete economic forms. Just as the latter can survive only if they are continually "adapted," so instinctual tendencies can survive only when the conditions that gave rise to them continue to apply, or when the "instinct" in question derives a new purpose from new conditions. The "instinct" that is *only* "instinct," that has lost its purpose, languishes relatively quickly in the capitalist world, just as does an inefficient economic practice. We see this process of rationalization at work even in the case of the strongest impulses. We observe it, for example, in the facts of procreation. We must therefore anticipate finding it in the case of the imperialist impulse as well; we must expect to see this impulse, which rests on the primitive contingencies of physical combat, gradually disappear, washed away by new exigencies of daily life. There is another factor too. The competitive system absorbs the full energies of most of the people at all economic levels. Constant application, attention, and concentration of energy are the conditions of survival within it, primarily in the specifically economic professions, but also in other activities organized on their model. There is much less excess energy to be vented in war and conquest than in any precapitalist society. What excess energy there is flows

[5] See in this connection especially Lederer, "Zum sozialpsychischen Habitus der Gegenwart," *Archiv für Sozialwissenschaft und Sozialpolitik,* Vol. 44.

largely into industry itself, accounts for its shining figures—the type of the captain of industry—and for the rest is applied to art, science, and the social struggle. In a purely capitalist world, what was once energy for war becomes simply energy for labor of every kind. Wars of conquest and adventurism in foreign policy in general are bound to be regarded as troublesome distractions, destructive of life's meaning, a diversion from the accustomed and therefore "true" task.

A purely capitalist world therefore can offer no fertile soil to imperialist impulses. That does not mean that it cannot still maintain an interest in imperialist expansion. We shall discuss this immediately. The point is that its people are likely to be essentially of an unwarlike disposition. Hence we must expect that anti-imperialist tendencies will show themselves wherever capitalism penetrates the economy and, through the economy, the mind of modern nations—most strongly, of course, where capitalism itself is strongest, where it has advanced furthest, encountered the least resistance, and preeminently where its types and hence democracy—in the "bourgeois" sense—come closest to political dominion. We must further expect that the types formed by capitalism will actually be the carriers of these tendencies. Is such the case? The facts that follow are cited to show that this expectation, which flows from our theory, is in fact justified.

1. Throughout the world of capitalism, and specifically among the elements formed by capitalism in modern social life, there has arisen a fundamental opposition to war, expansion, cabinet diplomacy, armaments, and socially-entrenched professional armies. This opposition had its origin in the country that first turned capitalist—England—and arose coincidentally with that country's capitalist development. "Philosophical radicalism" was the first politically influential intellectual movement to represent this trend successfully, linking it up, as was to be expected, with economic freedom in general and free trade in particular. Molesworth became a cabinet member, even though he had publicly declared—on the occasion of the Canadian revolution—that he prayed for the defeat of his country's arms. In step with the advance of capitalism,[6] the movement also gained ad-

6This parallelism, of course, cannot be traced in every individual case. Countries and ideas differ far too greatly for that. Kant, for example, certainly did not have a pronounced capitalist background, though English influences did an important part with him. His case, by the way, offers the occasion to point out that we mean our assertions to apply to *all* types formed by capitalism, not merely, or primarily, to capitalistic classes in the sense of *propertied* classes—in other words

herents elsewhere—though at first only adherents without influence. It found support in Paris—indeed, in a circle oriented toward capitalist enterprise (for example, Frédéric Passy). True, pacifism as a matter of principle had existed before, though only among a few small religious sects. But modern pacifism, in its political foundations if not its derivation, is unquestionably a phenomenon of the capitalist world.

2. Wherever capitalism penetrated, peace parties of such strength arose that virtually every war meant a political struggle on the domestic scene. The exceptions are rare—Germany in the Franco-Prussian war of 1870-1871, both belligerents in the Russo-Turkish war of 1877-1878. That is why every war is carefully justified as a defensive war by the governments involved, and by all the political parties, in their official utterances—indicating a realization that a war of a different nature would scarcely be tenable in a political sense. (Here too the Russo-Turkish war is an exception, but a significant one.) In former times this would not have been necessary. Reference to an interest or pretense at moral justification was customary as early as the eighteenth century, but only in the nineteenth century did the assertion of attack, or the threat of attack, become the only avowed occasion for war. In the distant past, imperialism had needed no disguise whatever, and in the absolute autocracies only a very transparent one; but today imperialism is carefully hidden from public view—even though there may still be an unofficial appeal to warlike instincts. No people and no ruling class today can openly afford to regard war as a normal state of affairs or a normal element

---

the capitalist class. A misunderstanding in this respect would be regrettable. It should be further emphasized that utilitarianism was not a philosophy of capitalists, either by origin or social tendency, although it was a *capitalistic* philosophy in the sense that it was possible only in a world of capitalism. Indeed, the "capitalist class" in England preponderantly and sharply rejected utilitarianism, from its early beginnings to its culmination in the younger Mill, and so did the big landowners. This fact is commonly ignored, because utilitarianism fits in so well with bourgeois practice. It does so, however, only so long as its distorted journalistic projection in confounded with its true character, only when it is taken at face value. Actually it shows an unmistakable kinship to socialism, in its philosophic approach, its social orientation, and many of its practical demands. It is the product of capitalist development, but by no means of capitalist *interests*. Pacifism, for example, can be shown to flow from it—though not from it alone. Present-day pacifist tendencies have their roots largely elsewhere, notably in Christian thought, which, of course, preceded the capitalist era, though it could become effective in this direction only in the capitalist world. Unfortunately it is not possible here to set forth these things at length and thus to guard our views against the danger of being misunderstood.

in the life of nations. No one doubts that today it must be characterized as an abnormality and a disaster. True, war is still glorified. But glorification in the style of King Tuglâtî-palisharra is rare and unleashes such a storm of indignation that every practical politician carefully dissociates himself from such things. Everywhere there is official acknowledgment that peace is an end in itself—though not necessarily an end overshadowing all purposes that can be realized by means of war. Every expansionist urge must be carefully related to a concrete goal. All this is primarily a matter of political phraseology, to be sure. But the necessity for this phraseology is a symptom of the popular attitude. And that attitude makes a policy of imperialism more and more difficult—indeed, the very word imperialism is applied only to the enemy, in a reproachful sense, being carefully avoided with reference to the speaker's own policies.

3. The type of industrial worker created by capitalism is always vigorously anti-imperialist. In the individual case, skillful agitation may persuade the working masses to approve or remain neutral—a concrete goal or interest in self-defense always playing the main part—but no initiative for a forcible policy of expansion ever emanates from this quarter. On this point official socialism unquestionably formulates not merely the interests but also the conscious will of the workers. Even less than peasant imperialism is there any such thing as socialist or other working-class imperialism.

4. Despite manifest resistance on the part of powerful elements, the capitalist age has seen the development of methods for preventing war, for the peaceful settlement of disputes among states. The very fact of resistance means that the trend can be explained only from the mentality of capitalism as a mode of life. It definitely limits the opportunities imperialism needs if it is to be a powerful force. True, the methods in question often fail, but even more often they are successful. I am thinking not merely of the Hague Court of Arbitration but of the practice of submitting controversial issues to conferences of the major powers or at least those powers directly concerned—a course of action that has become less and less avoidable. True, here too the individual case may become a farce. But the serious setbacks of today must not blind us to the real importance or sociological significance of these things.

5. Among all capitalist economies, that of the United States is least burdened with precapitalist elements, survivals, reminiscences, and power factors. Certainly we cannot expect to find imperialist

tendencies altogether lacking even in the United States, for the immigrants came from Europe with their convictions fully formed, and the environment certainly favored the revival of instincts of pugnacity. But we can conjecture that among all countries the United States is likely to exhibit the weakest imperialist trend. This turns out to be the truth. The case is particularly instructive, because the United States has seen a particularly strong emergence of capitalist interests in an imperialist direction—those very interests to which the phenomenon of imperialism has so often been reduced, a subject we shall yet touch on. Nevertheless the United States was the first advocate of disarmament and arbitration. It was the first to conclude treaties concerning arms limitations (1817) and arbitral courts (first attempt in 1797) —doing so most zealously, by the way, when economic interest in expansion was at its greatest. Since 1908 such treaties have been concluded with twenty-two states. In the course of the nineteenth century, the United States had numerous occasions for war, including instances that were well calculated to test its patience. It made almost no use of such occasions. Leading industrial and financial circles in the United States had and still have an evident interest in incorporating Mexico into the Union. There was more than enough opportunity for such annexation—but Mexico remained unconquered. Racial catch phrases and working-class interests pointed to Japan as a possible danger. Hence possession of the Philippines was not a matter of indifference—yet surrender of this possession is being discussed. Canada was an almost defenseless prize—but Canada remained independent. Even in the United States, of course, politicians need slogans—especially slogans calculated to divert attention from domestic issues. Theodore Roosevelt and certain magnates of the press actually resorted to imperialism—and the result, in that world of high capitalism, was utter defeat, a defeat that would have been even more abject, if other slogans, notably those appealing to anti-trust sentiment, had not met with better success.[7]

These facts are scarcely in dispute.[8] And since they fit into

[7]It is an interesting fact, by the way, that while the peace policy is certainly not rooted in the capitalist upper class, some of the most eminent exponents of the political interests of the trusts are among the most zealous promoters of the peace movement.

[8]Rather, imperialist and nationalist literature is always complaining vociferously about the debility, the undignified will to peace, the petty commercial spirit, and so on, of the capitalist world. This in itself means very little, but it is worth mentioning as confirming a state of affairs that can be established from other indications.

the picture of the mode of life which we have recognized to be the necessary product of capitalism, since we can grasp them adequately from the necessities of that mode of life and industry, it follows that capitalism is by nature anti-imperialist. Hence we cannot readily derive from it such imperialist tendencies as actually exist, but must evidently see them only as alien elements, carried into the world of capitalism from the outside, supported by non-capitalist factors in modern life. The survival of interest in a policy of forcible expansion does not, by itself, alter these facts—not even, it must be steadily emphasized, from the viewpoint of the economic interpretation of history. For objective interests become effective—and, what is important, become powerful political factors—only when they correspond to attitudes of the people or of sufficiently powerful strata. Otherwise they remain without effect, are not even conceived of as interests. The economic interest in the forcible conquest of India had to await free-booter personalities, in order to be followed up. In ancient Rome the domestic class interest in an expansive policy had to be seized upon by a vigorous, idle aristocracy, otherwise it would have been ruled out on internal political grounds. Even the purely commercial imperialism of Venice—assuming that we can speak of such a thing, and not merely of a policy of securing trade routes in a military sense, which was then necessary—even such a policy needed to have examples of a policy of conquest at hand on every side, needed mercenary groups and bellicose adventurers among the *nobili* in order to become true imperialism. The capitalist world, however, suppresses rather than creates such attitudes. Certainly, all expansive interests within it are likely to ally themselves with imperialist tendencies flowing from non-capitalist sources, to use them, to make them serve as pretexts, to rationalize them, to point the way toward action on account of them. And from this union the picture of modern imperialism is put together; but for that very reason it is not a matter of capitalist factors alone. Before we go into this at length, we must understand the nature and strength of the economic stake which captialist society has in a policy if imperialism—especially the question of whether this interest is or is not inherent in the nature of capitalism—either capitalism generally, or a special phase of capitalism.

It is in the nature of a capitalist economy—and of an exchange economy generally—that many people stand to gain economically in any war. Here the situation is fundamentally much as it is with the familiar subject of luxury. War means increased demand at panic prices, hence high profits and also high wages in many parts of the national economy. This is primarily a matter of money incomes, but as a rule (though to a lesser extent) real incomes are also affected There are, for example, the special war interests, such as the arms industry. If the war lasts long enough, the circle of money profiteers naturally expands more and more—quite apart from a possible paper-money economy. It may extend to every economic field, but just as naturally the commodity content of money profits drops more and more, indeed, quite rapidly, to the point where actual losses are incurred. The national economy as a whole, of course, is impoverished by the tremendous excess in consumption brought on by war. It is, to be sure, conceivable that either the capitalists or the workers might make certain gains as a class, namely, if the volume either of capital or of labor should decline in such a way that the remainder receives a greater share in the social product and that, even from the absolute viewpoint, the total sum of interest or wages becomes greater than it was before. But these advantages cannot be considerable. They are probably, for the most part, more than outweighed by the burdens imposed by war and by losses sustained abroad. Thus the gain of the capitalists as a class cannot be a motive for war—and it is this gain that counts, for any advantage to the working class would be contingent on a large number of workers falling in action or otherwise perishing. There remain the entrepreneurs in the war industries, in the broader sense, possibly also the large landowner—a small but powerful minority. Their war profits are always sure to be an important supporting element. But few will go so far as to assert that this element alone is sufficient to orient the people of the capitalist world along imperialist lines. At most, an interest in expansion may make the capitalists allies of those who stand for imperialist trends.

It may be stated as being beyond controversy that where free trade prevails *no* class has an interest in forcible expansion as such. For in such a case the citizens and goods of every nation can move in foreign countries as freely as though those countries were politically their own—free trade implying far more than mere freedom from tariffs. In a genuine state of free trade, foreign raw materials and foodstuffs are as accessible to each nation as though they were within its own territory.[9] Where the cultural backwardness of a region

[9]The stubborn power of old prejudices is shown by the fact that even today the demand for the acquisition of colonies is justified by the argument that they are necessary to supply the demand for food and raw materials and to absorb the energies of a vigorous, rising nation, seeking world outlets. Since the

makes normal economic intercourse dependent on colonization, it does not matter, assuming free trade, which of the "civilized" nations undertakes the task of colonization. Dominion of the seas, in such a case, means little more than a maritime traffic police. Similarly, it is a matter of indifference to a nation whether a railway concession in a foreign country is acquired by one of its own citizens or not—just so long as the railway *is* built and put into efficient operation. For citizens of any country may use the railway, just like the fellow countrymen of its builder—while in the event of war it will serve whoever controls it in the military sense, regardless of who built it. It is true, of course, that profits and wages flowing from its construction and operation will accrue, for the greater part, to the nation that built it. But capital and labor that go into the railway have to be taken from somewhere, and normally the other nations fill the gap. It is a fact that in a regime of free trade the essential advantages of international intercourse are clearly evident. The gain lies in the enlargement of the commodity supply by means of the division of labor among nations, rather than in the profits and wages of the export industry and the carrying trade. For these profits and wages would be reaped even if there were no export, in which case import, the necessary complement, would also vanish. Not even monopoly interests—if they existed—would be disposed toward imperialism in such a case. For under free trade only *international* cartels would be possible. Under a system of free trade there would be conflicts in economic interests neither among different nations nor among the corresponding classes of different nations.[10] And since protectionism is not an essential characteristic of the capitalist economy—

---

flow of food and raw materials from abroad is only impeded by tariffs at home, the justification has no rhyme or reason even in our world of high protective tariffs, especially since in the event of war traffic with colonies is subject to the same perils as traffic with independent countries. For the rest, the element of war danger circumscribes what has been said in the text to the extent that it creates an interest in the control of such food and raw material producing countries as are situated so as to offer secure access even in wartime. *In the case of universal free trade, however, the danger of war would be substantially less.* It is in this sense that the sentence about dominion of the seas, which follows in the text, must be understood.

[10]Even with free trade there would be capital exports to the countries offering the highest interest rate at any given time. But that flow would be lacking in any aggressive character, just as would be true of export of commodities, which would be regulated by the law of costs, or, if capital and labor were but incompletely mobile, by the law of comparative costs. Any forcing of exports, whether of commodities or of capital, would be senseless.

otherwise the English national economy would scarcely be capitalist—it is apparent that any economic interest in forcible expansion on the part of a people or a class is not necessarily a product of capitalism.

It is not true that the capitalist system as such must collapse from immanent necessity, that it necessarily makes its continued existence impossible by its own growth and development. Marx's line of reasoning on this point shows serious defects, and when these are corrected the proof vanishes. It is to the great credit of Hilferding that he abandoned this thesis of Marxist theory.[11] Nevertheless, the situation that has just been described is really untenable both politically and economically. Economically, it amounts to a *reductio ad absurdum*. Politically, it unleashes storms of indignation among the exploited consumers at home and the threatened producers abroad. Thus the idea of military force readily suggests itself. Force may serve to break down foreign customs barriers and thus afford relief from the vicious circle of economic aggression. If that is not feasible, military conquest may at least secure control over markets in which heretofore one had to compete with the enemy. In this context, the conquest of colonies takes on an altogether different significance. Nonmonopolist countries, especially those adhering to free trade, reap little profit from such a policy. But it is a different matter with countries that function in a monopolist role *vis-à-vis* their colonies. There being no competition, they can use cheap native labor without its ceasing to be cheap; they can market their products, even in the colonies, at monopoly prices; they can, finally, invest capital that would only depress the profit rate at home and that could be placed in other civilized countries only at very low interest rates. And they can do all these things even though the consequence may be much slower colonial development. It would seem as though there could be no such interest in expansion at the expense of other advanced capitalist countries—in Europe, for example—because their industry would merely offer competition to the domestic cartels. But it is sufficient for the industry of the conquering state to be superior

[11]Capitalism is its own undoing but in a sense different from that implied by Marx. Society is bound to grow beyond capitalism, but this will be because the achievements of capitalism are likely to make it superfluous, not because its internal contradictions are likely to make its continuance impossible. This is not properly part of our subject. I do wish, however, to preclude any interpretation that I regard capitalism as the *final* phase of social evolution, as something that exists of natural necessity, that cannot be adequately explained. Still less do I regard it as an ideal in any sense. I do not go along with Hilferding, incidentally, in anticipating that trustification will bring about a stabilization of capitalism.

to that of the one to be subjugated—superior in capital power, organization, intelligence, and self-assertion—to make it possible to treat the subjugated state, perhaps not quite, but very much like a colony, even though it may become necessary to make a deal with individual groups of interests that are particularly powerful. A much more important fact is that the conqueror can face the subjugated nation with the bearing of the victor. He has countless means at his disposal for expropriating raw material resources and the like and placing them in the service of his cartels. He can seize them outright, nationalize them, impose a forced sale, or draft the proprietors into industrial groups of the victor nation under conditions that insure control by the domestic captains of industry. He can exploit them by a system of quotas or allotments. He can administer the conquered means of communication in the interests of his own cartels. Under the pretext of military and political security, he can deprive the foreign workers of the right to organize, thus not only making cheap labor in the annexed territory available to his cartels, but also holding a threat over the head of domestic labor.

Thus we have here, within a social group that carries great political weight, a strong, undeniable, economic interest in such things as protective tariffs, cartels, monopoly prices, forced exports (dumping), an aggressive economic policy, an aggressive foreign policy generally, and war, including wars of expansion with a typically imperialist character. Once this alignment of interests exists, an even stronger interest in a somewhat differently motivated expansion must be added, namely, an interest in the conquest of lands producing raw materials and foodstuffs, with a view to facilitating self-sufficient warfare. Still another interest is that in rising wartime consumption. A mass of unorganized capitalists competing with one another may at best reap a trifling profit from such an eventuality, but organized capital is sure to profit hugely. Finally there is the political interest in war and international hatred which flows from the insecure position of the leading circles. They are small in numbers and highly unpopular. The essential nature of their policy is quite generally known, and most of the people find it unnatural and contemptible. An attack on all forms of property has revolutionary implications, but an attack on the privileged position of the cartel magnates may be politically rewarding, implying comparatively little risk and no threat to the existing order. Under certain circumstances it may serve to unite all the political parties. The existence of such a danger calls for diversionary tactics.

Yet the final word in any presentation of this aspect of modern economic life must be one of warning against overestimating it. The conflicts that have been described, born of an export-dependent monopoly capitalism, may serve to submerge the real community of interests among nations; the monopolist press may drive it underground; but underneath the surface it never completely disappears. Deep down, the normal sense of business and trade usually prevails. Even cartels cannot do without the custom of their foreign economic kin. Even national economies characterized by export monopoly are dependent on one another in many respects. And their interests do not always conflict in the matter of producing for third markets. Even when the conflicting interests are emphasized, parallel interests are not altogether lacking. Furthermore, if a policy of export monopolism is to be driven to the extremes of forcible expansion, it is necessary to win over all segments of the population—at least to the point where they are halfway prepared to support the war; but the real interest in export monopolism as such is limited to the entrepreneurs and their ally, high finance. Even the most skillful agitation cannot prevent the independent traders, the small producers who are not covered by cartels, the "mere" capitalists, and the workers from occasionally realizing that they are the victims of such a policy. In the case of the traders and small producers this is of the possibility of "dumping" capital in order to raise the domestic quite clear. It is not so clear in the case of the capitalists, because interest rate. Against this, however, stands the high cost of such a policy and the curtailment of the competition of entrepreneurs for domestic capital. It is of the greatest importance, finally, to understand that export monopolism injures the workers far more unequivocally than the capitalists. There can be no dumping of labor power, and employment abroad or in the colonies is not even a quantitative substitute. Curiously enough, this injury to the working class is a matter of controversy. Even neo-Marxist doctrine—and not merely those writers properly characterized as "vulgar Marxists," who in every respect resemble their ilk of other persuasions—is inclined to admit that the workers derive temporary benefits from export monopolism,[12] limiting the polemic against it to proof that the ultimate

[12]The reasons may, in part, lie in the fact that orthodox socialism has always been inclined to regard the question of protective tariff *vs.* free trade as something of essential concern only to the bourgeoisie, something almost unworthy of socialist attention, to be left to literary polemicists who are in the habit of compromising with the existing order. Tactically this attitude can scarcely be maintained any longer today, nor *is* it maintained with respect to export mono-

effects—economic and especially political—are doubtful, and that even the temporary benefits are purchased by an injury to foreign workers which conflicts with the spirit of socialism. There is an error here. Apparently it is assumed that production for export—and, to the extent that it fosters such production, monopoly capitalist expansion as well—increases the demand for labor and thus raises wages. Suppose we accept as correct the premises implied in this argument, that the increase in demand will outweigh any decrease flowing from monopolistic labor-saving production methods, and also that it will outweigh the disadvantage flowing from the fact that the workers are now confronted, rather than by many entrepreneurs in a single industry, by a single party of the second part who, on the local labor market at least, can engage in monopolistic policies with respect to them, both as workers and as consumers. Even if we accept these premises—which seem doubtful to me—the balance is not even temporarily in favor of the workers. We have already pointed out that the interest of workers in export, even when free trade prevails, is essentially a consumer interest; that is, it is based on the fact that exports make imports possible. But as a producer the worker will usually fare no worse without exports, since the lack of exports must also eliminate imports. The workers, moreover, have no interest whatever in exports that may result from a policy of export monopolism—in other words, that would not otherwise be exported at all. For if it were impossible to dump these quantities they would by no means remain unproduced. On the contrary, most, if not all, would be offered at home, in general affording the same employment opportunities to the workers and in addition cheapening consumption. If that is not possible—that is to say, if the profit from the increased supply at home, together with the profit from the

---

polism. Yet it was tactically comprehensible in Marx's own time, for any other stand would have compelled him to admit a community of interests between the proletariat and the contemporary bourgeoisie—in England an interest in free trade, in Germany an interest in an "educational tariff," which he and Engels acknowledged. The stand, however, did impair theoretical understanding. It was one of the elements in the incorrernt total evaluation of the effects of the system of free competition: especially of what Marx called the "anarchy of production," but also of the suicidal stimulus of profit, and finally, of the movement toward concentration. What was indirectly at stake was the entire concept underlying the theory of underconsumption, impoverishment, and collapse. Adherence to these views, regarded as essential to "scientific socialism," has led to far too favorable an evaluation of export monopolism, which is supposed to have brought "order" into "anarchy." See Lederer's excellent study: "Von der Wissenschaft zur Utopie," *Archiv für die Geschichte des Sozialismus und der Arbeiterbewegung,* Vol. VII.

reduced supply abroad, fails to cover total costs including interest—then the industry in question is expanded beyond economically justifiable limits, and it is in the interest of all the productive factors concerned, excepting only the cartel magnates, for capital and labor to move into other industries, something that is necessary and always possible. This constellation of interests is not altered by the circumstance that export monopolism is often able and willing to do things for its workers in the social welfare sphere, thus allowing them to share in its profits.[13] For what makes this possible is, after all, nothing but exploitation of the consumer. If we may speak of the impoverishment of the workers anywhere within the world of capitalism, then a tendency to such impoverishment is apparent here, at least in a relative sense—though actually that tendency has slowed up since the turn of the century. If it is ever true that there is not a trace of parallelism of economic interests between entrepreneurs and workers, but instead only a sharp economic conflict—and usually there is much exaggeration in such statements—then this is true here. Chamberlain had every reason to appeal to national sentiment, to mock the petty calculation of immediate advantage, and to call out to the workers: "Learn to think imperially!" For the English worker knew what he was about, despite the banner headlines on the front pages of the yellow press: "Tariff Reform Means Work For All," and so on.

The fact that the balance sheet of export monopolism is anything but a brilliant success, even for the entrepreneurs, has been glossed over only by an upswing that stemmed from sources other than export monopolism itself. The hope of a future of dominion, to follow the struggles of the present, is but poor solace for the losses in that struggle. Should such a policy become general, the losses—admitted or not—of each individual nation would be even greater, the winnings even smaller. And if the export monopolists have not done too well, the nonmonopolist industries of England have

[13]An imperialism in which the entrepreneurs and other elements woo the workers by means of social welfare concessions which appear to depend on the success of export monopolism may be called "social imperialism," a term appropriate to the factual situation, but certainly not implying imperialism on the part of the working class. Social imperialism in the sense of an imperialism rooted in the working class does not exist, though agitation may, of course, succeed in kindling such a mood locally and temporarily in the working class. Social imperialism in the sense of imperialist interests on the part of the workers, interests to which an imperialist attitude ought to correspond, if the workers only understood it correctly—such an imperialist policy oriented toward working-class interests is nonsensical. *A people's imperialism is today an impossibility.*

hardly suffered from the dumping policies followed by other nations. The British steel industry may have suffered (though it was by no means in serious danger), but in return all the other English industries actually enjoyed, at the expense of the foreign dumpers, a production premium in the form of abnormally low prices for iron and ferrous products. The sugar industry may have been unable to maintain itself in England, but in return sugar-using industries developed in England as they did nowhere else. To those entrepreneurs, moreover, who never succeeded in gaining leading positions in the cartels, the enjoyment of an assured return is often but a poor substitute for lost opportunities for growth. Thus we can understand the fact that even in entrepreneurial circles dissatisfaction with such a policy arose, and while one group entertained the thought of forcible expansion as a last resort, another was led into an attitude of opposition. In all the protectionist countries, therefore, we have had, for the past twenty years, anti-dumping legislation, primarily as an instrument of tariff policy. This legislation, it is true, is directed primarily against foreign dumping rather than against dumping by domestic enterprise, and hence it becomes a new weapon in the hands of the monopoly interests. But it is also true that its political basis lies partly in circles and attitudes opposed on principle to export aggression and for this reason anxious to make such a policy impossible for domestic enterprise. It must be admitted that such opposition often suffers from inappropriate techniques and from the influence of lay catchwords. But given peaceful development, it may be assumed that the opposition would gradually turn directly against dumping by domestic cartels.

This countermovement against export monopolism, within capitalism rather than opposed to it, would mean little if it were merely the political death struggle of a moribund economic order which is giving way to a new phase of development. If the cartel with its policy of export aggression stood face to face with noncartelized factory industry, as that industry once faced handicraft industry, then even the most vigorous opposition could scarcely change the ultimate outcome or the fundamental significance of the process. But it cannot be emphasized sharply enough that such is not the case. Export monopolism does *not* grow from the inherent laws of capitalist development. The character of capitalism leads to large-scale production, but with few exceptions large-scale production does *not* lead to the kind of unlimited concentration that would leave but one or only a few firms in each industry. On the contrary, any plant runs up against limits to its growth in a given location; and the growth of combinations which would make sense under a system of free trade encounters limits of organizational efficiency. Beyond these limits there is no tendency toward combination inherent in the competitive system. In particular, the rise of trusts and cartels—a phenomenon quite different from the trend to large-scale production with which it is often confused—can never be explained by the automatism of the competitive system. This follows from the very fact that trusts and cartels can attain their primary purpose—to pursue a monopoly policy only behind protective tariffs, without which they would lose their essential significance. But protective tariffs do not automatically grow from the competitive system. They are the fruit of political action—*a type of action that by no means reflects the objective interests of all those concerned* but that, on the contrary, becomes impossible as soon as the majority of those whose consent is necessary realize their true interests. To some extent it is obvious, and for the rest it will be presently shown, that the interests of the minority, quite appropriately expressed in support of a protective tariff, do not stem from capitalism as such. It follows that *it is a basic fallacy to describe imperialism as a necessary phase of capitalism, or even to speak of the development of capitalism into imperialism.* We have seen before that the mode of life of the capitalist world does not favor imperialist attitudes. We now see that the alignment of interests in a capitalist economy—even the interests of its upper strata—by no means points unequivocally in the direction of imperialism. We now come to the final step in our line of reasoning.

This significant dichotomy in the bourgeois mind—which in part explains its wretched weakness in politics, culture, and life generally; earns it the understandable contempt of the Left and the Right; and proves the accuracy of our diagnosis—is best exemplified by two phenomena that are very close to our subject: present-day nationalism and militarism. Nationalism is affirmative awareness of national character, together with an aggressive sense of superiority. It arose from the autocratic state. In conservatives, nationalism in general is understandable as an inherited orientation, as a mutation of the battle instincts of the medieval knights, and finally as a political stalking horse on the domestic scene; and conservatives are fond of reproaching the bourgeois with a lack of nationalism, which, from their point of view, is evaluated in a positive sense. Socialists, on the other hand, equally understandably exclude nationalism from their general ideology, because of the essential interests of the proletariat, and by virtue of their domestic opposition to the conservative stalking horse; they, in turn, not only reproach the bourgeoisie with an excess of nationalism (which they, of course, evaluate in a negative sense) but actually identify nationalism and even the very idea of the nation with bourgeois ideology. The curious thing is that both of these groups are right in their criticism of the bourgeoisie. For, as we have seen, the mode of life that flows logically from the nature of capitalism necessarily implies an antinationalist orientation in politics and culture. This orientation actually prevails. We find a great many antinationalist members of the middle class, and even more who merely parrot the catchwords of nationalism. In the capitalist world it is actually not big business and industry at all that are the carriers of nationalist trends, but the intellectual, and the content of *his* ideology is explained not so much from definite class interests as from chance emotion and individual interest. But the submission of the bourgeoisie to the powers of autocracy, its alliance with them, its economic and psychological patterning by them —all these tend to push the bourgeois in a nationalist direction; and this too we find prevalent, especially among the chief exponents of export monopolism. The relationship between the bourgeoisie and militarism is quite similar. Militarism is not necessarily a foregone conclusion when a nation maintains a large army, but only when high military circles become a poltical power. The criterion is whether leading generals as such wield political influence and whether the responsible statesmen can act only with their consent. That is possible only when the officer corps is linked to a definite social class, as in Japan, and can assimilate to its position individuals who do not belong to it by birth. Militarism too is rooted in the autocratic state. And again the same reproaches are made against the bourgeois from both sides—quite properly too. According to the "pure" capitalist mode of life, the bourgeois is unwarlike. The alignment of capitalist interests should make him utterly reject military methods, put him in opposition to the professional soldier. Significantly, we see this in the example of England where, first, the struggle against a standing army generally and, next, opposition to its elaboration, furnished bourgeois politicians with their most popular slogan: "retrenchment." Even naval appropriations have encountered resistance. We find similar trends in other countries, though they are less strongly developed. The continental bourgeois, however, was used to the sight of troops. He regarded an army almost as a necessary component of the social order, ever since it had been his terrible taskmaster in the Thirty Years' War. He had no power at all to abolish the army. He might have done so if he had had the power; but not having it, he considered the fact that the army might be useful to him. In his "artificial" economic situation and because of his submission to the sovereign, he thus grew disposed toward militarism, especially where export monopolism flourished. The intellectuals, many of whom still maintained special relationships with feudal elements, were so disposed to an even greater degree.[14]

Just as we once found a dichotomy in the social pyramid, so now we find everywhere, in every aspect of the bourgeois portion of the modern world, a dichotomy of attitudes and interests. Our examples also show in what way the two components work together. Nationalism and militarism, while not creatures of capitalism, become "capitalized" and in the end draw their best energies from capitalism. Capitalism involves them in its workings and thereby keeps them alive, politically as well as economically. And they, in turn, affect capitalism, cause it to deviate from the course it might have followed alone, support many of its interests.

Here we find that we have penetrated to the historical as well as the sociological sources of modern imperialism. It does not *coincide* with nationalism and militarism, though it *fuses* with them by supporting them as it is supported by them. It too is—not only historically, but also sociologically—a heritage of the autocratic state, of its structural elements, organizational forms, interest alignments, and human attitudes, the outcome of precapitalist forces which the autocratic state has reorganized, in part by the methods of early capitalism. It would never have been evolved by the "inner logic" of capitalism itself. This is true even of mere export monopolism. It too has its sources in absolutist policy and the action habits of an essentially precapitalist environment. That it was able to develop to its present dimensions is owing to the momentum of a situation once created, which continued to engender ever new "artificial" economic structures, that is, those which maintain themselves by political power alone. In most of the countries addicted to export monopolism it is also owing to the fact that the old autocratic state and the old attitude of the bourgeoisie toward it were so vigorously maintained. But export monopolism, to go a step further, is not yet imperialism. And even if it had been able to arise without protective tariffs, it would never have developed into imperialism in the hands of

14Methodologically, it is interesting to note here that, though nationalism and militarism are not "reflexes" of the capitalist alignment of interests, neither did they emerge as what they are today during the periods in which they had their roots. Yet they do not necessarily escape the focus of the economic interpretation of history. They are the forms assumed in the environment of the modern world by habits of emotion and action that orginally arose under primitive conditions.

an unwarlike bourgeoisie. If this did happen, it was only because the heritage included the war machine, together with its socio-psychological aura and aggressive bent, and because a class oriented toward war maintained itself in a ruling position. This class clung to its domestic interest in war, and the pro-military interests among the bourgeoisie were able to ally themselves with it. This alliance kept alive war instincts and ideas of overlordship, male supremacy, and triumphant glory—ideas that would have otherwise long since died. It led to social conditions that, while they ultimately stem from the conditions of production, cannot be explained from capitalist production methods alone. And it often impresses its mark on present-day politics, threatening Europe with the constant danger of war.

This diagnosis also bears the prognosis of imperialism. The pre-capitalist elements in our social life may still have great vitality; special circumstances in national life may revive them from time to time; but in the end the climate of the modern world must destroy them. This is all the more certain since their props in the modern capitalist world are not of the most durable material. Whatever opinion is held concerning the vitality of capitalism itself, whatever the life span predicted for it, it is bound to withstand the onslaughts of its enemies and its own irrationality much longer than essentially untenable export monopolism—untenable even from the capitalist point of view. Export monopolism may perish in revolution, or it may be peacefully relinquished; this may happen soon, or it may take some time and require desperate struggle; but one thing is certain—it *will* happen. This will immediately dispose of neither warlike instincts nor structural elements and organizational forms oriented toward war—and it is to their dispositions and domestic interests that, in my opinion, much more weight must be given in every concrete case of imperialism than to export monopolist interests, which furnish the financial "outpost skirmishes"—a most appropriate term—in many wars. But such factors will be politically overcome in time, no matter what they do to maintain among the people a sense of constant danger of war, with the war machine forever primed for action. And with them, imperialisms will wither and die.

It is not within the scope of this study to offer an ethical, esthetic, cultural, or political evaluation of this process. Whether it heals sores or extinguishes sins is a matter of utter indifference from the viewpoint of this study. It is not the concern of science to judge that. The only point at issue here was to demonstrate, by means of an important example, the ancient truth that the dead always rule the living.

The Concept of Economic Imperialism[1]

Richard Koebner

Richard Koebner, who died in 1958, taught at Breslau University and from 1934 to 1955 occupied the chair of Modern History at the Hebrew University of Jerusalem. Apart from many scholarly articles he published several books in German. His major works on imperialism, besides the article reprinted here, are *Imperialism: The Story and Significance of a Political Word, 1840-1960* (1964, co-author H. D. Schmidt) and *EMPIRE* (1961).

The author traces the development of the concept of economic imperialism with its beginnings in France to the era prior to World War Two. Koebner detects three different strands of thought in economic imperialism—Marxian, Fabian, and American. All three are interdependent and appear to agree basically with the Hobsonian thesis.

I

The term 'imperialism' has in the course of its rapid career become variegated and elusive to a degree. The word has been accepted as a key to the understanding of contemporary history. But there is reason to doubt whether the writers, who in the past used it most confidently in this sense, were certain of what they meant by it, and did not, in fact, become enmeshed in its ambiguity. There is, however, one connotation which tends to overshadow all others and to convey to the reader a clearcut meaning tantamount to a great historical revelation. This connotation is implied most clearly when the noun 'imperialism' is qualified by the adjective 'economic'. Indeed authors and propagandists are sometimes so certain of the economic interpretation as to drop the adjective and to assume that the reader cannot but think of special economic interests whenever the word imperialism is brought out.[2]

The meaning of the word in this application is as follows. The men representing the interests of capital in the greater countries of the West have obtained control of the foreign and colonial policy

[1]Reprinted from *The Economic History Review*, second series, Vol. II, No. 1, 1949, pages 1–29.

[2]Cf. for example F. Sternberg, *Der Imperialismus* (1926), p. 49: '. . . Imperialismus, das heisst Kapitalexpansion in nichtkapitalistischen Territorien.'

of their governments. The nations which are commonly referred to by the term of 'western civilization' have been goaded by their capitalists into bringing weaker peoples oversea within their grip and into exploiting them. The same had been done by Venetians, Dutchmen and Englishmen in former centuries; but—so the doctrine runs—getting hold of undeveloped countries did not become a dominant factor in politics until capitalism reached its full efflorescence—that is to say, until the last decades of the nineteenth century. It is then that the age of imperialism—or of economic imperialism or of modern imperialism—came into being. How long it lasted—whether imperialism is still vigorous in our days or already far on its decline—on this question opinions differ. They differ on other points too. Is the capitalist interest which dominates the whole movement rooted in the first place in great industrial enterprises, or in the profit-making of financiers and speculators? Are the instigations of capitalists the only decisive factors in the expansionist activities of Western countries or have other motives, especially national pride, been of more than subsidiary influence?

Besides differences of historical interpretation there are others concerning the application of the term to individual cases. To many people it will sound absurd if a minor state, as for instance Belgium or the Netherlands, is credited with 'imperialism' in its colonies; nevertheless, this is done. But all such divergences are of minor importance in relation to the general point of view represented by the term 'economic imperialism'; modern foreign and colonial policies obeying the dictates of capitalist interests.

At the time when this view of modern history was wedded to 'imperialism' the word had already been for some time a topic in animated controversies.[3] But accentuated by the economic connotation it was eventually to become a powerful irritant. Whatever the truth of its assertion concerning economic influences on modern politics—its claim to expose these influences has conferred on the word the quality of a powerful factor in modern public life.

The term 'imperialism' is altogether of recent origin. It started its career when Europe, and especially England, pondered over the destinies of the second French Empire. Twenty years later it was called in to denote contemporary ways of English foreign politics, the politics of Disraeli. After one more decade it began to be accepted

---

[3]In the following, I sometimes venture to anticipate results of a study, to be published later, concerning the career of the term 'imperialism' and cognate notions.

as an expression which embodied belief in the British Empire. This last meaning has endured to our own day. But most people who value the Empire connexion have become shy of styling themselves imperialists. They cannot but be conscious of the ominous connotations which have accrued to both 'imperialism' and 'imperialist'. In these connotations the original bias of the term which implied criticism of Louis Napoleon and of Beaconsfield is still to be traced; but this bias has been resuscitated and applied to the objects of enthusiasm which inspired the 'imperialism' in the 1890's. This enthusiasm was then itself expanding its meaning. While at first it had given pride of place to the connexion between the mother-country and the self-governing dominions, in the last years of the century the Asiatic and especially the new African dependencies came to be valued no less highly. The African exploits led to grave political repercussions, internationally as well as internally, and it was in this connexion that a bad name attached again to 'imperialism'. An echo arose across the Atlantic. In the United States the expansionist moves, prominent during the war of 1898, were dubbed 'imperialism' by their opponents. The danger of imperialism was proclaimed in both countries, and in connexion with this the economic explanation entered the field. Imperialist maxims and imperialist politics were said to be the chosen creed of sections of society which were materially interested in activities such as the conflict with the Transvaal which led to the Boer War and the bid for annexations which emerged from the Spanish-American War.

The fundamental notions of economic imperialism were conceived in this atmosphere. They were welded into a theory by that great advocate of a co-ordination between economic effort and social progress, John Atkinson Hobson. In his *Imperialism, A Study* (published in 1902), the concept was given a place in the critical analysis of capitalist economics. Such an interpretation implied that the concept was applicable not only to the politics of Britain and the United States but also to those of other countries especially France and Germany. A world-wide application had in fact been given to the word by authors who did not approach imperialism from the economic point of view. The attempts of the great European powers to secure spheres of interest in China were thus resented. English and American writers were the first to see the light. In the first years of the present century German, French and Italian writers followed suit and discussed the newly-discovered spirit of the time. It was, however, well noticed on the continent that there was a special connexion between imperialism and the British Empire. The French and—still longer—the German public employed the word imperialism to describe and to criticize either the ascent of the British Empire or modern endeavours to strengthen its coherence. These uses of the word were, of course, also frequent in English public opinion. Here an assertive as well as a negative ring could be given to the term. In Germany the circumstantial scholarship of Schulze-Gaevernitz tried to interpret British imperialism as the joint result of diverse historical factors: Puritan education of will-power, new national restlessness and economic apprehension.

These new vicissitudes of the term suggest that the exclusive association of imperialism and capitalist acquisitiveness had so far failed to establish itself. The vogue attained by the word contributed only to still more meanings being read into it. It was also applied to the history of empires generally. 'In a sense it may be said that imperialism is as old as the world'; so Lord Cromer justified his thoughtful comparison between 'Ancient and Modern Imperialism', the first of many disquisitions to which the concept meant neither more nor less than the phenomenon of empire-building throughout history. Before 1914 the line indicated by Hobson was followed only by socialist authors in Germany and Austria who incorporated the imperialist policy of capitalist expansion into the framework of ideas of Karl Marx, i.e., by O. Bauer, K. Hilferding, Rosa Luxemburg. But they were as yet of little consequence, even in the Marxian camp.[4] Another adept was won during the war. While German socialists were still quarrelling whether the concept of imperialism was to be adopted into their system of thought, Lenin was studying Hobson's book in Zurich and basing on it the far-reaching conclusions of his pamphlet *Imperialism the Highest State of Capitalism*. This pamphlet was printed in Petrograd when its author returned there in 1917.

Lenin wished to make the Russians understand that fighting the war against Germany was nothing but bleeding for international capitalism. It would be interesting to know whether and with whom his argument carried influence while Russia's adherence to the Allied cause was still in suspense. The world-wide influence of his pamphlet dates, however, from 1920 when it was translated into German and French and helped to enhance the reputations of the earlier books of Hilferding and Rosa Luxemburg with the Marxists. But by that time doctrines of economic imperialism directly derived from Hobson had found favour with socialists too, who did not profess Marxian

[4]The same holds true of H. N. Brailsford's *War of Steel and Gold* (1914).

orthodoxy. Leonard Woolf by his *Empire and Commerce in Africa* and his more popular pamphlet *Economic Imperialism* started the campaign of the English Labour Research Department for winding up colonial empires. In 1921 'economic imperialism' was the subject of a series of lectures delivered by the French Professor Achille Viallate at the Institute of Politics, Williams College, Mass. These lectures were published in English and French in 1923. The author, who twenty years earlier had interpreted the protectionist imperialism of Chamberlain as a contribution to British self-sufficiency,[5] enlarged now on the subject of imperialist expansion. It was, according to him, dictated by the desire of the 'great industrial nations' to find 'outlets both for the utilization of their available capital and for the surplus of their production'. This economic imperialism, he said, had worsened international relations before the war; people ought to be warned against the portent of its being intensified now.[6] Soon afterwards economic imperialism in this meaning became a topic of a vast American literature which was by no means intended to further the cause of socialism. W. S. Culbertson emphasized the influence of surplus capital on the scramble for raw materials and the ensuing international frictions. Carlton Hayes and Parker T. Moon set out to see recent European history in the light of 'substitution of the more peaceful and subtle methods of economic imperialism, of invest-ment and trade for the aggressive military imperialism of the old regime'. A flood of publications written in the same vein followed. Economic imperialism was made more or less responsible for the World War. 'Dollar diplomacy', the name once chosen for the politics of Presidents Th. Roosevelt and W. Taft, was now taken to represent the American brand of a world-embracing movement. J. Viner stated in 1929 that the term imperialism had become 'a downright nuisance'; but in the meantime the economic views expressed by it had been adopted in general historical literature.[7]

The three groups of thought and propaganda which we may call the Marxian, the Fabian and the American by no means represent an identical attitude towards contemporary society and politics. But their mutual independence gives only greater importance

[5]*La Crise Anglaise. Impérialisme et Protection* (1905). Cf. especially p. viii.

[6]*Economic Imperialism and International Relations during the last fifty years* (New York, 1923), pp. 62 f., 167 f.

[7]American writing based on the concept has been reviewed by E. M. Winslow, 'Marxian, Liberal and Sociological Theories of Imperialism', *The Journal of Political Economy*, vol. 39 (1931), pp. 737 fl. IV. 'The Formula of Economic Imperialism and the Historians.'

to the facts that they all at the same time have seen reason to elaborate J. A. Hobson's ideas and that they have arrived at views on history much akin to each other. They have joined in achieving a victory for the concept of economic imperialism. This success has indeed been frequently and—as we may assume—convincingly contested by historians and sociologists. But scholarly criticism was unable to prevent the forming of an international *communis opinio* for which economic imperialism has become an accepted fact. This acceptance has had enormous consequences. The historical view expressed in the term has gone far to stereotype popular attitudes to western civilization and western states. For communists, all the world round, it has given shape to the background against which their new world is to emerge. But it has had an impact no less vehement on consciences not converted to communism. It may have greatly contributed to the American distrust of western Europe and the British Empire. In England it has been a moral solvent. It has made people averse to colonial activity of every kind and apathetic towards imperial misfortunes; these could be easily construed as retributions for the economic imperialism of former days. The concept has finally become widely known among the peoples who had reasons to regard themselves as objects of 'imperialist' expansion. It has inspired and embittered national movements in Asiatic nations, in colonies, and in mandatory countries; it has widened the gulf between their intellectuals and the western nations, Great Britain in particular.

In all these directions the impact is still felt. To trace its channels and to measure its range is no task for the historian yet. But to ask how modern political and economic developments came to be understood by the terms of economic imperialism, and how this interpretation was able to carry conviction, is to put questions capable of historical investigation.

The questions would be easily answered if the advocates of the concept had succeeded in making good its postulates. For this purpose they would have had to clear the concept of its ambiguities and show it to embody an adequate interpretation of a certain category of political and administrative actions. This brought out, it should have shown that in these actions groups of capitalists have taken a leading part. The activities of these capitalists ought finally to be demonstrated as consequences of the economic structure of capitalist society. If all this were a matter of convincing proof there would be no need to ask why the concept has proved convincing.

Some advocates of the historical view implied in the concept have indeed been very active in explaining it and in collecting evidence

in its proof. But the criticism with which they have met has been
based on arguments more conclusive than the thesis itself. The criticism is equally convincing when it dissects the Neo-Marxian tenets
(as J. A. Schumpeter has done)[8] as when (as in the writings of
J. Viner and E. M. Winslow) it exposes the exaggerations and
misconstructions which have marred American scholarship. It has been
demonstrated again and again that statistical data do not in fact,
as has been asserted, bring out a tendency of surplus capital to
flow into colonial and other 'imperial' enterprises rather than into
other investments.[9] It has been shown (by W. K. Hancock and
S. H. Frankel) that the practical problems of colonial economics are
by far too serious to be disposed of by the indictment of imperialist
greed.[10] Research on diplomatic history even if prepared to accept
economic influences in general terms has seen no occasion to trace
them individually.

In short the critics of the concept have done enough to show
that the assurance with which it is proclaimed and the confidence
with which it is accepted are not based on its demonstrability.
This negative result adds special importance to the questions: How
did the concept emerge, how came it to carry conviction?

II

The concept of economic imperialism thus passed through four distinct
stages. The first stage saw the emergence of its characteristic motifs
which were finally arranged into a system by J. A. Hobson. The
second stage was one of adaptation of Hobson's views to the framework
of Marxist thought. In the third stage, since 1920, the doctrine that
mankind was fettered by economic imperialism was widely propagated,
not only in the Marxist-Leninist version but in specifically British
and American versions as well. This promulgation was in the fourth
stage followed by the concept becoming a powerful political ferment
all over the world. We are especially concerned with the first of
these stages.

At the beginning of this century the economic interpretation
of imperialism was a special instance of a certain historical view.
This was the view that the nations of the west were obsessed by

[8]*Capitalism, Socialism, and Democracy* (1943), pp. 49—55.

[9]Lately by W. K. Hancock, *Survey of British Commonwealth Affairs* (1940),
vol. 11, pt. 1, pp. 26 f., and by Louis M. Hacker, *England and America; the ties
that bind.* Inaugural Lecture (Oxford, 1948), pp. 19 f.

[10]Hancock, *Survey*, etc. vol. 11, pt. 2, pp. 300—2; Frankel, *Capital Investment
in Africa* (1938), p. 28.

a common tendency to expand their dominance over the world and that this tendency impressed its character on the age. In this way one historical generalization—the economic one—was quickly superimposed upon another relating to modern 'world politics'. Both generalizations implied a historical retrospect. According to them the age of imperialism, whether economically interpreted or not, had started in the 1880's and was now in its prime. This view has since become a part of school-book history. It cannot, however, be thought insignificant to note that this historical doctrine was not widely accepted until the very end of the century whose last decades it purported to interpret. It was so obviously influenced by contemporary events and actions, that we are bound to ask: Do these challenges perhaps apply, in fact, not to the whole period but only to those few years in which the term 'imperialism' came to be used in that far-reaching application?

This application had no basis in tradition. Reminiscences of the Roman Empire had little or nothing to do with its cropping up. It was not customary as yet to speak of 'Roman imperialism' to describe the rise and growth of this classical empire, and its Mediterranean scope offered no obvious analogy to the overseas ventures of modern European powers. The word 'imperialism' was used somewhat traditionally only in the English language and only with regard to the British Empire. In this context it did not, in the first place, apply to every extension of the Empire. If abusively used it meant Disraelian adventures; if used sympathetically it meant strengthening the ties between the mother-country and the self-governing colonies. In continental countries a word implying the notion of empire ought to suggest meanings very different from that of acquisitions overseas. The Austro-Hungarian and the Russian empires had no possessions of this kind. Germany and France had both laid claim to such possessions; but it was by no means natural to call their colonial aspirations 'imperial'. The German Emperor and Empire (Kaiser und Reich) were symbols of regained national unity and strength. In France 'imperial' phraseology recalled the two Napoleons.

But apart from the name—what about the identity of purpose which the term implies existed in the far-flung enterprises of western nations? These activities ranged—it is true—over the whole globe and had followed one another very quickly. But to represent them as if they had originated in the same motives impelling all nations alike—these interpretations conflicted with well-known facts. Let us take our stand at a date in the middle of the period, about 1892. Western European nations had by then proceeded rather far in the activities which are thought to have brought about the imperialist age. After Salisbury's treaties of 1890 the 'partition of Africa' was on the whole settled. France had extended its dominance from Algiers to Tunis and from Cochin-China to Annam and Tongking. Britain's Eastern Empire had been rounded off in Burma and Baluchistan. Britain would not retreat from Egypt within a measurable space of time; that had become certain. In the twentieth century all these facts were to be regarded as initial phases of one and the same movement. But they were scarcely seen in this light at the time when Wilhelm II took over from Bismarck and Rosebery from Salisbury. And it is easy to see why contemporaries did not indulge in such sweeping concepts. They knew better. The Dark Continent, Egypt, the Far East—these regions of the globe had attracted the interest either of volunteers in colonial enterprise or of statesmen or of both. But this interest was obviously not the same at every place. To trade with Negroes was not the same as to trade with Chinese. To control the Khedive and the Suez Canal was a task obviously different from controlling African or Polynesian chieftains. Furthermore, the move oversea was not a spontaneous move everywhere and at every moment. Britain had taken the largest share. Nevertheless, it was an obvious fact that the rulers of the nation had not spontaneously set out for expansion, as Jules Ferry and Bismarck had done. They had been 'forced by stress of circumstances,[11] in Egypt first and afterwards still more unmistakably, in tropical Africa and Polynesia. When Gladstone's cabinet slowly approached the question of taking New Guinea, Derby was shocked by the apprehension that Australian claims extended 'to the possession of (virtually) all the South Pacific Islands within 1000 miles' of the continent.[12] It was not easy for Salisbury to satisfy the forwardness of the Australians. He offended their delegates at the colonial conference of 1887 by his chilly attitude towards their complaints concerning French intrusion in the New Hebrides.[13]

11Ch. W. Dilke, *Problems of Greater Britain*, 11, 164—6, passages summarizing the author's cabinet experience and later observation.

12Letter to Gladstone, 13 September 1883. Brit. Mus. Add. MS. 44141, fol. 146. The reluctance with which the question of New Guinea was handled in Gladstone's Cabinet is vividly mirrored in Dilke's diaries (Gwynn and Tuckwell, *The Life of Sir Ch. W. Dilke*, vol. 11, passim). 'Anti-imperialistic grounds' made Gladstone and Harcourt refuse at first (loc. cit. p. 82).

13Dilke, *The Present Position of European Politics* (1887), pp. 347—9. With regard to Africa, the decisive steps which secured England's share in the partition are, indeed, to be credited to Salisbury. But that is not to say that he wished for

Imperial responsibilities were enlarged step by step by a hesitant government. One must not imagine a strong popular will to have been the driving force. It is a striking fact that the imperial nation manifested no interest to see its empire extended. That the occupation of Egypt should not be maintained for the duration was not only a dogma for Gladstone and his cabinet but also a leading maxim for Salisbury until 1887, and at that time it was accepted opinion in England generally.[14] *The Times,* indeed, spurred by its Cairo correspondent, demanded an Egyptian protectorate while Gordon's mission to London still looked hopeful.[15] But after the catastrophe a publicist like Edward Dicey who maintained this claim, found himself in mournful isolation.[16] The builders of the new African empire, Goldie, MacKinnon, Johnston and Rhodes, did their work without encouragement from home and did not ask for it. Rhodes, eager to have Afrikander support for going north, was for a time even anxious not to attract English popular acclamation which might conjure up the portent of the 'imperial factor'. In this device he was rather too successful. He was suspected to go out for a great South African republic with himself as President.[17] The 'Mercantile Company' by dint of which Rhodes wished to make his way was a danger signal to W.A. Henley, who was one of the few men at home who

---

them; he always held back until the last moment. The delays which taxed the patience of Mackinnon (McDermott, *British East Africa or IBEA*, pp. 11 ff.) are more characteristic of him than the somewhat complacent conclusions which H. H. Johnston drew from a conversation at Hatfield. *(The Story of my Life,* pp. 204 f.)

14Allegations that secret intentions inside the Gladstone cabinet were at variance with public declarations concerning the temporary character of the occupation of Egypt are easily disposed of by Dilke's diary entries, May 1884, summarized in his autobiography and published by Gwynn and Tuckwell, 11, 52 f. Of Dilke's letter to Grant Duff, 22 May, which is quoted there, a copy is preserved with the Gladstone Papers (Add. MS. 44149, fols. 215, 216). An occasional remark of Derby in a letter to Gladstone concerning Zululand is if possible, still more expressive: 'It might be openly announced that we governed the country only *ad interim*—much as we do Egypt' (18 December 1883, Add. MS. 44142, fol. 27). With regard to public opinion, Chamberlain's view is worth noting. Like most members of the cabinet he welcomed Dilke's suggestion to propose an international guarantee of the neutrality of Egypt. He gave as one of his reasons: 'To make Egypt the Belgium of the East is an object easily popularized. The phrase will carry the proposal' (Gwynn and Tuckwell, loc. cit.).

15*The History of 'The Times'* (vol. 111), *The Twentieth Century Test* (1947), pp. 20–38.

16'The Khedivate of Egypt', *The Nineteenth Century*, vol. XVIII (1885), p. 1.

17E. A. Walker, 'The Jameson Raid,' *Camb. Hist. Journ.* vol. VI (1941), p. 236.

in 1889 believed in a British mission in these regions.[18] When New
Guinea and Zululand were discussed in 1883-4, Derby's remark that
'England has already black subjects enough' became again a winged
word.[19] Public attitudes towards the affairs of Zululand are especially
characteristic. It was clearly a British responsibility to care for a
stable regime in this native community whose strength and cohesion
had been broken by British arms. An extension of the protectorate
was the only promising way for giving effect to this responsibility.
Gladstone and most of his colleagues were not ready for such a
step. But they were allowed, too, by public opinion, to cling to
an irresolute attitude for two years. In July 1884 the matter was
suddenly brought up for discussion in the House of Commons by
conservative members who branded this default 'of a power which
boasted that in its dominions the sun never set' as a shameful betrayal.
But when in the debate speakers on the Government benches referred
to the conservative appeal as an 'imperial spread-eagle policy' this
was thought to be an insult. Press comments on the whole betrayed
only embarrassment and did not urge more resolute action.[20] Impending enlargements of the colonial area were not chosen as a topic
of propaganda, when the Prince of Wales and his assistants cared
to bring home to the English public the value of the Empire by
the foundation of the Imperial Institute. Generally, the response with
which the exhibition met must not be thought to have been very
vivid. *Punch* sometimes satirized the public's obtuseness, but on occasion it satirized the Institute itself. And in Queen Victoria's Golden

[18]*Scots Observer* (25 May 1889), p. II ('Sir Hercules Robinson').

[19]Cf. J. S. Cotton, *Colonies and Dependencies,* 1883 (part of the text-book
series, *The English Citizen,* as aptly emphasized by Dilke, *Problems,* loc. cit.), p. 114.
That 'the Cabinet do not want more niggers', was Kimberley's comment on the
meeting of 22 March 1884 which decided against an increase of the Zulluland
protectorate. (Dilke's diaries, Gwynn and Tuckwell, loc. cit. p. 86.)

[20]Hansard, 3rd ser. vol. 291, pp. 1050—1126, especially the speech of Dawnay
explaining the motion (p. 1054), Randolph Churchill's menaces (pp. 1100f.), P.
Ryland's and W. E. Forster's altercation on the question whether the speech of
the seconder Wodehouse was advocating 'imperial spread-eagle policy' or not (pp.
1081, 1103). Of prominent London papers only the *Standard* fell in with the
opposition. Stead, in *Pall Mall Gazette,* somewhat timidly offered the opinion that
British responsibilities towards the natives went further than the Prime Minister
assumed. In the same year, 1884, 'the Empire Theatre in Leicester Square opened
its doors'. Was the name (as assumed by A. Cobban, 'The New Imperialism',
The Listener, vol. XXXIX, p. 776), 'calculated to appeal to a new generation'?
One has to consider that at that time preventing the dismemberment of the
Empire was the rallying-cry against the Irish demand for Home Rule.

Jubilee national satisfaction was not as yet, as in the Diamond Jubilee, mixed with imperial pride and exotic glamour.[21]

In the two countries, whose statesmen really initiated the 'scramble' for colonies, enthusiasm was no greater. Bismarck's forwardness in South-west Africa was a surprise for his people no less than for the Earl of Granville. Ferry's achievements in Africa and Indo-China did not endear him to the French who never gave him power again after his misfortune in Tongking.

Now, if the great territorial acquisitions of the 1880's were so clearly not the outcome of strong national passions, were they forced upon governments and nations by economic interests? 'Colonization and empire-building', it has been said, 'are above all economic acts, undertaken for economic reasons and very seldom for any others.'[22] Though there is truth in this statement some distinctions are necessary. Economic reasons are at work, if colonies are what was once called 'plantations'—when lands are to be settled, first of all by agricultural immigrants, and for that end claimed by governments. Economic interests of another kind are furthered when trade is made or assumed 'to follow the flag'. Other economic reasons for occupying a country may be the exploitation of its mineral wealth or prospects of its internal development, which are to be achieved by organizing native agriculture and by introducing transport and machinery. This last motive may go together with that of advancement of commerce, and in most cases some or all these motives may come into play together. But in every one of these cases the measure and structure of the economic energies which take an active interest in the occupation make a great difference. Considerable numbers of emigrants willing to live on the land may be at hand or on the contrary the promoters of the foundation may only expect that settlers will come in due course. The country may be desirable to important groups of traders, importing industrialists and investors—or private interests involved at the initial stage may be insignificant, compared to interests on behalf of which the State has entered upon its new responsibilities. It is furthermore, important, whether or not the interests of trade, industry and finance involved in the dependency are in a prominent position in the occupying nation. The term 'economic imperialism'—this much should be clear—has a meaning only when the 'interests' belong to the spheres of trade, industry, or investment; when these 'interests' are in the hands of discernible groups of capitalists who

[21]Tennyson's Odes offer, of course, no proof to the contrary.
[22]R. Pares, *Econ. Hist. Rev.* vol. VII (1937), p. 119.

put the dependency to their own use, when they form an essential part of the economic interests to which the home government (the 'imperial' government) must pay attention. Only if all these conditions are fulfilled can there be reason for saying that the government and the nation which make themselves responsible for the dependency have become 'tools of capitalism'.

To define thus this contingency is as much as to state that, until very late in the century, little had happened to justify the belief that powerful economic considerations were taking shape. Ferry was unable to point to concrete advantages when he spoke of the prospects which his colonial policy would open for commerce and investment. Bismarck made Hanseatic merchants hoist the German flag in Angra Pequena and in the Cameroons; but his colonial annexations were not followed by large economic enterprises. His expectation that private organizations, comparable to the British Chartered Companies, would bear the burden of colonial administration came to nothing. When in the course of the quarrels concerning colonial boundaries in East Africa Bismarck was represented to be powerless against the obstinacy of German traders the news could be ridiculed in England.[23] In England the prospects of the African market were glowingly depicted to the Manchester Chamber of Commerce by H. M. Stanley. But he did not then advocate British colonization in the Congo basin. He spoke in favour of King Leopold's 'association'; he wished it to be protected against Portuguese encroachments on the lower reaches of the river. The merchants of Manchester gave a ready response; they published a report of the meeting and fervently endorsed Stanley's entreaties on behalf of 'the earnest efforts of His Majesty the King of the Belgians to establish civilization and free trade on the Upper Congo'.[24] The year after they—and the London Chamber of Commerce with them—gave also a support to Taubman Goldie's endeavours for wringing a Charter for his National African Company. But this time when existence of a nascent British colony was at stake the businessmen did not emphasize national trade interests. They only demanded 'the establishment of an adequate police force to overawe predatory tribes as well as to enforce the decisions of judicial officers.'[25]

[23]*Scots Observer* (20 April 1889), pp. 595 f. ('Our Traders in Africa').

[24]'Manchester Chamber of Commerce,' special meeting of members, 21 October 1884, etc. *Report of Proceedings*.

[25]William N. M. Geary, *Nigeria under British Rule* (1927), p. 182.

Of the Chartered Companies the eldest, that of North Borneo (1881), was perhaps the most optimistic about the prospect of attracting capital from Great Britain. Their managers inspired an English journalist to write a colourful propaganda book in which the foundation was called the 'New Ceylon'. He compared the firm with the old East India Company and prophesied that its work would initiate 'a new era in the history of the colonizing aspirations of the Anglo-Saxon'.[26] His book has since been forgotten and the colony has not become one of the most renowned parts of the British Empire. Goldie's Royal Niger Company kept to practices and earned successes which, on first sight, have some similarity with what was represented later as 'economic imperialism'. The commercial monopoly which had been planned by Goldie in his treaties with the native chieftains, but was decidedly rejected by Salisbury, was carried into effect by his managers. Salisbury took offence and authorized the inquiry of 1889. Sir Claude Macdonald reported that the manner in which the Company directed the channels of local commerce was to the unqualified detriment of native traders and that it robbed of their markets those of the western Niger delta, direct subjects of the Crown. Nevertheless, the government did not take action. It swallowed also the injunction of the Company on its servants not to make public any facts concerning the administration and business of the Company. That was certainly capitalist high-handedness, from which the shareholders got benefit. Nevertheless, it would have been difficult to make the case appear a major instance for the dependence of colonial regime on the ascendancy of 'monopolist capitalism'. For the financial interests, which were stimulated by Goldie's creation, were not large and widespread enough. The manifest reason why the government, in the end, withheld interference was that it accepted the reasons which had made Goldie insist on monopoly rights. Restoring unhampered competition in the oil trade on the river might have resulted in such a decline of the Company's returns that its whole activities—including new governmental work—would have been paralysed.[27] MacKinnon of East Africa could less than any other man be suspect of capitalist ambitions. When after his and H. H. Johnston's protracted struggles with the Germans he finally founded the 'Imperial British East African Company', he had, like Goldie before him, to

[26]Joseph Hatton, *The New Ceylon. Being a sketch of British North Borneo, or Sabah* (1881), especially pp. 2, 30.
[27]Geary, loc. cit. pp. 177, 183, 188—92.

enlist subscribers in order to make certain that the Company would be equal to its administrative undertaking. In the list the names of Sir John Kirk and of military men are prominent; it is certainly not a galaxy of big capital interests.[28] Rhodes's South African Company was more closely connected with speculative capitalism. Of its original stock one-fifth represented the investment of the profits of De Beers. The exclusive claim to the exploitation of mineral resources, which was granted to this company as to the others, was in its case bound up with fresh speculative expectations. But in the opinion of Rhodes, as well as in that of the wary Charles W. Dilke,[29] the likelihood of the country being opened up rested on its being specially suitable to agricultural development, and it was expected to attract numerous British settlers. Finally, the fact that British capital was at all available for colonial enterprises was not yet known as a cause for complaint. The enthusiast Henley mentioned it, by the way, as one of the advantages which the imperial country could offer as no other one could.[30]

Salisbury's treaties of 1890 with Germany, France and Portugal coincided with signs of growing sympathy with and belief in the work of the African companies. Rhodes on his visits to England won the confidence and even the admiration of important men. The 'studied plainness' of his appearance made his successes in South African business and Cape politics appear to forbode the greatest accomplishments in the service of the race. Henley, who brought out this impression in an inimitable character sketch, was now ready to drop his misgivings about the 'mercantile company'; he became convinced that 'financier, filibuster, statesman' was 'a typical hero for a commercial age'. W. T. Stead discovered in him the man destined by Providence for making Englishmen understand their own providential mission in 'the upward trend of human progress'.[31] Chamber-

[28]McDermott, op. cit. p. 14.

[29]'The Uganda Problem', *Fortnightly Review*, vol. CIII (1893), p. 148.

[30]*Scots Observer* (2 March 1889), p. 405, 'Nyasaland'.

[31]Henley, *National Observer* (18 April 1891), pp. 556 f. 'The Hon. Cecil Rhodes.' To Stead's enthusiasm Edmund Garrett's reports from South Africa, 1889—90, made an important contribution. Cf. J. A. Spender and Cyril Asquith, *Life of H. H. Asquith* (1932), 1, 147. The passage quoted above is from the appeal 'To all English-speaking Folk', *Review of Reviews* (1891). The only disquieting element in 'the potentialities that lie hidden in this remarkable personality' was for Stead at the time that Rhodes was 'deficient in his appreciation of existing factors in our home politics'; he wished to improve upon the great man's erudition by providing him with instructive books and asked Gladstone for advice, which, of course, was withheld (Add. MS. 44303, fol. 462, 17 August 1891). Dilke's attitude

lain, who not long ago had thought the Boers to be indispensable instruments of civilization in South Africa, forgot his anxiety lest injustice should be done to them by English expansion.[32] Rosebery made this expansion the main object of his enthusiasm for the imperial mission of the race. Gladstone, who could not share such belief without reserve, admitted in private that he had 'fallen behind the age in point of colonial information'[33] and desisted from obstructing the growth of imperial feeling in the liberal ranks. Harcourt, indeed, was known to have remained immovably inimical to colonies; but poured out in letters only his anger at liberal apostates to 'Jingoism'.[34] The very fact that in 1892 Gladstone had to entrust Rosebery with the Foreign Office indicated that the African policy to which Salisbury had become converted would be continued by the Liberal cabinet. The new Foreign Secretary felt entitled to proclaim that the nation was 'engaged . . . in pegging out claims for the future' and that it was 'part of our responsibility and heritage to take care that the world as far as it can be moulded, shall receive the Anglo-Saxon, and not another character'.[35]

The phrase was understood to refer to a topic of the day. The East African Company faced great difficulties; the financial responsibilities which it had to face surpassed its means even if railway building was postponed. Its enterprise would be jeopardized, unless parliament agreed to expenses on its behalf. The discussion of the Uganda problem extended quite naturally to the whole African policy which was under way. It is interesting to see how the economic aspects were handled on this occasion. The irreconcilable radicals exposed, of course, the dangers of financial waste, of which the small expenditure demanded at first would be only the prelude. One of them declared himself to be bound in honour and as a Christian to protest against a government which might be prepared to expend millions of sterling in Central Africa while in their own country 'millions of people were living under shameful and insanitary condi-

---

to the same question was characteristically different; he was simply annoyed by Rhodes's 'avowed intention of ultimately coming to England to take part in English politics' (Gwynn and Tuckwell, loc. cit. p. 301).

[32]Cf. Chamberlain's speech in the Zululand debate, 1884 (Hansard, loc. cit. pp. 1113 f., and Johnston, loc. cit. p. 223).

[33]Letter to Stead (28 May 1889), Add. MS. 44303, fol. 406.

[34]Gardiner, *Life of Harcourt*, 11, 151, 192, 195, 198, 227. Harcourt believed, so Balfour said, 'in the curtailment of the British Empire if he believed in nothing else' (Fred Whyte, *The Life of W. T. Stead*, 11, 31).

[35]Speech at the Royal Colonial Institute, 1 March 1893.

tions'. But such social objections were not yet accentuated by the charge that the expense was to serve class interests. The sin which Labouchere felt bound to stigmatize was simply lust for aggrandisement: 'Jingoism'. 'These Jingoes were most remarkable men; they did not seem to care whether the land they required was valuable or valueless. They were like magpies, they loved stealing for the pleasure of staling.'[36] Dilke, on the occasion of the Uganda problem, restated his confidence in Rhodes's enterprise, but disapproved of the inclination of the Liberal party to enter into 'a rivalry with the Conservative in the race for the heart of Africa'. In his opinion nothing 'likely to prove profitable' to the nation could be gained there. His dislike of chartered companies, which dated from the days of the North Borneo affair, required substance now that a company was about to commit the imperial parliament 'to the costly occupation of unhealthy districts, exposed to war, and out of reach'. But he, too, had no scruples as yet about the gains which a company might earn while committing the nation.[37] On the other hand the government and the conservative and unionist supporters of the Uganda grant had little to say about economic prospects. They laid stress on the obligation to civilize Africa, to fight slavery, to come up to expectations and, besides this, mentioned strategical needs concerning the Nile valley. Lugard in his *Rise of Our East African Empire*, which was written as an appeal to the national interest, emphasized the same reasons and mentioned only by the way the 'commercial necessity of finding new markets'.[38] Chamberlain in the Commons debate enlarged on this point only a little more. In answer to the member who postulated priority for social misery at home, he called attention to the 'great proportion' of the people which 'earned its livelihood by the trade brought to this country in consequence of the action of our ancestors, who were not ashamed . . . to peg out claims for posterity'. He went on to glorify 'the spirit of travel and adventure and enterprise distinguishing the Anglo-Saxon race'.[39] He thus inaugurated the style in which he was to co-ordinate economic and patriotic arguments when conducting colonial, and a good deal of the foreign, policy of his country.

After Chamberlain came into office two years later, the whole aspect of colonial policy and of oversea engagements changed within

[36]Hansard, 4th ser. vol. 10, pp. 560 (Storey), 547 (Labouchere).

[37]*Fortnightly Review*, loc. cit. In 1895 Dilke sold his South African Company shares, 'not thinking them things for a politician'. Gwynn and Tuckwell, op. cit. 11, 496.

[38]Ibid. p. 592.

[39]Hansard, loc. cit. pp. 593 f.

a very short time. Economic arguments were, by advocates as well as by adversaries of such engagements, discussed far more specifically. Out of the discussions arose an indictment against capitalist rapacity. This was the power which was now seen to bring in its train fateful commitments for the English in South Africa, for the Americans in the Pacific and for the western nations generally in China. The portent was discovered which was to go under the name of 'economic imperialism'.

The facts which gave occasion for this dismal comment are well known. There was the gold of the Rand. There was the sugar of Hawaii. There were, in 1898, voices heard from America, which cried out for the Spanish island colonies in the interests of trade and surplus capital. 'We must have them if we would not drop out of the procession of the nations struggling for the commerce of the world.'[40] 'There is but one choice—either to enter by some means upon the competition for employment of American capital and enterprise in these colonies or to continue the needless duplication of existing means of production and communication.'[41] Finally, there was the spectacle of the French, German and British governments competing with each other in earmarking for their respective capitalists priorities of trade and of railway construction in China. There was, once again, reason to warn against lust of conquest reaching out overseas. But there was also apparent reason to think that such ambitions were allied to particular financial interests, which were or would soon be prominent on the Stock Exchange and might clandestinely influence the press and public men.

III

It is profitable to consider the manner in which the word imperialism was used during the critical years after 1895. Sometimes it occurs in contexts where it appears to bear the full meaning of 'economic imperialism', but, in fact, the appearance is deceptive. For, very often, the word has reference not to the structure of politics generally, but to the British Empire and to the attitude of Englishmen towards its values. In the understanding of this attitude there are differences which deserve to be noticed in just those cases in which emphasis is laid on economic interests.

[40]Cf. Fred. Greenwood, 'The Anglo-American Future', *The Nineteenth Century*, vol. XXXXIV (July 1898), p. 10.

[41]Ch. A. Conant, 'The Economic Basis of Imperialism', *North American Review*, CLXVII, 339.

'The results of free trade have led our manufacturers and merchants to become imperialists.' Having read only these words written in November 1897, we might understand the author—J. Holland Rose—to assume that English businessmen, harassed by foreign competition at home, are eagerly interested in new markets to be opened by imperial expansion. But he goes on to say: '... the great manufacturing towns, which were once the strongholds of a somewhat narrow Radicalism, now vie with London and the counties in their desire to maintain our naval supremacy and to secure the co-operation of all parts of the empire'.[42] The British imperialism, to which Holland Rose alluded, was speculating neither on conquest nor on share quotations.

It was both, it was 'stock-jobbing imperialism', in the verdict which in 1896 Harcourt passed upon the evidence of the 'cipher telegrams' as to the complicity of Rhodes's Chartered Company in the Jameson Raid. But this censure, too, must be read in its full context. An 'unlawful conspiracy', he told the House of Commons, had been promoted 'by de Beers Company and the Gold Fields Company of Pertoria. There is something, I think, inexpressibly revolting to any high-minded man in the low morality and vulgar slang of these communications. It is a squalid and a sordid picture of stock-jobbing imperialism.'[43] Here a distinction between different shades of imperialism is in the speaker's mind. But that 'imperialism', against which the new monetary one is set off, is not the loyalty to the Empire, of which we have just heard; it is craving for boisterous adventure at the expense of the nation—the meaning which had been annexed to the word at the time when Harcourt took part in the Liberal strictures on Disraeli's Turkish and Afghan politics.

Financial intrigue and bellicose aggressiveness were together contrasted implicitly with creditable British imperialism in the resolution submitted to the Fabian Society in December 1899: 'That the Society should dissociate itself from the imperialism of capitalism and vain glorious nationalism.[44] The juxtaposotion of the words 'imperialism' and 'capitalism' is not equivalent to 'economic imperialism', though to readers of to-day it might possibly suggest this concept. Capitalism and vainglorious nationalism are thought to have united in degrading British imperialism and causing an unjust war.

In the following year, Francis W. Hirst alleged that Britain had passed through three stages of imperialism: 'The first species

42*The Rise and Growth of Democracy in Great Britain* (1898), p. 246.
43H. o. C. 8 May 1896, Hansard, 4th ser. vol. 40, p. 889.
44Edward R. Pease, *The History of the Fabian Society* (1925), p. 130.

was the bluff military imperialism of Lord Palmerston. Then shot up the sham imperialism of Lord Beaconsfield. The third and most poisonous species grows in auriferous soil; it is the financial or speculative imperialism of Mr. Rhodes.'[45] The qualifications bestowed on 'the third species' could be used as variants of 'economic imperialism'. Here, however, the word 'imperialism' is called in to denote consecutive stages of British politics; to the stalwart radical the name of Rhodes conjures up those of Palmerston and Disraeli.

But the difference is no longer very great. In the same year 1900 the full doctrine of economic imperialism was implied in a resolution submitted to the 5th International Socialist Congress at Paris by its 5th Committee:

> . . .que le développement du capitalisme mène fatalement à l'expansion coloniale, cette cause de conflits entre les gouvernements; que l'impérialisme qui en est la conséquence excite le chauvinisme dans tous les pays et force à des dépenses toujours grandissantes au profit du militarisme; que la politique coloniale de la bourgeoisie n'a d'autre but que d'élargir les profits de la classe capitaliste et le maintien du système capitaliste, tout en épuisant le sang et l'argent du prolétariat producteur, et en commettant des crimes et des cruautés sans nombre envers les races indigènes des colonies conquises par la force des armes.[46]

The language of the resolution is French; the reasoning and terminology are not. They are doubtlessly inspired by the English members of the committee. These had taught their comrades how a discussion of 'la politique coloniale' ought to co-ordinate Marxist doctrine with what they believed to be the experience gained during the last years in England.

The actual experience which was most fresh in their minds, and which must have been persuasive for the delegates from other countries, was that to which our previous quotations referred: the Transvaal question, connected as it was with the activities and aspirations of the South African Company. The emergence of this problem was seen as a typical instance of what 'imperialism' could mean in practice. This view of the case was by no means restricted to the opponents of the politics into which Rhodes and the Rand interests had drawn Chamberlain and the nation at large. The henchmen of

[45]*Liberalism and the Empire*, three essays by F. W. Hirst, Gilbert Murray and J. L. Hammond (1900), p. 4.
[46]Compte rendu sténographique, *Cahiers de la Quinzaine* (1901), p. 175.

Rhodes had, after the Jameson Raid, contrived to bring home to
the British public that his cause was that of the empire, and ought
to be supported by true imperialism. 'If Mr Rhodes had not been
an avowed imperialist we should have been spared nine-tenths of the
criticism lavished upon his aims, objects and ambitions.' So wrote
'an imperialist' in his 'Vindication of the principle... of Chartered
Companies, with special reference to the British South African Company', published in 1896 under the name of *The Pioneers of Empire*.[47]
The assertion was still in need of justification for those who remembered that ten years ago Rhodes 'avowed' abhorrence of the 'imperial
factor' in South Africa. It was for this reason that soon afterwards
'imperialist', aided by Dr Jameson, provided the public with 'a
biography and appreciation' which, by personal anecdotes and plausible explanations, established the view that 'the expansion of our
Empire' had always been 'the paramount idea' in Rhodes's mind and
that only, 'an imperialism, as intense as it was enlightened' had
guided him at the time, when the sympathies of the imperial government were less important to him than those of the Cape Dutch.
Now the latter had been irretrievably lost. In view of this change,
it was to the interest of Rhodes's party that the English nation should
be prepared for a policy such as had been adumbrated by Sir Hercules
Robinson in 1889: 'Colonialism through imperialism; in other words,
colonial expansion through imperial aid, the home government doing
what the colonies cannot do for themselves, having constitutionally
no authority beyond their borders.'[48] In the eyes of the Cape English
and of the Uitlanders in Johannesburg the occasion on which this
obligation was to be honoured had now come. And they realized
that the aid of the 'Home government' could be effective only if
it was endorsed by enthusiasm on the part of the 'home country'.

This meant that activities 'beyond the borders' of a colony
should be thought a national cause in Great Britain. The English
had lately become used to the conviction that the colonials were
precious sections of their own nation, that 'Greater Britain' was the
real 'Great Britain'. And this creed was—though Seeley, who had done
most for making it accepted, did not like 'imperial' language—express-

---

[47]*The Pioneers*, etc. p. 1. *Cecil Rhodes. A Biography and Appreciation*, by
Imperialist, with personal reminiscences by Dr. Jameson (1897), p. 33. 'The Plain
Truth about Mr. Rhodes and the Transvaal', *Fortnightly Review* (1 June 1896),
pp. 839 ff., is signed 'Imperialist' too, while Elisabeth Lecky wrote at the same
time 'A Warning to Imperialists' against those who 'obscured the issues' with
regard to the Jameson Raid (*The Nineteenth Century*, XC, 19 ff.).

[48]*The Times* (20 May 1889), p. 6, col. 1.

ed in the word 'imperialism'. But to follow colonials in South Africa beyond their borders might mean aggressiveness, and a resuscitation of that 'Disraelite imperialism or jingoism' which even a conservative had, on the morrow of the election of 1895, deemed to be the object of an 'unquestionable and, as I think, just aversion'.[49] If the aspirations of Rhodes's party—and those cherished by Chamberlain and Milner too—were to have their way, this aversion had to be overcome and both brands of 'imperialism' blended in the minds of the nation at large. The fervour of imperialist aggressiveness was to be firmly rooted in the sympathies of imperialist solidarity. And this union of feeling had to embrace solidarity with groups of people who were, to a large extent, neither English nor Colonial in origin: the capitalists interested in the goldfields of the Rand. Milner fully realized that this was a dangerous issue and during the first year of his South African mission (1897-8) refused to adopt the legitimate grievances of the mining companies against Kruger's monopoly, and to make them a reason for imperial interference.[50]

In England, however, just at that time, popular sentiment gave the impression that such fastidiousness had become out of date. Growing masses were caught by a vision of the Empire, in which loyalty to its common causes figured not as the counterpart of, but as an incitement to, adventures which were to give palpable proof of the superiority of the race. And those business interests which might be the first to profit from such ventures could rely on being glorified in the halo of this vision. They would be trusted as carrying out pioneering activities for the common welfare of the nation, its empire and the peoples under its sway. We have seen Rosebery and Chamberlain designing publicly the frame work of these opinions when, in connexion with the Uganda grant of 1893, they gave out the watchword of 'pegging out claims'. The fact that, immediately afterwards, the opening of the Imperial Institute met with far more sympathetic interest from the middle-class public than had its foundation in 1887, gave colour to the assumption that the future of the empire had decisively risen in popular favour, just because of its economic prospects. 'Material interests, measurable in terms of £. s. d., are what pervade and regulate the public judgement; and rightly so.' Still G. Baden-Powell, who interpreted the event in these terms,[51] related the material interests to the existing empire only—with special reference to

[49]J. S. Stuart-Glennie, *Fortnightly Review* (December 1895), p. 854.
[50]E. A. Walker, *Lord Milner and South Africa* (1942), p. 11.
[51]*Fortnightly Review*, vol. 53, p. 892.

its self-governing colonies—and not to additions to its sphere of dominance. And confidence that 'jingoism' in colonial affairs would not be encouraged from above seemed justified even after the Jameson Raid. Chamberlain's influence was considered just then to be an element of circumspection and restraint.[52] Nevertheless, popular responses to the Raid gave grounds for the expectation that public opinion would concur with more spirited interpretations of empire causes in official demonstrations and politics. The Poet Laureate of the day was by no means disgraced by his eulogy of the conspirators. 'The country's love' was pledged to them by the *Evening News,* whose editors after a few months proclaimed the other pledge, to make their new paper, the *Daily Mail,* 'the embodiment and mouthpiece of the imperial idea'.[53]

For the first time in England this emotion was represented as an idea. The government rose to the situation in two ways. To the surprise of Lord Cromer it initiated the conquest of the Sudan. Chamberlain chose to make the Queen's Diamond Jubilee the occasion not only for disclosing his views on empire reform to the conference of Colonial Prime Minister, but also for arranging the pageant of 22 June 1897 which made the man in the street visualize his empire more tellingly than the Imperial Institute had done. 'Imperialism in the air—all classes drunk with sightseeing and hysterical loyalty'; so Beatrice Webb noted in her diary. For once her feelings were shared by Rudyard Kipling, who saw his countrymen 'drunk with sight of power' and invoked the merciful castigation of the Lord. But the self-satisfaction which had been sanctioned by the Jubilee celebrations did not die away after they were over. When in the following month, the Report on the Jameson Raid had been discussed in parliament and Rhodes's honour declared by Chamberlain to be unblemished, *The Times* wrote that the Raid had 'taken its place in the perspective of empire building'. For John Morley this view was, naturally, a proof that the whole perspective was wrong. He ventured to direct the attention of his constituents in Cornwall to the ominous implications of the case: 'All this empire building—why, the whole thing is tainted with the spirit of the hunt for gold. . . . I do not say of Mr Rhodes himself that his imperialism is a mere veil for stock operations and company operations; but this I do say that he is surrounded with men with whom imperialism is,

[52]Beatrice Webb's Diaries, *Our Partnership,* p. 131.
[53]Kennedy Jones, *Fleet Street and Downing Street* (1919), pp. 144-6. W. L. Langer, *The Diplomacy of Imperialism,* vol. 1 (1935), p. 83.

and cannot be anything else, but a name for operations of that ignoble kind.'

The effect of this censure was lost at that time just because of its wording. The *Spectator*, who professed to think of Rhodes no less severely, regretted that Morley had not realized, 'that the way to fight the dangerous and sordid Rhodesian imperialism is not by condemning the Empire altogether but by contrasting Rhodesian imperialism with the truer, nobler, and saner imperialism which, whether sound or not in policy, is at any rate clear and honest'.[54]

The paper saw 'the true English imperialism . . . working on well-tried Indian lines', expounded by Sir Harry Johnston. Yet to the popular mind this imperialism was, a year later, exemplified not by acts of colonial administration but by Omdurman and Fashoda. The cause of the Empire was again a matter of excitement, even military excitement.

In this view people became confirmed by the triumphs and aspirations which resulted from the war of 1898 in which the other great English-speaking nation was involved. There was much talk that year on both sides of the Atlantic about the superiority and the destinies of the Anglo-Saxon race.[55] Hopes were held out for realising these destinies by co-operation in world affairs. Chamberlain himself hinted at this prospect. He did it just at the time when Admiral Dewey's fleet attacked Manila and the acquisition of the Philippines became the foremost topic in American discussion on war-aims. This moment opened a new chapter not only in American politics but also in the development of 'imperial' ideas. Americans had heeded the rise of these ideas in England. Now many of them were eager either to adopt them or to show that their implications were at variance with the hallowed traditions of the republic. For some weeks the former of these attitudes prevailed. 'We see the beginning of an "Imperial" party here' wrote W. H. Page to James Bryce on 9 May. And a few weeks later the *Washington Post* asserted that empire had become the cry of American democracy. 'A new consciousness seems to have come upon us. . . . We are face to face

[54]*The Times* (29 September 1897), p. 4, col. d. *Spectator* (2 October), p. 428.

[55]For early comments, cf, the letter of W. H. Page quoted below (Burton J. Hendrick, *The Earlier Life and Letters of W. H. P.* (1928), p. 264); *New York Nation* (July 1898); O. Flower, *The Arena* (Boston, 1898); F. Greenwood, 'The Anglo-American Future', *Nineteenth Century*, vol. XCIV. In England Edward Dicey, the veteran of anti-Gladstonianism, became a most eloquent champion of the case in 'The New American Imperialism', *Nineteenth Century*, loc. cit. pp. 487 ff.

with a strange destiny.... The taste of empire is in the mouth of
the people even as the taste of blood in the jungle.' 'It means an
imperial policy. . . .' The *Washington Post* enjoyed the fame of being
a level-headed paper and has been respected just because of its
caution; its acceptance of imperial feelings as an irreversible current
was therefore particularly noticed.[56] Congressmen and publicists were,
indeed, quick to denounce 'the spectre of imperialism'—and the advocates of annexation themselves came to think unfavourably of imperial phraseology.[57] But, in fact, it was the attitude implied in
this phraseology which prevailed.

At the end of the year it was said to have become the state
of mind of the English too. 'At the moment when I write these lines
there is noticeable through the British Empire a very strange alertness
of concentrated attention ... my own memories go back faintly, so
far as the Crimean War; never in all those variegated years have
I seen anything approaching the attentive silence of to-day. The lion
has straightened his front paws, and rises, and listens.'

In such terms were Englishmen represented to Americans by
Edmund Gosse at New Year 1899.[58] Observers who were less given
to rhetorical images found the temper of the nation by no means
'silent'. The *Spectator* stated that current 'talk about "empire" was
at once eternal and exaggerated'.[59] Foreign writers who stayed in
London then were startled by the fervour of the 'imperial' ideas
which were current everywhere. They became aware of the passions
symbolized and the problems implied in these topics as something
relatively new. The German anglicist W. Wetz noted that the press
spoke no longer of the Kaiser and the Czar as of 'emperors'. Words
relating to 'imperial' causes had by the British become reserved for
their empire, Great Britain. This was, he thought, the result of
'the imperialist movement in England', which expressed itself in newspaper discussions, associations, and books. The movement, he confessed, had made him reverse his views on the spirit of the nation.[60]

[56] Congress. Record, 55th Congress, 2nd Session, Appendix, p. 573. *Kölnische
Zeitung* (21 June), p. 1, col. 3.

[57] The discussion includes Bryan's speeches, Karl Schurz, 'American Imperialism' and, on the other hand, President McKinley's message to Congress concerning the annexations. It has given rise to important scholarly comment, but
deserves special surveying with regard to the concepts of 'empire' and 'imperialism'.

[58] 'The Literature of Action,' *North American Review*, vol. CLXVII (January
1898), p. 14.

[59] 'Mr. Morley on Jingoism' (21 January 1899), p. 77.

[60] 'Die imperialistische Bewegung in England,' *Die Grenzboten* (58. Jahrgang,
1. Vierteljahr 1899), pp. 14 f. The first German student of the movement was,

Olindo Malagodi, who visited London clubs found their members since 1898 constantly involved in 'quella capitale questione che e scoppiata improvvisamente, col folgore di un gigantesco fuoco artificiale sulla frontiera oscura di due secoli: la questione dell' imperialismo'.[61] And Francois de Pressense asked Englishmen to consider the 'curious thing, but a fact beyond dispute, that when the masses are on the verge of rising in their majesty and asking for their rights, the classes have only to throw into their eyes the powder of "imperialism", and to raise the cry of the fatherland is in danger'.[62]

These observations are strikingly unanimous and strikingly simultaneous. They go far to show that, though prepared by manifold antecedents, the surge of imperial sentiment in 1898 was, like the corresponding excitement in America, remarkably sudden. Attempts to interpret it in terms of sociology and to trace it back to literary influences have been made by the same contemporary writers who directed attention to it. But no explanation can be adequate which does not take full account of the one fact: that the waves of 'imperialism' between 1897 and 1899 were not only in the nature of a social phenomenon, but also in the nature of historical events.

The upheaval of 1898 evoked an antagonism no less influential than the sympathy which it aroused. This antagonism had two lasting effects, both of them foreshadowed already in the discussion of the Philippines problem in the United States.[63] To the notion of imperialism it attached the stigma which was finally to obscure its nobler meanings. Moreover, it demanded a vigorous inspection into the particular economic interests which could be suspected of forcing the hands of statesmen and of inspiring the emotions of the multitude in affairs called 'imperial'.

This effect was not intended by the man who started the campaign. John Morley on 17 January 1899 informed his constituents of his resolve 'no longer to take an active and responsible part in the formal counsels of the heads of the Liberal party'. He summarized the dividing issue in two words which had, he insisted, recently becomes nearly synonymous: 'you may call it jingoism, you may call it

---

however, the socialist refugee, M. Beer, who in the Jubilee year 1897 wrote an article, 'Der moderne englische Imperialismus' for *Die Neue Zeit* (Jahrg. 16, 1), pp. 300 ff.

61*Imperialismo. La civiltà industriale et le sue conquiste. Studii Inglesi* (Milano, 1901), Prefazione. The book had been in preparation since 1898.

62'England and France. An examination and an appeal.' *Contemporary Review*, vol. LXXV (February 1899), especially pp. 158–60.

63See the quotations above, pp. 82–83.

imperialism'. Remembering the censures he had incurred sixteen months earlier he recognized this time the 'imperialism' could be interpreted in a favorable sense: 'national duty, not national vainglory . . . the guardianship and the guidance of a great state'. But that was not 'what "imperialism" is in the sense in which it is now used'. The current significance of the word was exhibited in the Sudan expedition with its cruel incidents, in the Fashoda crisis, which was the only palapable result of this expedition, and in the prospect of militarism, which meant gigantic expediture and inevitably led to war. Imperialism was the state of mind which acquiesed in all this, as the liberal leaders were doing.[64] The tenor of the speech was not very different from that of the essay in which twenty years earlier Robert Lowe had launched the indictment of 'imperialism' against Beaconsfield's Oriental policy, and by this attack given the word a meaning in English public life.[65] But the situation was different. Consequences far more momentous than those which had immediately resulted from Lowe's invective ensued now from Morley's solemn confession of faith. It gave the cue to a lively discussion which focused on the concept of imperialism, and was protracted for months in party speeches and dignified addresses, in newspaper articles and pamphlets, until late in the year it was merged in the altercations aroused by the outbreak and conduct of the Boer War.[66]

In this discussion champions of imperialism were the first to raise the question of economic interests. Chamberlain was not the only one who emphasized the interconnexion of empire and commerce. George Wyndham at the War Ministry defined an imperialist as 'a man who realizes . . . that those places which were recondite, visited at great intervals by travellers, are now the markets, the open ports, the exchanges of the world to which every energetic Briton should

[64]Speech at Brechin, *The Times* (18 January), p. 6, col. b.

[65]'Imperialism', *Fortnightly Review*, vol. XXIV (1 October 1878), pp. 453 ff. The important article started the debate which caused Lord Carnarvon to speak in Edinburgh (15 November) of 'imperialism' as 'a newly coined word' *(Fortnightly Review*, loc. cit. p. 760).

[66]Among political speeches those of Hicks-Beach, Chamberlain, G. Wyndham, Asquith, 18, 19 and 28 January, and the address of Campbell-Bannerman to the National Liberal Federation on 8 March, are notable for being reported and commented upon copiously in the daily and weekly press. Sir R. Giffen's paper on 'the Relative Growth of the Component Parts of the Empire,' read at the Royal Colonial Institute on 14 February and Rosebery's address at the Cromwell tercentenary belong to the series as well. Of articles in periodicals, 'Imperialism' by J. Lawson Walton, *Contemporary Review*, vol. LXXV (March), pp. 305 ff., deserves notice; it challenged R. Wallace to his article quoted below.

tend his footsteps and where a great part of the capital of Great Britain is invested'. *The Times* railed at Morley who still clung to the ideals which had been valid in the year of the Great Exhibition 'while the world has not stood still . . . and nations . . . have learned that wealth and progress, like all other good things, have to be guarded by strong hands and stout hearts'. This assertion was somewhat more militant than the similar remark of J. Holland Rose a year earlier; and so was that of the liberal J. L. Walton that 'the motive for the Manchester School has outlived the pacific philanthropy. . . . Now that . . . markets are in danger of closing, the industrial spirit is imperialist and even warlike and demands that they be kept open.'

Such opinions were certainly voiced among the businessmen themselves.[67] But, in the course of the year, they encountered answers. Demonstrations of protest and distrust followed three different lines. One was that indicated by Morley: disgust with the bravado and the reckless desire for further expansion. This sentiment was expressed most forcefully by Leonard Courtney and John L. Hammond;[68] it was countenanced by Campbell-Bannerman who thought abjuring 'the vulgar and bastard imperialism of irritation, and provocation, and aggression' a hopeful device for avoiding an incurable rift within the Liberal party. Other critics, who like him did not wish to be mixed up with Little Englanders and would even agree to well-considered imperial expansion, discovered that economic repercussions might be provoked by expanding finance. They warned against the dangers of 'the capitalist era which is now slowly superseding the industrial era'. Capital flowing abroad into the spheres of 'imperial interest' would soon stimulate the productive forces of other nations instead of those of the mother-country. From colonial countries in particular it would in fact not come back, and only shareholders would benefit from this investment. This was the economic reality into which 'pegging out for posterity' was about to be transformed, as long as 'a sham imperialism turns our heads'. The economist who uttered this warning[69] directed attention to an aspect of the

67Cf. Fred Greenwood, 'The Cry for new Markets, *Nineteenth Century,* vol. XLV (April 1899), pp. 538 ff., especially pp. 541, 543.

68And satirically by *Punch* (24 May): 'Private Views: Mostly Unpopular. No. II, Empire Makers.'

69Ritortus, 'The Imperialism of British Trade', *Contemporary Review,* vol. LXXVI (July, August), pp. 132—52, 282—304, especially pp. 145 f., 295 ff, where the author referred also to similar warnings of the *Financial News.* F. Greenwood, 'The Cry', etc., states that 'the lords and princes of British commerce are not in all things and in all ways the patriots they probably believe themselves to be',

case which a special group of critics thought to be no less morally revolting than were the militant emotions and, indeed, suspiciously allied to these. In the 200-odd pages in which John M. Robertson expatiated upon the mutual relations between 'patriotism and empire' this alliance between 'the temper of national pride' and the interests of investment which cried for new markets was reserved for the concluding chapter. The 'commercial aristocracy and rich middle class' was about to occupy the place which feudalism and the landlord system had held before. Among them 'the sinister interest of those industrial sections which thrive on the production of war material' was notable. Alongside the 'mere pride and passion of nation and race which had been characteristic of Disraelian Imperialism', there was now 'the concept of commercial interest' emerging more and more distinctly. It was more dangerous because it could hold its own better against criticism. And it was all directed only 'to the end of heaping up more capital for investment', while 'our own toilers are not to do more consuming'. Finally, besides the commercial and capitalist interest there was another stigmatized, though only occasionally, by the author: the service interest, which, since Gladstone abolished purchase in the army, had also become a middle-class interest.[70]

These short indictments were to become headlines in later anti-imperialist literature. Upon contemporaries their impression was lost because they were ejaculated only in passing and because Robertson repelled readers by his disparagement of patriotism. Another radical, however, made a great impression by attacks in a similar vein. Robert Wallace exposed 'the seamy side of Imperialism'. He wished to back Morley, but surpassed him in that he charged the Liberal party with having become dependent on 'a thousand firms, financiers, adventurers and company promoters who seize on every new market'. More important still, he extended the charge to the businessmen who traded and made money in the colonies, and thereby he extended it to the dependent empire at large. The native was to these people merely an object of manifold exploitation, now by dispossessing him of his land, now by selling him gin; 'and then expansionists boast

---

since they do not 'fill the markets they have already got' and are comparable to farmers who look out for new virgin soil when they are no longer surrounded by wilderness. G.'s principal concern is not, like that of Ritortus, misdirection of capital, but the efficiency of German competition. He too, however, deprecates being suspected of having become a Little Englander or declaring 'against further expansion'.

[70]Pp. 140, 172-8.

that trade is following the flag'. And Wallace saw no difference between these modern ways and 'the mode in which the Empire generally had been acquired'.[71]

The stirring effect of these strictures is best measured by the fact that Mary Kingsley singled them out for special refutation when in autumn 1899 she went on a lecture tour in order to make the manufacturing towns of the North share her interest in West Africa. She was appalled by 'the spectacle of a distinct outbreak of anti-imperialism up here in England'. In a way she thought men like Morley, Courtney and Wallace deserving the gratitude of the nation 'for their honest endeavours to keep England's honour clean and to preserve her imperialism from sinking into being in our times a stockbroker's nigger business'. But she felt, of course, compelled to emphasize the national merit of the 'buccaneers, privateers, pirates' of yore without whom 'we should not be Imperial England', and to defend the honour of the colonial merchants of the present day to whose expert understanding she would have chosen to confide the empire in Africa.[72] The *Spectator* held, like Mary Kingsley, 'that it is the business of England ... to take over and rule the inferior races of mankind'. But in October the paper saw reason to speak of people who nowadays practised this 'taking over' in terms not very different from those of Wallace. 'New jingoism' was afoot, which was 'tainted by the desire for great and rapid gain. ... From China, from Central Africa, from West Africa, from South Africa and from the Pacific we receive the same messages which mean: use force, coerce the dark men, defy the white men in battle, and then Englishmen will have new trades, new concessions, new mines, new pecuniary prosperity.' The writer was satisfied that the wrongdoers had 'little hold on Parliament and none on the Administration'; probably, by censuring the new jingoes he wished also to parry the detractions of anti-imperialists.[73]

War at the Transvaal border was imminent when the article appeared; but the author made no sign of being disquieted by the fact that the British government had espoused the Uitlanders' demands, which were prompted by 'the desire for great and rapid

[71]*Contemporary Review*, vol. LXXV (June), pp. 788 f., 792.

[72]*West African Studies* (2nd ed. 1901), pp. 415 ff., especially pp. 419, 423 ff. On Mary Kingsley's attitude to colonial economics, cf. Hancock, *Survey*, 11, 2, pp. 332 f.

[73]'The New Jingoism', vol. LXXXI (8 October), p. 480—preceded by an appeal for imperial concentration, loc. cit. (30 July), p. 137; the tendency of which is similar to that of Greenwood's article quoted above.

gain'.[74] An economist to whom the relation of capital accumulation to social welfare had been for years the crucial problem of modern economics held other views. J. A. Hobson had gone out to South Africa in order to inspect the conditions underlying the crisis. He was horrified by the mentality which pervaded the society of Johannesburg, and gave vent to his impressions and conclusions in reports to a London paper. These letters were, in the first year of the war, republished in his book *The War in South Africa. Its causes and effects.*

I V

Thus, when the South African War broke out, thoughtful and courageous Englishmen were just in the mood to inquire severely into the prospects as well as into the roots of all that was now called imperialism. In this inquiry economic acquisitiveness was the object of special suspicion. The manner in which England was drawn into the war could not but make such reflections highly unpopular. To all appearance the Empire was attacked. To say, or even to suggest that the war was the responsibility of the men in charge of imperial policies, or, still worse, of pecuniary interests countenanced by such men was to lower the national spirit. And the maintenance of this spirit was urgently necessary in view of the initial reverses and of the light which they threw on the national preparations. But it was just this situation which aroused searchings of the heart which could not be satisfied by overcoming the danger, still less by conquering the Boer countries. The depth of the shame with which conscientious hearts watched the next months is impressively brought out in reflexions which high-minded women confided to their diaries.[75] But, at the same time, such sentiments stimulated a resolute approach to systematic thought. To accept the war and to carry it on until the republics were brought under the British flag was thought a touchstone of imperialism by the great majority of the nation. If that was true, then for people with a conscience the

[74]In the renewed criticism of South African politics, voiced in the Commons debates of 28 July 1899, the question of economic interests was not prominent, while the debates concerning transfer of administration from the Royal Niger Company to the Imperial Government, on 3 and 26 July, had enlarged upon the subject of commercial monopoly (Hansard, 4th ser. vol. 75).

[75]Beatrice Webb, *Our Partnership*, pp. 190, 194 f. A. Ruth Fry, *Emily Hobhouse* (1929), p. 74. (A mournful strophe added by E. H. to Kipling's *Recessional.*)

imperialism which had brought about this war against a small brave people was a hideous power to be brought down by all intellectual means.

In this reasoning three groups of argument were prominent. They corresponded, broadly speaking, to the themes which had turned up in the discussions of 1899. The first argument fastened on the international situation. Anglophobia had been increased in France as well as in Germany and might be welcome to statesmen of both continental power-groups. To contemplate this danger was the more painful because it was now difficult for a scrupulous mind to draw a distinctive line between British imperialism on the one hand and German militarism or French chauvinism on the other. This trend of thought had historical implications. it was no longer of first importance that in the overseas expansion of the last two decades French and German politicians had shown more initiative and lust for prestige than those of Great Britain. There was, in fact, one imperialism which pervaded all the great nations, including America and Russia. But—and that was a second line of thought—England had a responsibility of her own rooted in a past which was wholly her own. England had grown into the British Empire which had become the model for the other nations. Was not imperial greatness a doubtful boon, fraught not only with political and financial risks but no less necessarily with moral evils? The young joint-authors of *Liberalism and the Empire,* who were 'blind neither to the glories nor yet to the responsibilities of the British Empire' expressed regret that the 'ambiguous and unfortunate' word 'empire' had blurred the great distinction to be made between the relations of England to free Canada and free Australia on the one hand, and her rule over 'all those tropical provinces which she has won as a conqueror and holds as a foreign despot'.

The third topic was the connexion between politics and economics. It was attached to two main issues. One was the danger threatening the great national principle of free trade. Was not 'every imperialist' at heart an 'emporialist'?[76] The second dominating issue was the particular connexion which to all appearances existed between imperial expansion and capital accumulated at home. It was the animating influence of overseas enterprises on the Stock Exchange, which made thousands of agents busy for a considerable section of society. And it was the reciprocal influence which these interests might bring

[76]Hirst in *Liberalism and the Empire,* pp. 72-4.

to bear on an obliging press which made them indiscernible from the national cause.[77] Both these dangerous elements of capitalist society, abettors of protection and speculators in exotic investments, had been shown up before the war. But the second species appeared an ominously commanding power now that it might be identified with those capitalists who had handled transactions in and earned big gains from Transvaal mines and the Chartered Company. The 'average citizen' was to be informed that his empire so 'magnificent and once so magnanimous' was liable to be overruled by the 'black magic of imperialism' which made sordid motives direct the actions of 'little minds' in government and parliament.[78]

All these indictments were inspired by spontaneous disgust and sincere moral apprehension. Nevertheless, one cannot fail to discover in them the influence of two master-minds—one of them long dead and often declared to be completely out of date, the other to many people still the 'Grand Old Man'—Cobden and Gladstone. The ethics were Gladstone's; the teachings were Cobden's. Fabians, indeed, wished to part with Gladstonian liberalism which 'thinks in individuals';[79] but at that time there were other things than that to be learned from liberalism, and from Cobden in particular. Cobden had spoken with disrespect of the intellects working in Foreign and Colonial Offices. Cobden had preached to his people that economic wisdom and peace would prevail in the world if only England would take the lead. Cobden had been convinced that the Empire connexions of Britain were obstructing this prospect. Cobden, finally, had denounced particular class interests as being the ultimate mischief-makers, whose unearned privileges barred the path to material and moral progress. These interests, indeed, had been different from those which had to be faced now. They had been those of the feudal landlord class, whereas now the economic antagonists of peace, humanity and public welfare

---

[77]Hirst, loc. cit. pp. 63 f. More sarcastically, Bernard Shaw, *Fabianism and the Empire* (1900), pp. 9 f.

[78]Hirst, loc. cit. pp. 43-57. Occasional remarks of the author (pp. 4, 39) hit ironically upon the Jewish element in South African finance, which was more sharply censured in a special chapter of Hobson's *War in South Africa* and elsewhere. The intense anti-Jewish feeling of the labour leader John Burns burst out, together with compassion on Kruger, in a diary-entry upon the outbreak of war (Add. MS. 46317; 10 October 1899).

[79]Beatrice Webb's diary-entries of September and October 1901 (*Our Partnership*, pp. 220—3), compared with those of January 1900 (loc. cit. p. 194) show how socialist thinking at this time was not necessarily bound to take up an anti-imperialist line. The closing pages of the book (pp. 488 f.) are remarkable for mirroring the change of mind after the Great War.

were detected in the capitalist class, whose enlightened self-interest was according to him a steady element of progress. This made it difficult for a liberal to weld all the indictments against imperialist statecraft and imperialist society into a coherent system of interpretation. To attain such a high goal and to form a real theory of imperialism was possible only to a mind which was prepared to combine the Cobdenian motives with unorthodox views concerning the mechanism of society.

This it is that J. A. Hobson did. In many respects his study *Imperialism,* which came out in the year of the peace treaty, is only an amplified restatement of all the charges which had been voiced before and during the war against perverted feelings and against harmful interests which played upon these feelings. But the argument concerning 'the economics of imperialism' reaches out further. Hobson surveys 'the measure of imperialism'. Taking as example Great Britain, because it has 'travelled so much faster and further along this road', he tabulates chronological data which show the overseas areas acquired during the previous twenty years. Thus he makes clear that he wishes to bring the whole colonial development of this period under the head of 'imperialism'. He gives historical definiteness to this term. He then proceeds to show that these imperialist acquisitions have been valuable neither as 'outlets for population' nor as markets for the commerce of the metropolitan country, such as former colonial foundations had been. He thinks relatively little of the imperialist driving force domiciled in mercantile counting houses. These exclusions appropriately lead to the inference that only 'certain sectional interests that usurp control of the national resources' can have made for imperialist expansion. The 'economic parasites of imperialism' are on the one hand the industries and professions which profit immediately from annexation and war: the 'services', the armament industry. More fundamentally significant are, however, financial parasites: investors, dealers in investments, or 'financiers', and certain industrial magnates which look out for big establishments in undeveloped countries because the home market is bound to render diminishing returns. And here Hobson finds the way to connect imperialism with the great defect which earlier meditation had led him to discover in the capitalist system. 'The taproot of imperialism' is inadequate distribution of industrial gains at home, 'under-consumption' and 'over-saving'.

Parasites are discovered who are sheltered by the prevailing economic system. They make this system act against the true interest of society. They make it pervert politics. They find the way to foster passions, romantic as well as savage. In this edifice of ideas a Cobdenite ground-plan is unmistakable. But the original motive has been transferred, so to speak, to another historical level. The pernicious parasites are no longer identified with the privileged remnants of feudal society; they are the outgrowth of capitalist society. The process of capitalist profit-making has developed so far that it sees no prospects of further expansion other than those opening in colonial and other exotic investments. This discovery entails a historical conclusion. Colonial enterprises, and other political operations overseas which made investment necessary, are to be understood solely on the basis of the urge of accumulated capital to be turned to profit in undeveloped countries. This urge, at the same time, can work only because capital is not put to healthier social use at home. It follows that the whole recent colonial development which clearly coincided with large capitalist gains, can be understood only as a consequence of the unhealthy organization of society. The driving force issuing from these conditions necessarily forced the hands of the men who had been active in these enterprises. It is this interpretation that gives unity to the whole process. It explains, in very fact, the dimensions of modern colonial exploit, the 'measure of imperialism'. The 'age of imperialism' assumes a shape under this one aspect. 'Imperialism' is really one and the same as 'economic imperialism'.

It would not be impossible to weigh against each other the modicum of historical facts to which this deduction can be supposed to refer, and the volume of other facts which make its full implications appear a distortion of historical evidence. This, however, is not our task here. It will have become clear that economic experience was only a part though an indispensable one of the reality which brought to birth the concepts of 'the age of imperialism' and of 'economic imperialism'. Motives of political morality were the most powerful and these motives were deeply rooted in the English tradition, as indeed was the Empire with which they found fault. We need not show why Hobson's views were attractive to Marxian economists some of whom had in fact (as the Paris resolution of 1900 shows) learnt to think similarly, before they knew Hobson. To study how the concept restarted its career and grew into a world-power during and after the Great War would be another task which cannot be tried here. Probably close inquiry would show moral and political forces to have been primarily at work again: this time strong reasons of expediency in the communist camp, but once more moral misgivings concerning the national past in England and second thoughts concerning recent politics in America. In both countries the situation in which consciences had found themselves in the years 1898 to 1900 was renewed on a very much greater scale.

'Imperialism'

An Historiographical Revision[1]

D. K. Fieldhouse

D. K. Fieldhouse was born in India in 1925. From 1950-52 he taught history at Haileybury College and from 1953-57 was Lecturer in History at the University of Canterbury, New Zealand. Since 1958 he has been Beit Lecturer in the History of the Commonwealth at Oxford. In 1965 he was Visiting Lecturer and Fellow at the Australian National University. He is a Fellow of Nuffield College, Oxford.

Fieldhouse's article is an outstanding example of the large body of literature that is critical of Hobson's interpretation of the so-called "new imperialism". He tries to show that it is mostly a political phenomenon rather than an economic one.

I

It is now nearly sixty years since J. A. Hobson published *Imperialism: a Study*,[2] and thereby gave the word the connotation it still generally carries. His conception of the nature of 'imperialism'[3] has, indeed, been almost universally accepted and, partly through the expository literature it has generated, may be said to have exercised a significant historical influence. Yet, for all its success, Hobson's argument has always been extremely vulnerable to criticism: and it is therefore surprising that those historians and economists who have argued effectively that his analysis is basically unsound should have received so little attention. The aim of the present article is to draw together some of the more important arguments that have been put forward

[1]Reprinted from *The Economic History Review*, second series, Vol. XIV, No. 2, 1961, pages 187—209. This essay arose out of reading the following recently published books: John Strachey, *The End of Empire* (London: Victor Gollancz Ltd., 1959); W. M. Macmillan, *The Road to Self-rule* (London: Faber and Faber, 1959); A. P. Thornton, *The Imperial Idea and Its Enemies)* (London: Macmillan & Co. Ltd., 1959); B. Semmel, *Imperialism and Social Reform* (London: George Allen & Unwin Ltd., 1960); H. Brunschwig, *Mythes et Réalités de l'impérialisme colonial français* (Paris: Librairie Armand Colin, 1960). The essay has benefited from being read by Miss M. Perham and A. F. McC. Madden.

[2]Published in 1902. References are to the third edition (1954).

[3]When used in Hobson's sense, the word will here be printed in inverted commas.

for and against his thesis, and to suggest that, on balance, the noes have it.

Hobson's own claim to importance and originality lies simply in his having induced British, and subsequently world, opinion to accept his own special definition of the word imperialism. Professor Koebner has already examined the various meanings given to the word before 1902.[4] He has suggested that, as used in England, it had two general connotations in the 1890's, both of which were morally neutral. In one sense, it was being used of those who wished to prevent the existing British settlement colonies from seceding and becoming independent states, and was therefore a conservative factor. In another, and increasingly common, sense, it was being used to indicate an expansionist and 'forward' attitude towards problems connected with the future control of the 'uncivilized' parts of the world, such as Africa, the Middle East and the Pacific. Salisbury was, in this sense, regarded as an imperialist in accepting the need for Britain to share in the partition of East Africa. Gladstone, in opposing the acquisition of Uganda, was emphatically anti-imperialist, even though he had acquiesced in the need to gain some control over Egypt in 1882. In the eyes of the anti-imperialists the sin of expansionism lay in the waste of moneys entailed on armaments, in the cost of colonial governments, and in the danger of international conflicts over intrinsically unimportant territories which it would be wiser to leave alone. As a rule no worse motive was attributed to the imperialists than 'jingoism' or excessive concern with Britain's position as a great power.

But, between 1896 and 1902, imperialism, as a word, began to lose in innocence. Koebner has shown that events in South Africa, and particularly the Jameson Raid, gave rise to a suspicion that, here at least, the expansive urge was motivated by something other than a concern for national greatness by what Harcourt called 'stock-jobbing imperialism'—based on the interests of financiers. This was, of course, a special case; and a distinction remained between an honest, even if misguided, imperialism, and the debased variety to be seen on the Rand. Yet the idea now gained ground that South Africa might not, after all, be a special case, but might exhibit in an extreme form a factor inherent in all expansionism. By 1900 radical opinion had moved so far in the direction that the

[4]R. Koebner, 'The Concept of Economic Imperialism,' *Economic History Review*, 2nd ser. 11, no. 1.

Fifth International Socialist Congress, taught probably by its English delegation, could resolve

> . . .que le développement du capitalisme mène fatalement à l'expansion coloniale . . .: que la politique coloniale de la bourgeoisie n'a d'autre but que d'élargir les profits de la capitaliste et le maintien du système capitaliste . . .[5]

Here, in a nutshell, was Hobson's doctrine of 'imperialism'. But it remained to be seen whether such a dogmatic interpretation would ever command a wide support: and it was essentially his achievement to ensure that, in his own non-Marxist form, it should become the generally accepted theory.

Hobson's *Imperialism* therefore came out at a time when British public opinion, disillusioned by the Boer war, was already profoundly suspicious about the motives behind recent imperial expansion. It was, in fact, a pamphlet for the times, rather than a serious study of the subject; and, like all pamphlets that achieve influence, it owed much of its success to the fact that it expressed a current idea with peculiar clarity, force and conviction. It arose immediately out of Hobson's visit to South Africa during the war, and derived from reports he sent back to *The Speaker,* which were published as a book in 1900 as *The War in South Africa, Its Causes and Effects.* Yet, paradoxically, Hobson was not primarily concerned with imperial problems: and *Imperialism* can only be properly understood on the basis that his interest, then and throughout his life, was with the social and economic problems of Britain. In a sense, this book was primarily a vehicle for publicizing the theory of 'underconsumption', which he regarded as his main intellectual achievement, and which he expressed more fully in *The Evolution of Modern Capitalism,* and other works. In brief, the theory, which was an alternative to the Marxist concept of surplus value as an explanation of poverty, saw excessive investment by the capitalist, with its concomitant of underconsumption by the wage-earner, as the root cause of recurrent slumps, of low interest rates, and of permanent under-employment. Hobson thought there were only two answers to this problem. The correct one—which would also be the answer to the 'condition of England question'—was to increase the buying power of the workers by giving them a higher share of the profits of industry. The wrong

[5]*Ibid.* p. 16.

one, which was no answer to the social question, was to invest the surplus capital overseas, where it could earn a high interest rate, and thus sustain domestic rates of interest, without benefiting the British worker. And this, he held, was what Britain had been doing since at least the middle of the nineteenth century.

To this point the economic theory, though highly vulnerable, has no apparent relevance to the phenomenon of overseas expansion, that is, to imperialism. The key to Hobson's theory of 'imperialism' lies in the connexion he makes between the two.

> Overproduction in the sense of an excessive manufacturing plant, and surplus capital which could not find sound investments within the country, forced Great Britain, Germany, Holland, France to place larger and larger portions of their economic resources outside the area of their present political domain, and then stimulate a policy of political expansion so as to take in the new areas.[6]

Thus 'imperialism', in the special sense used by Hobson, is an external symptom of a social malady in the metropolitan countries. Without this domestic pressure for investment overseas, there would be no effective impulse towards the acquisition of new colonies. Conversely, without colonies, capital would lack an outlet, and domestic rates of interest would sink. Thus the need to export capital and to make it politically secure overseas was what Mr John Strachey has recently called the 'prime mover for the modern imperialist process . . .'[7] And 'imperialism', on this assumption, is not variously 'sound' or 'stock-jobbing'; but, without exception, results from the special economic interests of the capitalist, and is therefore 'economic imperialism'.

It is not proposed at this stage to examine Hobson's theory in detail: but some comment must be made on the logical value of the argument he uses to demonstrate the historical truth of this hypothesis. Does he, in fact, supply any evidence to support the claim that colonies were the product of a demand either for new investment opportunities, or for security for existing investments? He begins with a straightforward account of the expansion of the European empires since 1870, printing a list of territories acquired by Britain, which Lenin, and later Mr Strachey, have reproduced. Then, in chapter two, he demonstrates that the expansion of the British empire had been of little apparent value to British trade;

[6]Hobson, p. 80.
[7]Strachey, *op. cit.* p. 123.

that trade with these recent acquisitions was the least valuable part of intra-imperial trade; and that British trade with all colonies was declining in relation to trade with the rest of the world.[8] Clearly, then, 'imperialism' was not good for trade. Nor was it good for emigration (which, in any case, he thought unnecessary), since these new tropical colonies were quite unsuited to white settlement.[9] And his conclusion was that

> The Imperialism of the last six decades is clearly condemned as a business policy, in that at enormous expense it has procured a small, bad, unsafe increase of markets, and has jeopardised the entire wealth of the nation in arousing the strong resentment of other nations . . .[10]

How then can a motive be found for this imperial expansion? The motive is to be seen if, alongside the list of territorial acquisitions, is placed a table showing the increase of British overseas investments in the same period.[11] It then becomes obvious that, during the period in which British possessions had increased by 4,754 m. square miles and by a population of 88 millions, British overseas investments had also increased enormously—from £144 m. to £1698 m. between 1862 and 1893 alone. Could there be any doubt that the two sets of figures were intimately connected as cause and effect? Hobson had no doubts about it: 'It is not too much to say that the modern foreign policy of Great Britain has been primarily a struggle for profitable markets of investment'.[12]

But it is immediately apparent that Hobson had in no sense proved that there was any connexion between the investments made overseas and the territory acquired contemporaneously. His table of investments[13] makes no differentiation between the areas in which investment had taken place, beyond such classifications as 'Foreign',

---

[8]Hobson based this conclusion on figures taken from Cd. 1761, p. 407, which are quoted in Hobson, p. 33. These were inaccurate. A. K. Cairncross (*Home and Foreign Investment 1870-1913*, Cambridge University Press, 1953), p. 189, shows that British exports to the empire increased from 24 per cent to 33.6 per cent of the total British trade between 1870-2 and 1890-2, and imports from 21.9 per cent to 22.9 per cent in the same period. Both percentages continued to increase to 1910-12. But Hobson was right in saying that the new colonies contributed little to the increased volume of intra-imperial trade.

[9]Hobson, pp. 41—5.

[10]Hobson, p. 46.

[11]Hobson, p. 62.

[12]Hobson, p. 53.

[13]Hobson, p. 62.

'Colonial', 'U.S.A.' and 'Various', and, in fact, he assumes quite arbitrarily that the new colonies had attracted a high proportion of the investment called 'Foreign' (i.e. before they were annexed) or 'Colonial' (subsequent to annexation). This, it will be suggested below, is a basic fault of his theory of 'imperialism'. Indeed, to put the case bluntly, Hobson performed an intellectual conjuring trick. Convinced of the essential truth of his economic theory, he deceived the eye by the speed of his hand, creating the illusion that, of the two sets of statistics he held up, one was the cause of the other.

It is not possible here to consider the rest of Hobson's *Imperialism*, interesting though it is in relation to related controversies over protection, tariff reform and imperial unity. But two additional points in his main argument must be mentioned because they were intrinsic to his definition of the origins and nature of 'imperialist' expansion.

The first of these concerns the relationship between the financial interest and other 'imperialists', and is therefore crucial to his theory. He was aware that, contrary to his argument, the obvious driving force of British expansion since 1870 appeared to lie in the explorers, missionaries, engineers, patriotic pressure groups, and empire-minded politicians, all of whom had evident influence, and had demonstrable interests, other than those of investment, in territorial acquisitions. And he was equally aware that if the impulse to expansion could be satisfactorily explained in the old-fashioned terms of their idealism, their ambition, or their concern with the status of Britain as a world power, rather than in terms of the self-interest of the capitalist, his own central thesis would collapse. It was therefore necessary that these men—the Lugards, the Milners, the Johnstons, and the Roseberys —should be shown to be mere puppets—the tools of 'imperialism' rather than its authors. Hobson did this by falling back on what may be called the 'faceless men' gambit:

> Finance manipulates the patriotic forces which politicians, soldiers, philanthropists, and traders generate; the enthusiasm for expansion which issues from these sources, though strong and genuine, is irregular and blind; the financial interest has those qualities of concentration and clear-sighted calculation which are needed to set Imperialism to work. An ambitious statesman, a frontier soldier, an overzealous missionary, a pushing trader, may suggest or even initiate a step of imperial expansion, may assist in educating patriotic public opinion to the urgent need of some fresh advance, but the final determination rests with the financial power.[14]

14Hobson, p. 59.

In this ingenious way Hobson inverted the apparent relationship between the obvious 'imperialists' and the investor. Instead of the financier being induced to invest in new possessions, with more or less enthusiasm, once political control had been imposed for other reasons, he becomes the essential influence in the take-over itself. Investment no longer follows the flag: it decides where it is profitable to plant it, and tells the government whether it is to follow the advice of men of action or of ideas in each particular case. Thus, 'imperialism' can never be interpreted as the spontaneous expression of the idealism, the chauvinism or the mere energy of a nation. In its practical form it is the expression of the special interests of the financier behind the scenes, who decides whether it is worth his while to allow a dream to become a reality, and who alone will reap the benefits.

This assumption, which has been adopted by most subsequent supporters of Hobson's thesis, will be examined later.

The other essential point in the theory of 'imperialism' is the suggestion that the possession of colonies by individual capitalist states results automatically in the exploitation of the indigenous peoples of Africa and Asia. In his long chapter 'Imperialism and the Lower Races',[15] which is in many ways one of the most undogmatic and constructive parts of the book, Hobson argued that exploitation, whether by appropriation of land, or by the use of cheap labour—forced or nominally free—in mines, farms and factories, had been a general feature of the colonies of all the European powers. Hobson, in the British humanitarian tradition, thought such exploitation to be both wrong and inexpedient. Economic development was good for undeveloped colonies and for the world as a whole. The danger lay in allowing the financiers to use the political power of the imperial authority for their own purposes; and the solution was for international control of colonies—the germ of the later mandate concept—and patience in allowing normal economic forces to give the natives an inducement to work freely in European enterprises. Sensible as his general attitude was, it is clear that Hobson had thus included in 'imperialism' the suggestion that countries possessing colonies were almost certain to exploit them in their own interests; and this argument was to become a staple of later critics of 'colonialism'.

II

The theory of 'imperialism' as it developed after the publication of Hobson's *Study* continued to be founded on the three main concepts outlined above. Yet, in examining its historiography, it is clear that

[15]Hobson, pp. 223–84.

it was Lenin, writing in 1916, rather than Hobson himself, who gave 'imperialism' its dogmatic coherence and much of its eventual influence. It is therefore necessary to consider briefly the extent to which Lenin modified Hobson's ideas.[16]

The greatest difference lies in the first and most important part of the argument; that is, in the nature of the internal pressure in the capitalist countries which forces them to expand their colonial possessions. Hobson had explained this pressure in terms of 'under-consumption': but Lenin naturally had a more orthodox theory to hand. Capitalism as a system was approaching the apocalypse Marx had foretold. Competitive capitalism had, in the late nineteenth century, been replaced by 'monopoly capitalism', with its characteristic agencies, the cartels, trusts and tariffs. It was no longer dynamic, but anxious only to maintain its profit margins by more intensive exploitation of limited and protected markets. Moreover, the 'finance-capitalists'—the banks and trusts—who now largely controlled capital itself, found that, under monopoly conditions, it was more profitable to employ surplus capital abroad than in domestic industry. At home, it could only increase production, lower prices, and raise wages. Abroad it could give a high interest return without any of these consequences. But, to gain the highest return from overseas investment it was desirable to have some political control over the territory in which the investment was made. This might be in the limited form of a 'semi-colony', such as the Argentine. But only in the colony proper could really comprehensive economic and political controls be imposed which would give investments their highest return. The result had been the competition between the great powers to acquire new colonies after 1870, which would continue until the whole uncivilized world had come under imperial rule. Then would follow the inter-imperial wars for the redivision of the empires, leading to proletarian revolutions in the 'imperialist' states, the creation of 'socialist' states, and so, automatically, to the end of 'imperialism'.

How much, then, does Lenin's explanation of the force behind 'imperialism' differ from that of Hobson? Fundamentally, only in this: that, whereas Hobson used his theory as evidence that social-democratic reform at home was necessary and possible to eliminate the evil of 'under-consumption' and therefore make 'imperialism' unnecessary,

---

16V. I. Lenin, *Imperialism, the Highest Stage of Capitalism* (1916). References are to the Moscow edition of 1947. For the genesis of Lenin's ideas on the Marxist side see W. K. Hancock, *Survey of British Commonwealth Affairs,* vol. II, part I (1940). Appendix I, by W. H. B. Court, pp. 393–395.

Lenin made 'imperialism' the definition of an inherent and unavoidable stage in the growth of capitalist society which could not be 'reformed'. Hobson was a doctor prescribing a remedy, Lenin a prophet forecasting catastrophe.[17] But, while they disagreed as to the precise causes, both maintained that there existed in the 'capitalist' countries a tremendous pressure for overseas investment, and that this was the main factor in producing 'imperialist' expansion after 1870.

On Hobson's second point—the control and influence exercised by 'finance' over government and over the men who actually carved out the new empires—there is little difference between them. Lenin, if anything, went further, ignoring the theory that in a democratic country like Britain Hobson's 'imperialists' found it necessary to corrupt public opinion through the press; and assuming, on the basis of Marxist theory and German experience, that the financial power of the banks and trusts was now so great that governments virtually did as they were told by the 'finance-capitalist'. Moreover, Lenin rejected entirely the possibility that the drive behind imperialism might have been the natural product of nationalism in international politics. To him as a Marxist such arguments were superficial. The only true explanation must lie in the fundamental economic environment which dictates political interests: and he castigates the unfortunate Kautsky on the grounds that he 'detaches the politics of imperialism from its economics . . .'[18] Economic factors are the root of all features of the 'imperialist' state; and even Franco-German competition for Alsace-Lorraine exists 'because an essential feature of imperialism is the rivalry between a number of great powers in the striving for hegemony, i.e. for the conquest of territory, not so much directly for themselves as to weaken the adversary and undermine *his* hegemony'.[19] There is no room here for explaining the actions of governments in any terms other than of the economics of 'imperialism'.

On Hobson's third point, Lenin had little explicit to say. As a Marxist he assumed it to be axiomatic that all workers were exploited by capital; so that a colony would differ from the metropolis only in the fact that the exploiting capitalist was an alien, and colonies merely added to the pool of labour from which he could extract 'surplus value'.

---

[17]There are, of course, many other differences which cannot be considered here, e.g. Hobson ignored 'semi-colonies', and throught of 'finance' as operating in an essentially free-trade environment.

[18]Lenin, p. 112.

[19]Lenin, p. 111.

With the publication of Lenin's book it may be said that the concept 'imperialism' had reached its mature form; for, on points on which they differed, Lenin's interpretation has generally been the dominant one. The subsequent historiography of the subject on the 'imperialist' side of the argument has tended to fall into two main categories—either glosses on the theory or applications of it to the actual events of the period after 1870, and a few of the more important books in the English canon may be mentioned. First, in point of time, came Leonard Woolf's *Empire and Commerce in Africa* (1920), which was influential in British Labour Party thinking on the subject. P. T. Moon's *Imperialism and World Politics* (1928) used the theory to interpret the international politics of the age of 'imperialism'; and in 1942 P. M. Sweezy restated Lenin's theory in relation to the central Marxist argument with considerable clarity and some minor modifications in *The Theory of Capitalist Development*. Finally, in 1959, Mr John Strachey published *The End of Empire* which, as the most recent work of apologetics, deserves some comment as an honest and intelligent attempt to assess and defend the theory after the experience of half a century.

Like Professor Sweezy, Mr Strachey is aware that the theory, as stated by Hobson and Lenin, had important limitations, of which the most obvious was that it related only to the period after 1870, and therefore offered no explanation of earlier empires, or of developments since the First World War. It was Mr Strachey's main aim to demonstrate that at least one concept of 'imperialism'—that empire consists primarily in the exploitation of a dependent territory for the economic advantage of the metropolis—holds good for all empires at all times; and that it is the means, not the fact, of exploitation that varies. For the period after 1870 itself he thinks Hobson and Lenin were right in seeing 'imperialism' as the external expression of the surplus capital of the European states; preferring Lenin's theory of 'finance-capital' to Hobson's 'under-consumption' as the basic factor. But he recognizes also that Lenin was less successful as a prophet, for he ignored the reformative capacity of political democracy to modify the structure of a capitalist society to such an extent as to make both 'imperialism' and eventual revolution unnecessary. Much of the book consists of an attempt to apply the view that exploitation was the basic factor in the 'imperialism' of the period after 1870 to other empires; and to suggest that the characteristic feature of each empire has been its own peculiar method of exploiting its dependencies. In the modern empires this was, as Hobson had said, to make wage-slaves of indigenous peoples by exporting capital to their countries, and forcing them to work within the capitalist economy, and he instances copper-mining in Rhodesia as a typical example. But other empires had their own characteristic methods. In India, the British began in the eighteenth century with mere plunder, which they later rationalized into the system of revenues exacted from Bengal, and replaced in the nineteenth century by the enforcement of the open door to British exports at the cost of ruining indigenous industries. Further back in time, Mr Strachey suggests that the empires of the ancient world were based on the exploitation of slave labour—the original 'surplus value': 'Imperialism in its original form could almost be called enslavement applied externally ...'[20] The medieval European empires he calls 'peasant empires'; and he thinks they were based on the 'invention of a way in which men could be exploited without the cumbrous and difficult business of directly enslaving them'.[21] After them came the mercantile empires, which ingeniously combined all known forms of exploitation—plunder (as in India or Mexico), enslavement for the silver mines and plantations, and trade on a one-sided basis with unsophisticated peoples.

Mr Strachey's book covers far more ground than can be suggested here, and deserves a place in the 'imperialist' canon both because of the ingenuity with which it attempts to give universality to the basic ideas of Hobson and Lenin, and because it shows the extent to which a confessed 'revisionist' can adapt these ideas to the circumstances of the mid-twentieth century. But, without following his arguments further, it is necessary to turn to a critical examination of the central theory of 'imperialism', and to alternative interpretations of the facts that first gave rise to it.

III

The central feature of the theory of 'imperialism', by which it must stand or fall, is the assertion that the empires built up after 1870 were not an option but a necessity for the economically advanced states of Europe and America: that these capitalist societies, because of their surplus of domestically produced capital, were forced to export capital to the under-developed regions of the world: and that it was only this investment—prospective or existing—that supplied a motive for the acquisition of new colonies.

Faced with this theory, the historian who does not take its

---

[20]Strachey, p. 322.
[21]Strachey, p. 327.

truth for granted is likely to be sceptical on at least three main grounds. First, his instinct is to distrust all-embracing historical formulas which, like the concept of 'the rise of the middle class', seek to explain complex developments in terms of a single dominant influence. Again, he is likely to suspect an argument that isolates the imperial expansion of the period after 1870 from all earlier imperial developments if only because he is aware of so many elements of continuity in the history of overseas empires over the past few centuries. But, above all, he must be aware that the theory simply does not appear to fit the facts of the post-1870 period as he knows them. Looking, for example, at Hobson's list of territories acquired by Britain after 1870, it seems, at first sight at least, difficult to believe that any considerable part of them were annexed either because British capitalists had already invested much of their surplus capital there, or because they regarded them as fields for essential future investment. In some cases, perhaps, it seems that a *prima facie* case could be made out on these lines—for Egypt, the Transvaal and Rhodesia, to take Hobson's three main examples. But, even in these, further consideration must arouse doubts. Surely the strategic importance of the Suez Canal was as good a reason for controlling Egypt in 1882 as the preservation of the interests of the bond holders in the Canal Company. Was it really necessary, on purely economic grounds, to annex the Transvaal in 1899 when the British mine-owners were making vast fortunes under Kruger's government, and had shown themselves so divided over the question of the Jameson Raid and the independence of the Republic?[22] Again, granted that Rhodes and the British South Africa Company had excellent economic reasons for wanting British control over Rhodesia, was their anxiety really due to the pressure of British funds waiting for investment opportunity?

Doubts such as these concerning even the key examples chosen by Hobson inevitably stimulate further examination of his list: and this makes it clear that not even a *prima facie* case could be made out for most of the territories he includes. To take a random selection, it would surely be ludicrous to suggest that Fiji, British New Guinea or Upper Burma were annexed in order to protect large British investments, or even as a field for subsequent investment. In each case secular explanations seem fully to account for their annexation, the chaotic condition of a mixed society in the Pacific, the fears of Australia for her military security, and the frontier problems of India. And even where, as in Malaya, large capital investment did

[22]See J. S. Marais, *The Fall of Kruger's Republic* (Oxford, Clarendon Press, 1961, pp. 62–3, 138–42, 162 and n. 3, 228–9, 233–4, 247–56, 324–5.

take place after annexation, the time factor must be considered. Were the British investor and the government really so alert to the possible future need for fields for investment? Or did annexation in fact take place for quite other reasons, being followed by investment when new conditions and new possibilities arose which were then totally unforeseen?

Yet, obvious though the weakness of the theory of 'imperialism' may seem when applied in specific cases, it is also clear that it would be extremely difficult to invalidate Hobson's model by a process of piecemeal examination. For the adherents of this, as of most comprehensive formulas, could counter, as Mr Strachey does, by asserting that an analytical explanation of the phenomenon merely supplied 'an unaccountable jumble of facts and dates...'[23] or, as Professor Sweezy does, by calling all annexations that do not fit demonstrably into the pattern 'protective and anticipatory', or based on 'considerations of a strategic nature'.[24] That is, they could fight an indefinite rearguard action, retreating, as Mr Strachey does, on to the ultimate citadel of the historicist, with the assertion that 'After all, each of these things [capital exports and colonial annexation] undeniably existed. Only the intentionally blind will deny a connection between them'.[25] Moreover, if the theory is false, it should be possible to demonstrate that its premises are false also. And, since the essential premise of 'imperialism' is the belief that the drive to acquire colonies after 1870 was the direct and necessary result of the need of the capitalists to export capital, this proposition demands careful examination.

It has been seen that this theory of surplus capital being forced out into the undeveloped world was expressed differently by Hobson and Lenin, and it will be convenient to consider Lenin's theory first. This was, it will be remembered, that the centrifugal force in the capitalist countries was the interest of the monopolistic 'finance-capitalists' who stood only to lose by investment at home.

In this the fallacy is immediately obvious. If it was true of any country, it was not true of Britain; for no one could maintain that British capital was then controlled by a few trusts or even cartels. These, of course, did exist in Britain, such as the Salt Union of 1888, the United Alkali Company of 1897, and others in textiles, shipping and steel. But, whatever the desires of their founders, they were in fact small, tentative and generally unsuccessful. British capital,

---

23Strachey, p. 123.
24Sweezy, p. 303.
25Strachey, p. 124.

whatever its tendencies, was still 'competitive' on Lenin's definition: and he in fact admitted that in Britain 'monopoly' must be taken to mean the reduction of the competing enterprises to 'a couple of dozen or so'.[26] This is hardly a satisfactory explanation of the need to export capital on a vast scale; so, presumably, Britain must have other reasons both for this and for territorial annexation. But, for different reasons, other countries also escape from the formula. Germany was Lenin's main example of the country dominated by trusts: but, as Professor Hancock has pointed out,[27] the age of German cartels came only after about 1900, while the main German grab for colonies had taken place during the previous twenty years. And America, which certainly had vast industrial and financial combinations, proved, in spite of Roosevelt's attempt to create an expansionist movement, to be the least 'imperialist' of all the capitalist states. It would therefore seem reasonable to conclude that Lenin's narrow explanation for the export of capital and the concurrent extension of European political control overseas is unacceptable.

Yet, whatever reasons are assigned to it, the fact of vast capital exports from the advanced countries in the period after 1870 remains. Sir G. Paish, in his much quoted article,[28] estimated that British overseas investment had increased between 1871 and 1911 from £785 m. to £3500 m., with a possible margin of error of 10 per cent either way. These figures are necessarily highly speculative; but there is no question that they were extremely large. And it is quite possible, even while rejecting Lenin's doctrinaire explanation, to see in the fact of this investment support for Hobson's theory that the urge to invest was the main cause of imperialist expansion. Hence, the important questions must be faced. Was there in fact a vast reservoir of capital, generated (for example) in Britain, which was available for overseas investment? Why was it invested abroad rather than at home? And was it in fact invested in those areas which were annexed as colonies after 1871?

The publication in 1953 of Professor A. K. Cairncross's *Home and Foreign Investment 1870-1913*[29] has made it possible to approach these questions from a new and non-doctrinaire angle. The key to his

26Lenin, p. 26.

27W. K. Hancock, *The Wealth of Colonies* (Cambridge, 1950), pp. 11–12.

28G. Paish, 'Great Britain's foreign investments', *Journal of the Royal Statistical Society*, LXXIV, 27.

29*Op. cit.* Since the present essay was written, an article has been published by M. Blaug, 'Economic Imperialism Revisited', *Yale Review*, L, no. 3 (1961), 335–49, which supports most of the arguments put forward in this section.

interpretation lay in his rejection of Hobson's naive model of the British capitalist, embarrassed by an excess of capital, which could not be invested at home because of the 'under-consumption' factor, sending it abroad into undeveloped tropical territories where it would produce a high rate of interest. Instead, it is necessary to see that capital exports were not divorced from the economy of Great Britain but were in fact a necessary concomitant of the pattern of British trade and development. It can be shown that in fact the great majority of this capital went to the 'new' countries—to the United States, Canada, Argentine, Australasia and South Africa in particular—who were producing the primary materials that the British economy needed, and who had to have capital to expand their production for British consumption. To invest in these countries was therefore, in one sense, to invest in a primary sector of the British economy itself. And the return to Britain was not entirely, or even primarily, in a tribute of money, but in cheap and plentiful raw materials and food.

Moreover, far from weakening the British economy and reducing the living standards of the working class as both Hobson and Lenin thought they did, these capital exports were essential to both. Indeed, Cairncross argues convincingly that, by creating a demand for British products, these investments simultaneously kept up the level of profits at home, kept down the level of unemployment, and maintained wage levels. And, as the rate of overseas investment seems to have been greatest when the terms of trade were against Britain—the 1880's being an exceptional period when special factors in the United States offset the general tendency—Cairncross concludes that 'it was foreign investment that pulled Britain out of most depressions before 1914'.[30]

Seen, therefore, from the point of view of Britain's part in the world economy, rather than in purely domestic terms, capital exports no longer seem to have been forced out of the British economy by the selfish interests of the capitalists to maintain artificially high interest rates, and become, as Professor Nurkse has described them, 'a means whereby a vigorous process of economic growth came to be transmitted from the centre to the outlying areas of the world'.[31] That is to say that the force behind the export of capital was the pull exerted by urgent need for capital in the newly-developing countries, who, because of their higher potential productivity and because markets were available for their exports, could afford to pay

[30]Cairncross, p. 188.
[31]R. Nurkse, *Patterns of Trade and Development* (Stockholm, 1959), p. 14.

higher rates of interest than were obtainable in Britain. Yet, important though it was in explaining why the British and European investor chose to send his capital abroad, this differential in rates of interest should not be overestimated. For the years 1905-9 Lehfeldt calculated the average interest on home, colonial and overseas investments to be 3.61 per cent, 3.94 per cent and 4.97 per cent respectively.[32] But even this to some extent obscures the real facts of the situation. The interest on British consols might be only 2.88 per cent: but rates of over 5 per cent were available on other British stocks, such as railway debentures and industrials. Equally, in railway loans, which were the most popular type of British overseas investment in the years before 1914, the interest rates varied from a mere 3.87 per cent on India railways to 4.7 per cent in foreign railways.[33] In fact it can be said that the British investor did not choose to invest abroad simply to get high interest rates, but, by and large, to get a slightly higher rate than on an equivalent type of stock at home. Above all, if he chose to invest in a British colony, it was not because he expected higher interest, but because he wanted greater security than he would get in an equivalent foreign investment. If he wanted a 'risk' investment—diamonds, copper, gold, nitrates, etc.—he went for it wherever the enterprise happened to be situated. But, in proportion to the whole, investments of this type were very small in 1911.[34]

But, for the present argument, the third and most important fact that emerges from the work of Paish, Cairncross and Nurkse is that Hobson was entirely wrong in assuming that any large proportion of British overseas investment went to those undeveloped parts of Africa and Asia which were annexed during the 'imperialist' grab after 1870. As Professor Nurkse has remarked of Hobson:

> Had he tried to do what he did for trade, that is, to show the geographical distribution of overseas investment, he would have found that British capital tended to bypass the primitive tropical economies and flowed mainly to the regions of recent settlement outside as well as inside the British Empire.[35]

And the figures published by Paish in 1911 demonstrate this conclusively.[36] The bulk of British investment then lay in the United States, £688 m., South America, £587 m., Canada, £372 m., Au-

---

[32]Quoted by Cairncross, p. 227.
[33]*Ibid.*
[34]Paish, *loc. cit.* tables on pp. 180, 182, 184.
[35]Nurkse, p. 19.
[36]Paish, *loc. cit.* p. 186.

stralasia, £380 m., India and Ceylon, £365 m., and South Africa, £351 m. By contrast, West Africa had received only £29 m., the Straits and Malay States, £22 m., and the remaining British possessions, £33 m. These last were, of course, by no means negligible amounts, and indicate clearly that in some at least of the tropical dependencies which had been recently acquired, British finance was finding scope for profit and investment. But this does not make Hobson's thesis any more valid. The sums invested in these tropical areas, whether newly annexed or not, were quite marginal to the total overseas investment, and continued to be relatively very small in the years immediately before 1911. Hence, to maintain that Britain had found it necessary to acquire these territories because of an urgent need for new fields for investment is simply unrealistic: and, with the rejection of this hypothesis, so ingeniously conjured up by Hobson, the whole basis of his theory that 'imperialism' was the product of economic necessity collapses.

IV

But to suggest that Hobson and Lenin were mistaken in thinking that the need to export capital from Europe after 1870 was so intense that it made the colonization of most of Africa and the Pacific necessary as fields for investment is merely to throw the question open again. The essential problem remains: on what other grounds is it possible to explain this sudden expansion of European possessions, whose motive force is called imperialism?

For the historian it is natural to look for an explanation of these developments which is not based on *a priori* reasoning, does not claim to be a comprehensive formula, and is not out of line with long-term historical developments. It would, of course, be unreasonable to expect to find in the late nineteenth century any precise repetition of earlier patterns of imperial expansion: at the same time it would seem reasonable to look carefully for evidence of continuity of motive and policy with earlier periods before falling back on the conclusion that events after 1870 were unique.

Looking broadly over the four centuries since the early Portuguese discoveries, it may be said that, although European motives for acquiring colonies were extremely complex, they fell into two general categories. First was the specifically economic motive, whose aim was to create a lucrative trade for the metropolitan country.[37]

[37]R. Pares, 'The economic factors in the history of the Empire', *Economic History Review*. VII (1937), 2, for a fuller discussion of this. His interpretation of the period after 1870 differs from that of the present writer.

Its typical expression was the trading base or factory, secured by some form of agreement with the local ruler: but, where no commodities already existed for trade, it could result in territorial possessions, like the sugar islands of the Caribbean, or the spice islands of the East; the fur-producing parts of North America, and the silver mines of Peru. The export of capital played no significant part in this economic activity, for Europe had little surplus capital before the nineteenth century, and investment was restricted to the immediate needs of trade itself, of the mines, sugar estates, etc.

By contrast, it is clear that from the earliest days of European expansion the margin between economic and other motives was small, and that many colonies were rather the product of political and military rivalries than of the desire for profit. The mercantile practices followed by all European states were as much concerned with national power as with economic advantage, and tended, as Adam Smith pointed out, to subordinate opulence to the needs of security. Indeed, by the eighteenth century, imperial policies had come to be largely a reflection of European power politics: and the struggle for territorial supremacy in America, India and the strategic bases on the route to the East were the outcome of political rather than of strictly economic competition. Britain's decision to retain Canada rather than Guadaloupe in 1763 may perhaps stand as an example of preference given to a colony offering mainly military security and prestige over one whose value was purely economic.

If, then, a general view of pre-nineteenth century imperial policies shows the complexity of its aims—made still more complicated in the early nineteenth century by the important new element of humanitarianism—it must seem surprising that Hobson should have interpreted post-1870 imperialism in narrowly economic terms, and have ignored the possibility that strictly political impulses may once again have been of major importance. The reason would seem to be that the evolution of imperial practices since about 1815 appeared, at the end of the century, to have constituted a clear break with earlier methods; to have made both the economic and the political criteria of earlier times irrelevant; and thus to have made comparison pointless. With the independence of almost all the American colonies, and the subsequent adoption by Britain—the chief remaining colonial power—of the practices of free trade, the possession of colonies no longer offered any positive economic advantage. The colonial trades were now open to all; bullion-hunting became the function of the individual prospector; and emigration, although it led to new British colonies in Australasia, flowed more naturally into the existing states of the new world. On the political side also, colonies had ceased to play an important part in diplomacy. With the preponderance of Britain as a naval power, and the weakness of most European states, power politics were largely restricted to Britain, France and Russia. As between them competitive aggressiveness was recurrent: but, except briefly in the Pacific, and more frequently in the Near East and on the borders of India, their rivalry did not produce any major competition for new territory. And this seemed to imply that the end of mercantilism had been followed by the end also of political imperialism: which in turn suggested that the renewal of a general international desire for colonies after 1870 must have sprung from some new phenomenon—the unprecedented need to acquire openings for the safe investment of surplus capital.

It is mainly because Hobson's theory of 'imperialism' in his own time was based on this theory of discontinuity in nineteenth century history that it must be regarded as fallacious. For there had, in fact, been no break in the continuity of imperial development; merely a short-term variation in the methods used, corresponding with a temporary change in world conditions. In the first place, the extension of the territorial possessions of the three surviving great powers continued intermittently throughout: and the list of British acquisitions between 1840 and 1871 alone bears comparison with those of the following thirty years. On what grounds, in this period of so-called 'anti-imperialism', are these to be explained? Obviously no single explanation will serve. Hong Kong stood alone as a trading base with a specifically economic function. Queensland was the result of internal expansion in Australia, British Columbia of rivalry from the United States. But the rest—the Punjab, Sind, Berar, Oudh and Lower Burma on the frontiers of British India; Basutoland, Griqualand and (temporarily) the Transvaal on the Cape frontier; and small areas round existing trading bases in West Africa—stand as evidence that an existing empire will tend always to expand its boundaries. They were not the product of an expansive British policy, but of the need for military security, for administrative efficiency, or for the protection of indigenous peoples on the frontiers of existing colonies. Basically, they demonstrated the fact, familiar in earlier centuries, that colonies which exist in a power vacuum will tend always to expand slowly until they meet with some immovable political or geographical obstacle; and that a metropolitan government can do little more than slow down the speed of movement. For the purpose of the present argument this process may be said to indicate that Hobson needed no new explanation for the bulk of British acquisitions after 1870: for, as has already been pointed out, most of the new colonies on his list differed little in type or situation from those just mentioned—and were indeed mostly the extension of the same colonial frontiers. And, to this extent, late nineteenth century imperialism was merely the continuation of a process which had begun centuries earlier.

At the same time, it must be said that this 'contiguous area' theory does not fully cover certain of the new British possessions on Hobson's list. For some of them, like East Africa, were not strictly contiguous to an existing British colony; and others, such as Nigeria or Rhodesia, were clearly annexed too suddenly and on too large a scale to be seen as the product of the domestic needs of Lagos or the Cape. These therefore suggest that some other factor was at work—competition for new colonies on political grounds—which will be considered later.

Again, in the sphere of economic policy, the antithesis between different parts of the nineteenth century were greatly exaggerated and misunderstood by Hobson. The rejection of most of the mercantile devices for stimulating European trade had not meant that trade ceased to be a matter of national concern, or that governments ceased to use political means to support their men of business; the contrast with earlier centuries lay mainly in the methods now used. Hobson seemed to think that free trade had ended 'economic imperialism' of the mercantile variety simply because political control was no longer regarded as a prerequisite for economic exploitation of an undeveloped area. But, as Messrs. Gallagher and Robinson have pointed out,[28] 'formal' control, as in a colony, was not the only way in which 'economic imperialism' could operate; indeed, it now had two complementary features. On its specifically economic side it implied, as always, the control of the economic assets of some other country for the advantage of the metropolitan state. And the essential weapons of the European trader or financier were economic—the demand for his goods, his capital or his credit, and the effectiveness of the organization he built up in a country lacking business organization. The stranglehold he thus obtained differed only in detail from that held in the eighteenth century by British firms in the American colonies, transferred now to the similarly defenceless, though politically independent, states of South America, the Middle

[28]'The Imperialism of Free Trade', *Economic History Review*, 2nd ser. VI. no. 1 (1953).

and Far East. By the end of the nineteenth century most of the world had been thus brought under the economic control of European, and now also United States, business enterprise: their trade was organized and carried by foreign merchants, their revenues mortgaged to the loans they had received. This indeed was 'economic imperialism' in its purest form; cosmopolitan in outlook, unconcerned with political frontiers, showing no interest in the creation of 'formal' colonies except where, as in China, the formula of the open door proved otherwise unworkable. Only in the absolute volume of its activity, and in the increasing competition between rivals from newly industrialized countries, did the character of 'economic imperialism' change before 1914. And, while it remained thus strictly economic and cosmopolitan, the 'division of the world among the international trusts', which Lenin prophesied, remained a possibility.

Yet, even in its classical form, 'economic imperialism' required political support from governments at home: and, in view of developments after about 1870, it is important to define the nature of the support it received. Essentially the men of business needed only two things which their own enterprise could not supply: a minimum standard of political security at the periphery, and the solution of the quasi-political problems arising out of their relations with foreign rivals by diplomatic action at the centre. The first need was met by the network of treaties made for them with their client countries which secured equality of opportunity and reasonable tariffs, and was backed up, where necessary, by the use of threats and force. In the environment of the free world economy, these were the equivalents of the commercial monopolies of the mercantile period in that they supplied the political basis for successful business enterprise in undeveloped countries.

Second, and parallel with this, went the constant diplomatic work of the foreign offices of Europe in maintaining the balance between their nationals at the circumference. On the common assumption that it was to the general interest that competition should remain fair, that an artificial monopoly was to the advantage of none, and that such problems must not be allowed to harm international relations, diplomacy sought to settle these disputes without taking refuge in unilateral annexation of the area concerned. In this it was generally successful, where the will to succeed existed: and the Anglo-French condominium of 1906 in the New Hebrides stands as a late example of how such problems could be met.

It is now possible to place the imperialism of the period of Hobson's *Study* in its historical context, and to attempt a definition of the extent to which it differed from that of earlier years. The

most obvious fact on which his theory was based was that, by contrast
with the preceding half-century, vast areas of the world were quickly
brought under European control for the first time: and it is now
evident that this cannot be explained in terms of either of the
two tendencies operating throughout the earlier nineteenth century.
Although the break with the past was not as sharp as Hobson seemed
to think, it remains true that many British annexations cannot be
explained on 'the 'contiguous area' theory: and the new possessions
of France, Italy and Germany were quite definitely in a different
category. But neither can these facts be explained on Hobson's theory:
for, as has been said, the places now to be taken over had hitherto
attracted little capital, and did not attract it in any quantity subsequently. Nor, again, can an explanation be found in the more
general theory of 'economic imperialism', for these places in the
Pacific and in Africa for which the nations now competed were
of marginal economic importance; and, on the assumptions of the
past fifty years, governments might have been expected to reject demands by their nationals for annexation of territories whose administrative costs would be out of all proportion to their economic value
to the nation. In sum, the most obvious facts of the new phase
of imperialism cannot be explained as the logical continuation of
the recent past, nor in Hobson's terms of a new economic factor.
What, then, was the explanation?

An answer is not, of course, hard to find, and indeed emerges
clearly from the vast literature now available.[39] With the exception
of the supporters of the 'imperialism' thesis, the consensus of opinion
is very marked. The new factor in imperialism was not something
without precedent, certainly not anything uniquely economic, but
essentially a throw-back to some of the characteristic attitudes and
practices of the eighteenth century. Just as, in the early nineteenth
century, the economic interests had demanded effectively that imperial
questions should no longer be decided on political grounds, demanding
opulence in place of security, so, at the end of the century, the
balance was again reversed. The outstanding feature of the new situa-

39It is impossible to give an adequate list. On the British side a good bibliography, to about 1957, is available in the *Cambridge History of the British Empire*,
vol. III. Later works include: M. Perham, *Lugard* (2 vols. London, 1956 and 1960);
R. Oliver, *Sir Harry Johnston* (London, 1957); and W. M. Macmillan, *The Road
to Self Rule* (London, 1959). For France there is a good bibliography in H.
Brunschwig, *Mythes et Réalités de l'impérialisme colonial français* (Paris, 1960).
For Germany see M. E. Townsend, *Origins of Modern German Colonization, 1871-
1885* (New York, 1921), and *The Rise and Fall of the German Colonial Empire,
1884-1918* (New York, 1930).

tion was the subordination of economic to political considerations, the preoccupation with national security, military power and prestige.

Again, reasons are not hard to find. The significant fact about the years after 1870 was that Europe became once again an armed camp. The creation of a united Germany, the defeat of Austria and, above all, of France were to dominate European thinking until 1914. Between Germany and France there stood the question of Alsace-Lorraine: and for both the primary consideration was now a system of alliances which would, on the German side, prevent French counter-attack, on the French side, make revenge possible. Inevitably the rest of Europe was drawn into the politics of the balance of power between them; and for all statesmen military strength became once again the criterion of national greatness. Inevitably too this situation, with its similarities to the politics of the eighteenth century, brought in its train a return to many of the attitudes of mercantilism. Emigration to foreign states, instead of being regarded as an economic safety valve, became once again a loss of military or manufacturing manpower; and population statistics became a measure of relative national strength. Protective tariffs came back also, with the primary aim of building up national self-sufficiency and the power to make war.

Under such circumstances it was only to be expected that colonies would be regarded once again as assets in the struggle for power and status: but in fact the attitude of the powers to the imperial question was not at first a simple one. Indeed, it cannot be said that the attitudes characteristic of 'the imperialism of free trade' were seriously weakened until the mid-1880's; and until then it seemed possible that the colonial question might be kept clear of European politics. This is not in fact surprising. For most of the men who then ruled Europe retained a realistic appreciation of the potential value to their countries of those parts of the world that were available for annexation. Bismarck in particular recognized that, as sources of raw materials, as fields for emigration or as spheres for trade, the areas available in Africa and the Pacific had little to offer Germany, whatever national advantages those with private interests there might claim. At best they might offer naval bases, a strictly limited trade, and bargaining counters for use in diplomacy. It is improbable that Bismarck ever really changed this opinion: and, while he held off, it was unlikely that any other power would feel strong enough to precipitate a rush for new colonies. Even Belgian and French action in the Congo failed to do this; although their ambitions showed the probable trend of future events.

It was, therefore, Bismarck's action in 1884-5, in announcing the formal control by Germany over parts of West and South West Africa, and of New Guinea, that really began the new phase of political imperialism: and it is therefore important to consider his reasons for giving Germany a 'colonial policy'. Was it, as Miss Townsend has argued,[40] that the pressure of the commercial interest involved in these places, and the arguments of the new colonial party in politics convinced him that colonies were an economic necessity to Germany? The answer must be that it was not. In 1884 Bismarck seems to have decided that it was time for him to stop playing the honest broker in the disputes of other powers over their own possessions —such as Egypt and the Congo—and that, on two counts, both essentially diplomatic, Germany should now stake her own claims to colonies. The first was that it was politically desirable to show France that his recent support for Britain on the Egyptian question did not imply a general hostility towards her, since he was now prepared to take action resented by Britain: the second that Britain should be made to see that German support for her in the colonial field must be repaid by closer co-operation in Europe.[41]

In a narrow sense, then, the race for colonies was the product of diplomacy rather than of any more positive force. Germany set the example by claiming exclusive control over areas in which she had an arguable commercial stake, but no more, as a means of adding a new dimension to her international bargaining power, both in respect of what she had already taken, and of what she might claim in the future. Thereafter the process could not be checked; for, under conditions of political tension, the fear of being left out of the partition of the globe overrode all practical considerations. Perhaps Britain was the only country which showed genuine reluctance to take a share; and this was due both to her immense stake in the continuance of the *status quo* for reasons of trade, and to her continued realism in assessing the substantive value of the lands under dispute. And the fact that she too joined in the competition demonstrated how contagious the new political forces were. Indeed, until the end of the century, imperialism may best be seen as the extension into the periphery of the political struggle in Europe. At the centre

[40]*Origins of Modern German Colonization, 1871—1885* (New York, 1921).

[41]A useful summary of the arguments and the evidence is in the *C.H.B.E.* III, 114—22. Mr. A. J. P. Taylor described Bismarck's action as 'the accidental by-product of an abortive Franco-German entente. Taylor, *Germany's First Bid for Colonies, 1884–1885* (London, 1938), p. 6.

the balance was so nicely adjusted that no positive action, no major change in the status or territory of either side was possible. Colonies thus became a means out of the impasse; sources of diplomatic strength, prestige-giving accessions of territory, hope for future economic development. New worlds were being brought into existence in the vain hope that they would maintain or redress the balance of the old.

This analysis of the dynamic force of the new imperialism has been stated in purely political terms. What part was played in it by the many non-political interests with a stake in the new colonies: the traders, the investors, the missionaries, and the speculators? For these were the most vociferous exponents of a 'forward' policy in most countries: and to men like Hobson it seemed that their influence, if backed by that of the greater interest of the financier, was decisive in causing the politicians to act.

Again the problem is complex. In general terms the answer would seem to be that, while statesmen were very much aware of the pressure groups—conscious of the domestic political advantage of satisfying their demands, and often themselves sympathetic to the case they put up—they were not now, any more than earlier in the century, ready to undertake the burden of new colonies simply on their account. What made it seem as if these interests were now calling the tune was that the choice facing the statesman was no longer between annexation and the continued independence of the area in question: it was now between action and allowing a rival to step in. Salisbury and Rosebery may well have been convinced by the argument of men like Lugard that, on humanitarian grounds, it would be desirable for Britain to bring law and order to Uganda. But it was the threat of German or French occupation of the key to the Nile and Egypt that decided them to act. Yet if, in the last resort, the decision by Britain or any other country to annex was based on the highest reasons of state, it is also true that the very existence of these hitherto embarrassing pressure groups now became a diplomatic asset, since they were the obvious grounds on which valid claims could be made, an approximation to the principle of effective occupation.

Thus the relative importance of the concrete interests and demands of the various pressure groups, as compared with the political criteria of the statesmen, was the reverse of that assigned to them by Hobson; and, if the word 'investment' is taken to cover the whole range of these interests, the point has been well summarized by Professor E. Staley:

Conflicts between the great powers over private investment matters
have rarely, almost never, reached a state of dangerous international tension except in cases where the powers have been led
into conflict by the pursuit of political policies extraneous to
the investment affair itself. The best explanation of these facts
runs in terms of the way in which those in charge of foreign
policies interpret national advantage. Where investments can be
regarded as economic aids to established lines of foreign policy,
they are supported most vigorously; investments receive least
vigorous political backing where they are not in any sense tools
of national policy or where they run counter to national policy.[42]

Yet, if the first, and territorially decisive, factor in the imperialism
of the post 1870 period was this unemotional, almost cynical, policy
of the statesmen, it cannot be said that it was the only new feature,
nor, in the long run, the most important one. For by the time Hobson
wrote in 1902, those who supported a 'forward' policy were no longer
the few diplomatic chess-players, nor even the relatively small pressure
groups, but millions of people for whom an empire had become
a matter of faith. Indeed, the rise of this imperialist ideology, this
belief that colonies were an essential attribute of any great nation,
is one of the most astonishing facts of the period. It was, moreover,
an international creed, with beliefs that seemed to differ very little
from one country to another. Its basic ideas had been clearly expressed
as early as 1879 by a German, Treitschke:

> Every virile people has established colonial power ... All great
> nations in the fulness of their strength have desired to set
> their mark upon barbarian lands and those who fail to participate
> in this great rivalry will play a pitiable role in time to come.
> The colonizing impulse has become a vital question for every
> great nation.[43]

By the end of the century, the 'imperial idea', as it has significantly
been called,[44] after twenty years of propaganda by such groups of
enthusiasts as the German *Kolonverein* and the British Imperial Fed-

---

[42]E. Staley, *War and the Private Investor* (Chicago, 1935), pp. 387–8. It
remains true, however, that in the aftermath the main, possibly the only, advantage
of the new colonies went to these special interests, particularly the soldiers and
administrators, to whom they offered careers; the missions, who gained security;
and the wide range of concession-hunters and government contractors who swarmed
in all the new colonies.

[43]Quoted in M. E. Townsend, *Origins of Modern German Colonization,
1871–1885*, p. 27.

[44]By A. P. Thornton, *The Imperial Idea and its Enemies.*

eration League, had become dominant. The process of educating the public has now been examined in detail:[45] and it is interesting to see that in each case the historian has found it necessary to deal almost entirely in ideas, rather than in concrete facts. This is no accident. The imperialism of the early twentieth century, although ironically the product of the power politics of the previous two decades, bore little resemblance to the ideas of men like Bismarck and Salisbury. It was the generation of Kaiser Wilhelm II, of Theodore Roosevelt and of Chamberlain (in his later years) that came to adopt for the first time this mystical faith in the value of an empire. Chamberlain's tariff campaign of 1903-5 indicates that such tenuous links as the imperial movement had ever had with precise calculations of economic—and even of political—advantage had now ceased to be of primary importance.

For, by that time, imperialism had been shown to be a delusion. It was already the common experience of all the countries that had taken part in the partition of Africa and the Pacific that, except for the few windfalls, such as gold in West Africa, diamonds in South West Africa, and copper in the Congo and Rhodesia, the new colonies were white elephants: and that only small sectional interests in any country had obtained real benefits from them. Whether German, French, British or Italian, their trade was minute (German trade with her colonies was only $\frac{1}{2}$ per cent of her external trade); their attraction for investors, except in mines, etc., was negligible; they were unsuitable for large-scale emigration, and any economic development that had taken place was usually the result of determined efforts by the European state concerned to create an artificial asset. Moreover, in most cases, the cost of administration was a dead weight on the imperial power. By 1900 all these facts were apparent and undeniable. They were constantly pressed by opponents of colonial expansion in each country; and Hobson's book consisted primarily of an exposition of these defects. Yet public opinion was increasingly oblivious to such facts: the possession of colonies had become a sacred cow, a psychological necessity. While the financiers continued to invest their money, as they had done in the previous fifty years, in economically sound projects, such as the Baghdad railway, in the non-tropical settlement colonies and independent countries, and in places like India—remaining true to the criteria of true 'economic

45For Britain, C. A. Bodelsen, *Mid Victorian Imperialism* (Copenhagen, 1924, reprinted 1960); B. Semmel, *op. cit.*; Thornton, *op. cit.* and J. E. Tyler, *The Struggle for Imperial Unity, 1868–95* (London, 1938), in particular. For France, H. Brunschwig, *op. cit.* For Germany, Townsend, *op. cit.*

imperialism'—the politicians, pressed on now by a public demand they could not control, even if they had wanted to, continued, with increasing bellicosity, to scrape the bottom of the barrel for yet more colonial burdens for the white man to carry.

v

The reassessment of so abstract a concept as 'imperialism', particularly within the present limitations of space, cannot hope to prove or to disprove anything. At the most it may lead to the suggestion that an earlier synthesis does not appear to fit the facts. How far can it be said that the arguments put forward above make necessary a revision of the theory of 'imperialism' which derives from Hobson and Lenin?

The general conclusion would seem to emerge that, as an historical interpretation of the expansion of European empires between 1870 and 1914, it is unacceptable. As an economic theory it is unsatisfactory because detailed investigations have shown that the alleged need of the European investor, monopolist or individual capitalist, to find outlets for his surplus capital had little or nothing to do with the division of Africa and the Pacific between the European powers. Again, as a theory of historical development, which makes this expansion seem to be a unique phenomenon, capable of being understood only in terms of the special methodology used by Hobson and Lenin, it ignores both the continuity of nineteenth century developments, and also its similarity to earlier periods of European imperialism. In most respects, indeed, there was no break in continuity after 1870. On the political side, many of the new annexations of territory, particularly those made by Britain, resulted from the situation of existing possessions: and, on the economic side, the rapid expansion of European commercial and financial influence throughout the world—the true 'economic imperialism'—did not change its character after 1870; and was no more likely then than before to have resulted in significant acquisitions of land. The real break in the continuity of nineteenth century development—the rapid extension of 'formal' control over independent areas of Africa and the East—was a specifically political phenomenon in origin, the outcome of fears and rivalries within Europe. The competition for colonies, being as characteristic of economically weak countries like Italy as of others which had large resources of capital available for overseas deployment, was indeed more obviously a throw-back to the imperialism of the eighteenth century than the characteristic product of nineteenth century capitalism in an advanced phase. And the ideological fervour that became the dominant feature of the imperial movement after about 1890 was the natural outcome of this fevered nationalism, not the artifact of vested economic interests.

Yet, in conclusion, a paradox must be noted. Hobson's analysis of 'imperialism' was defective: but the fact that it was defective was probably the result of his having grasped one essential truth about the imperial movement—that it had become irrational. Seeing clearly that the new tropical colonies could not be justified in terms of their economic value to the metropolitan powers—the criterion a nineteenth century rationalist would naturally apply—he was forced back on the theory that they must have been of value to sectional interests at least; and that these had succeeded in hoodwinking a presumably sane public opinion. Seen in this light, Hobson's sinister capitalists and their 'parasites' were nothing more than a hypothesis, a *deus ex machina,* to balance an equation between the assumed rationality of mankind and the unreasonableness of imperial policies: and the book was a plea for a return to a sane standard of values.

His mistake, then, was to think that the equation needed such artificial adjustment. For, in the second half of the twentieth century, it can be seen that imperialism owed its popular appeal not to the sinister influence of the capitalists, but to its inherent attractions for the masses. In the new quasi-democratic Europe, the popularity of the imperial idea marked a rejection of the sane morality of the account-book, and the adoption of a creed based on such irrational concepts as racial superiority and the prestige of the nation. Whether we interpret it, as did J. A. Schumpeter in 1919,[46] as a castback to the ideas of the old autocratic monarchies of the *ancien régime,* or as something altogether new—the first of the irrational myths that have dominated the first half of the twentieth century—it is clear that imperialism cannot be explained in simple terms of economic theory and the nature of finance capitalism. In its mature form it can best be described as a sociological phenomenon with roots in political facts: and it can properly be understood only in terms of the same social hysteria that has since given birth to other and more disastrous forms of aggressive nationalism.[47]

[46]*Imperialism and the Social Classes* (reprinted by Basil Blackwell, Oxford, 1951).

[47]Since this essay went to press. *Africa and the Victorians*, by R. E. Robinson and J. Gallagher, with A. Denny (London: Macmillan & Co. Ltd. 1961. Pp. XII +491, 4 maps. 45s.) has become available. In relation to the present essay the book would appear to give strong support to the central argument on the political nature of post-1870 imperialism. On the other hand it puts forward a specific motive for British participation in Africa—the security of the Suez Canal: and it makes British action there in 1882, rather than Bismarck's claims in 1884, the starting point of the general grab for African territory.

The Nature of
Economic Imperialism[1]

David S. Landes

Professor Landes was born in New York City in 1924. He has taught at Columbia University and the University of California in Berkeley, and at present he
is a professor of economic history at Harvard University. He is also the author
of *Bankers and Pashas: International Finance and Economic Imperialism in
Egypt, The Rise of Capitalism* (1966); *The Unbound Prometheus: Technological Change and Industrial Development in Western Europe Since 1750.*

   While accepting the primacy of the economic pressures towards empire,
David Landes feels that it explains only some of the facts. According to him
imperialism is a "multifarious response to a common opportunity that consists simply in disparity of power."

   Landes points out that formal imperialism was seldom worthwhile in
terms of economic payoff. It always paid for some people, and this is what
is of importance. It was not necessary to have a certain economic system to
create demand for an empire; all that was necessary was a group of interested
people who could influence the decision-makers of the country.

One should distinguish from the start between the economic interpretation of imperialism and economic imperialism. The one is an explanation, an essentially monistic explanation, of an historical phenomenon.
The latter is an aspect of the phenomenon itself: if imperialism
is the dominion of one group over another, economic imperialism
is the establishment or exploitation of such dominion for continuing
material advantage. The definition assumes that economic imperialism
is more than simple, once-for-all pillage; rather that it tries to
cultivate relationships that yield a recurrent harvest of profit, as the
ground its corn. Moreover, it makes no distinction between dominion
established for economic motives and dominion that, for whatever
reasons established, is maintained and exploited primarily for material
ends. Finally, it does not confine imperialism to cases of formal

   [1]Reprinted from "Some Thoughts on the Nature of Economic Imperialism,"
The Journal of Economic History, Vol. XXI, No. 4, 1961, pages 496-512.

rule or protectorate, but includes that "informal" dominion that is often far more effective and lucrative than direct administration.[2]

It is not easy to write about imperialism. So much has been written about it already. One would think that all this learned and not-so-learned polemic would have settled some issues; in particular, that the massive attacks by historians, sociologists, and even economists on the economic interpretation of imperialism would have long since buried it in the graveyard of historical myths. Yet cherished myths are not easily abandoned, and this one is at least as lively today as it was over a decade ago when Koebner, in a memorable article, wrote of the "international *communis opinio*" for which the economic interpretation of imperialism was an "accepted fact."[3]

Under the circumstances some will wonder why it is necessary to reexamine the question: those who are historically sophisticated are already enlightened; and those who accept the economic interpretation are impervious to reason and facts. To this I can only plead that if the target is old, the ammunition may be new; and a reconsideration may suggest a new way of looking at the entire problem.

The economic interpretation of imperialism has many faces. It goes back almost a hundred years and derives from a number of separate sources. Koebner distinguished three streams—the Marxian, Fabian, and American—and each of these is a blend of varied currents. All of them agree, however, on the essential: that the taproot of imperialism is the appetite for material gain; that this appetite grew appreciably in the nineteenth century as a result of structural changes in the industrial economies of Europe; and that modern imperialism is the work of monopoly capitalism. (There are some interesting variations at this point, some like Hobson stressing the role of high finance in promoting the drive for empire, others singling out industrial trusts and monopolies, still others equating the two.)

2The definition does not comprise the range of phenomena covered by François Perroux's concept of economic domination. This includes involuntary as well as voluntary subordination by one economic entity of another, whether at the level of enterprises, national economics or regional groups of economies; there may or may not be control or constraint. Such a concept is at once more comprehensive than imperialism as defined above, in that it embraces all interrelationships of strong and weak economic units, whether or not there is dominion; and at the same time less comprehensive, in that it does not include imperialism of non-economic origin or character. See F. Perroux, "Esquisse d'une théorie de l'économie dominante," *Economie appliquée*, I (1948), 243–300.

3R. Koebner, "The Concept of Economic Imperialism," *Econ. Hist. Rev.*, 2d Ser., II (1949), 5.

One should first do justice to this argument. In its intelligent versions (and it has been distorted to the point of caricature by polemicists pro and con), it does not pretend that only capitalism in its monopolistic stage produces imperialism; on the contrary, it specifically distinguishes between the "colonial policy of capitalism in its *previous* stages" and that of "finance capital." Nor does it attribute imperialist ambitions exclusively to monopoly capitalism; on the contrary, it recognizes the importance of "politico-social roots," though these in turn grow in and are nourished by economic ground.[4] Nor does it make the mistake of thinking that the only imperialism consists in formal occupation of colonial territory. On the contrary, it is well aware of the existence of informal domination—too well aware, for it tends to see it almost everywhere.

If the economic interpretation of imperialism is not foolish, neither is it empty. There is no question of the great importance of material incentives to imperialism in any period, or of their special and increasing importance in the nineteenth century. We are all familiar with the stimulus given the drive for empire by the enormously increased productive capacity of a technologically transformed industrial system. From the first years of the century, the need and hence incentive to increase overseas outlets became acute for Britain: witness Popham's picaresque expedition to Buenos Aires in 1806; and Raffles' attempt to displace the Dutch in Indonesia after 1811.[5] And concomitant with this went a sharpening hunger for raw materials; it is no coincidence that even Victorian Britain

---

[4]These points are phrased by Lenin. The edition used is that of E. Varga and L. Mendelsohn (eds.), *New Data for V. I. Lenin's 'Imperialism, the Highest Stage of Capitalism'*, New York; International Publishers, n.d.), pp. 174, 182.

[5]Commander Popham took it upon himself to sail his squadron from African waters to Buenos Aires in time of war. When His Majesty's Navy took umbrage at this and instituted court-martial proceedings, Popham saved himself by rallying the British mercantile community to his defense. See H. S. Ferns, *Britain and Argentina in the Nineteenth Century* (Oxford; Clarendon Press, 1960), ch. I. Note that Britain's interest in new markets in this period was much stimulated by the commercial dislocations of war. Even before the formal institution of the Continental Blockade, the rich European market had become precarious and costly of access—a foretaste of things to come. See F. Crouzet, *L'économie britannique et le blocus continental* (1806-1813) (2 vols.; Paris: Presses Universitaires, 1958). On Raffles, there is abundant literature. See especially the article by H. R. C. Wright, "The Anglo-Dutch Dispute in the East, 1814—1824," *Econ. Hist. Rev.*, 2d ser., III (1950), 229—39; also the highly critical Dutch viewpoint of Bernard H. M. Vlekke, *Nusantara: A History of the East Indian Archipelago* (Cambridge: Harvard University Press, 1945), ch. XII.

abated its allegiance to free trade to protect the tin of Malaya from foreign interlopers.[6]

Clearly the economic interpretation is not a figment of doctrinaire imagination. It casts light on an important causal relationship, and the effort of certain anti-Marxists to dismiss it completely has only compelled them to erect other myths in its place. Its essential failing lies in the discrepancy between its pretensions and accomplishments. It explains part and claims to explain all—not every trifle and detail, but all that really matters. And this discrepancy, embarrassingly enough, is especially marked for the formal imperialism of the late nineteenth century. Nothing fits the economic interpretation so poorly as the partition of Africa (South Africa and the Congo excepted) —that frantic scramble of industrial, industrializing, and preindustrial European countries for some of the most unremunerative territory on the globe.

As is often the case, much of this explanatory inadequacy derives from the premises, explicit and implicit, on which the structure rests. There are at least three of these:

a. There is a cohesive business class—in Marxian terminology a bourgeoisie—conscious of a common economic interest.

b. In so far as relations with other peoples are concerned, this economic interest lies in the furtherance of imperialism. For dominion, formal or informal, makes it possible to extract wealth from another society, either directly by expropriation on artificially favorable terms, or indirectly by exploiting the labor of the indigenous population. It is precisely in this ability to use force for gain where resides the advantage of imperialism over free contractual relations.

c. That this business class or bourgeoisie controls the state, whose officers of government are in effect its servants.

We need not tarry long on the first of these. Even the most rudimentary knowledge of European history makes clear how divided the so-called bourgeoisie was on any and every issue, economic or noneconomic. It could not agree as a class on tariff questions, the suffrage, the tax system, public works, or factory laws; why

---

[6]S. B. Saul, "The Economic Significance of 'Constructive Imperialism,'" *The Journal of Economic History*, XVII, No. 2 (June 1957), 184—86; Wong Lin Ken, "Western Enterprise and the Development of the Malayan Tin Industry to 1914" (mimeographed paper presented to the Study Group on the Economic History of Southeast Asia of the School of Oriental and African Studies, University of London, July 1961).

should it be expected to agree on colonial policy? In fact, as we shall see, it really did not matter whether or not the business class, or classes to be more precise, acknowledged as a group the material advantages of imperialism. The motor of imperialism lay elsewhere; and the sanction of the bourgeoisie, as well as of the rest of society, could as easily be gained on noneconomic as on economic grounds.

The second premise deserves more detailed examination, not only because it has given rise to its own myths but also because through it we may be able to arrive at a more exact understanding of the actual workings of imperialism.

To begin with, what is exploitation? Few words have been so freely bandied about; this one has come to be almost a battle cry. For most people the word simply means low wages, low in relation to profits, low in relation to wages in other places or occupations—the content is rarely precise, but the disapproval and moral stigma are inescapable.

For serious work as against polemic, this kind of imprecision simply will not do, and I would propose in its stead a definition linked to the exercise of political dominion, formal or informal: imperialist exploitation consists in the employment of labor at wages lower than would obtain in a free bargaining situation; or in the appropriation of goods at prices lower than would obtain in a free market. Imperialist exploitation, in other words, implies nonmarket constraint.[7]

So defined—and I submit that this is the only significant definition of the word—exploitation is by no means the universal concomitant of imperialism that it is frequently alleged or assumed to be. It makes no sense, for example, to talk of exploitation by oil companies in Venezuela or sugar refineries in Cuba when these not only pay a freely negotiated wage, but a wage distinctly higher than that prevailing in the sector of indigenous enterprise. (My own

---

[7]The point is to distinguish between relationships real or latent in any market situation and those specific to imperialism, that is, to separate out from the range of phenomena embraced by the concept of the *économie dominante* those deriving from the exercise or threat of superior force. The two definitions most current in the economic literature will not do this. One—payment to labor of less than its marginal product—relates to any deviation from perfect competition; the second—payment of less than marginal revenue product—is relevant to cases of *monopsony or collusion*.   A third definition, the Marxian one, is based on a normative judgment of social deserts: the appropriation by employers of the so-called surplus value of labor. Because of its tautological character—exploitation is built into the Marxian definition of capitalism—it is neither susceptible of verification or disproof nor applicable to exploitation by noncapitalist systems.

ironic experience has been that some of those who cry out most bitterly against exploitation are the first to complain about foreigners who spoil the market by tipping too generously or overpaying domestic servants.) Nor is it reasonable to decry as exploitation every fall in the price of coffee, cocoa, or palm oil even when due to the normal interplay of supply and demand.

Yet even in the strict sense, exploitation has been a widespread concomitant of imperialism. So far as labor is concerned, one has only to think of the discharge ticket system of Malaya, the head taxes of Africa, and such thinly disguised forms of bondage as the plantation gangs of Angola and the Congo. This recourse to constraint has been based partly on the assumption that forced labor is more profitable than free—a dubious assumption, as Marx himself implied— even more, on the absolute shortage of voluntary labor. In primitive areas, especially those where nature requires little work for subsistence and where much of such work as has to be done is performed by women, it is often impossible to attract labor by means of money, at least at first; and even such labor as is recruited is relatively unresponsive to increasing reward (the supply curve bends backwards once income expectations are fulfilled).

Similarly, with commodities: the most notorious example is the "Culture System" of the Dutch East Indies, under which the peasants of Java, and to a small extent Sumatra, were required to devote a part of their lands to certain cash crops and to deliver these to the government at fixed prices. Such institutional arrangements have been exceptional, however, partly because of the difficulty of compelling satisfactory performance from otherwise free native cultivators, partly because the system is a closed preserve and does not generate wealth for the nationals of the imperialist power. Instead, the proceeds go to the occupying authorities, in lieu of tax payments, as it were, and to such enterprises as they choose to employ.[8] As a result, economic imperialism prefers direct occupation and cultivation of the soil, whether by plantation-sized estates or small homesteads;

[8] Thus the Dutch gave their officials a portion of the proceeds of the system; and crops that required processing, such as sugar, were turned over to factories managed by Europeans or Chinese and worked for or financed by the government. J. A. M. Caldwell, "Indonesian Export Production from the Decline of the Culture System to the First World War" (mimeographed paper presented to the Study Group on the Economic History of the East and Southeast Asia of the School of Oriental and African Studies, University of London, July 1961); C. Day, *The Policy and Administration of the Dutch in Java* (New York: Macmillan Company, 1904), chs. VII–IX.

and if there is to be exploitation, it prefers exploitation of labor to forcible appropriation of commodities.

It is one thing, however, to note the existence of exploitation and its profitability, and another to argue or assume that it is always the most remunerative possible arrangement and that it constitutes therefore an implicit incentive to economic imperialism. There have been, on the contrary, numerous instances of abstention from dominion on the ground that it would not pay. The history of the British East India Company, for example, is full of this—the directors were inclined to look at territorial ambitions as a bottomless drain of men and money, to the intense frustration of some of their ambitious servants. Or of abstention on the ground that it was not necessary: businessmen in the field rarely lacked for native commercial co-operation, even in illicit ventures, and free bargaining generally proved more than lucrative enough.

Thus in the recruitment of labor: neither slavery nor the more subtle forms of bondage that followed it proved satisfactory for large-scale undertakings. The quality of performance was invariably low, and the quantity of labor offered was often inadequate. As a result, employers preferred when possible to find their manpower in the open market. In the Eastern hemisphere and certain parts of the Western, the most important source of labor for capitalist colonial enterprise was the teeming multitudes of the Orient. Tens of thousands of Indian coolies mined diamonds and harvested sugar in Natal, and immigration was halted only by the South Africans' fear of commercial competition (the Indian proved to have a talent for retail trade) and India's resentment of South African discrimination. Gangs of Chinese mined tin in Malaya and Sumatra, cultivated sugar in Cuba, cocoa and rubber in Samoa.[9] These workers were generally recruited by contractors of their own nationality, men whose rapacity and cruelty far surpassed those of the white planters or European corporations who were the ultimate employers. One writer, generally sympathetic to Dutch rule in the Indies, described "this trade in human cattle" as follows:[10]

[9]Cf. Persia C. Campbell, *Chinese Coolie Emigration to Countries within the British Empire* (London: P. S. King, 1923); also Watt Stewart, *Chinese Bondage in Peru: A History of the Chinese Coolie in Peru, 1849–1874* (Durham: Duke University Press, 1951).

[10]A. Cabaton, *Java, Sumatra, and the Other Islands of the Dutch East Indies* (New York. Scribners; London: T. Fisher Unwin, 1911), p. 301 f.

The coolie's agent or labour contractor receives all the expenses of importing him, including passage money, cost of engagement, commission, and medical examination, and the value of his wages at the rate of 1 florin 20 (two shillings) per diem; but the coolie himself receives only a fraction less than 4d. per diem for food, and wages at the rate of 12s. 6d. per month. He must engage himself for at least a year: tempted by opium, driven by the physical distress that follows its discontinuance, and obliged to obtain all that he needs upon credit; clothed and fed at usurious prices by the stores run or leased by the labour agent himself; burdened with debts and with vices, he can no longer hope to escape from the mine, and only too often dies in abject poverty in sight of the natural treasure-house that has taken his life.

In the acquisition of commodities, take that strangest and most evil of commodities, the human being reduced to chattel: the opposition to the abolition of the slave trade was just as strong among those African tribes that had made a business of taking and selling captives as it was among the European traders who bought and resold them. In 1850 the King of Dahomey rejected a British offer of a subsidy to give up the slave trade, on the ground that his people were too "manly" for agriculture and had laid waste by their raids all the arable land around.[11]

I am reminded here of that illuminating story of British reluctance to extend His Majesty's authority in West Africa. In 1807 the Ashanti[11] pursued two enemy chiefs into the territory of the Fanti; these refused to give up the refugees and were themselves attacked and driven toward the coast town of Anamabo, where there was a British fort. In spite of the British commander's offer to mediate, the townspeople elected to fight and were slaughtered; the British garrison, which was also attacked, barely held out. At this point the Ashanti king negotiated a peace with Colonel Torrane, governor of Cape Coast. Torrane agreed to turn over the refugee chiefs, as well as up to half the Fanti who had sought asylum in the Anamabo fort; he and his council then turned the rest to profit by selling most of them as slaves. The best comment on the proceeding is that of the Ashanti king: "From the hour Governor Torrane delivered

11S. O. Biobaku, *The Egba and Their Neighbours,* 1842–1872 (Oxford: Clarendon Press, 1957), p. 40. (Ironically, the Dahomi were famous—or infamous—throughout West Africa for their women soldiers.)

up Tchibbu [one of the fugitive chiefs] I took the English for my friends, because I saw their object was trade only and they did not care for the people. Torrane was a man of sense and he pleased me much."[12]

In the presence of such mutual esteem, imperialism was often an embarrassment. The hard-bitten sea captain of fiction, scouring exotic seas for any and all business—Have tub, will travel; no questions asked—is not a figment of the imagination. Many traders preferred to keep their activities secret, to conceal their profits or the way in which they made them. And the last thing they wanted was "nosy" officials and Her Majesty's law, hence numerous instances of appeals by missionaries for political intervention to defend the native from free enterprise.

As for businessmen at home, they entertained far less illusions about the profitability of colonial ventures than the adventurers, chauvinists, and statesmen who exhorted them to invest and become rich. Bismarck had to instruct his bankers to drum up interest in the South Pacific and Africa—to little avail.[13] Leopold's warm invitations to the financiers of Europe to fructify the resources of the Congo got a lukewarm response.[14] Bouet (the later Admiral Bouet-Willaumez), France's Popham, found the chambers of commerce of Le Havre, Nantes, and Marseilles despairingly indifferent to his campaign to establish French power in the Gulf of Guinea.[15] And so on—it was a veritable epic of obtuseness, or rationality, depending on the point of view. In so far as the promoters of empire succeeded in whipping up the enthusiasm of business groups at home, they

---

12A. B. Ellis, *A History of the Gold Coast of West Africa* (London, 1893), p. 117 f.

13There is material on this in the archives of the banking house of S. Bleichröder, graciously lent me by Mr. F. H. Brunner, of Arnhold and S. Bleichröder, New York. Among the numerous but scattered printed sources, see H. Feis, *Europe, the World's Banker, 1870—1914* (New Haven: Yale University Press, 1930); and G. Diouritch, *L'expansion des banques allemandes à l'étranger* (Paris: A. Rousseau, 1909), pp. 738—63.

14Again there is information in the Bleichröder archive on Leopold's efforts to draw in German capital. The story of the reserved reaction of the Belgian business community remains to be examined in detail. Cf. P. A. Roeykens, *La période initiale de l'oeuvre africaine de Léopold III* [Memoires de l'Académie Royale des Sciences Coloniales, Brussels, Classe des Sciences Morales et Politiques, Nouvelle Série in —8°, Tome III, fasc. 3] (Brussels, 1957), p. 85.

15B. Schnapper, "La politique des 'points d'appui' et la fondation des comptoirs fortifiés dans le golfe de Guinée (1837—1843)," *Revue historique*, CCXXV (1961), 99—120.

had their greatest success with those whose interests were remote from the acquisitions in question and those who had nothing to lose and possibly something to gain, manufacturers for example. And they had their least success with those made wary by experience, above all, with those who would have to prove their faith with cash.

At this point the economic interpretation of imperialism would argue that such abstinence was exceptional—a temporary aberration—and that increased international competition toward the end of the century encouraged European powers to seek closed rather than open markets. Here, too, the picture is not so simple as that. There were closed markets and preferential systems; but there were also large colonial areas where free trade prevailed, or where foreign enterprise was invited—reluctantly perhaps, but deliberately—to make up for the shortcomings or hesitations of home entrepreneurs, as in German Africa, where most of the trade remained in British hands.[16] Nor is this surprising: many of these territories were acquired not as a by-product or for the sake of economic expansion, but for political, military, or psychological reasons; their shape and size were a function not of rational market considerations but of negotiation and accident. Once one had them, one made the best of them; and the best rarely coincided with neat patterns of international economic rivalry.

What is more, those very monopolies and trusts that critics of economic imperialism have been wont to inveigh against were themselves forces for international co-operation: the bigger they got, the more they understood the advantage of sharing resources and markets rather than fighting over them. Oil is the best example of this trend, which would not have surprised Marx: even in so closed a colony as the Dutch East Indies, more than half the investment in extraction and refining came from Britain and France.

Indeed, one may well argue that in the long run, exploitation is no more a rational motor of imperialism in nonindustrial areas than it is in industrial ones; and that this same free contractual

---

[16]W. O. Henderson, "British Economic Activity in the German Colonies, 1884—1914," *Econ. Hist. Rev.* XV (1945), 56—66. In the case of the Congo, it was Leopold's declared intention from the start to establish a free-trade area, not only because any other policy would have alienated potential support from abroad, but because this was the way to maximize return from what was intended to be the biggest personal domain of the age (or the ages). At the same time, he wooed his countrymen by stressing the contribution the Congo would make to Belgian prosperity, without, however, making any promises of special treatment. This all-things-for-all-men technique is closely analogous to that employed by Lesseps in his promotion of the Suez canal.

nexus that Marx felt to be indispensable to the development of
capitalism in Europe is equally advantageous elsewhere, and while
not all merchants, manufacturers, and planters dealing with or working
in colonial areas were prepared to recognize this, many did. Ironically,
the best examples of the latter are the great international bankers—
Hobson's villains—who have always understood that prosperous, independent states make the best clients.

Related to this matter of exploitation is the general question:
did imperialism pay? Books have been written on the subject, which
we can hardly do justice to here. Suffice it to say that most informal
imperialism paid—in spite of occasional crashes and repudiations, if
only because the use of power in such situations was minimal and
the outlay of funds was based on essentially rational grounds. Formal
imperialism, on the other hand, rarely paid (India, the East Indies,
Malaya and the Congo are egregious exceptions), for precisely the
opposite reasons.[17]

Yet for some people imperialism has always paid: energetic
traders, enterprising (corrupt?) officials, manufacturers of cheap, color-
ful wares. And in the last analysis that is what counts. The advocates
of the economic interpretation have tried to prove too much. One
does not need a business class or an economic system to create
a demand for empire. All one needs is a few interested people who
can reach the ears or pockets of those who command. It is sufficient
for the others to stand passively by, absorbed by their own cares
or convinced that their opinions are of no weight anyway—as often
they were. For imperialism was in large measure built on the *fait*

---

[17]Even with those colonies that clearly paid, however, the historian must
take care not to overestimate their contribution to the economy of the imperial
country, the more so as this contribution hardly requires exaggeration. It was
greater for small nations like Belgium and Holland. It was less important for
Britain. It is an article of faith among many Indian historians that the Indian
market was the key to British industrial growth and prosperity; indeed, that the
"exploitation" of India accounts for the Industrial Revolution. In fact, it was not
until after 1815 that exports of British manufacturers to the East began their rapid
growth. Thus in 1814 less than one million yards of cotton cloth were sent to ports
east of Suez, or less than one half of 1 per cent of the total exports. By 1830 the
figure was 57 million; by 1860, 825 million to India alone. At the last date, British
shipments accounted for perhaps 35 per cent of the consumption of the Indian
market, as against some 4 per cent in the early thirties, and almost a third of
total British exports of cloth. In the course of these years, therefore, Indian production for home consumption actually increased; but Indian exports were virtually
driven from the world market. Th. Ellison, *The Cotton Trade of Great Britain*
(London, 1886), p. 63; S. B. Saul, *Studies in British Overseas Trade, 1870–1914*
(Liverpool: Liverpool University Press, 1960), p. 14 and n. 2.

accompli—the Jameson raid is the most famous example—with the state almost always ready to pull its nationals' chestnuts out of the fire. And it was ready to do this, at some risk and expense, not for material reasons, but for face; for nations as for men, *amour-propre* is the most powerful of drives.

If ever it proved advisable, moreover, to whip up general support for these *faits accomplis,* this could usually be accomplished by appeals to lofty sentiments of prestige and humanity. To material interests, too, but I am inclined to think these less important: first, because people are better judges of their own than of national interests, and second, because they do not like to think they are acting for selfish reasons. Hence their powers of rationalization on the one hand, and credulity on the other, know no bounds. Nothing illustrates this sugar-coating better than the following sincere defense of the hut tax, the basis of forced labor in much of Africa:[18]

> The direct taxation of the native is desirable in order to create in him a sense of responsibility, without which a settled condition of society is difficult to attain. It is essential to impress upon the native mind the fact that they can and must participate in the government of the country. This can only be done by getting them to contribute towards the expenses of admistration. They are likely to value more highly a government for which they have to pay directly. Moreover, direct taxation fosters commerce, and settled habits of life. In order to pay the hut tax or gun tax, or both, the natives must work. Commerce will be fostered in two directions: firstly, by providing labour for the extension of commercial enterprise; secondly, by supplying the natives with wages which will be spent increasingly upon the imports of European trade. There is, also, the broader question of political ethics—what the native receives he should pay for. The former government by tribal chiefs gave no security for life and property. This has been introduced by the British administration. It is only fair to ask the native to contribute to the cost of the benefits which he now enjoys.

There is, of course, a big "if" here. To make this kind of economic imperialism effective, interested parties had to be able to call on power. And this brings us to the third premise of the economic interpretation, that the state was in the hands or service of the business class.

[18]A. J. MacDonald, *Trade, Politics and Christianity in Africa and the East* (London: Longmans, Green, 1916), p. 114.

Once again, the facts belie the assumption. We have, to begin with, numerous instances of governments refusing to annex territory or bring pressure on weaker states in order to protect or further the material interests of their nationals. Britain in particular repeatedly rejected the importunities of empire builders and businessmen, partly on moral grounds, partly because of economic principle—the Liberals clung wistfully to the ideal of a free-trade, free-enterprise world well into the period of renewed territorial expansion—and not least because she was rich with empire already and could assume a disenchanted stance. The pique of Kimberley, frustrated in his desire to establish a protectorate over Zululand in 1884, is classic: "I see the cabinet do not want more niggers."[19] The correspondence of the Foreign Office is full of lamentations by conscientious consuls of the abuse of power and privilege by European fortune hunters in hapless quasi-colonial lands; and of injunctions from London to observe that golden rule of international relations: treat the stranger as you would your own. The whole makes a fascinating story of an honorable effort to build policy on right rather than expediency. The attempt, for reasons to be examined, was condemned to failure from the start.[20]

Other countries were less scrupulous, but there other considerations often served to hamper collaboration between economic interests and the political arm. At least British diplomatic and military personnel recognized the principle of the state in the service of *legitimate* trade. When the Shah of Persia asked British support against Russian encroachment in 1884, the cabinet decided to ask the Shah to open the rivers of Persia to British trade as "an earnest of his good intentions." Dilke notes in his diary: "Not a bad touchstone." It was a typically British touchstone.[21]

Elsewhere, however, officials, while paying lip service to the importance of trade, were less than sympathetic to the activities and personalities of their compatriot entrepreneurs. French traders and chambers of commerce, for example, complain repeatedly of lack of co-operation from consular and naval officers, even of hostility.

19S. Gwynn and G. M. Tuckwell, *The Life of the Rt. Hon. Sir Charles W. Dilke* (2 vols.; London: J. Murray, 1917), II, 86.

20Thus Britain made repeated efforts to defend the government of Egypt in the 1850's and 1860's against the extortions of foreign businessmen, adventurers, and confidence men, extortions condoned and connived at by the consular representatives of the European powers and effected thanks to a system of extra-territorial privilege and the threat of superior force; to no avail. See D. S. Landes, *Bankers and Pashas* (London: Heinemann, 1958), ch. III, especially the sources cited in p. 94 n. 3.

21Gwynn and Tuckwell, *Life of Dilke*, II, 87.

The following letter of April 1847, from Victor Régis of Marseilles, pioneer of the French palm-oil trade in West Africa, to Captain Bouet-Willaumez, Governor of Senegal, is indicative of a larger conflict:[22]

> Do we want to confine ourselves to making Gabon a military station from which traders must be excluded? If such a policy has not been decided in principle, it exists in fact, and I am pained to conclude that we shall have to start all over with a war in the newspapers to enlighten the government on the consequences of the conduct of several officers towards trade. It is distasteful to me to resort to such an extreme measure, but I refuse [*je ne serais nullement disposé*] to submit to injustices.

Nor is this conflict surprising. On the one side stood a gentleman or presumed gentleman, often drawn from a milieu traditionally hostile to business; on the other, tough, grasping men anxious to get rich as quickly as possible and get out. To those charged with maintaining order and securing territorial gains, the trader looked like a bull in a china shop. Even British officials—and there were none more sympathetic to commerce and cognizant of its importance as means and end—felt a certain impatience with the lesser vision of the money makers. Listen to the tone of a letter from Harry Johnston, "Commissioner and Consul-General for the territories under British influence to the north of the Zambezi," to the British South Africa Company:[23]

> There is nothing for it. You must make up your minds to trust me, for say one year, with the supreme direction of all things in British Central Africa. I must be able to say to one of your trading agents 'build a store here', 'Give six and threepence a pound for ivory', 'You are selling that cloth too dear', 'You must send an indent for twelve gross of brass pans', 'Supply Crawshay instantly with one dozen child's tops, 26 wax dolls, 3,000 yards of cotton, 30 packets of fancy stationery, five bales of imitation cashmere shawls, and send them off to Lake Mweru tomorrow'. I know as much about your African trade as your Moirs and your Ewings. It is twelve years ago to-day since I landed in Tunis and I have studied Africa ever since. Besides,

22P. Masson, *Marseille et la colonisation française* (Marseilles: Barlatier, 1906), p. 387.

23Roland Oliver, *Sir Harry Johnston and the Scramble for Africa* (New York: St. Martin's, 1958), p. 198 f.

for the first year or two in my great task of bringing five hundred thousand square miles of Central Africa under British control, the shop is only second to the sword. But it is a shop which must be wisely and judiciously managed, and its shopboys must not be allowed to baulk my efforts by cheating an African chief over damaged jam or pretending that half a crown and a rupee are just the same value. In plain words the African Lakes Company is loathed by everyone in the land. Its policy has been idiotic because its silly little frauds have not even profited it. However enough on this score. If you start your Trading Department in the way I have sketched out, send out, with public or private instructions to work under my direction in all things, two good men of the accountant type, and for a change, just for a change, send Englishmen.

One final point: even when one considers the numerous instances of collaboration between economic interests and the state, it would be a mistake to assume that there is a simple one-way pattern of influence. In fact, it was often business that was in the service of diplomacy, when necessary at some disadvantage to itself. Moreover, this relationship grew steadily more important in the course of the century, as the development of a world market for goods and capital, with its concomitant patterns of dependency, made economic pressure an ever more effective diplomatic weapon. I cannot do justice to the subject here, but nothing offers so instructive a commentary on the oversimplicity of the economic interpretation than the record of lending as an instrument of foreign policy in pre-World War I eastern Europe.[24]

The foregoing analysis of the complexity of imperialism, with its stress on what we may call countervailing forces—avoidance of or opposition to territorial expansion; conflicts between business ambitions, state policy and personnel; subordination of economic interests

[24]The records of the Service du Mouvement des Fonds of the French Ministry of Finance are full of evidence of this subordination of banking to politics. The dossiers on Rumania (Archives Nationales, F03 327) are particularly suggestive, not only for what they show of government attitudes, but also for the evidence they offer of the ability of the state to impose its will on reluctant enterprises in a nominally free economy. The Deutsches Zentral Archiv in Potsdam contains similar material on German lending policy, among other things, on Bismarck's famous decision to cut off credit to Russia in 1887 in order to bring pressure on the Tsarist government.

to diplomatic considerations—suggests a question: in view of all this tugging and hauling, how does one account for the remorseless if spasmodic advance of imperialism over the course of the century? Surely all these contradictory tendencies and hesitations are only the surface detail that characterizes any broad historical movement. Surely, once one cuts away the brush one finds firm ground—the ground of economic motivation that changes its form of expression but not its meaning. This is the argument advanced, for example, by Gallagher and Robinson, in their article on the "Imperialism of Free Trade": that dominion is essentially a device for the integration of new areas into the expanding industrial economy of Britain; and that the form of control—explicit or implicit, manifest or latent, simply reflects need and opportunity.[25]

While accepting this point about the persistence and indeed primacy of the economic pressures toward empire, especially informal empire, in nineteenth-century Britain, I would dissent from this interpretation on a ground already adduced: that it will account for only a part—an important but nevertheless insufficient part—of the facts. In particular, it will not account for a major historical phenomenon, the occupation of large areas of the world for noneconomic reasons. The correct observation that Africa was "the bottom of the [imperialist] barrel,"[26] far from disposing of the significance of this occupation, only heightens it.

A more general interpretation would seem desirable; and to that end I should like to hazard an equilibrium analysis that transcends place and circumstance. It seems to me that one has to look at imperialism as a multifarious response to a common opportunity that consists simply in disparity of power. Whenever and wherever such disparity has existed, people and groups have been ready to take advantage of it. It is, one notes with regret, in the nature of the human beast to push other people around—or to save their souls or "civilize" them, as the case may be. To be sure, there is such a thing as morality, and occasionally a nation or part of a nation, as in nineteenth-century Britain, develops ideals concerning freedom and self-determination that put an obstacle in the way of unrestrained exploitation of superior strength. But here the best of intentions are eroded in the long run by the inner logic of dominion. This inner logic finds expression

25J. Gallagher and R. Robinson, "The Imperialism of Free Trade," *Econ. Hist. Rev.*, 2d ser., VI (1953), 1—15.
    26*Ibid.*, p. 15.

in two fields: within the context of a given area of imperialistic influence; and in the larger context of the international relations of imperial powers.

Concerning the first, the decisive determinant at the working level—as distinguished from the level of plans and intentions—is the instability of any relationship of unequal power. In the long run, the weaker party will never accept his inferiority, first because of the material disadvantages it entails, but even more because of the humiliation' it imposes. In return, the stronger party must ceaselessly concern itself with the security of its position. Hence this imperialism of the "turbulent frontier" so well described by John Galbraith: each strong point requires outposts to defend it, and each outpost calls for new ones beyond it.[27] The spiral of increasing commitments and "obligations" is limited only by the balance of power.

This pattern of pressure or the threat of pressure from the weak side and response from the strong has its counterpart in initatives from the strong side and responses from the weak. Whatever may be the policy of the imperial nation, however restrained it may be in its application of power, its citizens—businessmen, missionaries, soldiers of fortune—exploit on their own initiative the opportunities offered. Moreover, there is no necessity here of concerted action. The situation is analogous to a market in which equilibrium may be upset by the action of only one competitor. All that is needed is one man to place the prestige of the dominant group in the scales or put its security in jeopardy, and corrective action is inevitable. It may occasionally take the form of restoring the previous equilibrium, but it will not do this indefinitely. Sooner or later the fatal words will be pronounced: "We're going to get no rest until . . ."

In the second or international arena, an analogous situation prevails. It matters not what the intentions; each nation operates in a universe peopled by other nations, and its actions are determined as much by their moves as by its own objectives. Under the circumstances, principle and morality must yield to tactical necessity—on a small scale, as in mid-century Egypt, where Britain found herself obliged to follow the example of the other European powers in extorting advantages for her nationals, if only to maintain her prestige in the area;[28] or on a large scale, as when the transpiring ambitions

27J. S. Galbraith, "The 'Turbulent Frontier' as a Factor in British Expansion," *Comparative Studies in Society and History*, II (1960), 150—68.

28Thus in the enforcement in 1868-1869 of British claims against the Egyptian government in the liquidation of the Société Agricole. F. O. 78—2166 and 2167, especially F. O. 78—2167, Clarendon to Stanton, teleg. 23—4—1869, letter 30—4—1869.

of other European powers led Britain in the 1880's to adopt the policy of a pre-emptive veto on the acquisition of any of the unclaimed areas of the world.

So if one seeks to understand the imperialism of the nineteenth century, one must take into account not only stronger economic motives, among others, but even more those technological changes that increased the disparity of force between Europe and the rest of the world and created the opportunity for and possibility of dominion. It is no coincidence that the Araucanian Indians of South America repeatedly defeated and humiliated the Spanish invaders in the eighteenth century (as they had the Incas earlier) but succumbed to Chilean troops in the nineteenth, while at the same time, but thousands of miles away, settlers from the north succeeded in subduing the Plains Indians of the southwestern United States, where the Spanish and Mexicans had failed. The key to conquest in both cases was essentially improved firepower through the introduction of repeating weapons.[29]

In this sense, the expansion of the nineteenth century is only the last phase of a millennial explosion that goes back to the turning point of the Middle Ages when the peoples of Europe, long compressed and pierced by stronger enemies, halted their incursions and beat them back—on the plateau of Castile, on the east Elbian plain, along the shores of the Mediterranean. The explosion is not even or continuous; the frontier of dominion retreats as well as advances. But in the long run the great tide swells inexorably, for it expresses a fundamental and continuing shift in the balance of power between Europe and the rest of the world. And power, like nature, abhors a vacuum.

[29]On the Araucanian Indians, see R. C. Padden, "Cultural Changes and Military Resistance in Araucanian Chile, 1550–1730," *Southwestern Journal of Anthropology*, XIII (1957), 103–21. On the Plains Indians of North America, the discussion of Walter P. Webb, *The Great Plains* (Boston: Ginn and Co., 1931), chs. IV and V, is a classic. Eric A. Walker, *A History of Southern Africa* (London: Longmans, Green, 1957), p. 429, has a ghastly phrase about the effect of military technology on British dominion over the Matabele: "The machine guns, a novelty in warfare in those days [1893], worked wonders at Shangani and Imbembezi, and the volunteers entered the ruins of Bulawayo to find the king fled." Compare the change in British fortunes (and policy) in the Sudan, from the days of Gordon (fall of Khartum, 1885) to those of Kitchener (battle of Omdurman, 1898). It is one of the ironies of history that the machine gun, which long met with skepticism in the planning rooms of European war ministries, was proved and perfected in combat with the colonial peoples of the world, so that when World War I came, with its trench warfare, the now much improved weapon was able to slaughter the children of its European developers. Cf. G. S. Hutchison, *Machine Guns: Their History and Technical Employment* (London: Macmillan, 1938).

Economic Imperialism Revisited[1]

Mark Blaug

Mark Blaug was born in the Netherlands and has lived and worked in the U.S.A., the U.K., France, and South-East Asia. He has taught at Yale University for many years and at present is Professor of Economics of Education at the University of London. He has always had a great interest in Marxian economics, on which he has written at greater length in his book *Economic Theory in Retrospect*.

Blaug's article is a sweeping criticism of the Hobson-Lenin theory of Imperialism. The question he examines is whether a capitalist economy can expand on its own resources. If so, then the elimination of imperialism would not mean the doom of the capitalist system. (The reader is referred to Tapan Mukerjee's doctoral dissertation, *Economic Impact of Decolonization: The Britain India Case;* University of Colorado, 1970.)

Endlessly debated, frequently attacked, still controversial, the theory of economic imperialism is currently enjoying a new lease on life in the underdeveloped countries. When Premier Khrushchev tells an Indian audience that capitalist countries will never extend genuine aid to backward nations "because it would deprive them of their own profits and markets for their goods," he is thinking of Marx and Lenin, not of the record of American foreign aid. But his words find a quick response with most of the nationalist leaders of the newly created countries, providing further evidence of the amazing vitality of the Marxist doctrine of imperialism. In the decades before the First World War it played an important role in socialist debates over the impending breakdown of capitalism; in the 1920's it served to explain the origin and nature of the First World War; in the 1930's it was linked up with the popular view of how Fascism arose in certain Central European countries; and now, since the Second World War, it has turned up in a new guise to discredit Western aid and assistance to the underdeveloped nations.

And yet when explained at all closely, the theory of economic imperialism seems to rest upon slippery grounds; indeed, its proponents

[1]Reprinted from the *Yale Review*, Vol. 50, March 1961, pages 335–349.

142

have hardly bothered to present a theoretical argument. They have relied for the most part upon familiar underconsumptionist fallacies or simply upon selected descriptions of imperialist policy. No doubt, the history of colonialism does not make edifying reading: the story of the imposition of foreign rule never does. But this is not what is at issue. Economic imperialism is a foreign policy that seeks political and economic control over backward areas to guarantee an outlet for idle savings and surplus manufactured goods in exchange for strategic raw materials. Marxist theory supposes that a closed capitalist economy—an economy having no trading relations with other countries—must suffer from chronic insufficiency of effective demand, from a basic imbalance that can only be corrected by the opening of foreign markets. Imperialism, the direct or indirect exploitation of backward areas, is therefore an inherent feature of mature capitalism. It would follow that one cannot seriously expect the West to work actively for the raising of living standards in the poor countries of Asia and Africa: the all-round industrialization of these areas would simply spell the doom of capitalism.

This is the thesis I want to examine. Can a closed capitalist economy in principle expand indefinitely on its own resources? If so, the elimination of imperialism would not mean the end of the capitalist system. But if the Marxist argument stands up, only a socialist society can break away from the imperialist pattern. The question is not whether, say, British rule in Africa was ruinous or beneficent, but whether the Dark Continent was plundered to sustain capitalism in England. Not whether the United States did or did not practice dollar diplomacy in Latin America with the aid of the Marines, but whether a free enterprise economy can help to raise incomes in the Caribbean or Southeast Asia without committing economic suicide. The brute facts marshalled by Lenin and his disciples are all too frequently beyond dispute, but my concern is with the inferences they have drawn from them.

Let us for a moment consider the doctrinal roots of the argument. Lenin's *Imperialism* is thoroughly permeated by Marx's vision of capitalism, subject to chronic underconsumption because wages are slow to rise, if they rise at all, and because investment opportunities dry up as the rate of profit declines. Marx himself talked of colonies as a thing of the past—in his day Britain was said to have acquired her colonies "in a fit of absence of mind"—and abstracted from foreign trade in his central analysis. He believed that on the whole labor was not a beneficiary of economic progress but he refused to be committed to any definite opinion. Even the basic notion that the rate of profit on capital tends to fall through time he only demonstrated by the seemingly plausible but arbitrary assertion that profits per man can never rise as fast as capital per man. Still, Marx, and for that matter John Stuart Mill, did argue that the export of capital, by draining off excess savings, counteracts the decline of the rate of profit in a country. It was not difficult to stretch this into the proposition that the inability to profitably dispose of goods and capital at home leads inevitably to imperialist ventures. The entire theory of economic imperialism was ready made for Lenin by the German followers of Marx and he took it over without further examination, neatly combining in his emphasis upon foreign investment the high-profit pull of backward areas with the low-profit push of late-stage capitalism:

> In backward countries, profits are usually high, for capital is scarce, the price of land is relatively low, raw materials are cheap. *The possibility of exporting capital* is created by the entry of numerous backward countries into international capitalist intercourse; main railways have either been built or are being built there; the elementary conditions for industrial developments have been created. *The necessity of exporting capital arises* from the fact that in a few countries capitalism has become over-ripe and (owing to the backward state of agriculture and the impoverished state of the masses) capital cannot find profitable investments.

Underlying Lenin's reasoning is the familiar notion of chronic deficiency of markets under capitalism. This is not the vulgar fallacy that capitalists must seek foreign outlets because workers cannot buy back the whole current product, receiving as they do less than the value of the output which they create. The gap between total income or output and total payrolls is just what makes investment possible, and investment creates purchasing power without creating goods which must be bought by workers. Lenin, like Marx, was perfectly well aware that aggregate effective demand consists of consumption *plus* investment. What he had in the back of his mind was something more sophisticated. Investment creates capacity as well as income and the growth of capacity coupled with the rising productivity of labor leads to an ever larger excess of income over consumption, to an ever increasing portion of unconsumed income that is saved and that must be invested to maintain a given rate of growth of income. But why invest when consumption is lagging behind? Isn't it obvious that investment for investment's sake cannot continue indefinitely?

This obvious argument, unfortunately, has an equally obvious retort. While the investable "surplus" increases absolutely, it does not necessarily increase relative to total income. Assuming with Marx that all wages are spent on consumption and all profits on investment, the system encounters difficulties only if profits grow not just absolutely, but as a fraction of income. But even Marx did not claim that this would happen, and in fact it has not happened: the relative share of profits in national income has shown a downward, not an upward, trend in all advanced countries since 1870 or thereabouts, while the flow of savings over that period rose in the same proportion as income.

The Marxist conviction that capitalism is subject to under-consumption in the broader sense harks back to two doctrinal pillars: the concept of the absolute impoverishment of the working class and the theory of the tendency of the rate of profit to fall in the course of capital accumulation. How can domestic markets expand, argues the Marxist, when incessant laborsaving technical change holds down wages even as the eagerness to mechanize and to accumulate capital chokes off investment opportunities? This is the kind of under-consumptionist argument that every Marxist insists upon. It is as implicit in Lenin as in Marx. Capitalism, Lenin declares, is bound to fall victim either to the Scylla of "the impoverished state of the masses" or the Charybdis of insufficient "profitable investments"; imperialism is merely "the monopoly stage of capitalism" attempting to solve this fundamental contradiction.

We might take comfort in the fact that real wages have risen continuously in all capitalist countries, that labor's relative share of income has increased over the last century, and that the rate of return on capital over the same period shows only a mild downward tendency. But the idea that a mature economy tends to produce a flow of savings so large as to outrun all feasible domestic investment opportunities, driving investors to seek foreign outlets, has a familiar ring. It is reminiscent of the Hansen-Keynes thesis of secular stagnation so much in vogue in the days of the Great Depression. Indeed, some quasi-Marxist writers, like John Strachey (*The End of Empire*), have not been averse to borrowing a leaf from Keynes to prove their case. After all, Keynes did show that private investment in an advanced economy is likely to be inadequate to mop up the savings forthcoming at a full employment income level. And what is the Keynesian "deflationary gap" but academic jargon for a tendency toward under-consumption? But this ignores the fact that Keynes's central argument is concerned with business cycles, not with secular trends. For purposes

of analyzing the causes of a depression, consumption may be taken
to be a stable function of income; thus, in the short run, the only
way to eliminate a deflationary gap is by additional private or
public investment. But in the long run one would expect the consumption function to shift upwards as the growth of income generates
rising wants. This means that a community that consumes 80 per
cent of current income in 1900 may also consume 80 per cent in
1950 although incomes may then have doubled. And, as a matter
of fact, the consumption-income or saving-income ratio has remained
remarkably stable over long periods of time in mature economies,
suggesting that capitalism is not necessarily subject to a secular tendency toward underconsumption or oversaving. Indeed, since the
Second World War it has been more reasonable to assert a tendency
toward secular exhilaration: the inflationary pressures experienced almost everywhere imply that the flow of savings has proved insufficient
to satisfy the demands for investment. How often are we told that
post-war prosperity in the United States is utterly dependent upon
armament spending because military hardware does not enter the market for sale. The fact that such expenditures since 1945 have been
almost entirely financed by taxing current income, so that the net
expansionary effect may well be nil, is simply forgotten. Moreover,
the prosperity of such capitalist countries as Western Germany, Holland, Belgium, Norway, and Sweden, all of which have spent very
little on arms, is conveniently explained away as "special cases."

Supposing that a closed capitalist economy can theoretically
grow along an equilibrium path, we have not yet disposed of the
high-profit pull thesis. Surely, the prospect of super profits in the
poorer countries will induce an outflow of capital from the richer
nations? The yield of capital is necessarily higher in backward areas
because capital is scarce there and labor is artificially cheap. This
kind of argument had considerable a priori appeal in days when
foreign investment was a significant fraction of total investment, but it
fails to explain, as we shall see, why foreign investment took the
pattern it did and why the flow of funds to the backward areas
was so limited even in the nineteenth century. Nor can it account
for the common observation that domestic savings in underdeveloped
countries are often hoarded or exported to the advanced capitalist
world; if the rate of return is really as high as it is claimed, what
prevents local capitalists from emerging?

Contrary to popular belief, however, the yield of capital is
generally higher in a capital-rich economy than in an underdeveloped
country, because capital in the advanced country is invested in a

complementary fashion in basic industry, transport, and power. The potential high yield in capital-poor areas cannot be exploited in the absence of social overhead facilities, such as roads, railways, harbors, docks, dams, power plants, and schools. It rarely pays the individual to invest in these lines since he himself cannot reap their social benefits—this is precisely the argument nowadays for public investment in the underdeveloped countries. Backward countries are generally *not* attractive outlets for private capital. Lenin made his case by simply assuming that social overhead capital, what he called "the elementary conditions for industrial development," was already in existence in the backward areas. But when this was the case, as in Canada and Argentina, the areas did not long remain under-developed.

Other things being equal, investors prefer to place their capital at home rather than abroad. The fact that capital was nevertheless exported does indicate that foreign investment offered higher rates of return than domestic investment. But taking into account the risk of inadequate information and the possibility of default, the differential yield was usually more modest than might be expected. Super profits and huge windfalls did occur but losses were not uncommon and on the average it is doutbful whether profits on overscas investment in the nineteenth century exceeded earnings at home by more than one or two per cent. There is very little reliable information on this score but it has recently been shown that the average annual income from the entire British investment of nearly a thousand firms in Latin America rarely rose above five or six per cent of the par value of the investment; these rates are quite comparable to British stock yields during the past century. Latin American government bonds were bringing as much as 8 per cent but almost half of these were in default by the close of the century (J. F. Rippy, *British Investments in Latin America*, 1822-1949).

Neither the push nor the pull version of economic imperialism stands up under analysis. But weak in theory, Lenin's book has nevertheless been praised as giving a succinct review of the facts. The presentation of the record, however, is if anything more suspect than Lenin's theoretical arguments and has given rise to a total misconception of the typical pattern of foreign investment in the heyday of imperialism. I will pass over his belief that modern imperial-ism is characterized by bank participation in the conduct of business enterprises, and by the growth of monopoly. Finance capitalism, as Lenin defines it, never did establish itself in Great Britain, which had the largest empire of all, and even in Germany and America it largely disappeared after the First World War. Nor is there evidence of any long run trend in Great Britain or the United States in the concentration of industry over the last forty years. But these issues do not touch the heart of the matter. The picture of foreign investment which Lenin projects in his book is that of capital exported to low-income staple-producing areas under the direct political control of the major powers concentrating almost exclusively upon the extractive industries, and earning enormous rates of return for a narrow class of investors at home; an accompanying feature is the deliberate dumping of excess supplies upon restricted colonial markets. It is not too much to say that the whole of this is an elegant fiction. Lenin granted, for example, that the bulk of French capital held abroad was invested in Russia, not in the French colonies, while German capital was mostly invested outside her own negligible holdings in Africa. But he insisted that "the principal sphere of investment of British capital is the British colonies," while in fact over half of Britain's foreign assets in the decades before 1914 were held outside the Empire. Even within the Empire, Canada, Australia, and New Zealand—hardly outstanding examples of the ruinous effect of imperialism—accounted for one-half of British investment, and more was invested in Australia and New Zealand alone than in India and the whole of Africa. Outside the Empire the United States and Argentina took the lion's share of British capital. Instead of capital flowing to densely populated China or India, where capital was scarce and labor cheap, two-thirds of Britain's overseas investment in the years 1870-1914 went to the so-called regions of recent settlement, stimulated and complemented by the migration of something like 60 million people. The unique element of capital movements in the classic era of imperialism was just this: capital and labor flowed together from the Old World to the New, a striking fact completely ignored in the Marxist literature. And instead of the backward areas with their "teeming millions" providing the dumping ground for surplus goods, the greater part of British manufactured exports likewise flowed to the regions of recent settlement in the wake of capital and labor.

The preoccupation with the extraction of mineral and plantation products for export to the industrial countries, so often thought to be the typical imperialist pattern of international investment, played a minor role in the period before 1914. The demand for foreign capital came to a large degree from public development schemes. At the outbreak of the First World War, 30 per cent of Britain's overseas investment consisted of loans to public authorities, another 45 per cent of railway securities to finance construction undertaken by governments in the borrowing country, leaving only 25 per cent for the strictly "colonial" type of investment in agriculture, industry, and mining. The proportion of government loans and other public investment was even higher in French and German than in British foreign investment, and in each case over half of the capital invested abroad was placed in other European countries, with less than 10 per cent of the total invested within the respective colonies (H. Feis, *Europe: The World's Banker, 1870-1913*).

The fact that very little capital went to the densely populated countries and that most of it was put into fixed-interest bearing government bonds or securities directly guaranteed by some branch of government is surprising only to those held in the grip of the Leninist conception of foreign capital ruthlessly exploiting native labor. Even today, 30 per cent of American total direct investment abroad, 37 per cent of the foreign branches of American firms, and 50 per cent of all American foreign investment in manufacturing is located in Canada, the country with the second highest per capita income in the world. Once again, the developed countries like Canada, Great Britain, France, Germany, and Australia together account for about one-half of all direct American foreign investment. What is even more striking is that rates of return on foreign investment in the Persian Gulf are as high as 20 per cent in contrast to 11 per cent in Latin America and 8 per cent in Canada; yet the Persian Gulf attracts less than one-tenth of American foreign investment and the rate of increase of foreign investment in the post-war years has been higher in Canada than in the oil-soaked regions of the Middle East. The preference of American investors for relatively developed and culturally familiar economies is a fact difficult to fit into the Leninist theory. And yet it is clear that non-pecuniary motives have always loomed large in determining the flow of international capital. The Marxist theory of imperialism, by stressing the prospect of super profits from the exploitation of colonial labor, provides no guide to the pattern which foreign investment took in the nineteenth century or which it is taking today.

There remains the Marxist suggestion that the high standard of living of workers in the advanced countries is somehow due to the "exploitation" of the colonial masses. This notion is almost impossible to get hold of because its meaning is not at all clear. Lenin talked vaguely of the "aristocracy of labor" in the home country sharing in the superprofits of imperialism, but the extra yield of foreign over domestic investment has not been such as to reasonably account for a tripling of real wages over the last century. Moreover, taken at face value, this would mean that the rise in wage rates and in general working conditions in the advanced countries has been matched by a deterioration of living standards in the colonies. I know of only one Marxist writer who has had the courage of his convictions to claim that "the law of absolute impoverishment of the working class" holds strictly, not for individual countries, but for the whole labor force employed within a given capitalist society both at home and abroad. He carried out a series of statistical studies designed to verify the thesis but, after one inconclusive volume on the British Empire, abandoned the project (J. Kuczynski, *A Short History of Labour Conditions under Capitalism*). I think one may be allowed to draw the obvious inference.

Another possible interpretation of the argument is that unemployment in the major capitalist countries would have been much worse in the absence of imperialism. After all, Great Britain in the years 1870-1914 did invest abroad something like half of her domestic savings, whose interests and dividends amounted to one-tenth of her national income. Surely, the transfer of so much saving must have reduced potential domestic deflationary pressures and stabilized national income? But it is a mistake to assume that savings which went overseas would have existed at all in the absence of capital exports: foreign investment, by stimulating exports, generates income and hence saving just as much as domestic investment. Without foreign investment, British income would no doubt have grown less rapidly but so would domestic savings. Moreover, most overseas investment after 1870 did not offset domestic savings in any sense whatever: the bulk of it was due to the reinvestment of undistributed profits on previous investment. No matter how interpreted, the idea that the British worker was better off at the expense of the Indian peasant or African miner carries no conviction.

In its persistent emphasis upon the notion of surpluses seeking outlets in the colonies, the Marxist theory of imperialism loses sight of Germany and the Scandinavian countries which achieved high levels of income per head without benefit of colonial possessions, of countries like the United States, Japan, Russia, Sweden, Canada, Australia, New Zealand, and South Africa, which achieved high rates of growth over decades with the aid of substantial capital imports and then sustained high income levels to this day without becoming significant exporters of capital. China, India, tropical Africa, and Central and South America (excepting Argentina), which were little "exploited" by British capital in the nineteenth century, remained underdeveloped, while incomes in the regions receiving foreign capital soared upwards. It is true that the most developed country in Asia, Japan, was also the only one to escape colonization or dependency upon European capitalism. But the reluctance to invest in backward areas shows up once again in the fact that more European capital flowed to Japan in the years 1890-1914 than to all the rest of Asia.

The case of the United States proves particularly troublesome to Marxist doctrine. America's colonies in the Pacific have had little significance from an economic standpoint and even Latin America, her principal sphere of influence, never attracted as much American capital or commodity trade as the Dominions. The standard Marxist reply to this observation is that the United States has been able to practice internal imperialism by pushing out her economic frontier and exploiting Negro labor in lieu of colonial labor. But the wage-differential between Negroes and Whites is narrowing and the frontier no longer absorbs surplus capital. Yet American foreign investment is now an even smaller fraction of total domestic capital formation than in the past. Since the Second World War, the net outflow of private long-term capital (including reinvested profits) has amounted on the average to no more than 4 per cent of total gross private domestic investment, with earnings from overseas investment accounting for only about one-half of one per cent of national income. It has been estimated that if the United States were exporting capital today on a scale equivalent in terms of real income per head to that of the United Kingdom at the turn of the century, the total value of American foreign investment would be $600 billion instead of the $30 billion it is, and annual earnings would be ten times as large as they are; each year, the United States would have to lend abroad a sum equal to twice the aid given under the entire Marshall Plan. Adding to direct plus portfolio investment abroad, all public loans and grants as well as outlays on military establishments overseas, we reach an average annual sum of about 5 per cent of national income. Is it possible that these relatively minor expenditures provide a vital outlet for idle funds without which American capitalism could not be maintained, as Marxists are wont to claim? These sums at best bear no comparison to overseas spending in the Edwardian imperial heyday, which suggests the paradoxical conclusion that capitalism requires foreign outlets less the more advanced it is.

Although international capital movements and the structure of world trade now show no similarity whatever to the pre-1914 pattern which gave rise to the theory of economic imperialism, the Leninist doctrine shows no sign of waning. Khrushchev may declare that wars are no longer inevitable despite imperialist rivalry but his Chinese colleagues cling to the standard propositions, while Western Marxists continue to insist upon the unreformed nature of contemporary imperialism and its inherent animosity toward all efforts at economic development of the backward countries. In a recent book, *The Political Economy of Growth,* Paul Baran argues that the liquidation of the British and other empires since 1945 does not herald the passing away of imperialism: old-style colonialism is merely being replaced by a new policy of supporting puppet-governments in the ex-colonies, representing a coalition of "wealthy compradors, powerful monopolists, and large landowners" who are dedicated to the defense of "the existing feudal-mercantile order." He rests his case squarely on the allegation that economic progress in the underdeveloped countries is inimical to business interests in the advanced countries: "providing their corporations with vast profits and investment outlets, the backward world has always represented the indispensable hinterland of the highly developed capitalist West." He interprets the Western clamor for foreign aid as a scheme for bribing the backward peoples to refrain from demanding rapid industrialization and sweeping political reform. Only government planning, he concludes, can provide the all-out mobilization of resources which will move the backward economy off dead center and only a social revolution can make it possible for the government to plan effectively.

Baran's reasoning is grounded upon an underconsumptionist view of the capitalist process and a misinterpretation of the classic pattern of long-term capital movements. But as a description of postwar American foreign policy, his analysis rings all too true. There is no doubt that the urge for economic development is a force profoundly subversive of the prevailing social order in many backward countries. Furthermore, under existing conditions in Asia and Africa, industrialization seems to require a degree of state planning that the average congressman would call socialism. Given the risk of nationalization one cannot expect much help from private foreign investment and it is probably true that the only way to remove the uncertainty which now deters the private investor is to obtain such concessions and guarantees as would seem to threaten the national independence of the backward countries. Faced with a Congress hostile to generous foreign aid and obsessed with the Communist Menace at the expense of every other consideration, the State Department swung over to the easy view that the best aid is military aid. And since neutralism was regarded as a half-way house to Communism, most military aid was given to Turkey, Korea, and Pakistan, while India—the backward country with the best chance of early rapid development—went neglected. But this only shows that the United States has failed to develop any definite point of view about the backward areas, not that Washington watches over the interests of the business community who are inevitably hostile to economic growth in the low-income countries.

When the Second World War drew to a close Great Britain was quick to realize that her former colonies could no longer be returned and was generous in granting independence. Even Malaya, with its immense dollar-earning capacity, was given up. Holland and France, on the other hand, refused to surrender their colonies until forced to do so at gun-point. But in the Suez incident and the Cyprus War Britain denied her own claim that colonial rule is justifiable only in so far as it trains a people for self-government. America fulfilled her democratic promises to the Philippines but in Guatemala and Guam took upon herself the mantle of imperialism. The inconsistency of behavior in each case suggests the dominance of political over economic considerations. Time and time again in the last fifteen years we have witnessed cases in which the major powers have set into motion every lever of diplomatic intrigue, economic pressure, and political subversion to overthrow some recalcitrant national government and to replace it with a dependable regime. But Yugoslavia and Hungary remind us that these incidents prove nothing about the nature of capitalism or of economic imperialism.

Most of the underdeveloped nations in the world are located in the tropical zones below the equator and have only recently emerged from colonial status. But before we conclude that economic backwardness is due to climate or to imperialism, let us recall that incomes per head are higher in Venezuela, Argentina, and Brazil than in Greece, Portugal, and Southern Italy; that Catholic Spain is no more industrialized than Catholic Ireland or most of Catholic Central America; that the regions of recent settlement were once colonies but colonies settled by migrants imbued with the philosophy of capitalism; that India and Egypt, thanks to the British legacy, are the two backward countries most likely to attain self-sustaining economic growth in the near future, and that Puerto Rico has already done so by creating a favorable climate for investment from the mainland; that Indonesia lags generations behind India owing to the Dutch system of legal pluralism and the dual civil service, combined with discriminatory treatment of native entrepreneurs. It is difficult to see how such differences could be explained on the basis of the Marxist theory of economic imperialism. Indeed, nothing is more curious than the compliment which Marxism is forever paying to the science of economics by attempting to subordinate all political and cultural considerations to economic ones. It seems clear, however, that neither the pattern of territorial expansion nor the foreign policy of the Great Powers, nor even the differential impact of capitalism upon the various regions of the world can be traced exclusively or even predominantly to forces one could properly describe as economic.

Nothing that is said, however, against the Marxist conception of imperialism should prevent us from examining the free play of certain economic forces which have operated adversely to the underdeveloped areas. A criticism of the Leninist doctrine merely clears the way for an adequate explanation of the widening income-gap between the developed and the underdeveloped nations. For it is a striking fact that almost every densely populated ex-colonial country has failed to achieve self-sustaining economic growth. If imperialist exploitation is not the answer, what is? Some economists have argued that the terms of trade have long been relatively unfavorable to the primary producing countries—the prices of raw materials and foodstuffs falling relative to the prices of manufactured goods—not because of monopolistically regulated trade or even low labor costs but because productivity has improved less rapidly in primary production than in manufacturing activity. In this way, the pattern of world trade in the last century has tended to widen the gap in income between the rich-industrial and poor-rural countries. Others have noted that the capital which is nowadays flowing to underdeveloped areas gravitates predominantly to the Middle East to exploit natural resources, not native labor. In so doing it creates a dual economy: on the one hand a highly developed foreign enclave, and on the other an insulated subsistence-economy which remains impervious to the forces of growth. This implies no sinister conspiracy to prevent development: the poverty of local consumers and the absence of social overhead facilities simply provide no incentives for investment in domestic manufacture. No wonder foreign capital prefers to work for export to the industrial countries. But this is only to say that concerted planning will be necessary to produce growth in all sectors.

Whatever the benefits of Western enterprises in raising the incomes of the native population directly employed, in providing tax receipts for local government, in constructing roads, railways, and power stations, in conveying technical skills and knowledge, the truth remains that the indigenous culture is often disrupted without putting anything in its place, while the introduction of Western public health schemes generates dangerous population explosions. The legacy of imperialism in the ex-colonies does pose a problem that cannot be solved by automatic market forces working themselves out. The West can do much to promote development of the backward areas, but not until both sides abandon the idea that colonies are indispensable to advanced capitalist countries and that the developed economies are rich only because they plundered Asia and Africa.

The Marxist doctrine of economic imperialism is after all only a genus of a species: to wit, the art of attributing all the ills of mankind in the last 200 years to capitalism. When anti-Communist writers play the game in reverse—making forced labor camps and political purge trials the inevitable products of socialism—Marxists are the first to object. But they cannot have it both ways: what is sauce for the goose is sauce for the gander.

Notes on the Theory of Imperialism[1]

Paul A. Baran
and Paul M. Sweezy

Paul Sweezy taught at Harvard University from 1934 to 1946. He has also been a visiting professor of economics at Cornell University, Stanford University, and the New School of Social Research. Besides being a co-editor of *Monthly Review,* he has published several books, which include *The Theory of Capitalist Development* (1942), *The Present as History* (1943), *Monopoly Capital: An Essay on the American Economic and Social Order* (with Paul Baran, 1966).

Paul A. Baran was, until his death in 1964, Professor of Economics at Stanford University. Born in the Ukraine, he was educated in Germany and the Soviet Union and moved to the United States on the eve of the Second World War. After wartime military service, he joined the staff of the Federal Reserve Bank of New York, leaving to become a member of the Stanford economics faculty in 1949. His book *The Political Economy of Growth* (1947) is recognized as one of the most important contributions to Marxian thought in recent decades.

The authors, perhaps the two foremost scholars of Marxian thought in the United States, point out that the traditional Marxist view of the industrialists and the bankers as the important actors on the imperialist stage does not explain the phenomenon as it exists today. It is through the analysis of the giant corporation of today that one can comprehend the functioning of contemporary imperialism.

The Marxian theory of imperialism, as developed chiefly by Hilferding, Rosa Luxemburg, and Lenin and since accepted with but few modifications by most Marxists, has served at least three major purposes. First, it provides a theory of international relations within the capitalist world, encompassing not only relations between advanced and underdeveloped countries but also among the advanced countries themselves. Second, it contributes to the clarification of the development of social and political conditions within the various capitalist countries, both advanced and underdeveloped. And third, it purports to provide an important part of the explanation of strictly economic tendencies and

[1]Reprinted by permission of Monthly Review Inc. from *Monthly Review,* Vol. 17, No. 10, March 1966.

trends within the advanced capitalist countries. In this third connection, two points have been usually stressed. The unequal relations between the developed and underdeveloped countries result in the establishment of terms of trade which greatly favor the former at the expense of the latter. In this way wealth is transferred from the poor countries to the rich, and the disposable surplus of the rich—which can be used to support parasitic classes, a "workers' aristocracy", as well as for normal purposes of capital accumulation—is vastly expanded. But imperialism, by putting capital export at the very center of the economic stage,[2] is also supposed to provide a crucially important outlet for the surplus of the rich countries. In the terminology of bourgeois economics, capital export expands effective demand and thereby raises income and employment above what they otherwise would have been. It is this last aspect of the traditional theory of imperialism which seems to us to be in particular need of rethinking in the light of conditions existing today, nearly half a century after publication of Lenin's classic work. As we hope to make clear, even within the confines of a brief exploratory essay, the problem is very much more complicated than Marxists have been wont to think, and the breadth and depth of its ramifications can hardly be exaggerated.

I

At the outset it must be stressed that the familiar national aggregates—Gross National Product, national income, employment, etc.—are almost entirely irrelevant to the explanation of imperialist behavior. In capitalist societies, these are *ex post* calculations which play little if any causal role.[3] Nor does it make any difference whether the "costs" of imperialism (in terms of military outlays, losses in wars, aid to client states, and the like) are greater or less than the "returns", for the simple reason that the costs are borne by the public at large while the returns accrue to that small, but usually dominant, section of the capitalist class which has extensive international interests. If these two points are kept firmly in mind, it will be seen that

2"Under the old type of capitalism," Lenin wrote, "when free competition prevailed, the export of commodities was the most typical feature. Under modern capitalism, when monopolies prevail, the export of *capital* has become the typical feature." *(Imperialism, the Highest Stage of Capitalism, Chapter 4).*

3To be sure, depressions and mass unemployment have pushed capitalist governments into armaments expansion, agressive foreign policy and even war, but the analysis of these crucially important problems is a task of the general theory of monopoly capitalism which is obviously much broader than the classical "pure" theory of imperialism.

all liberal and Social Democratic efforts to refute Marxian, or for that matter any other predominantly economic theories of imperialism on the ground that in some sense or other it "doesn't pay", have no claim to scientific standing.[4]

All of which is only another way of saying that the relevant actors on the imperialist stage are classes and their subdivisions down to and including their individual members. And this means in the first instance the dominant classes in the most advanced capitalist countries to which the less developed and underdeveloped countries stand in various relations of subordination. In terms of the total system, these are the classes which have the power of initiative: they are, so to speak, the independent variables. The behavior of other classes—including the subordinate classes in the dominant countries as well as both the dominant and the subordinate classes in the subordinate countries—is primarily reactive. One of the most important tasks of a theory of imperialism is therefore to analyse the composition and interests of the dominant classes in the dominant countries.

At the expense of some oversimplification, we can say that the traditional Marxist view has been that the imperialist ruling classes are made up of industrialists and bankers and that a certain characteristic evolution has taken place in the relations between the two groups. In the first phase—up to the closing decades of the 19th century—the industrialists played the leading role. Their interests in the underdeveloped countries were of two kinds: as sources of cheap food and raw materials which would have the effect of raising the rate of surplus value and lowering the organic composition of capital, thus doubly boosting the rate of profit, and as markets for manufactured goods which would help to solve the realization problem. Both these ends would best be served by free trade and free competition which could be counted upon to turn the underdeveloped countries into complementary appendages of the advanced countries.

The second phase, beginning around 1880 or so, is characterized by the dominance of finance capital. Concentration and centralization

---

[4]It should perhaps be added that in addition to being based on a fatal methodological error, these alleged refutations of economic theories of imperialism usually rely on arguments which can only be described as nonsensical. In this connection a good recent example is Hans Neisser's *Economic Imperialism Reconsidered,* "Social Research," Spring 1960. Neisser would like to compare what the capitalist world is like today with what it would have been like "if western economic penetration of the rest of the world had stopped at the beginning of the nineteenth century" (p. 73.). That this involves a wholly fanciful and arbitrary invention of a century and a half of world history does not trouble him in the least.

of capital lead to spread of the corporate form, of stock markets, etc. In this context, bankers (investment bankers in the United States) seize the initiative, promote mergers and monopolies over which they establish their dominance, and thus become the leading echelon of the capitalist class. Since the bankers deal in capital rather than in commodities, their primary interest in the underdeveloped countries is in exporting capital to them at highest possible rates of profit. This end, however, is not furthered by free trade and free competition. Finance capitalists in each imperialist country want to establish an exclusive domain out of which they can keep their rivals and within which they can fully protect their investments. Hence the vigorous revival of empire-building—somewhat in abeyance since mercantile days—in the closing decades of the 19th century. There is, of course, no implication that export of capital is in conflict with the aims of the preceding period—raw materials and markets—for, on the contrary, they complement each other nicely. It is only that in the Hilferding-Lenin theory it is the export of capital which dominates imperialist policy.

This theory, taken together with Lenin's very important Law of Uneven Development, worked well in explaining the main lines of development of the world economy and of world politics in the period before the First World War. Since then, however, certain changes in the characteristics of the ruling classes in the dominant countries have taken place which need to be taken into account in the development of the theory.

II

One can no longer today speak of either industrialists or bankers as the leading echelon of the dominant capitalist classes. The big monopolistic corporations, which were formed and in their early years controlled by bankers, proved to be enormously profitable and in due course, through paying off their debts and plowing back their earnings, achieved financial independence and indeed in many cases acquired substantial control over banks and other financial institutions. These giant corporations are the basic units of monopoly capitalism in its present stage; their (big) owners and functionaries constitute the leading echelon of the ruling class. It is through analysing these corporate giants and their interests that we can best comprehend the functioning of imperialism today.

In size, complexity of structure, and multiplicity of interests the corporate giant of today differs markedly from the industrialist or the banker of an earlier period. This can be most graphically illustrated by an actual case, and for this purpose we can hardly do better than select Standard Oil of New Jersey (hereafter referred to as Standard or Jersey). This corporation was the earliest of its kind anywhere in the world; it is today the second largest industrial corporation in the world (second only to General Motors); and its international ramifications are at least as complicated and far reaching as those of any other corporation. It shows in clearest and most developed form the "ideal type" to which hundreds of other giant corporations, both in the United States and in the other advanced capitalist countries, are more or less close approximations.

Here, in brief summary form, are some of the most important data about the size, structure, and operations of Jersey.[5]

Size. As of December 31, 1962, Jersey had total assets of $11,488 million. Its aggregate revenues for the year 1962 came to $10,567 million, and its net income to $841 million (*Form 10K*).

Geographical distribution of assets and earnings. As of the end of 1958, the percentage distribution of earnings and assets by various regions was as follows *(Notice)*:

	Assets	Earnings
U.S. and Canada	67	34
Latin America	20	39
Eastern Hemisphere	13	27
Total	100	100

Rate of return on stockholders' equity. During 1962 the percentage rates for return on stockholders' equity in different regions were as follows *(Annual Report)*:

United States	7.4
Other Western Hemisphere	17.6
Eastern Hemisphere	15.0

Number of subsidiaries. As of the end of 1962, Jersey owned 50 per cent or more of the stock in 275 subsidiaries in 52 countries. The following is a list of the number of such subsidiaries by country or organization (*Form 10K*):

[5]The sources are the company's *1962 Annual Report,* its *Notice of Special Stockholders' Meeting* (October 7, 1959), and its *Form 10-K for the Fiscal Year Ended December 31, 1962,* filed with the Securities and Exchange Commission pursuant to Section 13 of the Securities Act of 1934. These sources are identified as *Annual Report, Notice,* and *Form 10-K* respectively.

U.S.A.	77	Neth. Antilles	3
Canada	37	Norway	3
Great Britain	24	Austria	2
Panama	17	Belgium	2
France	12	Bermuda	2
Bahamas	8	Iraq	2
Italy	6	Malaya	2
Morocco	2	Egypt	1
Switzerland	2	El Salvador	1
Uruguay	2	Finland	1
Venezuela	2	Hungary	1
Algeria	1	India	1
Dominican Republic	1	Indonesia	1
Sweden	6	Kenya	1
Colombia	5	Luxemburg	1
Netherlands	5	Madagascar	1
Australia	4	Mexico	1
Brazil	4	New Zealand	1
Chile	4	Paraguay	1
Germany	4	Peru	1
Philippines	4	Republic of Congo	1
Argentina	3	Singapore	1
Denmark	3	South Africa	1
Ireland	3	Spain	1
Japan	3	Surinam	1
		Tunisia	1

Recapitulating by regions, we find that Jersey had 114 subsidiaries in the United States and Canada, 43 in Latin America, 77 in Europe, 14 in Asia, 9 in Africa, and 18 in other regions.

Countries marketed in. According to the *Annual Report,* Jersey sold to "more than 100" countries in 1962.

It would obviously be wrong to expect a corporation like this to behave like a British cotton mill owner interested in getting his raw cotton from abroad at the lowest possible price and in exporting his products to a duty-free India, or like a Rothschild or a Morgan disposing over great amounts of liquid capital and interested in investing it abroad at the highest attainable rate of profit. Standard's interests are much more complicated. Take, for example, the question of exports and imports. Though Standard, through its principal U.S. affiliate, Humble Oil and Refining Company, is one of the biggest producers in the country, the company is definitely not interested in protectionist measures. Quite to the contrary, it is a strong opponent of the present system of controls which limit the importation of fuel oil.[6] "In the interests of consumers, the national economy, and the international relations of our country", states the 1962 *Annual Report,* "we hope that these unnecessary controls not only will be relaxed...but will be completely removed". Behind this public spiritedness, of course, lies Standard's interest in having its relatively low-cost Venezuelan subsidiary, Creole Petroleum, sell freely in the lucrative East Coast fuel-oil market.

Or take the question of capital exports. On the face of it, one might be tempted to conclude from the tremendous magnitude and variety of Standard's foreign operations that over the years the corporation has been a large and consistent exporter of capital. The conclusion, however, would not be justified. From the data presented above, it appears clearly that foreign operations are much more profitable than domestic, and this has been the case since the early days of the corporation. Under these conditions, a small initial export of capital could, and undoubtedly did, expand rapidly through the reinvestment of its own earnings. Not only that. So great have been the profits of foreign operations that in most years even after the needs of expansion have been covered, large sums have been available for remittance to the parent corporation in the United States. The year 1962 may be taken as an example: Standard paid out dividends to its shareholders, the vast majority of whom are resident in the United States, a total of $538 million. In the same year, however, operations in the United States produced a net income of only $309 million. It follows that some 40 per cent of dividends plus whatever net investment may have been made in the United States during the year were financed from the profits of foreign operations. Far from being an exporter of capital, the corporation is a large and consistent *importer* of capital into the United States.

The foregoing gives hardly more than a hint of the complexity of Standard's interests. It takes no account of the fact that the oil industry as organized by the giant international corporations is in reality a congeries of businesses: extraction of the raw material from the subsoil, transportation by pipe-line and tanker, processing in some of the most technologically advanced plants in the world, and finally selling a variety of products in markets all over the world. Nor is Standard confined to the oil industry even in this comprehensive sense. It is a large and growing supplier of natural gas to the gas pipe-line companies; it is a major producer of artificial rubber, plastics, resins, and other petrochemical products; and it re-

[6]The existence of these import restrictions is a reflection of the great political power of the oil- and gas-producing states, especially exercised through the Democratic Party.

cently entered the fertilizer business with plans which, according to the 1962 *Annual Report,* "will make Jersey an important factor in the world fertilizer industry". Finally, Jersey, like other giant corporations, maintains a large research and development program the purpose of which is not only to lower costs and hence increase profits from existing operations but also to invent new products and open up new lines of business. As an illustration of the latter, we may cite the following from the 1962 *Annual Report*: "Food from oil through biological fermentation is an intriguing possibility. Esso Research, in a small pilot plant, has produced a white powder that resembles powdered milk or yeast. It is odorless, has a bland taste, and is high in protein and B vitamins. The first goal is to develop food supplements for animals, but it is hoped that the technique may one day help to improve the diet and health of the world's growing population". Quite a promising market, one must admit.

This is, of course, not the place for a detailed examination of the structure and interests of Standard Oil or any other corporation. But enough has been said, we hope, to carry the conviction that such a huge and complicated institutional "capitalist" can hardly be assumed to have exactly the same attitudes and behavior patterns as the industrial or finance capitalists of classical Marxian theory. But before we explore this subject further, we must ask whether Standard Oil is indeed an ideal type which helps us to distil the essence of capitalist reality, or whether on the contrary it may not be an exceptional case which we should rather ignore than put at the center of the analytical stage.

III

Up to the Second World War, it would have been correct to treat Standard Oil as a sort of exception—a very important one, to be sure, exercising tremendous, and at times even decisive, influence on United States world policy. Nevertheless, in the world-wide scope and ramifications of its operations not only was it far ahead of all others; there were only a handful that could be said to be developing along the same lines. Many U.S. corporations of course had large interests in exports or imports, and quite a few had foreign branches or subsidiaries. In neither respect, however, was the situation much different from what it had been in 1929. Direct investments of U.S. corporations indeed declined slightly between 1929 and 1946.[7] Most

7The figure was $7.5 billion in 1929 and $7.2 billion in 1946. U.S. Department of Commerce, Office of Business Economics, *U.S. Business Investments in Foreign Countries: A Supplement to the Survey of Current Business,* 1960, p. 1.

of the giant corporations which dominated the U.S. economy were, in the words of "Business Week", "domestically oriented enterprises with international operations" and not, like Standard Oil, "truly world oriented corporations."[8]

A big change took place during the next decade and a half. To quote "Business Week" again: "In industry after industry, U.S. companies found that their overseas earnings were soaring, and that their return on investment abroad was frequently much higher than in the U.S. As earnings abroad began to rise, profit margins from domestic operations started to shrink ... This is the combination that forced development of the multinational company."[9] The foreign direct investments of U.S. corporations increased sharply—from the already cited figure of $7.2 billion in 1946 to $34.7 billion in 1961.[10] While this tremendous jump of course involved actual capital exports by many individual companies, it cannot be over-emphasized that for the United States as a whole the amount of income transferred to the United States on direct investment account far exceeded the direct capital outflow. The two series, which can be constructed from official government statistics for the years 1950 and later, are shown on the opposite page.

From the figures presented it will be seen that from 1950 through 1961, U.S. corporations were able to expand their direct foreign investments by $27.5 billion while at the same time taking in as income $9.5 billion more than they sent out as capital. Foreign investment, it seems, far from being a means of developing underdeveloped countries, is a most efficient device for transferring wealth from poorer to richer countries while at the same time enabling the richer to expand their control over the economies of the poorer.

But this is not the aspect of the matter which primarily concerns us at the moment. The point is that in the course of expanding their foreign assets and operations in this spectacular way, most

---

[8]*Multinational Companies,* A Special Report, "Business Week," April 20, 1963. It is interesting to note that in the United States, the business press is often far ahead of economists in recognizing, and even attempting to analyse, the latest developments in the capitalist economy.

[9]*Ibid.* The shrinkage of profit margins in the U.S. economy, beginning as early as 1950 and in spite of unprecedentedly rapid technological progress and slowly rising unemployment, is a complete mystery to bourgeois thought, both journalistic and academic. Since it is obviously impossible to pursue this subject within the confines of this essay, we must be content to refer the reader to a forthcoming work, tentatively entitled *Monopoly Capital,* by the present authors.

[10]U.S. Department of Commerce, *Survey of Current Business,* August 1962, p. 22.

Year	Net Direct Investment Capital Outflow ($ Millions)	Direct Investment Income ($ Millions)
1950	621	1.294
1951	528	1.492
1952	850	1.419
1953	722	1.442
1954	664	1.725
1955	779	1.975
1956	1.859	2.120
1957	2.058	2.313
1958	1.094	2.198
1959	1.372	2.206
1960	1.694	2.348
1961	1.467	2.672
Totals	13.708	23.204

Sources: U.S. Department of Commerce, *Survey of Current Business*, November 1954, pp. 9, 13; August 1955, pp. 18, 20; August 1957, p. 25; August 1959, p. 31; August 1961, pp. 22-23; August 1962, pp. 22-23.

of the corporate giants which dominate the U.S. economy have taken the road long since pioneered by Standard Oil. They have become, in "Business Week's" terminology, multinational corporations.[11] It is not enough that a multinational corporation should have a base of operations abroad; its true *differential specifica* is that "its management makes fundamental decision on marketing, production, and research in terms of the alternatives that are available to it anywhere in the world."[12] This, of course, is what Standard Oil has been doing since roughly the beginning of the century. The difference is that what was then the exception has today become the rule.

I V

One cannot say of the giant multinational company of today that it is primarily interested, like the industrialist of the 19th century, in the export of commodities; or, like the banker of the early 20th century, in the export of capital. General Motors, for example, produces automobiles for the rapidly expanding European market not

[11]The term seems to have originated with David E. Lilienthal, Director of the Tennessee Valley Authority under Roosevelt and of the Atomic Energy Commission under Truman, and now Chairman of the Development and Resources Corporation which appears to be backed and controlled by the international banking house of Lazard Freres. A paper delivered by Mr. Lilienthal at the Carnegie Institute of Technology in April, 1960, and later published by Development and Resources Corporation, bears the title *The Multinational Corporation*.

[12]*Business Week's* "Multinational Companies."

in Detroit but in Britain and West Germany; and it probably exports many more from its European subsidiaries to the under-developed countries than it does from the United States. In many cases, indeed, the foreign subsidiaries of U.S. companies are large-scale exporters to the U.S. market. In 1957, for example, the aggregate sales (excluding intercorporate petroleum sales) of direct-investment enterprises abroad was $32 billion. Of this amount, more than $3.5 billion (11 per cent) was exported to the United States.[13] Considering that aggregate merchandise imports into the United States in 1957 came to $13.2 billion, it is a most striking fact that more than a quarter of this total was supplied by the foreign subsidiaries of U.S. companies. And as for capital export, we have already seen that U.S. multinational companies are on balance massive importers, not exporters, of capital.

What all this means is that one must beware of easy generalizations about the specifically economic interests of the leading actors on the imperialist stage. Their interests are in fact variegated and complex, often contradictory rather than complementary. Subsidiaries of a U.S. company in two foreign countries may both be in a good position to export to a third country. If one gets the business, the interests of the other will be damaged. Which should be favored? Or a certain company produces raw materials through a subsidiary in one country, processes the materials through another subsidiary in a second country, and sells the finished product through yet another subsidiary in the United States. Intercorporate prices can be so fixed as to allocate revenues and profits in any number of ways among the subsidiaries and countries. Which set of prices should actually be selected? These examples illustrate the kind of problem which the top managements of the multinational corporations have to solve every day; and about the only valid generalization one can make is that in every case they will seek a solution which maximizes the (long-run) profits of the enterprise as a whole. And this of course means that whenever necessary to the furtherance of this goal, the interests of particular subsidiaries and countries will be ruthlessly sacrificed. This is admitted with refreshing candor by the authors of the "Business Week" report already cited: "The goal, in the multinational corporation, is the greatest good for the whole unit, even if the interests of a single part of the unit must suffer. One large U.S. manufacturer, for example, concedes that it penalizes some

---

[13]U.S. Department of Commerce, *U.S. Business Investments in Foreign Countries*, p. 3.

of its overseas subsidiaries for the good of the total corporation by forcing them to pay more than necessary for parts they import from the parent and from other subsidiaries. Says one of the company's executives: 'We do this in countries where we either anticipate or already face restrictions on profit repatriation. We want some way to get our money out.' "

A whole treatise could—and should—be written about the way the national interests of the subordinate countries fare under the regime of multinational corporations. Here we will have to be content with one illustration—a case which is less well known than it deserves to be but which we believe to be fully typical. One of the most important natural resources of the Caribbean area is bauxite. Jamaica, Surinam, British Guiana, and the Dominican Republic are all important producers, with operations being organized and controlled by a few U.S. and one Canadian corporate giants. Separate figures on the operations of these subsidiaries are not published. However, the U.S. Department of Commerce does report the profits accruing to U.S. mining companies on their operations in Western Hemisphere dependencies of European countries, at least 90 per cent of which must be attributable to bauxite production in Jamaica, Surinam, and British Guiana. Adding a conservatively estimated figure for profits of the Canadian company, profits from operations in these three countries in 1961 were between $70 and $75 million on an investment estimated at between $220 and $270 million.[14] This profit rate of between 26 and 34 per cent suggests, in the opinion of Philip Reno, that "this could well be among the most profitable U.S. investment structures in the world." However, this is only part of the story. Commerce Department figures give current costs of U.S. aluminum company operations in the three countries for 1957. Of the total of $81 million, no less than $31 million, or almost 40 per cent, are classified under the heading of "Materials and Services." Since it is simply incomprehensible how materials and services could constitute so large a share of the costs of an extractive operation of this kind (more than 50 per cent greater than wages and salaries), one can only conclude that this item is artificially padded to cover excessive payments to U.S. shipping, insurance, and other interests. In this manner, profits (and hence taxes) can be kept down and funds can be remitted from the colony to the metropolis.

[14] All figures are from an article "Aluminum Profits and Caribbean People," by Philip Reno, *Monthly Review,* October 1963. Mr. Reno spent several months in British Guiana studying the operations of the aluminum companies.

Nor is even this all. The price of bauxite produced in the United States doubled in the two decades from 1939 to 1959, while the price of bauxite imported from Surinam and British Guiana remained almost the same throughout the whole period. This means that profits which should have been realized by the subsidiary companies and been taxed by the Surinam and British Guiana governments were in fact realized in the United States. At length, however, the parent aluminum companies, with one exception, began to alter this price structure, and here we get a revealing glimpse of the kind of considerations that determine the policy decision of the multinational corporations. In Philip Reno's words: "The prices set on bauxite from all the Caribbean countries except British Guiana did finally begin to rise a few years ago. The explanation lies with the law granting tax concessions to U.S. companies operating in other countries of this Hemisphere through what are called Western Hemisphere Trade Corporations. Instead of a 52 per cent corporate income tax, Western Hemisphere Trade Corporations pay the U.S. only 25 per cent. By raising the price of bauxite, U.S. companies could now reduce their total income taxes. The price of bauxite began to rise for the first time in 20 years, except for British Guiana bauxite mined by Altd, Canada-based and unaffected by Western Hemisphere Trade Corporation maneuvers."

If this is a fair sample of how the underdeveloped countries are treated by the multinational companies, it does not follow that these giant enterprises are any more concerned to promote the national interests of the advanced countries, including even the one in which their headquarters are situated. Quite apart from particular actions—like the Ford Motor Company's remittance abroad of several hundred million dollars to buy out the minority interest in Ford of Britain at a time when the U.S. government was expressing serious concern about the state of the country's balance of payments—a plausible argument could be made that in the last fifteen years U.S. corporations have developed their foreign operations at the expense of, and often in direct competition with, their domestic operations and that these policies have constituted one of the causes of the lagging growth rate of the U.S. economy and hence of the rising trend of unemployment which is now perhaps the nation's number one domestic problem. Whether or not this is really the case—and it would probably be impossible to *prove* either that it is or isn't—it remains true that the decisions and actions of the multinational companies are taken solely with a view to promoting the interests of the companies themselves and that whatever effects, beneficial or injurious, they may

have on the various countries in which they operate are strictly
incidental.

V

Does this mean that the giant multinational companies have no interests in common on which they can unite? Are there no *general*
policies which they expect their governments—and the governments
of the dominant imperialist states are indeed theirs—to follow? The
answer is that there are common interests and desired general policies,
but that for the most part they are not narrowly economic in nature.
The multinational companies often have conflicting interests when it
comes to tariffs, export subsidies, foreign investment, etc. But they
are absolutely united on two things: First, they want the world
of nations in which they can operate to be as large as possible.
And second, they want its laws and institutions to be favorable
to the unfettered development of private capitalist enterprise. Or to
put the point in another way, their ideal would be a world of nations
in every one of which they could operate uninhibited by local
obstacles to their making and freely disposing of maximum attainable
profits. This means not only that they are opposed to revolutions
which threaten to exclude them altogether from certain areas—as,
for example, the Cuban Revolution excluded all U.S. corporations
from Cuba—but also that they are adamantly opposed to all forms
of state capitalism (using the term in its broadest sense) which
might tend to hamper their own operations or to reserve potentially
profitable areas of economic activity for the nationals of the countries
in question.[15] Their attitude is well expressed in the 1962 *Annual
Report* of Standard Oil on which we have already drawn for illustrative
material: "Both at home and abroad, a greater awareness is needed
of the importance of private investment to economic progress. Some
countries have shown a trend toward state enterprise both through
government participation in new commercial ventures and through
nationalization of established private businesses. The interest of these
nations will best be served, however, by fostering societies that are
based on those principles of free enterprise which have produced the
outstanding economic development of many other nations. It is reassur-
ing to see steps taken—such as the Hickenlooper Amendment to the
Foreign Assistance Act of 1961—to ensure that economic assistance

---

[15]This does not mean, of course, that they oppose foreign governments' undertaking public works—roads, harbors, public health and education programs, etc.,
etc.—of a kind that will benefit their own operations. For such beneficent activities
they even favor generous "foreign aid" from their own government.

funds from the United States encourage a climate of progress by emphasizing the importance and protection of private investment in nations receiving aid from the United States." It would be wrong to think that the management of Standard Oil opposes government enterprise in the subordinate countries because of a naive belief that state action is identical with socialism. The explanation is much more rational: government enterprise and state action in these countries generally represent attempts on the part of the native bourgeoisies to appropriate for themselves a larger share of locally produced surplus at the expense of the multinational companies. It is only natural that such attempts should be resolutely opposed by the multinational companies.

The general policy which the multinational companies require of their government can thus be summed up in a simple formula: to make a world safe for Standard Oil. In more ideological terms, this means to protect the "free world" and to extend its boundaries wherever and whenever possible, which of course has been the proclaimed aim of U.S. policy ever since the promulgation of the "Truman Doctrine" in 1947. The negative side of the coin is anti-Communism. The necessary complement is the building up and maintenance of a tremendous global military machine.

All the major struggles going on in the world today can be traced to this hunger of the multinational corporations for maximum *Lebensraum*. And the connection usually has a direct, immediate, and visible aspect. We cite just two facts relative to Cuba and Vietnam where the essence of present-day imperialist policy can be seen in its clearest form. Under the heading "Standard Oil Co. (New Jersey)", in Standard and Poor's *Standard Corporate Descriptions,* dated July 24, 1961, we learn that "loss of $62,269,000 resulting from expropriation of Cuban properties in 1960 was charged to earned surplus." And from the same company's 1962 *Annual Report* we learn that "Jersey continues to look for attractive opportunities both in areas where we now operate and in those where we do not," and that the following are among the measures being taken to implement this policy: "A refinery in which the company will have majority interest is under construction in Malaya, and affiliates have part interests in a refinery under construction in Australia and one that is being planned for Vietnam".

Losses in Cuba, plans for South Vietnam: what more eloquent commentary could there be on the struggles now going on in and around those two little countries on opposite sides of the globe?

The Effects of British
Imperial Policy[1]

Robert P. Thomas

Robert P. Thomas is Professor of Economics at the University of Washington in Seattle. The present article is in the tradition of the "new economic history." The author attempts to measure the impact of the imperial navigation acts on the welfare of the American colonies.

Historians have long debated whether the American colonies on balance benefited or were hindered by British imperial regulation. George Bancroft thought the regulations worked a definite hardship on the colonies. George L. Beer believed these regulations nicely balanced and that the colonies shared in the general advantages. Lawrence Harper, in a now classic article, actually attempted to calculate the cost and found that British policies "placed a heavy burden upon the colonies."[2] Oliver Dickerson wrote that "no case can be made . . . that such laws were economically oppressive,"[3] while Curtis P. Nettels, writing at the same time to the same point, stated: "British policy as it affected the colonies after 1763 was restrictive, injurious, negative."[4] It is quite evident that a difference of opinion

[1]Reprinted from "A Quantitative Approach to the Study of the Effects of British Imperial Policy upon Colonial Welfare: Some Preliminary Findings," *The Journal of Economic History*, Vol. XXV, No. 4, 1965, pages 615-638. The paper is a progress report on one aspect of a larger study of the effects of British imperial policy upon colonial welfare. All computations in this study are preliminary and subject to revision. I have benefited from conversations with many persons, especially Douglass C. North and James Shepherd. The former was especially helpful in pointing out several errors in a previous draft. Since I did not take all his advice, he is not responsible for any errors that may remain. J. N. Sharma and James Livingston served ably as my research assistants. The National Science Foundation provided support for the project on which this paper is based. An appendix explaining how the calculations were made has been deleted, but it is available to the interested reader from the author.

[2]"Mercantilism and the American Revolution," *Canadian Historical Review*, XXIII (Mar. 1942), 3.

[3]*The Navigation Act and the American Revolution* (Philadelphia: University of Pennsylvania Press, 1951), p. 55.

[4]"British Mercantilism and the Economic Development of the Thirteen Colonies," *Journal of Economic History*, XII, No. 2 (Spring 1952), 114.

exists among reputable colonial historians over this important historical issue.

In this paper an effort is made to meet this issue head on.
I shall attempt to measure, relative to a hypothetical alternative,
the extent of the burdens and benefits stemming from imperial regulation of the foreign commerce of the thirteen colonies. The main
instruments of this regulation were the Navigation Acts, and we shall
confine our attention to evaluating the effect of these Acts upon
colonial welfare. Various other imperial regulations such as the
Revenue Acts, enacted after 1764, the modification of naturalization
and land regulations, the interference with colonial issues of paper
money, and the various regulations discouraging manufactures will
not be dealt with in this paper. The assumption is that the direct
effects of these regulations upon the economic welfare of the American
colonists were insignificant compared to the effects of the Navigation
Acts.[5]

The hypothesis of this paper is that membership in the British
Empire, after 1763, did not impose a significant hardship upon the
American colonies. To test this hypothesis I shall endeavor to bias
the estimates against the hypothesis, thus not attempting to state
what actually would have happened but only that it would not
have amounted to as much as my estimate. The end result will,
therefore, err on the side of overstating the real costs of the Navigation
Acts to the thirteen colonies.

The traditional tools of economic theory will guide the preparation of these estimates. Two series of estimates will be prepared
where possible: one, an annual average for the period 1763-1772, based
upon official values; the other, for the single year 1770. The official
trade statistics for the year 1770 have been adjusted to make them
more accurate.[6]

I

*Is it legitimate for the historian to consider alternative possibilities
to events which have happened? ... To say that a thing happened
the way it did is not at all illuminating. We can understand the*

---

[5] The effects of British regulations not considered in this paper will be taken
into account in the larger study now in process.

[6] The statistics on colonial exports have been adjusted in a manner suggested
by James Shepherd and used by him in preparing his balance of payments for the
colonial period. Imports, due to a lack of prices, were adjusted by the Schumpeter-
Gilboy price index.

significance of what did happen only if we contrast it with what might have happened.

Morris Raphael Cohen[7]

All attempts at measurement require a standard to which the object being measured is made relative or compared. In the case of this paper, the colonies either on balance benefited or were burdened by British imperialism, relative to how they would have fared under some alternative political situation. The problem is to pick the most probable alternative situation.

The only reasonable alternative in this case is to calculate the burdens or benefits of British regulation relative to how the colonies would have fared outside the British Empire but still within a mercantilist world. Considered within this political environment there is little doubt that prior to February 1763, when the Treaty of Paris was signed, the American colonies on balance benefited from membership in the British Empire. Before that date, the colonies were threatened on two sides by two superior colonial powers. C. M. Andrews has pointed out that, before 1763, in addition to remaining within the protection of Great Britain, the American colonies had only one other alternative: domination by another European power, probably France or Spain. Clearly, from a colonial point of view, belonging to the British Empire was superior to membership in any other.[8]

The French and Indian War ended the menace of foreign domination through the cession to Great Britain of Canada by the French and of Florida by Spain.[9] Immediately, thereupon, several Englishmen voiced their fears that these spoils of victory, by removing the foreign threat, made inevitable the independence of the American colonies.[10] Even the French Foreign Minister, Choiseul, lent his voice to this speculation when, soon after the Treaty of Paris, he predicted the eventual coming of the American Revolution. In 1764, Choiseul went so far as to send his agents to America to watch developments.[11]

[7]Quoted in Robert W. Fogel, *Railroads and American Economic Growth* (Baltimore: Johns Hopkins Press, 1964), p. 17.

[8]*Journal of Economic History*, XII (1952), 114.

[9]In 1790, nearly 80 per cent of the residents of the United States traced their origin, or that of their ancestors, to the British Isles.

[10]Bernhard Knollenberg, *Origin of the American Revolution: 1759-1766* (New York: Collier Books, 1961), p. 18.

[11]Max Savelle. "The American Balance of Power and European Diplomacy, 1713-78," in Richard B. Morris, ed., *The Era of the American Revolution* (New York: Columbia University Press, 1939), p. 162.

Knollenberg has pointed out that English suspicions of a desire for independence on the part of the colonies do not prove that the suspicions were well founded.[12] They do, however, suggest that an independent America was, by 1763, a distinct possibility; and thereafter the American colonists possessed another alternative to membership in a European empire. This alternative was an independent existence outside the British Empire but still within a mercantilist world.

The alternative situation that I shall employ to calculate the economic effects of the Navigation Acts after 1763 is that of a free and independent thirteen colonies outside the British Empire. This new nation would, therefore, be subject to most of the same restrictions hindering foreign nations attempting to carry on commerce with the eighteenth-century British Empire.[13]

I I

Had the wealth and economic potential of the thirteen Atlantic colonies depended solely on farming, their growth history might have paralleled that of many another slowly developing agricultural settlement. However . . . as indigenous commercial economy developed, unique in colonial history and conducive to sustained growth.

George Rogers Taylor[14]

This "unique" commercial economy developed within the British Empire subject to the rules and regulations of the Navigation Acts. The American colonies in a sense grew up with the empire, which after the successful conclusion of the Seven Years' War in February 1763, was the wealthiest, most populous colonial empire in the world. It included the kingdom of Great Britain and Ireland with the outlying islands of Europe; trading forts on the Gold Coast of Africa; enclaves in India, and some minor islands in Asia; Newfoundland, Hudson Bay, Nova Scotia, Quebec, the thirteen American colonies, East Florida, and West Florida on the continent of North America; the Bahamas, Bermuda, Jamaica, Antigua, Barbados, and the Leeward and Windward groups of minor islands in the West Indies, as well as the settlement of Belize in Central America.

The American colonies by 1763 formed the foundation of Great Britain's Atlantic empire and had become, as a group, England's

---

[12]Knollenberg p. 19

[13]This was certainly the case after the American Revolution.

[14]"American Economic Growth Before 1850: An Exploratory Essay," *Journal of Economic History,* XXIV, No. 4 (Dec. 1964), 435.

most important commercial ally.[15] The basis of this commerce was a vigorous colonial export trade. The total exports in 1770 amounted to £3,165,225. Trade with Great Britain and Ireland accounted for 50 per cent of colonial exports. The West Indies trade constituted another 30 per cent, and commerce with southern Europe and the Wine Islands, another 17 per cent. Trade with Africa and South America accounted for most of the residual.

The colonists, of course, used their exports to purchase imports. They were Great Britain's most important customer and Great Britain their most important supplier. The British Isles shipped to the American colonies in 1768 (a year for which a detailed breakdown is available) £2,157,000 worth of goods, or nearly 75 per cent of all colonial imports, which totaled £2,890,000. Of this, £421,000 were British reexports from northern Europe.[16] The West Indies, the other important source of imports, accounted for 20.5 per cent of the colonial imports; southern Europe and the Wine Islands, 2.9 per cent; and Africa, a little less than 2.0 per cent.

The thirteen American colonies carried on this foreign commerce subject to the constraints of a series of laws designed to alter the trade of the British Empire in the interests of the mother country.[17] This commercial system can be viewed as being made up of four types of laws: (1) laws regulating the nationality, crews, and ownership of the vessels in which goods could be shipped; (2) statutes regulating the destination to which certain goods could be shipped; (3) laws designed to encourage specific primary industries via an elaborate system of rebates, drawbacks, import and export bounties, and export taxes; (4) direct prohibition of colonial industries and practices that tended to compete with English industries or to harm a prominent sector of the British economy or even, occasionally, the economy of a British colony.[18] These laws, it should

[15]B. R. Mitchell, *Abstract of British Historical Statistics* (Cambridge University Press, 1962) , p. 312.

[16]The values of imports are the official values f.o.b. Great Britain. For that reason, they are probably approximately 10 to 20 per cent too low. Import figures for 1768 were used because detailed breakdowns for 1770 were unavailable when this paper was written.

[17]Sir William Ashley thought the regulations of English mercantilism were pious formulas nullified in the actual world of commerce by fraud and evasion when they existed contrary to national commercial habits. Studies by Lawrence Harper have indicated that the burden of the Navigation Acts was in fact felt in transatlantic commerce.

[18]The Molasses Act of 1733 was a law enacted in the interest of the British West Indies. This law taxed foreign molasses sufficiently to make the molasses of the British West Indies competitive. The way was, however, widely evaded.

be stressed, did not regulate the American colonies alone, but with occasional local modifications applied equally to the entire British Empire.

The laws regulating the nationality of vessels were designed to insure a monopoly of the carrying trade of the empire to ships of the empire. In the seventeenth and eighteenth centuries the freight factor on goods traded internationally probably averaged at least 20 per cent, and these laws were designed to insure that this revenue stayed within the empire.[19] The Navigation Acts also insured, to the extent that they were effective, that England would be the entrepot of the empire and that the distributing trade would be centered in the British Isles.

The commodity clauses of these various regulatory Acts controlled the destination to which certain goods could be shipped. These enumerated commodities generally could be shipped only to England. The original list contained tobacco, sugar, indigo, cotton-wool, ginger, fustic and other dyewoods. Later, naval stores, hemp, rice, molasses, beaver skins, furs, and copper ore were added. The Sugar Act of 1764 added coffee, pimiento, coconuts, whale fins, raw silk, hides and skins, potash and pearl ash to the list. In 1766, the law was amended to prohibit the direct export of any colonial product north of Cape Finisterre.

There were exceptions and compensations to these commodity clauses which benefited the American colonies. Rice, after 1730, could be directly exported south of Cape Finisterre and, after 1764, to South America. Tobacco was given a monopoly in Great Britain, as its local cultivation was prohibited. While the list appears extensive, of the enumerated commodities only tobacco, indigo, copper ore, naval stores, hemp, furs and skins, whale fins, raw silk, and potash and pearl ash were products of the thirteen colonies, and only tobacco, rice, and perhaps indigo and naval stores could be considered major exports of the colonies that later became the United States.

An elaborate series of laws was enacted by the English Parliament to encourage specific industries in the interest of a self-sufficient empire. These included preferential tariffs for certain goods of colonial origin. A distinctive feature of these laws was an elaborate system

[19]Export commodities shipped to the West Indies were reputed by one source to be worth £ 275,000 when they left the American colonies and £ 500,000 when they arrived in the West Indies. The freight factor is thus over 30 per cent. The return trip saw excess cargo capacity and therefore lower rates. The freight factor on the return trip was but 5 per cent. Herbert C. Bell, "West Indian Trade before the Revolution," *American Historical Review*, XXII, No. 2 (Jan. 1917), 273-74.

of rebates and drawbacks to encourage the exports of certain commodities from England and extensive bounties to encourage the production of specific goods for export to Great Britain.

Most enumerated goods benefited from a preferential duty. These goods were thus given a substantial advantage in the markets of the mother country. Goods receiving preferential treatment included cotton-wool, ginger, sugar, molasses, coffee, tobacco, rice, naval stores, pitch, rosin, hemp, masts, whale fins, raw silk, potash and pearl ash, bar and pig iron, and various types of lumber. Certain of these goods also received drawbacks of various amounts upon their reexport from Great Britain. Foreign goods competing in the English market with enumerated colonial commodities were thus subject to a disadvantage from these preferential duties.

A system of bounties was also implemented to encourage the production of specific commodities in the colonies or to allow the British manufacturers to compete with foreign exports in the colonial markets. The production of naval stores, silk, lumber, indigo, and hemp was encouraged in the colonies with bounties. In the mother country the manufacture of linen, gunpowder, silks, and many non-woolen textiles was encouraged by a bounty to allow these products to compete with similar foreign manufactures in the colonial markets.

Certain of the colonial commodities favored by legislation were given what amounted to a monopoly of the home market of the mother country. The colonial production of tobacco, naval stores, sugar and sugar products was so favored. In the case of tobacco, the major share of total imports was reexported, so the local monopoly proved not a great boon.

In economic terms, the Navigation Acts were designed to insure that the vast bulk of the empire's carrying trade was in ships owned by Englishmen. The design of the commodity clauses was to alter the terms of trade to the disadvantage of the colonists, by making all foreign imports into the colonies, and many colonial exports whose final destination was the Continent, pass through England. The effect was to make colonial imports more expensive and colonial exports less remunerative by increasing the transportation costs of both. Finally, through tariff preferences, bounties, and outright prohibitions, resources were allocated from more efficient uses to less.

I shall approach the problem of assessing the overall effect of the various British regulations of trade by considering their effect on the following aspects of the colonial economy: (1) exports of colonial products; (2) imports into the colonies; (3) colonial foreign commerce; and (4) colonial shipping earnings. An assessment will then be undertaken of compensating benefits arising from membership in the British Empire. Finally, an attempt will be made to strike a balance on the total impact of British imperial policy upon the colonial economy.

I I I

The enumeration of key colonial exports in various Acts ... hit at colonial trade both coming and going. The Acts ... placed a heavy burden upon the colonies...

Lawrence Harper[20]

In spite of the extravagant language that has been used to condemn the system, the grower of enumerated commodities was not enslaved by the legal provisions of enumeration. ... Enumeration clearly did not hamper the expansion of the tobacco raising business in America. ... It has been assumed by many writers that enumeration imposed a serious burden upon rice planters. The ascertainable facts do not support this assumption.

Oliver Dickerson[21]

The export trade between the colonies and the mother country was subjected to regulations which significantly altered its value and composition over what it would have been if the colonies had been independent. The total adjusted value of exports from the American colonies to Great Britain in 1770 was £1,458,000, of which £1,107,000, or 76 per cent, were enumerated goods. Such goods were required to be shipped directly to Great Britain. The largest part, 85.4 per cent, of the enumerated goods was subsequently reexported to northern Europe and thus when competing in these markets bore the burden of an artificial, indirect routing through England to the Continent. The costs of this indirect route took the form of an added transhipment, with the consequent port charges and fees, middlemen's commissions, and what import duties were retained upon reexport. The enumerated goods consumed in England benefited from preferential duties relative to goods of foreign production. A few of these enumerated commodities also were favored with import bounties.

The additional transport costs borne by enumerated goods upon their reexport had the effect of lowering the prices received

---

[20]*Canadian Historical Review,* XXIII (1942), 3.
[21]Dickerson, p. 33.

by the colonial producer and depressing the quantity exported. In economic terms, the world market price as shown in Graph 1 would in the absence of regulation, be P_2 and exports would be Q_2. The effect of the additional cost of shipment through England is to raise the price to the consumer to P_3. Colonial exports, consequently, are reduced to Q_1. Therefore, both consumers and producers suffer from the enumeration of colonial exports whose final destination is not England.

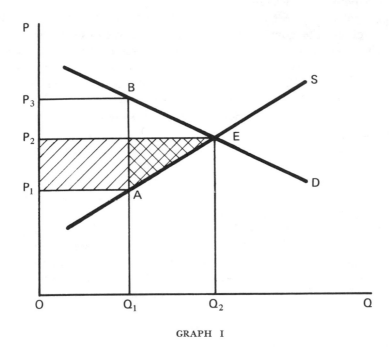

GRAPH I

The incidence of this burden depends upon the elasticities of supply and demand for the product. The direct cost to the producer as shown in Graph 1 is the unit burden times the quantity produced (P_2P_1 . Q_1).[22] The burden on the reduced output is equal to the return that would be earned on the additional output over what the resources would earn in their next-best alternative. This cost is illustrated by the shaded triangle in Graph 1 and represents the sum of the direct and indirect burdens.

[22]Since most tobacco was exported. exports for all practical purposes equal output of production.

In order to calculate the direct burden borne by the colonial producers of enumerated goods that were reexported from England, we need to know three separate time series. In the case of tobacco, we need to know the world market price in a European port, the price actually received in the colonies, and the actual reexports of tobacco from England—all three of which are readily available.[23]

The price that would have existed in the colonies in the absence of enumeration can be estimated, given the above information. It was estimated by dividing the observed Amsterdam price of Virginia tobacco before the Revolution by the ratio of Amsterdam to Philadelphia tobacco prices after the Revolution.[24] The postwar ratio of prices reflects the advantages received by the colonists by shipping directly to northern Europe rather than indirectly through England. This procedure provides us with an estimate of the price of tobacco in the colonies (P_2 on Graph 1) had tobacco not been subject to enumeration. The difference between the estimated price (P_2) and the actual price (P_1) is the unit burden suffered by reexported colonial tobacco.

Calculated in this manner, the price of tobacco in 1770 colonial America, had the colonies been independent, would have been over 49 per cent higher than it actually was. The average price for the decade 1763-1772 would have been 34 per cent higher than was actually recorded. These higher prices indicate that tobacco planters suffered a burden on the tobacco they actually grew in 1770 of £262,000 and, for the decade, an average annual burden of £177,000.

The direct burden is only a portion of the total colonial loss due to enumeration. The hypothetical higher tobacco prices would certainly have stimulated an increase in the supply of tobacco. Assuming that a 1 per cent increase in price would generate a 1 per cent increase in supply, the resulting increase in supply would have been about 39,000,000 pounds in 1770, or an annual average of 29,000,00

[23]For Philadelphia prices, Anne Bezanson, *et al., Prices and Inflation during the American Revolution: Pennsylvania, 1770-1790* (Philadelphia: University of Pennsylvania Press, 1965). For a European port, Amsterdam prices have been used as found in N. W. Posthumus, *Inquiry into the History of Prices in Holland* (Leiden: E. J. Brill, 1946). For tobacco quantities, see *Historical Statistics of the United States, Colonial Times to 1957* (Washington: U.S. Government Printing Office, 1960), series 230-37, p. 766.

[24]Albert Fishlow, discussion of a paper by Gordon Bjork, "The Weaning of the American Economy: Independence, Market Changes, and Economic Development," *Journal of Economic History*, XXIV, No. 4 (Dec. 1964), 565.

pounds for the decade.[25] The loss to the colonies of this foregone output is the calculated value of the shaded triangle in Graph 1, which is £64,000 for 1770, or an average of £30,000 for the decade.[26] Thus, the total burden on tobacco amounts to £326,00 for the year 1770, or an average of £207,000 for the period 1763-1772.

The calculation of the encumbrance suffered by rice proceeded in the same manner as the calculation of the burden on tobacco, except that Charleston prices were used instead of Philadelphia prices since South Carolina was the center of colonial rice production. The burden on the price of rice reexports was calculated to be an appreciable 105 per cent. This amounted to £95,000 in 1770, or £110,000 average for the decade 1763-1772.[27]

The indirect loss attributable to the expected increase in rice exports with the increase in price amounted to £25,000 for 1770, or an average of £29,000 for the longer period. In the case of rice, an elasticity of supply of .5 was assumed, due to the limited area of southern marshlands suitable to the cultivation of rice. The whole burden on rice products totaled £120,000 for 1770, or an average of £139,000 for the period 1763-1772.

Tobacco and rice together accounted for the vast bulk of the enumerated products that were reexported and therefore bore most of the burden. If we apply the weighted average of the tobacco and rice burden to the remainder of enumerated reexports, and adjust for the expected increase in supply, we obtain an estimated additional burden of £53,000 for 1770, or an annual average of £35,000 for the ten-year period.

However, to arrive at the total burden on enumerated exports we must allow for the benefits that colonial exports received from preferential duties or bounties. Most enumerated commodities benefited from one or the other: beaver skins, furs, and copper ore appear to be the only exceptions. Enumerated goods consumed in Great

25This amounts to assuming an elasticity of supply of one. This is probably optimistic since the average exports of tobacco between 1790 and 1793 were 28 per cent greater than the average for the period 1765-72 and 11 per cent greater than for 1770.

26The indirect burden suffered because of the loss of exports is calculated as the unit burden times the increased output that would have been exported, divided by two.

27For rice, the prices are to be found in Arthur H. Cole, *Wholesale Commodity Prices in the United States, 1700–1861, Statistical Supplement* (Cambridge: Harvard University Press, 1938). The rice estimate was made on the basis of but one observation in the colonial period (1760).

Britain amounted to £161,570 in 1770, or an average of £126,716 for the decade. The average preference amounted to 38 per cent of the price of enumerated products consumed in the mother country.[28] Again, assuming an elasticity of supply of one, we find that in the absence of these preferential duties the first-order effects would result in a decline in the amount of these enumerated commodities consumed in England of about £61,000 for 1770, or an average of £48,000 for the decade. The benefit of preferential duties to the colonists is the gain enjoyed by those exports that would have been sent to England in the absence of preferential duties had the colonies been independent (or £38,000 in 1770 and £30,000 average for the decade) plus the gain on the commodities actually sent that would not have been sent to England had the colonies been free. This amounted to £17,000 in 1770, or £9,000 as the annual average between 1763 and 1772. The benefit accruing to the colonies from preferential duties thus totals £55,000 for 1770, or £39,000 for the decade average.

TABLE 1

Net Burden on Colonial Foreign Commerce

	1770	1763-1772
Exports		
Tobacco	£ 326,000	£ 207,000
Rice	120,000	139,000
Other	53,000	35,000
Burden	499,000	381,000
Preference	55,000	39,000
Bounty	33,000	35,000
Benefit	88,000	74,000
Imports		
Burden	121,000	144,000
Net burden on foreign commerce	£ 532,000	£ 451,000
	or	or
	$ 2,660,000	$ 2,255,000

In addition to preferential duties, the Crown annually spent large sums in the form of bounties to promote certain industries.

---

[28] The average preference was figured from statistics presented in tables 2 and 3, found in Lawrence Harper, "The Burden of the Navigation Acts on the Thirteen Colonies" in Morris, ed., *Era of the American Revolution*.

The recorded bounties for the year 1770, for instance, totaled £47,344.[29] These payments were designed to divert resources from more efficient uses into industries where they were employed less efficiently but where, for political purposes, they were thought better occupied. Thus it was better to obtain naval stores in the American colonies at a higher cost than to rely upon foreign imports. Part of the bounty, therefore, was a payment for the inefficient allocation of colonial resources and was no gain to the colonies.

The calculation of the approximate proportion of these payments that exceeded the amount required to pay the cost of the inefficiency is not difficult. Since in every case Great Britain continued to import substantial amounts of these commodities from foreign as well as colonial sources, the demand for bountied goods from the colonies can reasonably be assumed to have been perfectly elastic. That is, the colonies could have sold as much of these goods in England as they desired without lowering the market price. This is shown in Graph 2 as a horizontal demand schedule (D) and OB is the market price of the commodity.

The effect of a per-unit bounty is to increase the supply of the commodity; this is shown as an increase in the quantity supplied from Q_1 to Q_2. The net benefit to the colonies of the total bounty (shown on Graph 2 as the area $ABCD$) is the shaded portion of that rectangle. The total bounty payment less the cost of an inefficient use of resources (the unshaded area of the rectangle $ABCD$) gives the net benefit, which must be less than the bounty payment. In order to measure the actual benefit derived by the colonies from the bounty payments we need know only the percentage of the market price represented by the bounty and the elasticity of supply of the commodity.

The export of colonial naval stores was stimulated by bounty payments in significant amounts. The average for the decade 1763-1772 totaled £33,000, and for the year 1770 the payment amounted to £29,803. The average bounty amounted to about 28 per cent of the price; therefore, assuming an elasticity of supply of one, the bounty was responsible for roughly 28 per cent of the exports of naval stores to Great Britain. Figured on this basis, the net

[29]Recorded bounty payments for the decade 1763-72 averaged:

Indigo	£ 8,065
Naval stores	32,772
Lumber	6,557
Total	£ 47,394

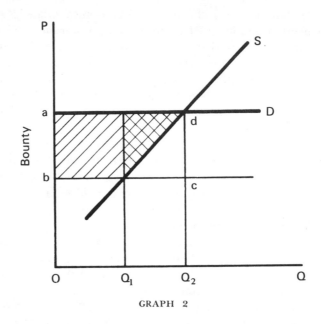

GRAPH 2

gain to the colonists from the bounty on naval stores was 86 per cent of the payment.[30] This amounted to an average of £28,000 for the decade, or £26,000 for the single year 1770.

The second largest bounty payments were for the production of indigo; in 1770 this amounted to £8,732 and for the decade an average of £8,065.[31] Evidently, the indigo bounty not only stimulated

[30]The gain to the colonists from the bounty payments was figured in the following manner. The gain is in two parts. First, the unit bounty times the quantity that would have been produced without the bounty gives us the clear gain. In order to find that portion of naval stores that would have been produced without the bounty, we assumed a supply elasticity of one, reckoned the percentage of the price of naval stores that the bounty represented, and thus easily estimated that portion of the supply of naval stores for which the bounty was responsible. The other part would have been produced anyway; on this portion the full amount of the bounty was clear gain. On the part stimulated by the bounty, only one half was gain to the colonists.

[31]This figure is taken from reports by the London Custom House, retained in Treasury 38, Vol. 363, Public Record Office, London, as originally stated in Dickerson, p. 28, and is accurate. Lawrence Harper "Navigation Acts" (cited in n.27) uses a figure of £ 23,086. While the Dickerson figure may possible exclude some payments, the Harper figure is calculated on the basis that all indigo received the bounty, which was not the case. Lewis Grey quotes a British official to the effect that about seven eighths of the indigo exported from South Carolina received the bounty, but much less deserved so, being poor in quality. On this basis the pay-

increased output but was responsible for the entire output, since the production of indigo in the colonies disappeared after independence. Therefore, the net benefits of the indigo bounty are derived by calculating the value of the triangle as shown in Graph 3. In the absence of the bounty, no indigo would have been exported. The effect of the bounty was to stimulate an export equal to Q_1. The net gain to the colonists from the indigo bounty at best is equal to, and is probably something less than, one half the amount of the bounty. We estimated that 50 per cent of the bounty payment for indigo was gain for indigo producers—gain they would not have enjoyed if the colonies had been independent. This totaled £4,400 in 1770, or £4,000 as the annual average for the decade.[32]

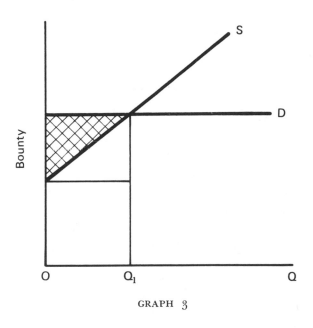

GRAPH 3

The importation of colonial lumber into Great Britain also received a bounty which, accordin to Beer, totaled £6,557 in 1769.[33] Sufficient data are not available to allow a calculation of the gain

ments could have reached as high as £ 20,000 a year. Lewis C. Grey, *A History of Southern Agriculture* (Washington: Carnegie Institution, 1933), p. 292.

32Figured on the basis of an annual bounty of about £ 20,000. Then around £ 10,000 would have been the value of the bounty to the producers of indigo.

33George Louis Beer, *British Colonial Policy, 1754-1765* (New York: Macmillan, 1907), p. 224.

to the colonists from this payment, but it appears that the bounty was just sufficient to pay the added cost of shipping lumber to England. This payment was necessary to divert lumber from the West Indies, which was the colonies' natural market, and to attract it to England. It appears justifiable to assign the entire payment as the cost of a less efficient use of resources. Nevertheless we shall include 50 per cent as a net gain to the colonists, which amounts to £3,300.

The total net gain to the colonies from the bounties paid for colonial products was, therefore, £33,000 in 1770 and an average of £35,000 for the decade. Our analysis of the effect of the Navigation Acts on colonial exports has included the burden on exports, the benefit of the preferential duties, and the net gain from bounty payments. The sum total of these burdens and benefits is a net burden upon exports of £411,000 for 1770. The average annual burden for the decade 1763-1772 was calculated to be £307,000.

IV

The extra expense of importing competitive European products from England acted as a protective wall which permitted increases in English prices. . . . Those [statistics] which exist tend to confirm . . . the theory that transshipment was costly.

Lawrence Harper[34]

The clauses of the Navigation Acts that sought to make England the chief source of supply for manufactured goods were not burdensome. . . . There was a distinct effort to make the British market attractive to colonial purchasers.

Oliver Dickerson[35]

British law required that the colonies purchase their East Indian and European goods in England. The colonies actually purchased three quarters of their imports from the mother country, of which about 20 per cent were goods originally manufactured in Europe or Asia. These imported goods also bore the burden of an indirect route to the colonies, analogous to that borne by tobacco destined to be consumed in Europe. This burden was reflected in higher prices for goods of foreign manufacture in the colonies than otherwise would have been the case.

Our method for calculating the burden borne by colonial imports of foreign manufactures is similar to the method used to calculate the cost of enumeration on colonial goods reexported to

[34]"Navigation Acts," p. 36.
[35]p. 70.

Europe. Two commodities, tea and pepper, for which both colonial and Amsterdam prices are available, were selected as our sample.[36] Tea and pepper accounted for about 16 per cent of the value of foreign goods imported into the colonies through England. The price that would have obtained in the colonies had they been independent was calculated for these goods exactly as in the case of tobacco. The alternative prices of these commodities, according to our estimates, would have averaged 16 per cent lower than they in fact were.[37] Thus, the colonists paid more for their imports of foreign origin than they would have paid had they been independent.

The colonies actually imported foreign goods to the average value of £412,000 for the decade 1763-1772 and of £346,000 for the single year 1770. The burden on the goods, according to our measurement, averaged £66,000 for the decade, or £55,000 for 1770. However, the burden on imports should not be calculated on the basis of foreign goods alone. The burden should also be calculated on goods of English manufacture which were made competitive in the colonial markets by virtue of the artificially increased cost of foreign goods forced to travel an indirect route to the colonies.

The bounty laws benefiting English manufactures which were designed to make Enlish goods competitive with those of foreign manufacture give us a clue to the identity of these English manufactures. If goods of English manufacture required a bounty to compete with similar foreign goods suffering the handicap of an indirect shipment, then the colonists, if independent, would have purchased foreign instead of English goods. Thus, some English goods actually purchased by the colonists would not have been purchased if the colonies had been independent.

Linen was the most important of these goods; the list also included cottons and silks. The colonies thus paid more for most nonwoolen textiles than they would have if they had existed outside the British Empire. The additional monetary loss resulting from the purchase of English rather than foreign goods was calculated to average £73,000 for the decade or £61,000 for 1770 alone.[38] The

[36]Colonial prices are to be found in Bezanson and Amsterdam prices in Posthumus.

[37]Bjork, *Journal of Economic History*, XXIV, (1964), 554, found that goods of foreign manufacture (his Index A) fell dramatically in price after the Revolution, while goods in which Britain had a comparative advantage fell little if at all in price (his Index B).

[38]This loss was calculated by taking the percentage unit burden on the price of such imports times their total value.

colonists thus paid a total of £116,000 more in 1770 or £139,000 average for the decade for their imports than they would have if independent. If we assume, for convenience, a price elasticity of demand for imports of one, the colonists would have spent the same amount on imports but they would have received more goods for their money.[39]

The results of this preliminary investigation into the effects of the Navigation Acts upon the foreign commerce of the American colonies are found in Table 1. The result is an overall burden for the year 1770 of £532,000, and an average of £451,000 for the decade.

v

The fact is that colonial shipowners suffered, directly, and colonial shipowners, indirectly, under the Navigation Acts.

Lawrence Harper[40]

Instead of being oppressive the shipping clauses of the Navigation Acts had become an important source of colonial prosperity which was shared by every colony. As a device for launching ships these clauses were more efficient than the fabled beauty of Helen of Troy's face.

Oliver Dickerson[41]

The purpose of the various clauses in the Navigation Acts dealing with shipping was to insure that ships built and manned by Englishmen monopolized this aspect of the foreign commerce of the empire. Colonial vessels, for all intents and purposes, were considered English and shared in the benefits of the monopoly.

Calculation of the resultant colonial benefits was hampered by a lack of available data; therefore, the conclusions should be considered tentative. The estimate was constructed in the following manner: an estimated percentage of the total tonnage entering and clearing colonial ports in 1770 that was colonial owned was calculated from the American Inspector General's ledger. Using an estimated average earnings per ton, it was possible to approximate the shipping earnings deriving from the foreign commerce of the American colonies.[42] The

[39]The consumer surplus lost to the colonists because of higher import prices could be easily calculated in the Hotelling-Harberger manner.

[40]*Canadian Historical Review*, XXIII (1942), 4.

[41]p. 32.

[42]See James Shepherd, "Colonial Balance of Payments," p. 691, for a discussion of how this estimate was obtained.

total earnings from shipping the foreign commerce of the thirteen colonies were calculated to be £1,228,000, of which 59.4 per cent, or £730,000, was earned by American vessels.

The next question considered was what these earnings would have been had the colonies been independent. Using as a guide what actually did happen between 1789-1792, after the Revolution but before the outbreak of the war in Europe, I found that the colonies' share of the trade carrying their own commerce declined from 59.4 per cent to 53.2 per cent. On this basis, their shipping earnings in 1770 would have been £653,000 instead of £730,000—a difference of £77,000.

However, as we have seen, had the American colonies been independent their volume of foreign commerce would have been greater. Their ships would have carried a portion of the increased amounts of tobacco, rice, and other exports that would have been shipped, as well as a portion of the larger volume of imports.

My calculations suggest that the volume of shipping required to carry this additional output would have amounted to over 53,000 tons. If American vessels had carried the same percentage of this increased volume as they carried of the total volume in 1789, their earnings in 1770 would have increased to over £742,000—or a little more than they in fact were during the late colonial period. The composition of the trade, however, would have been different.[43]

Thus, it seems fruitless to do more with the effect of the Navigation Acts upon shipping earnings until we know more about shipping rates before and after the Revolution. The best guess, at this time, is that on balance the colonial shipping industry neither gained nor lost from the Navigation Acts.

V I

Indeed, the question ought not be separated from the larger one of the savings offered Americans by the military and naval protection of the British.

Stuart Bruchey[44]

The main obligation of the mother country to its colonies in a mercantilist world was to provide protection. In this area lies the

[43]Colonial vessels probably would have carried relatively less of the trade with the West Indies, assuming that (as happened after the Revolution) they were excluded from the British West Indies. However, they would also presumably have carried relatively more of the transatlantic trade.

[44]*Roots of American Economic Growth* (New York: Harper and Row, 1916), p. 74.

significant benefit to the colonies from membership in an empire. The empire of course also performed certain administrative functions for the colonies from which they benefited.

Great Britain in the defense of the empire could provide for the protection of the American colonies at very little additional expense to itself. That is to say that the colonies, if independent, would have had to expend more resources in their own defense than did England, just to maintain the same level of protection. Our estimate of the value of military and naval protection provided by the British to the colonists, since it is based in part upon actual British expenditures, is therefore too low.

The value of British military protection was estimated as follows. Great Britain, before 1762, maintained a standing army in America of 3,000 officers and men. After 1762, the size of this troop complement was increased to 7,500 men.[45] These troops were garrisoned throughout the colonies, including the frontiers where they served as a defensive force against the incursions of hostile Indians. Each man stationed in America cost the mother country an average of £29 a year, or annually a total expense of at least £217,500.[46]

The colonists constantly complained about the quality of the "redcoats" as Indian fighters. Furthermore, they believed the larger standing army in the colonies after 1762 was there not primarily to protect them but for other reasons. However, they found after independence that a standing army of at least 5,000 men was required to replace the British.[47] Thus the benefit to the colonies from the British army stationed in America was conservatively worth at least the cost of 5,000 troops, or £145,000.

Another large colonial benefit stemmed from the protection offered colonial shipping by the British navy, which included the Crown's annual tribute to the Barbary powers. The ability of the British navy to protect its merchant ships from the ravages of pirates far surpassed anything a small independent country could provide. This the colonies learned to their sorrow following the Revolution.

The value of such protection would be reflected in the rise in marine insurance rates for cargoes carried by American vessels after independence. Unfortunately, until research in progress is completed, I do not have sufficient data to directly calculate the value of the protection of the British navy in this manner.

[45]Knollenberg, p. 34.
[46]Great Britain, *House of Commons Journals,* King George III, Vol. XXXII (1768-1770), sessions no. 1768, 1803.
[47]*Historical Statistics,* p. 737.

However, this benefit can be tentatively measured in an indirect manner. Insurance rates during the 1760's on the West Indies trade one way averaged about 3.5 per cent of the value of the cargo.[48] Rates to England were higher, averaging 7 per cent. These rates on colonial cargoes existed while colonial vessels were protected by the British navy. During the French and Indian War, the risk of seizure increased the rates to the West Indies, which rose steadily until they reached 23 per cent, while rates to England climbed as high as 28 per cent,[49] indicating the influence of risk upon marine insurance rates.

The colonists upon obtaining their independence lost the protection of the British fleet. Insurance rates, as a result must have increased over the prerevolutionary levels. To estimate the approximate rise in insurance rates, we calculated the percentage decline in insurance rates for American merchant vessels following the launching in 1797 of three frigates which formed the foundation of the small, eighteenth-century American navy.[50]

The percentage difference between the rates on an unprotected merchant marine and those charged on the merchant fleet safeguarded by our small navy was applied to the insurance rates prevailing before the Revolution. The weighted difference in rates between a barely protected merchant marine and a totally unprotected one was slightly over 50 per cent.

Applying this percentage to existing prerevolutionary rates, it appears that the average cargo insurance rate, if the colonies had been independent, would have been at least 8.7 per cent of the value of the cargo instead of 5.4 per cent, a difference in rates of 2.7 per cent. Figuring this increase in insurance charges on the value of colonial cargoes in 1770 gives a low estimate of the value derived from British naval protection of £103,000. Three ships were not the British navy and could not be expected to provide equal protection. Marine insurance rates thus probably increased more than 2.7 per cent. An estimate that rates doubled does not seem unreasonable and would raise the annual value of naval protection to £206,000.

The estimate of the value of British protection for the American colonies is thus made up of the adjusted cost of the army in the colonies. £145,000, plus the estimated value of naval protection for

48Harold E. Gillingham, *Marine Insurance Rates in Philadelphia, 1721-1800* (Philadelphia: Patterson & White, 1933), pp. 18, 64.

49*Ibid.*

50Charles Goldsbourgh, *The United States Naval Chronicle* (Washington, 1824), pp. 109-10.

the merchant marine of £206,000. The estimated total value of the protection afforded the colonies by their membership in the British Empire was thus calculated to be at least £351,000.

By way of a check upon this estimate, the Government of the United States, during its first nine years under the Constitution, found it necessary to spend annually an average of $2,133,000, or £426,600, for national defense.[51] This included the purchase of arms and stores, the fortification of forts and harbors, and the building and manning of a small navy. In addition, an independent America had to bear the expense of conducting an independent foreign policy. The support of ministers to foreign nations, the cost of negotiating and implementing treaties, the payment of tribute to the Barbary nations, all previously provided for by Great Britain, now had to be borne by the independent colonies. These expenses alone cost the United States, during the last decade of the eighteenth century, annually over £60,000.

After achieving independence, the United States found it necessary to spend annually about £487,000 to provide certain functions of government formerly provided by Great Britain. This suggests that our estimate of £351,000 for the value of British protection to the American colonists is too low. It is doubtful, in the light of history, whether the new nation was able to provide this type of governmental services of equal quality to those furnished by the British. If not, even the £487,000 a year understates the value of governmental services supplied by Great Britain to her American colonies.

VII

For reasons which have been explained more fully elsewhere we shall reject Beer's claim that there was no exploitation.

Lawrence Harper[52]

Exploitation . . . by the home country is an economic myth.

Oliver Dickerson[53]

My findings with reference to the effect of the Navigation Acts upon the economy of the thirteen colonies indicate a net burden of £532,000, or $2,660,000, in 1770. The average burden for the decade 1763-1772, based upon official values, was somewhat lower—

[51]U.S. Congress, *American State Papers, Finance*, III, 14th Cong., 1st sess., 63, 69.

[52]*Canadian Historical Review*, XXIII (1942) 2.

[53]p. xiv.

£451,000, or $2,255,000. These estimates are near the lowest estimates made by Harper and seem to strengthen his case that exploitation did exist.[54]

TABLE 2

SUMMARY OF THE RESULTS

	1763-1772	*1770*
Burdens		
Burdens on colonial		
foreign commerce	£ 451,000	£ 532,000
	or	or
	$ 2,255,000	$ 2,660,000
Burden per capita[a]	$ 1.20	$ 1.24
Benefits		
Benefit of British		
protection	£ 351,000	£ 351,000
	or	or
	$ 1,775,000	$ 1,775,000
Benefit per capita	$ .94	$ .82
Balance[b]		
Estimate 1	$ —.26	$ —.42

[a] Population for the decade average was figured to be 1,881,000, and for 1770 to be 2,148,000.

[b] The balance was obtained by subtracting the per capita benefits from the per capita burden.

Considering for a moment only the value of the losses on colonial exports and imports, the per capita annual cost to the colonist of being an Englishman instead of an American was $1.24 in 1770. The average per capita cost for the decade based upon official values was a somewhat lower $1.20. The benefits per capita in 1770 were figured to be 82 cents, and for the decade 94 cents. Subtracting the benefits from the burdens for 1770 shows a per capita loss of 42 cents. The estimate for the decade shows a smaller loss of 26 cents a person. It is unlikely, because of the nature of the estimating procedures employed, that these losses are too low. Conversely it is not at all improbable, and for the same reasons, that the estimated losses are too high.

54Harper estimated that the burden on tobacco, rice, European goods imported, and the benefits of bounties together added up to a burden of between $2,560,000 and $7,038,000. Harper's estimate of the loss on tobacco and rice really measured the area $(P_1.A.B.P._3)$ in Graph 1 rather than $(P_1.A.E.P_2)$, which is the correct area. However his lower estimate is rather close to ours.

Suppose that these findings reflect the true magnitude of the cost of the Navigation Acts to the thirteen colonies. The relevant question becomes: How important were these losses? Albert Fishlow stated at last year's meetings that he believed that the average per capita income in the 1780's "could not have been much less than $100."[55] George Rogers Taylor, in his presidential address, hazarded a guess that per capita income did not grow very rapidly, if at all, between 1775 and 1840.[56] Therefore, assuming that average per capita income hovered about $100 between 1763 and 1772, what would it have been had the colonies been independent?

The answer is obvious from Table 2: it would not have been much different. The largest estimated loss on this basis is .54 of 1 per cent of per capita income, or 54 cents on a hundred dollars. Suppose for a moment that my estimates are off by 100 per cent; then, in that case the largest burden would be slightly more than 1 per cent of national income. It is difficult to make a convincing case for exploitation out of these results.

[55]*Journal of Economic History*, XXIV (1964), 566.
[56]*Ibid.*, p. 429.

Theory of Economic Drain

Impact of British Rule on the Indian Economy, 1840-1900

Tapan Mukerjee

Tapan Mukerjee has taught at the University of Colorado and is Assistant Professor of Economics at Callison College, University of the Pacific. His present area of research deals with international economic relations and the economics of imperialism. A slightly different version of the paper used in this reader was presented at the Western Economic Association Conference, at Long Beach, California, August, 1969.

In the literature of nineteenth-century Indian economic history opposing views have existed regarding the annual tribute demanded by Britain. One is that the tribute was a drain on India, a form of exploitation practiced by the Imperial country. The other maintains that the tribute did not result in a drain since there were many benefits accruing to the Indian economy in return. The author makes an attempt to resolve this dichotomy through an analysis of the costs and benefits of the "home charges." The reader should also consult the following papers on this topic:

B. N. Ganguli, "Dadabhai Naoroji and the Mechanism of External Drain," *Indian Economic and Social History*, II April 1965, pages 85-102.

John Strachey, *The End of Empire*, New York, 1964, pages 46-59.

The contents of this paper may be put into focus by examining the following quotations:

> Another—melancholy fact which we learned is the steady increase of the expenditure in England—the Home Charges. Great Britain and India were equally gainers by the establishment and maintenance of the British Empire in India, and the cost of the Empire should have been shared by the two countries. . . . But the sword of the conquerer is thrown into the scale today as it was in the days of Brennus, and financial arrangements are never dictated by strict justice between a subject and a ruling race. To India the annual Economic Drain was a pure loss; the money flowed out of the country never to return again: it went from a poor country to fructify the trades and industries of a rich country.[1]

[1]R. C. Dutt, *Economic History of India, Victorian Age*, 8th edition. London, 1950, p. 213.

The continuous surplus of the exports over the imports which had gone on since 1842-43 gave rise towards the end of the century to the theory of the "Drain". Sir Theodore Morrison has shown that the "Drain" of the decades 1899-1900 to 1908-9 was an average of 15,051,000 sterling per annum. This consisted of remittances to pay the interest on the loans which have done so much to develop the prosperity of the country by providing railway and irrigation works. In addition, the repayment of the capital borrowed is also met by the surplus exports, the payment for shipping services, and the remittance for pensions of Englishmen who have served in India. Roughly speaking, one third of the surplus payments in the shape of the exports was for good government, one third for the interest on the loans for the public works, and one third payment for bullion absorbed (by Indian citizens) . . . when one looks on those forty years between 1858 and 1899, one realizes the change that had come over the whole economic structure of India. . . . All this is inconsistent with any theory of exploitation.[2]

The first quotation is from a book published in 1903 by an Indian economist in which the author, R. C. Dutt, indicates that the annual tribute demanded by the British was a drain on the economy. The second quotation is from a book first published in 1924, by an English economist. The author, L. C. A. Knowles, points out that the home charges did not result in an economic drain, since there were many benefits accruing to the Indian economy from British rule. These quotations appear to be fairly representative of the two dominant viewpoints that have existed in the literature of nineteenth-century Indian economic history. Many other Indian writers have emphasized the fact that British economic policy was exploitative in nature and resulted in a heavy drain on the Indian economy.[3,4,5] Although L. Rai in his book makes a somewhat diluted attempt at considering the benefits of the home charges, his effort leaves much to be desired in terms of critical analysis. The problems are

[2]L. C. A. Knowles, *The Economic Development of the British Overseas Empire*. 2nd ed. London, 1928, vol. 1, pp. 392-93.

[3]L. Rai, *England's Debt to India*. New York, 1917, ch. 3, pp. 69-96.

[4]D. Naoroji, *Poverty and Un-British Rule in India*. Publication division, Ministry of Information and Broadcasting, Delhi, India, 1962, pp. 33-54. (First published in 1901).

[5]T. B. Desai, *Economic History of India Under the British*. Bombay, 1968, pp. 219-26.

similar in the case of the works by D. Naoroji and T. B. Desai. In Knowles' book and later in V. Anstey's work[6] the benefit side of the home charge, i.e., what India received in exchange is fairly well described, but neither is there an attempt to quantify them, nor is there an attempt to make a thorough appraisal of the deleterious effects of the home charges. Recent work by an Indian economist seems to be better balanced in analyzing the economic impact of British rule in India in the nineteenth century.[7,8]

In view of the controversy and lack of clarity that exists in the literature of nineteenth-century Indian economic history on the question of the impact of British rule on the Indian economy a reexamination of the subject seems justifiable. This paper examines the nature and the extent of the burden of home charges on the Indian economy in the period 1840-1900 and attempts to make a qualitative estimate of the cost and benefits of British rule in that period. In the first part of the paper the magnitude and financing of the home charge is discussed. Then an assessment is made of the unjustifiable segments of these charges in order to obtain estimates of the actual "drain" on the economy. The last section deals with an overall cost-benefit analysis in qualitative terms of British rule in India.

The major components of the annual charges made by Britain to the Indian economy consisted of interest on India's sterling public debt, military charges, expenditure connected with British administration of Indian affairs, and purchase of stores.[9,10] The home charges amounted to about 2.6 million in 1840 and by 1900 had gone up to about 25.8 million.[11] The growth pattern of these charges is illustrated in Figure 1. In the first eighteen years of the period under consideration India was under the domination of the East India Company, and from 1858 onwards it was under British rule.[12] The home charges

[6]V. Anstey, *The Economic Development of India.* London, 1929, Appendix G., pp. 509-11.

[7]N. V. Sovani, "British Impact on India Before 1850-57," *Cahiers d'histoire mondiale.* April 1954, pp. 857-82.

[8]N. V. Sovani, "British Impact on India After 1857," *Cahiers d'histoire mondiale.* July 1954, pp. 77-105.

[9]N. V. Sovani, *op. cit.,* p. 877.

[10]V. Anstey, *op. cit.,* p. 509.

[11]R. C. Dutt, *op. cit.,* p. 212 and p. 595.

[12]The Sepoy mutiny of 1857-58 was the turning point in the British rule of India. Initial British contacts with India were established as far back as 1600 through the trading company. Political and territorial influence of the British had become significant by the second half of the 18th century. In the next hun-

in the period up to 1856-57 stayed in the region of 2 million to 3 million, about ten per cent of the gross revenue of India. In 1857 there was a sudden jump in these charges mainly due to the fact that the cost of the mutiny was charged to the colony. All through the remainder of the 19th century, the steady increase in these charges was principally due to the fact that there was a continuous increase in debt service as the amount of the total sterling debt increased. The major components of the debt consisted of that incurred by military expenditures and by investment in the infrastructure. L. H. Jenks states ". . . something like one hundred and fifty million pounds of British capital were invested in India between 1854 and 1869. Capital continued to move in to India at the rate of about five million pounds a year during the seventies. But its climax in volume was reached immediately after the mutiny."[13]

The transfer of home charges was possible owing to the substantial trade surplus that the Indian economy registered throughout the period except for three short intervals—between 1855-1863, 1869-1873 and 1897-1900.[14] The trade surplus data are also plotted in Figure 1. In the last two intervals although the trade surplus was positive, the home charges were greater than the surplus. It is not exactly clear as to how the home charges were financed in these intervals. There are two distinct possibilities. First, an export of bullions took place from India, and second, sterling loans were taken out in Britain. Considering the fact that India suffered from an excess demand for precious metals for monetary and non-monetary needs, it is quite likely that the last course was followed.[15] If this were to be the transfer mechanism, then there was a further increase in the public debt and consequently the home charges.

---

dred years or so, British consolidation of the Indian empire was more less complete. In 1858 the British crown took over the administration of the country from the company and a new era began.

[13]L. H. Jenks. *The Migration of British Capital to 1875.* New York, 1927, p. 22

[14]N. K. Chaudhuri in his recent work on India's foreign trade states: ". . . the most remarkable feature of India's foreign trade during this period, and indeed to a certain extent throughout the nineteenth century, was the dominating influence exercised on it by the pressure of a unilateral transfer of funds. A massive outflow of funds took place in this period from India to Britain . . . the export of capital usually took the form of an active merchandise balance of trade (export surplus) in the current account of her balance of payment." N. K. Chaudhuri, "India's Foreign Trade and the Cessation of the East India Company's Trading Activities, 1828-40," *Econ. Hist. Review,* Vol. XIX, No. 2, August 1966, p. 355.

[15]N. V. Sovani, *op. cit.,* p. 877.

FIGURE 1. INDIA—HOME CHARGES & TRADE SURPLUS,
1834-1900

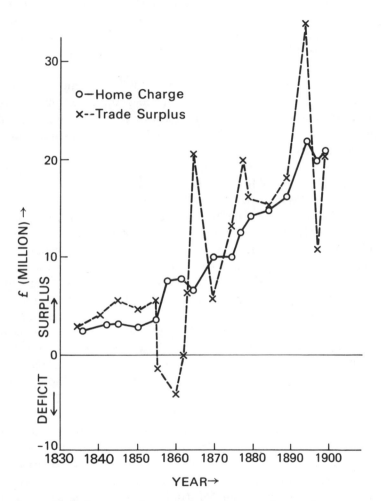

For the period 1840 to 1900 the sum of annual home charges amounted to about 335 million sterling.[16] In the period 1840 to 1858, under the rule of the East India Company, the total home charges amounted to about 52 million sterling and for the remaining period, under the rule of the British crown, the total charges amounted to about 283 million sterling. For the period under the company, the average annual charge comes out to be 2.8 million sterling, and for the period under crown rule it amounts to about 6.7 million sterling per year.

The amounts charged to India by Britain which appear to be of no direct benefit to the economy and therefore unjustifiable fall mainly in the category of expenditures for wars fought on the borders and outside the country, and administrative expenditures unconnected with India.

In the period under consideration, the cost of nine separate external military expenditures were charged to the colony.[17] These were the First Afghan war (1838-42) —total burden on India of 15,000,000 sterling;[18] the first China war (1839-40) —part of the cost was borne by India; the Persian war of 1850—major part of the charges were borne by India; the Abyssinian war (1867-68) —India paid 600,000 sterling; the Perak expedition of 1875—part of the charges were borne by India; the second Afghan war (1878-80) —India paid 18,000,000 sterling;[19] the Egyptian war of 1882—India paid 1,000,000 sterling;[20] Sudan War (1885-86) —part of the charges were borne by India; for the Gilgit and Chitral expeditions India paid 1,000,000 sterling.[21] The total expenditure on these wars, which could not be justified on the grounds of maintaining peace and security within the colony at the minimum amounted to about 40 million sterling. The cost of the Sepoy mutiny of 1857 which amounted to another 40 million sterling was also charged to India.[22] The annual charges also swelled considerably as a large contingent of British soldiers were maintained in the colony in order to undertake military expeditions in Asia and in Africa. Around 1860 there were 70,000 British and 135,000 Indian troops in the country. After the British crown had taken over the administration of India from the company, it had

[16]R. C. Dutt, *op. cit.*, pp. 212, 373, 595.
[17]L. Rai, *op. cit.*, p. 105.
[18]R. C. Dutt, *op. cit.*, p. 217.
[19]*Ibid.*, p. 55.
[20]*Ibid.*, p. 564.
[21]*Ibid.*, p. 571.
[22]*Ibid.*, p. 375.

become the launching ground for further expansion into Asia and Africa.

A large portion of the Indian expenditures were due to military needs. By 1878 the cost of the military machine was one third of the total revenue of the country, amounting to about 17 million sterling.[23] By 1891 the expenditure on military services had gone up to about 25 million sterling which amounted to about 41 per cent of the total Indian budget.[24] For the period under consideration the revenue and expenditure data is presented in Figure 2. From 1840 to 1890 there were continuous deficits in Indian finance. In order to obtain some idea of the frequency of the military campaigns during this period these events are noted down in a chronological order. In all there were at least about 20 different conflicts in and out of India which were financed wholly or partially by the colony. The deficit was maximum during the Sepoy mutiny, from 1857 to 1860. The Indian public debt during this period increased by about forty million sterling. The growth of the debt is illustrated in Figure 3. Up to the time of the mutiny and just before the crown took over from the company, the sterling debt in Britain, service charges on which formed a substantial part of the home charges, stood at about 10 million sterling. From 1858 onward the sterling debt in England increased at a very rapid rate. By 1880 this had increased to 70 million sterling, and by 1900 it was about 130 million sterling, about 60 per cent of the total Indian debt.

At the end of the nineteenth century an analysis of the various components of the home charges reveals that in 1901-02 out of the total of 17.3 million sterling, about 3 million went towards paying interest on debt, about 6.4 million towards interest and annuities on loans for railroads, etc. Military charges amounted to £3 million, and £2 million went for stores, including those for defense works.[25] In other words about 17 per cent of the home charges went for paying interest on debt, 37 per cent towards paying interest on loans about 17 per cent for military charges, about 14 per cent for civil charges, and about 11 per cent for stores, and the remaining 4 per cent was for miscellaneous items.

We have seen earlier that the total expenditure for the various external and border wars and military expenditures unjustifiably charged to India amounted to 40 million sterling for the period

[23]S. Wolpert, *India.* Englewood Cliffs, 1965, p. 104.
[24]V. Anstey, *op. cit.,* p. 391.
[25]R. C. Dutt, *op. cit.,* p. 604.

FIGURE 2. PUBLIC FINANCE—INDIA—1837-1900

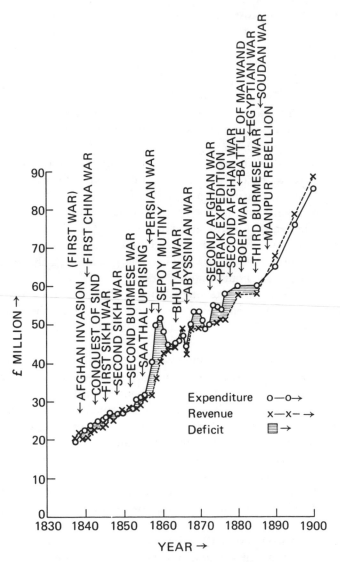

Source: R. C. Dutt, *Economic History of India; Victorian Age.*

FIGURE 3. INDIAN PUBLIC DEBT, 1837-1900

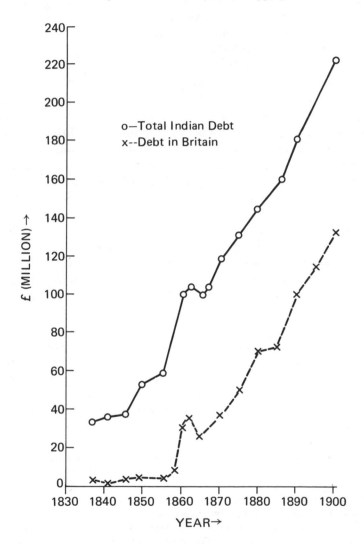

Source: R. C. Dutt, *op. cit.*, pages 217, 374.

1840-1900. This amounts to about 18 per cent of the public debt. It is fair to say that this percentage of the debt was not necessary for the welfare of India in terms of securing internal law and order in the country since these expenditures were only necessary for the British to maintain their military supremacy in the East. In other words, keeping the calculations simple, 18 per cent of the annual debt service was unjustifiable. This amounts to about 3 per cent of the total' home charges made by Britain for the year 1901.

If we consider the 3 million sterling annual military charges for 1901-1902 and assume, in view of the fact that a large number of British forces were garrisoned in India for fighting battles of the whole empire, that only half of this amount (1.5 million sterling) was necessary for maintaining peace and security in the colony, then another 9 per cent of the total home charges seem to be unnecessary.

As far as the civil charges are concerned, there were components in that which seem to have been unreasonably charged to India. For example a large part of the operating costs of the British mission in Persia was charged to the colony. For the period 1823 to 1900 this amounted to about 878,000 sterling,[26] or an average of about 11,500 sterling per year for this period. There were other civil charges which appear to have been unjustifiable.[27] Let us say that all these unfair claims amounted to 1 per cent of the total home charges.

Thus we find that about 13 per cent of the home charges (3 per cent for unjustifiable debt service, 9 per cent for unnecessary military adventures, and 1 per cent for unjustifiable civil charges) from 1901-02 could be designated as unnecessary. If we make the assumption that this was typical for the entire period under considera-

---

[26]L. Rai, *op. cit.*, p. 106.

[27]In this connection Jenks states: "The burdens that it was found convenient to charge to India seem preposterous. The cost of the military, the cost of the transfer of the company's rights to the crown, the expenses of simultaneous wars in China and Abyssinia, every governmental item in London that remotely related to India down to the fees of the charwomen in the India office and the expenses of ships that sailed but did not participate in hostilities and the cost of Indian regiments (British troops) for six months' training at home before they sailed,—all charged to the account of the unrepresented ryot. The Sultan of Turkey visited London in 1868 in state, and the bill was charged to India. A lunatic asylum in Ealing, gifts to members of a Zanzibar mission, the consular and diplomatic establishments of Great Britain in China and Persia, part of the permanent expenses of the Mediterranian fleet and the entire cost of a line telegraph from England to India had been charged before 1870 to the Indian treasury." L. H. Jenks, *op., cit.*, p. 106.

tion, not a very unrealistic assumption in view of the fact that military expenditures were higher in the middle of the nineteenth century rather than the end, then the total amount of unnecessary home charges would be approximately 42 million sterling. This amount may be denoted as the "effective drain" on the Indian economy, instead of the total home charges of 335 million for the period under study.

How much of a drain was this on the Indian economy? In order to obtain some idea it seems worthwhile comparing the magnitude of the drain to national income data. Table 1 exhibits statistics on per capita income and population for four selected years—1872, 1881, 1891 and 1900, for which census data were available. The per capita income data were obtained from the work of M. Mukerjee.[28]

TABLE 1

1	2	3	4	5	6	7	8	9
		Per Cap. Income					Home Charges	Drain
	Pop.	(Rs., 1948-	Nat. Inc.	Exch.	Nat. Inc.	Home Charges	as % of	as % of
Year	(Mil.)	49 prices)	(Rs. mil.)	Rate	(£mil.)	(£mil.)	N. Y.	N. Y.
1872	206	182	37,510	1 Rs-2/25	2,988	10	0.33	0.04
1881	253.8	220	55,830	1 Rs-2/25	4,467	14	0.31	0.04
1891	287.3	200	57,400	1 Rs-3/50	3,447	17	0.5	0.05
1900	291.0	190	55,290	1 Rs-3/200	3,783	20.5	0.55	0.07

Notes:

Column 2, V. Anstey, *op. cit.*, p. 515.

Column 3, data extrapolated from V. B. Singh, ed., *op. cit.*, pp. 689-90.

Column 4, obtained by multiplying cols. 2 and 5.

Column 5, R. C. Dutt, *op. cit.*, p. 529.

Column 6, obtained by multiplying cols. 4 and 5.

Column 9, Drain is equivalent to about 13% of the Home Charges; the percentage has been estimated in the text.

[28]V. B. Singh, editor, *Economic History of India—1857-1956.* Bombay, 1965, pp. 701-2; Mr. Mukerjee in the article entitled "National Income," pages 661 to 703, obtained the series after taking into account the various works on income estimates of people such as D. Naoroji, F. J. Atkinson, Major Baring, Horne, W. Digby, Lord Curzon, and R. Giffen. He derived the time series by using Atkinson's 1875 estimates as the base and carrying out calculations forwards and backwards with the help of population series and index number of wage rates. The estimates of Naoroji, Baring, and Horne were fitted in the series after making necessary adjustments for the sake of comparison. To obtain an idea of the problems involved in estimating national income of India, see "Long-term Trends in Output in India" by D. Thorner in *Economic Growth: Brazil, India, Japan.*, edited by S. Kuznets. Durham, N.C., 1955.

Simple calculations reveal that the drain for the period under consideration varies from 0.03 per cent to 0.05 per cent of the annual national income. Even if we consider the total home charge of 335 million sterling to be a "drain", an assumption heavily biased towards proponents of that theory, the percentage varies from 0.3 to 0.5 of national income. The home charges seem to be insignificant in relation to the national income. Perhaps the real "drain" was somewhere else, and not in these charges. If these amounts were to be invested in the social and physical infrastructure or other desirable projects the Indian economy would not have been significantly better off even if we assume a respectable incremental capital output ratio for the economy.

An analysis of home charges does not tell the full story as far as the impact of British rule on India is concerned. The total impact can only be assessed if one looks at the broader economic aspects of colonial rule in India.

On the benefit side several factors should be considered.

The creation of the infrastructure—railways, roads, and irrigation networks appear to have been beneficial to the Indian economy. The British invested large amounts in the railway with a 5 per cent public guarantee by the Indian government. The railroads were initially run privately, later on they were taken over by the government.

By 1909 the British investment in railways in India and Ceylon amounted to about 136,519,000 sterling. In 1856 there were only about 89 miles of railroad tracks in India; by 1900 this had increased to about 24,752 miles.[29]

The social, political and economic impact of the railway development in India was significant. Politically India became more of a closely-knit country. The civil and military administration improved considerably with the improvement of communications. People began to undertake long journeys which resulted in exchange of ideas among the various sections of the vast country which to some extent increased national unity by reducing traditional prejudices among the people.[30]

The railway system was a forerunner of modern industry in India. Cotton and woolen textile mills, sugar factories and tanneries were helped in their development by the railroads. India's export trade increased from 30 million sterling in 1859 to 76 million sterling

[29]Vinod Dubey, "Railways," *The Economic History of India*, ed. V. B. Singh. New Delhi, India, 1965, p. 336.
[30]Vinod Dubey, *op. cit.*, pp. 334-35.

in 1900. Import trade over the same period expanded from 34 million sterling to 60 million sterling.[31,32]

In 1800 a total of approximately 12,000,000 sterling was spent upon irrigation works.[33] At the end of the nineteenth century there were 15 major canal systems irrigating a land area of about 11,300,000 acres.[34] British investment in Government bonds which financed irrigation and other public works amounted to about 136,519,000 sterling by 1909.[35]

There is little doubt that investment in the infrastructure stimulated India's economic growth significantly. A commercial revolution in agriculture began in the country around 1860 as a result of the infrastructure development, the opening of the Suez canal, and increased demand for Indian cotton in the United States with the onset of the civil war. Between 1883 and 1906 the food crop output of India increased by 4 per cent in real terms.[36]

British rule in India was able to restore peace and security in the land on a scale that was not achieved in earlier periods. One of the direct results of this was the increase in total area under cultivation after 1840. In the Chingulput district of Madras the area under cultivation doubled in the period 1829-1850. In Nellore district cultivated area increased by about 60 per cent between 1801 and 1850. Between 1840 and 1850 in the Bombay region, cultivated area increased by a million and a half acres.[37] In 1891-92 the total cropped area in India was 188 million acres, by 1901-02 this had risen to about 200 million acres.[38,39]

With the coming of the British modern banking methods were

[31]R. C. Dutt, *op. cit.*, pp. 343, 529.

[32]The trade data are given in current prices. From 1859 to 1900 the prices doubled in the Indian economy according to the work of Mr. Mukerjee, *op. cit.*, p. 685; on this basis there is a small increase in exports and a small decline in imports of India in real terms.

[33]R. C. Dutt, *op. cit.*, p. 362.

[34]S. R. Sharma, "Irrigation," *Economic History of India*, ed. V. B. Singh, *op. cit.*, p. 165.

[35]Simon Kuznets, ed., *op. cit.*, p. 475.

[36]B. M. Bhatia, "Agriculture and Cooperation," *Economic History of India*, ed. V. B. Singh, *op. cit.*, p. 126.

[37]N. V. Sovani, *op. cit.*, p. 868.

[38]B. M. Bhatia, *op. cit.*, p. 127.

[39]The increase in acreage under cultivation was obviously not entirely due to restoration of law and order, a substantial part of the increase was a result of the development of the social and physical infrastructure.

introduced into India.[40] The Presidency Banks of Bengal, Bombay and Madras were established in the first half of the nineteenth century. In 1870 the total deposits and reserves of the Indian banking system amounted to about 125 million rupees and 37 million rupees respectively, by 1900 these figures had gone up to 343 million rupees and 69 million rupees respectively.

Britain endowed India with an efficient system of civil service, one that exists today in an Indianized version and perhaps is a model for many of the developing countries of the world. With the advent of the British crown in the second half of the nineteenth century, India was no longer ruled by ruthless adventurers bent upon enriching themselves. The excesses of eighteenth and early nineteenth centuries were gone. The ruling civil servants were able and were selected mostly from what Strachey calls "ordinary firsts "and "good seconds" of the British educational system.[41]

On the cost side of the picture, besides the home charges levied on India, several other factors have to be considered.

The construction of the railroads was achieved at a cost which was very likely much higher than what it would have been if free market conditions had prevailed. The contracts for railway construction were awarded to British companies on a cost plus five per cent profit basis. This arrangement did not result in cost minimizing behavior. Although the railroads were built rapidly and construction was sound, the costs were much higher than the initial estimates. In 1868 the cost per mile averaged about 18,000 sterling in place of estimated costs of 8,000 sterling. It is very likely that the cost of the railroad would have been cheaper even if the construction were to be handled by the state.[42]

Railroad construction in India was not primarily designed to stimulate well-rounded economic development of the country, but they were instituted primarily with British interests in mind. The railways were laid out in such a way that they provided rapid transportation of raw materials and produce from the interior to the chief ports. Thus Bombay, Calcutta, and Madras were connected to

[40]India possessed indigenous bankers from 500 B.C. onwards. Their chief function was to lend money to traders and kings. By the twelfth century Indian bankers were using a system of bills of exchange. S. G. Panandikar, "Banking," V. B. Singh, ed., *op. cit.,* p. 414.

[41]John Strachey, *End of Empire.* New York, 1964, p. 54.

[42]L. H. Jenks, *op. cit.,* p. 222.

the centers of raw material production, while the linkage between the interior cities was lacking or was very expensive due to different track sizes. The freight rates were favorable to long haul of primary products to the ports and movement of British manufactured goods from the ports to the interior. This pattern of railway development created structural deficiencies in the Indian economy by promoting growth of primary export industries at the expense of secondary ones.[43]

Although there is no question that a part of the military expenditures were essential for restoring law and order in the country, a considerable portion of the defense budget was spent on military expeditions which were of little value to the colony. With the advent of crown rule, India had become the imperial base in Asia and the Indian army was used in order to maintain the balance of power in the continent. The expenditures connected with these unnecessary military expenditures as shown earlier amounted to a sizable cost to the colony.

After the end of the Sepoy mutiny, the doctrine of racial superiority had hardened considerably in the minds of the British in India. Gunnar Myrdal points out that racial segregation policies had adverse effects on the Indian economy as a result of segregation of economic activities. British firms in India were outposts of Britain, they only employed unskilled Indian labor and the economy did not benefit in terms of externalities through valuable manpower training.[44] Similar detrimental policies also existed in the military and the civil services. In the armed forces until 1914 the Indians were confined to lower ranks, and the officers were mostly British. The Indian Civil Service was thrown open in 1858, but it was only a token gesture. Very few Indians were able to enter it because of exacting requirements. By 1933 the picture had improved; about 35 per cent of the higher level jobs were occupied by Indians.[45] The parliamentary returns of 1892 show that out of 2388 civil and military jobs paying Rs. 10,000 or more only 60 were occupied by Indians, 15 by Eurasians, and 2313 by Europeans. The small band of fortunate Indians were mostly concentrated in the civil departments. There was only one Indian in the military falling in this salary category.[46] The cost due to diseconomies of discrimination was

[43]S. Kuznets, *op. cit.*, p. 477.
[44]J. Strachey, *op. cit.*, p. 55.
[45]N. V. Sovani, *op. cit.*, p. 79.
[46]R. C. Dutt, *op. cit.*, p. 573.

probably very high during British rule of India. The problem had become very serious because of the dualistic development of the economic and social systems of India—one British, the other Indian.

While examining the variables in the cost-benefit equation, it becomes apparent that Britain's presence in India, in the second half of the nineteenth century, does not follow a pattern of ruthless exploitation as has been suggested by many. There seems to be little doubt that Britain came to India with economic ends in mind, and it is also true that she gained a lot throughout the seventeenth and eighteenth centuries, but, with the coming of the crown in the second half of the nineteenth century there were substantial improvements in the welfare of the colony.[47]

The major criticism of British rule in the second half of the nineteenth century would be what M. D. Morris calls the "night watchman" policy of the government. The policies, although not purposely designed to frustrate economic development, certainly did not actively encourage industrial development. The policy makers of British India felt that their role was to provide law and order and a minimum of infrastructure. The development of the colony was to take care of itself. The government was overly concerned with balancing the budget and this inhibited higher levels of investment in the infrastructure. The principle on which investment in social overhead was made was that the projects should begin to pay rapidly at the market rate of return. Such an investment criteria resulted in inadequate development of railways, roads, and canals.[48]

Perhaps it is appropriate to raise a question which has been raised many times in the past. Would India be more developed if the British had not conquered and ruled the country? The validity of this question is in serious doubt because the Sepoy mutiny, although militarily successful in its earlier states, had proven that India could not form itself into one nation due to a lack of national consciousness and adequate administration. This fact clouds the very first assumption necessary in order to analyze the course of Indian development—the existence of the colony as a nation without British rule. The alternate question to ask then is what would have been the course of India's development if the fractionated subcontinent had reacted to western

[47]The per capita income in the period 1857 to 1900 show a rising trend. See Figure 4 for data on per capita income in India. Income time-series for the remaining part of the period under consideration, 1840-1856, was not available.

[48]M. D. Morris, "Towards a Reinterpretation of 19th Century Indian Economic History," *Journal of Economic History*, 1963, vol. 23, no. 4, pp. 614-16.

FIGURE 4. INDIA: AVERAGE PER CAPITA INCOME AT 1948-49 PRICES FOR
OVERLAPPING NINE-YEAR PERIODS

(Each point represents the center of a nine-year period.)

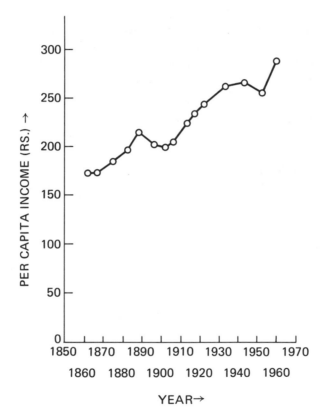

Source: V. B. Singh, ed., *op. cit.*, pages 701, 702.

influence without losing its independence? A tentative answer to this is provided by Sovani:

> In the 18th century when the British began to loom rather menacingly on the Indian horizon, the Indian princes of those days were struck by the magic of European arms and discipline and regarded it as the key to their success. Scindia, Mir Kasim, the Sikhs, engaged Europeans to train and discipline their troops, i.e., they began the process of learning from the west at the technical level much in the same way as the Japanese and Chinese did. If this is any indication, it can be said that the process of imitation of western techniques in the initial stages of India would not have been different from that in Japan or China if India had not been conquered by the British.[49]

Although I do not completely agree with the last part of Sovani's statement, where he claims that India would have followed Japan's development path, since there are vast differences between the two systems in social and cultural terms, it is probable that industrialization could have come to the various Indian national entities which comprised the subcontinent without British conquest and subjugation of the land.

[49]N. V. Sovani, *op. cit.,* p. 103.

Rising Demands and Insufficient Resources[1]

Harold and Margaret Sprout

Harold and Margaret Sprout are Research Associates in the Center of International Studies of Princeton University, where Harold Sprout is also Professor Emeritus of Geography and International Relations. They are co-authors of *The Rise of American Naval Power*, (1939); *Toward a New Order of Sea Power*, (1940); *Foundations of National Power*, (1946, 1951); *Foundations of International Politics*, (1962); *The Ecological Perspective on Human Affairs*, (1965); *An Ecological Paradigm for the Study of International Politics*, (1968); and numerous shorter writings on international and ecological subjects.

According to Harold and Margaret Sprout it was possible for Britain to maintain the empire as long as the common people in the United Kingdom and the colonies could be kept under control with relatively low cost. The empire became progressively insupportable as rising domestic demands and increasing resistance to foreign rule in the colonies coincided with increasing cost of maintaining Britain's Grandiose role in international politics.

I

One dictionary defines a dilemma as either (1) "a situation involving choice between equally unsatisfactory alternatives" or (2) "a problem seemingly incapable of a satisfactory solution." The dilemma examined in this review article exhibits both facets. It arises from the following conditions: In every political community there is, in any specified period, a certain aggregate of disposable goods and services, an aggregate that varies through time, generally though not necessarily expanding. All such communities exhibit a congeries of ongoing commitments, contractual or customary, that likewise tend generally to proliferate and enlarge through time. In most communities new demands for goods and services also tend to arise. With few exceptions ongoing commitments and new demands exceed, often greatly exceed, disposable resources. The chronic gap between commitments and demands, on the one hand, and disposable resources, on the other, poses the dilemma that our model is intended to identify and illuminate.

[1]Reprinted from "The Dilemma of Rising Demands and Insufficient Resources," *World Politics*, Vol. 20, No. 4, July 1968 (excerpts).

From the perspective of governing, the severity of the dilemma depends on various conditions. These include, among others, (1) the degree of consensus within the community regarding goals and (2) the level, or quality, of public order that prevails. Communities exhibit wide differences with respect to consensus and public order, with deterioration of one or both likely to accompany stresses set up by rapidly changing conditions.

This dilemma is not a new phenomenon. Resources available to rulers have rarely seemed adequate for the rulers' felt needs and those of their constituents. Allocations have just as rarely satisfied all claimants within the body politic. Moreover, the elements of the dilemma are familiar to political theorists as well as to politicans and administrators and are implicit in numerous models and theories.[2] However, it seems to us timely and useful to restate and reexamine the dilemma more explicitly and to suggest certain relatively new dimensions that may be clothing it with considerably greater salience for both domestic and foreign politics.

II

A convenient point of entry is 1815, the year the French wars finally ended, though, as others have demonstrated in detail, the roots of Britain's nineteenth-century naval primacy reach back at least to the reign of Elizabeth I.[3] In the generation of nearly continuous conflict with revolutionary France, the British navy had achieved a fairly comprehensive command of the sea. Specifically, British forces had prevented invasion of the home islands, protected movements of troops and matériel to foreign battlefields, maintained the flow of essential supplies into Britain, and driven enemy fleets and merchant shipping from the main sea routes, thereby cutting Napoleon and his satellites off from essential supplies and assistance.

[2] One thinks immediately of the ongoing work of James N. Rosenau; among other items that could be cited is his symposium *Domestic Sources of Foreign Policy* (New York 1967). The dilemma of insufficient resources is implicit in David Easton's concept of "input overload" *(A Systems Analysis of Political Life* [New York 1965], 58-59). The dilemma is likewise implicit in Harold Lasswell's "distributive" concept *(Politics: Who Gets What, When, How* [New York 1958]). The dilemma lurks in the cliché "revolution of rising expectations." It informs Paul Y. Hammond's essay "The Political Order and the Burden of External Relations," *World Politics,* xix (April 1967), 443-64. It enters into certain chapters of Samuel P. Huntington's *The Common Defense* (New York 1961), esp. chaps. 14-19; and into still other theoretical writings.

[3] See Alfred Thayer Mahan. *The Influence of Sea Power Upon History* (Boston 1890); also Strang. chaps. 1-6.

As the French wars receded, the Royal Navy's presence (often only a token presence) in foreign ports and upon the high sea served to keep memories of British naval prowess alive and to foster in other people's minds a presumption that the Royal Navy could again close the main seaways to its enemies in case of war.

No one can possibly know for certain how much political leverage British diplomats derived from this source. The materials for solving that riddle vanished with the men who dealt with Britons during the nineteenth century. However, from scattered and inconclusive clues in the surviving records, it seems credible that throughout most of that century, the legend of British naval invincibilty, firmly rooted in historic achievement, exerted a strong psychological influence both on Britain's adversaries and on British statesmen themselves.

It is clearer in retrospect than it was to most contemporary observers that Britain's historic (and presumptively continuing) ability to set the terms of access to the high sea in time of war derived from a rather extraordinary combination of environing conditions. And so pervasive was the myth that it diverted attention from changes—technological, economic, and broadly political—that gradually and insidiously eroded the foundation of British seapower during the later nineteenth century and thereafter to the present day.

Britain's influence on other nations reached its peak in a period when all the Great Powers were European states—the period when the expression "European states system" was nearly synonymous with international politics. It was also a period when overland transport was everywhere slow and costly. For most of the continental countries, access to the ocean and connecting seas was a condition of high priority, nearly as essential as for insular Britain. The bulk of their maritime traffic had to pass throgh one or more constricting seaways—the Channel, the North Sea, the Strait of Gibraltar, and (after 1869) the Suez Canal and the Red Sea. By occupying shore positions near those bottlenecks and by maintaining even nominal naval forces in the vicinity, British statesmen kept their continental adversaries perpetually reminded of the Royal Navy's presumptive ability to deny access to the oceans and lands beyond. Under conditions prevailing until near the end of the nineteenth century, presumptive control of the narrow seas of Europe entailed political effects felt around the world.

The global effect of presumptive local control of European waters was buttressed by ancillary geo-military patterns in the Indian Ocean and in other distant seas. By mid-century Britain held strategic shore positions close to all the passages into and from the Atlantic, Indian, and Pacific oceans. Nearly all of those established (or potential) naval stations were located either upon an island or at the foot of a peninsula or promontory or upon an isolated coast backed by desert, jungle, or mountains.[4] Before the spreading railway grids reached deeply into Africa and across Eurasia and North America, before the days of motor vehicles rolling along all-weather highways, above all before the advent of submarines and aircraft, neither the British Isles nor the bases overseas could be taken from an unprotected flank or rear. As long as the British navy retained control of the water's surface, all were secure.

All this was accomplished without the financial burden of a large military establishment on land. A relatively small army, manned by volunteers, garrisoned the colonies and naval bases and provided a nucleus for greater forces if required in case of major war in Europe or beyond the oceans.

In contrast to the astronomical cost of large military establishments in our time, the price of Britain's nineteenth-century global primacy seems incredibly cheap. From the 1830's until the end of the century, the combined cost of army and navy in time of peace varied between two and three per cent of the national income.[5] At the peak of British power and influence, the decade of the 1860's, total expenditures for military purposes averaged less than £30 million per year. Adjusting for inflation and changes in the dollar price of sterling, this works out to something in the range of one to two per cent of average U.S. military expenditures in the 1950's and early 1960's. In short, mid-nineteenth-century British governments policed a worldwide empire and a global net of seaways and exerted on other nations an influence as great as, if not considerably greater than, that the United States can achieve today at a real cost fifty to one hundred times larger.[6]

---

[4]A partial list of British strategic positions overseas includes, besides those mentioned above, the Cape of Good Hope, the Falkland Islands, Ceylon, Singapore, Hong Kong, Jamaica, Trinidad, Halifax, Vancouver Island, and several positions within the Mediterranean. In 1904, Admiral Lord Fisher penned the often quoted epigram, "Five keys lock up the world! Singapore, the Cape, Alexandria, Gibraltar, Dover. These five keys belong to England . . ." (quoted by Arthur J. Marder in *The Anatomy of British Sea Power* [New York 1940], 473).

[5]B. R. Mitchell and Phyllis Deane, eds., *Abstract of British Historical Statistics* (Cambridge 1962), 366-67, 396-97.

[6]This estimate is derived from the price indexes in *Abstract of British Historical Statistics*, 476; and in Alan T. Peacock and Jack Wiseman, *The Growth of Public Expenditure in the United Kingdom* (Princeton 1961), 153-54. Our estimate may be considerably in error, but is probably on the conservative side. In any case, the general order of magnitudes is all that matters.

III

As the nineteenth century drew to a close, a few observers were beginning to perceive, albeit dimly, that the British political community was the legatee of a depreciating estate, so to speak. In a slightly different metaphor, PEP (a British planning group active since the 1930's) characterized Britain at the end of the century as "in the position of a patentee whose patent is running out."[7]

Historians may disagree as to just when British statesmen began to be consciously aware of this erosive trend—when a sense of security and adequacy (with only occasional lapses into anxiety) gave way to chronic anxiety (relieved only sporadically by short intervals of relaxation). Lord Strang, a lifelong diplomat, has suggested that the turning point came between 1887 and 1897, the dates of the Golden and Diamond Jubilees of Victoria's reign.[8]

In any case, it is now possible, in longer historical perspective, to identify relevant antecedents of the change well back in the nineteenth century. These include technological innovations of many kinds, changes in the geopolitical structure and scale of international politics, erosion of Britain's industrial, commercial, and financial primacy, and profound stirrings within the British nation and in the colonies overseas.

The technological revolution included radical changes in the design, propulsion, and armament of naval ships—the transition from sail to steam, from solid shot to explosive shells, from smoothbores to rifled guns, from "wooden walls" to heavily armored steel decks and hulls; the invention of the automotive torpedo; and many other innovations—a transformation described with authority and in detail in Bernard Brodie's *Sea Power in the Machine Age*.[9]

Officers and seamen of the period of Elizabeth I could have "sailed and fought ... with considerable efficiency" the ships of Lord Nelson's navy 250 years later. But "Nelson's men ... would have been utterly bemused if called upon to go forward only a quarter of that period."[10] Naval ships in the 1830's were still in essence similar to those of the Napoleonic wars. But those of the 1880's had become much more like the ships that fought the Battle of Jutland in 1916.

[7]Political and Economic Planning, *Planning No. 24*, quoted by Stephen King-Hall, in *Our Own Times* (London 1935), Vol. I, 25.

[8]*Britain in World Affairs*, 188ff., 233ff.

[9](Princeton 1941). For an earlier account of the revolution in naval technology, from the standpoint of American power and policy, see our *Rise of American Naval Power* (Princeton 1939), paperback ed. (Princeton 1966).

[10]Michael Lewis, "Armed Forces and the Art of War: Navies," in *The New Cambridge Modern History*, Vol. X (Cambridge 1960), chap. 11, 274.

Other facets of the technological revolution entailed consequences no less destructive of the old order of seapower. The building
of canals and railways, with improved roads to follow and, eventually,
motor vehicles to travel upon them, made continental countries progressively less dependent upon seaborne transport. Improved overland
transport was part of a larger technological upsurge—for example,
in industrial chemistry (new metallurgical processes, synthetic sub-
stitutes for natural materials, and so on) and in engineering design
(the steam turbine, oil-fired boiler, internal combustion engine, electric
generator, and many, many others). Nearly all of the technological
innovations narrowed the potential effects of future naval blockades
or reduced the security of insular Britain, its oversea colonies and
naval stations, and the interconnecting seaways. As is well known,
submarines in the First World War and the combination of submarines
and aircraft in the Second nearly brought the British people to
starvation and the British economy to collapse.

Changes in the geopolitical structure of international politics
also worked adversely to Britain. Japan and the United States began
building modern navies in the 1880's. These expanded rapidly during
the 1890's and thereafter. By 1900 control of the ocean portals
of Europe no longer gave to the British navy a global command
of the sea. Only by redeploying major naval units to American
and Asian waters could the Admiralty have maintained its former
presumptive primacy in those distant seas. And whatever the inclinations of British naval authorities, developments nearer home precluded
any such redeployment. Accelerated naval building in Europe, especially in Germany after 1900, threatened Britain's historic predominance
in European seas. Thus, instead of strengthening its American and
Asian squadrons, the Admiralty had progressively to deplete them
in its effort to maintain a margin of superiority in the narrow seas
and eastern Atlantic.

Japanese, American, and German naval expansion was an outward manifestation of profound changes in international politics. The
historic European states system was becoming a global system, with
additional, widely separated centers of power and influence in North
America and Asia. Concurrently, the scale of everything—agriculture,
industry, communications, military forces—was increasing. These
changes moved the British geographer, Sir Halford Mackinder, to
conclude in 1902, on the final page of his book *Britain and the British
Seas,* that "in the presence of vast Powers broad-based on the resources

of half-continents, Britain could not again become mistress of the seas."[11]

British as well as foreign appreciation of these changes and their military-political implications lagged behind events. As late as 1948— three years after atomic bombs wrecked Hiroshima and Nagasaki—the Government's annual Statement on Defence still adhered in essential respects to the historic design. It was readily admitted that new weapons and other changes in the international milieu had rendered Britain's military problem more difficult and costly. But there was little evidence that the Defence Minister and his political and professional colleagues contemplated drastic reassessment of military objectives and strategy. It was still assumed that "balanced forces"—land, sea, and air, supplemented by suitable civilian defenses—could repel any assault on the home islands, keep open vital oversea communications, garrison the colonies, keep the economy running, and carry on offensive operations as required. Even as late as 1955, after the Soviet Union had successfully tested its own thermonuclear weapons, the traditional doctrine continued to show through a veneer of lip service to new weapons, increased vulnerabilities, and drastic changes in the international system.

Concomitant changes in economic conditions also weakened Britain's relative power position. For reasons beyond the scope of this discussion, the Industrial Revolution began earlier in Britain than elsewhere. For several decades British producers enjoyed a long head start over most foreign competitors. British imports of food and raw materials and exports of coal and manufactures came in the nineteenth century to constitute by far the largest national component of the total commerce among nations. Most of the profits from this enterprise were reinvested in Britain and also overseas. To facilitate this worldwide system of trade and investment, British bankers evolved an international monetary system based on unrestricted movement of gold and convertibility of sterling into all currencies. London became the capital, so to speak, of a commercial and financial community that came to embrace not only the British oversea colonies and dominions but also most of the politically independent communities in every continent.[12]

[11](New York 1902), 358.

[12]The standard authority on this aspect of British nineteenth-century primacy is Albert H. Imlah, *Economic Elements in the Pax Britannica* (Cambridge, Mass., 1958). In an overview of the period 1810-1850, the British historian David Thomson says: "The effect of economic changes in these four decades was that by 1850, Great

The deterioration of this economic order was as gradual and insidious as the erosion of Britain's military primacy upon the seas. As late as 1850 the British economy produced over half of the world's iron and steel. But before the end of the century both Germany and the United States produced more than Britain. That is not to say that British production declined. On the contrary, it went on rising. What gradually declined was Britain's share of the world total. British production simply expanded less rapidly than that of the newer industrial economies. What was true of steel was true, with variations of detail, of numerous other sectors of economic activity. The picture was much the same with respect to coal production, shipbuilding, ship operation, exports and imports of commodities, and other indicators of economic activity.

The two world wars accelerated the decline of Britain's industrial, commercial, and financial primacy. The first war entailed the sale of a considerable portion of foreign investments, income from which had long helped to pay for essential imports of food and raw materials. The second war further depleted the investment portfolio, while inflicting heavy damage on productive plant and delaying replacement of obsolescent plant and equipment. The war also disrupted established trade patterns and stimulated the growth of local industries in countries previously dependent on Britain for some or most of their manufactures. Thus Britain entered the post-1945 period with heavy economic handicaps, handicaps only partially offset by large-scale loans and subsidies, chiefly from the United States.

I V

It remains to examine still another set of conditions and events, the impact of which on Britain's external power and influence has received less attention than it deserves. Few subjects have been more diligently investigated in recent years than the condition of the British common people during the nineteenth and twentieth centuries, but rarely in the context of international politics. In the earlier years, the picture is one of unrelieved hardships and misery, a picture

---

Britain had triumphantly established herself both as the 'workshop of the world' and as the shipper and trader of the world. . . . Her [worldwide] interests . . . were soon to be deeply and severely affected by formidable rivals whose industrialisation had meanwhile taken place. The greatest of these were Germany and the United States. But until the decade after 1870 she continued to harvest very rich rewards, as the impetus of her growth and productivity carried her forward" ("The United Kingdom and Its World-wide Interests," in *The New Cambridge Modern History*, X, chap. 13, 333-34).

of a population barely literate, ignorant of affairs, geographically immobile in the main, grossly underpaid, poorly housed and fed— *above all a population with almost no effective access to government.*[13] Judges who administered the common law of crimes, torts, and property legitimized the existing order and denied redress of injustice to the poor. Lords and Commons resisted social reform, in part from conviction, in part from sheer parsimony. In a sense which most Americans today should comprehend, the common people of Britain were the "invisible poor"—invisible not so much in a literal as in a political sense. These were the people characterized in 1909 by C. F. G. Masterman as "that 80 per cent (say) of the present inhabitants of these islands who never express their own grievances, who rarely become articulate, who can only be observed from outside and very far away."[14] This "multitude," as Masterman also called them, were more or less effectively excluded from the British *political* community of which they were nominally members.

The Pax Britannica of the mid-nineteenth century rested, in both its economic and its military aspects, upon the social order sketched above. It was a social order that encouraged saving as well as affluent living by the well-to-do upper classes and denied to the vastly more numerous manual and clerical workers a large part of the fruits of their labor. In the historic words of John Maynard Keynes, the industrial growth that supported the military power of the European states, Britain included, depended on a "double bluff or deception."

"On the one hand, the laboring classes accepted from ignorance or powerlessness, or were compelled, persuaded, or cajoled by custom, convention, authority, and the well-established order of

---

13Among the works we have found most useful in this connection, special mention should be made of Henry Mayhew, *London Labour and the London Poor* (London 1861), 3 vols.; Charles Booth, *Life and Labour of the People in London,* 17 vols., published during the final years of the nineteenth century, and a recently published abridgment in one volume, *Charles Booth's London,* edited by Albert Fried and Richard M. Elman (New York 1967); C. F. G. Masterman, *The Condition of England* (London 1909); G. D. H. and M. I. Cole, *The Condition of Britain* (London 1937); G. D. H. Cole and Raymond Postgate, *The Common People, 1746-1938* (London 1938); Phyllis Deane, *The First Industrial Revolution* (Cambridge 1965), chap. 9; Herman Ausubel, *In Hard Times* (New York 1960); L. G. Johnson, *The Social Evolution of Industrial Britain* (Liverpool 1959); S. G. Checkland, *The Rise of Industrial Society in England* (London 1964); David Roberts, *Victorian Origins of the British Welfare State* (New Haven 1960).

14p. 85.

society into accepting a situation in which they could call their own very little of the cake that they and Nature and the capitalists were cooperating to produce. And on the other hand the capitalist classes were allowed to call the best part of the cake theirs and were theoretically free to consume it, on the tacit underlying condition that they consumed very little of it in practice."[15]

Some critics have contended that Keynes exaggerated the degree of exploitation and servitude to which the common people were subjected. There clearly is room for some debate as to how large a part of the population was so enthralled. That it ran to many millions cannot be doubted. After thorough research, it has been recently reaffirmed that "destitution was still the outstanding characteristic of our [British] industrial society up to the First World War. Between a quarter and a third of the whole population still lived in 'poverty,' carefully defined . . . as 'earnings . . . insufficient to obtain the minimum necessaries for the maintenance of mere physical efficiency'. . . ."[16]

In 1920, when Keynes penned the words quoted above, the British social order was in the early stage of a nonviolent but nonetheless sweeping revolution. Progressive taxation was beginning to transfer control over accumulated wealth and income from private owners to public authorities. And concurrently, politicians of all parties were becoming more attentive to the condition of the less privileged classes.

In the space available here we can mention only some of the dimensions of a process that began in the nineteenth century, gathered momentum in the early years of the twentieth, and eventually transformed the British political community. Those dimensions included extensions of the suffrage, mitigation of the rigors of the common law, legalization of unions, recognition of the right to strike, a gradual increase in the allocations of public resources to education, old-age pensions, and other social services, development of the Labour party, and the leveling side effects of two exhausting wars. Change was rapid in some decades, dragged in others. But the secular trend has been irreversible.

As the poor have become less poor, more articulate, more politically active, their demands in Britain (as elsewhere) have risen steadily and steeply, along with those of nearly all classes of society. Expressed in terms of domestic politics, these demands have become

[15]*The Economic Consequences of the Peace* (New York 1920), 19-20.
[16]John Burnett, *Plenty and Want* (London 1966), 93.

increasingly "hard" demands—hard in the sense that politicians, even the most conservative, have rather consistently given high priority to them in recent years, either from conviction or for reasons of expediency. Indeed, "pie in the sky," *now* or *soon*, not merely in some vague "by and by," has become a prime principle of prudential statecraft in Britain as it has increasingly around the world.[17]

Anyone who doubts the thrust of this trend in Britain should consider the picture that emerges from the statistical record. As indicated in Figure 1, in the 1890's annual expenditures of public authorities for social services averaged slightly over two per cent of GNP.[18] By 1913, the eve of World War I, these had risen to four per cent. In the last year before World War II, the allocation had risen to eleven per cent. In 1950, the first relatively "normal" year after the war, the allocation was eighteen per cent. From that level it declined to sixteen per cent in 1957 and since then has risen steadily to more than twenty-one per cent in 1966.

Turning to expenditures for military purposes, Figure 1 shows that the allocation before World War I was nearly the same as for social services, except during the Boer War at the turn of the century. In the interwar period (1920-1938), the military allocation ranged from over eight per cent of GNP in 1920 to less than three per cent in the late twenties and early thirties to nearly nine per cent on the eve of the Second World War. From 1921 to 1938, military expenditures were consistently lower than allocations to the social services. The widest spread came in the depression year of 1932, when military and social-service allocations were 2.8 and 12.9 per cent respectively.

For the 1950's and 1960's, the statistical contrast is just as striking and the trend even more so. In 1950, the military services took 7.2 per cent of the GNP; in 1952, 11.8 per cent in response to the Korean crisis. Thereafter the allocation to military purposes declined more

[17]Regarding this aspect of British political culture, see Richard Rose, *Politics in England* (Boston 1964), chap. 2; for a comparison of British and American political culture in these and other respects, see Kenneth N. Waltz, *Foreign Policy and Democratic Politics* (Boston 1967), chap. 2.

[18]The category "social services" covers "education and child care, health services, national insurance (unemployment, sickness benefits, retirement pensions, etc.), national assistance (relief of the poor and family allowances), housing (subsidies and capital expenditures), and food subsidies" (Peacock and Wiseman, 183). These subcategories are derived from the Central Statistical Office's annual handbook *National Income and Expenditure*. For the earlier years, many of these items were negligible or nonexistent. That is to say, public expenditures for social services have expanded in scope as well as in magnitude during the past half century.

FIGURE 1. GOVERNMENT EXPENDITURES, 1890-1966, FOR MILITARY PURPOSES AND SOCIAL SERVICES (as percentages of GNP)

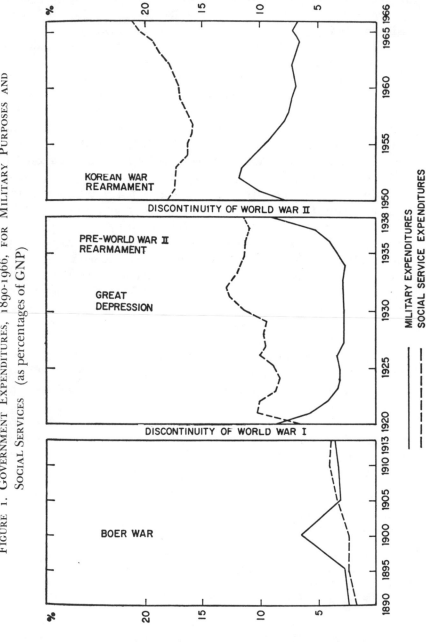

SOURCES: 1890-1955, Peacock and Wiseman, 190-91; 1955-1966, Central Statistical Office, *National Income and Expenditure, 1967.*

or less steadily to 6.9 per cent in 1966, with further decline in prospect.[19] In the same period, as noted above, public expenditures for the social services stood at 18 per cent of GNP in 1950, declined to 16 per cent in the middle fifties, and rose steadily thereafter to 21.2 per cent in 1966.

A similar picture emerges when expenditures for military purposes and for the social services are viewed as fractions *not* of GNP but of total governmental expenditures. This picture is graphically presented in Figure 2 (p. 234).

We leave this picture for the moment with the observation that, no matter what prime ministers and their fellow politicians *say* about maintaining the military posture and stature of a great power, the statistics of allocation tell us that the social services during the past seventeen or eighteen years have commanded higher priority than the military services. In short, compared with social welfare, military commitments are "soft" demands in the context of electoral and parliamentary politics. Barring dire emergency, such as an all-encompassing war, it is unrealistic, in our judgment, to expect any reversal of these priorities in the foreseeable future.

v

The prospect of continuing military retrenchment is further strengthened by extending the analysis to additional dimensions of the British *political* economy. As the readers of this journal are well aware, Britain is a densely settled, heavily industrialized country, but poor in indigenous material resources. The economy depends heavily upon imports. About fifty per cent of all food is imported. Coal is the only abundant indigenous raw material, and the cost of producing coal from old mines has risen sharply in recent decades. Total imports— chiefly foodstuffs and industrial raw materials—have regularly exceeded twenty-five per cent of GNP in recent years.

These imports are paid for mainly by current exports of goods and services. Given Britain's dependence on imports, the nation's ability to meet the various demands for goods and services depends, first of all, on correspondingly high exports. This requires not only that goods and services be available for export, but also that they compete effectively with the offerings of foreign competitors.

In order to keep British prices competitive in foreign markets, numerous conditions are necessary. One of these is that British equip-

[19]Statistics for 1967 were unavailable at the time of writing in early 1968.

ment and methods of production be kept up-to-date and efficient in a period of rapidly advancing industrial technology and consequent early obsolescence. This requirement entails large annual increments of new fixed capital. Furthermore, nearly all capital equipment manufactured in Britain—every turbine, generator, lathe, die, press, tractor, truck, and much of the rest—contains some amount, usually a good deal, of imported materials. Hence, keeping British industry abreast of foreign competitors not only requires large allocations from current output to investment, but also involves consumption of large quantities of imports. Nor is that the whole story! Most of the goods exported to pay for imports of raw materials also contain imported materials themselves. These, in turn, must be paid for by additional imports. Thus there is a sort of spiraling effect that presents special problems for an economy as dependent on imports as Britain's is these days.

Whenever the aggregate of purchases from foreign suppliers exceeds sales to foreign customers, the international account can be balanced only by some one or combination of the following: deferring payment or other borrowing abroad, receiving gifts from foreign governments, exporting gold or other monetary reserves, and lowering the official exchange value of sterling relative to other currencies. The problem can be severely aggravated by the traditional practice of many foreign governments as well as private individuals and companies of maintaining large sterling deposits in British banks. When international payments crises occur, as these have with painful frequency since World War II, foreign depositors are likely to withdraw some or all of their sterling deposits—that is, to sell sterling. Such withdrawals tend to depress the price of sterling, necessitating support from Britain's limited monetary reserves. Even without this added source of pressure, the British economy is extremely sensitive to changes in the international flow of goods and services.[20]

[20]Writing for the *District Bank Review* (London) in 1957, the British economist John Jewkes characterized Britain's international economic position in terms that still apply, with some changes in detail, a decade later: "Comparing 1939 with 1955, in pounds sterling of unchanged value, our gold and dollar reserves are now about five-eighths, our total overseas investments perhaps one-half, our returns on overseas investments perhaps three-fifths of what they formerly were. Hanging above our heads are the short-term external liabilities, standing mainly to the credit of sterling area countries, which are about three times as large as pre-war; and a £2,006 million of long-term dollar debts which have been incurred since 1945" (No. 121 [March 1957], 3-17).

The need to expand domestic investment and to increase exports has been a continuing theme in British political debate over recent years. The links between investments, exports, imports, and the international balance of payments have been reiterated hundreds of times in Parliament and the public prints. It has also been repeatedly argued that the only *feasible* way to achieve these ends is to reduce military expenditures. This argument rests upon the important premise —a premise rarely made explicit in public—*that it is politically inexpedient to dampen private spending severely or to cut back governmental spending for the social services.*

Foreign observers, especially Americans, harshly criticize the British Government's reluctance to curtail personal consumption and social-welfare goals, if necessary, to sustain military and military-related foreign commitments. Critics have accused British Governments of timidity, of abandoning Britain's "international responsibilities," of sacrificing national security and honor for partisan advantage, and more of the same. Leaving aside the dubious propriety of foreigners' telling Britons how to manage their public affairs, such criticisms often betray ignorance of widely held values, priorities, and other features of the British political scene.

The average standard of living in Britain has improved considerably in the past twenty-five years.[21] Compared to people in most societies, Britons live well, though on the average less well than the average in the United States. However, British attitudes reflect bitter memories of hard times: ten years of severe depression followed by nearly twenty years of bleak austerity—the years of the Second World War, the delayed postwar recovery, and the Korean War. In those years, rationing, high purchase taxes, still higher income taxes, stringent credit restrictions, and other government-imposed controls all severely curtailed personal consumption—far more severely than anything most of Britain's American critics have ever themselves experienced.

In a masterpiece of understatement in 1957, Professor Jewkes, in the article previously quoted, observed that "efforts to cut down consumption might encounter stronger . . . psychological resistance . . . than in 1939." This was definitely our own impression during our extended residence in Britain in 1955, 1957, and 1962. Austerity had become an odious word. People everywhere were hungry for better houses, new furniture, modern kitchens, new cars, oversea vaca-

[21]Burnett, chaps. 13-14.

tions, and all the other amenities that middle-class Americans simply take for granted. People were not only hungry for these things, but determined to have them. Since 1962 we have had to observe the British scene from a distance. But we know of no evidence that indicates any slackening of the popular demand for goods and services. This is politically a "hard" demand, and Labour and Conservative Governments alike have so recognized it.

Under 'conditions prevailing since World War II, this "hard" consumer demand has put heavy pressure on the British economy. Increased spending for immediate personal consumption, like investment in new capital, increases imports of food and raw materials. The imported materials that go into personal consumption, no less than those that go into new fixed capital, must be paid for with greater exports of goods and services. And, to reemphasize a point made previously, these greater exports of goods and services require in turn still further imports, since the exports themselves contain a substantial amount of imported materials.

What we have said with regard to personal consumption applies with comparable force to governmental spending for nonmilitary purposes. It applies to the cost of administration, to modernization and rationalization of the nationalized coal and transportation industries, to the building and maintenance of modern highways and other public works. It applies in particular to subsidized housing projects, to the national health service, to education and child care, to old-age pensions and unemployment compensation, and to other social services. Anyone who follows events in Britain is familiar with the outcry that greets any proposal to cut back severely, or even marginally, in the broad sector of social services and welfare.

Finally, as has frequently been emphasized by British and foreign commentators, the military services consume both labor and materials, including imported materials, that might otherwise go into exportable goods and services. In an economy as nearly fully employed as Britain's has been most of the time in recent years, the military establishment competes with the civilian economy for manual labor, for specialized skills, and for the output of industries, especially metal-using industries upon which the export trade also heavily depends. And British military forces overseas consume foreign services (which have to be paid for with exports) just as surely as do British tourists in the Alps.[22]

---

[22]This aspect of Britain's military problem is especially well covered in chap. 9 of Colonel Snyder's book. He also deals with the closely related issue of conscrip-

In the foregoing paragraphs we have assembled a picture of the British political economy as an intricate system of capital, materials, labor, and organization, producing and distributing goods and services to several more or less distinct sets of claimants. These claimants compete in the political forum as well as in the market place for shares of a supply of goods and services—a supply that increases through time, but remains grossly insufficient in the agregate to cover similarly increasing demands and commitments.

In times of acutely sensed peril, Britons have shown themselves as able as any nation, more able than many, to carry on under restrictions of many kinds. They did so with remarkable perseverance during World War II and for nearly a decade thereafter. But the prevailing mood in Britain, as elsewhere, has changed in recent years. Britons appear, in general, to view the world scene with less alarm. Except for the short-lived Suez crisis in 1956, local problems have tended to crowd foreign events and commitments from most people's attention. The weight of the evidence known to us suggests that Britons these days are more concerned about taxes, pay, new cars, better schools, and a host of other problems close at hand, than about Russia, China, communism, Vietnam, De Gaulle, or the H-bomb. If this is so, one speculates that the tenure of British cabinets is likely to depend more on maintaining and further improving the style of living than on pursuing a vigorous foreign policy, maintaining an impressive "military presence" overseas, contributing to European defense, supporting the United States, or otherwise preparing for hypothetical perils abroad.

Evidence also seems to indicate that leading politicians of both major parties clearly understand this mood of their constituents. At any rate, as previously shown, their decisions in recent years have rather consistently given high priority to personal consumption and the social services, nearly as high priority to exports and industrial modernization, and much lower priority to oversea commitments and the military establishment.

This schedule of priorities, we repeat, derives from two sets of imperatives: economic and broadly political. Domestic capital formation and exports of goods and services receive high priority because the economy's viability is at stake, and everything else depends on

---

tion. Growing resistance to conscription became evident in the middle fifties. Conscription was abolished after the Suez crisis of 1956-1957 by the reorganized Conservative Government headed by Harold Macmillan. Snyder covers the question of conscription in both its political and its military aspects (pp. 249-42 and elsewhere).

that. Personal consumption and the social services receive high priority because the tenure of the Government may be at stake. These imperatives take precedence over foreign commitments and military demands in the prudential calculus of contemporary British politics.[23]

V I

We turn now to the general pattern that emerges from the foregoing review of British experience with the dilemma of rising demands and insufficient resources. In the introductory paragraphs we suggested that certain relatively new dimensions of politics might be endowing this age-old dilemma with fresh salience, not only for Britain but for all, or nearly all, political communites as well.

One of these newer dimensions is the progressive enlargement in greater or lesser degree of the effective political community, in many if not most countries, by the processes sometimes called politicization. Until quite recent times, most of the population in nearly all countries were illiterate or barely literate, immobile and unorganized, ignorant and politically powerless. Britain's ill-fed, ill-clothed, ill-housed, long-suffering poor typified the condition of all but tiny privileged elites in even the most affluent and powerful societies of the past. It was a condition of virtual servitude, in effect if not in law, a servitude that more or less rigorously excluded large segments of the population from effective access to those who ruled in the name of the community. In the judgment of Keynes and other eminent authorities, such servitude was a requisite of rapid industrialization. Comparable servitude, with many local variations, was widely imposed on non-European populations, sustaining for a time the historic colonial empires and expediting the production of primary resources that contributed to the rapid industrial development of Europe and the societies of European origin overseas.

These conditions have changed in radical respects during the past seventy-five years. Nearly everywhere today, common folk, though far from well informed, are more aware of the gap between relative poverty and affluence both inside their own country and between their own country and others. Spreading knowledge has stimulated demands, gradual and hesitant at first, then insatiable. Less privileged classes have gained greater access to government, greater ability to

[23]The prevailing schedule of values was clearly evident in the Government's handling of sterling devaluation in November 1967—in particular, in the prominence given to further military retrenchment in connection therewith, and the patently evident reluctance to dampen consumer spending or to cut deeply into welfare services.

articulate their felt needs and to compel the society's rulers to pay attention. In the main this process has proceeded further in the democratic and quasi-democratic societies of the West, but the weight of the evidence known to us suggests that it is actually or potentially a universal phenomenon.

Increasing access to government derives in part from education, the spread of information, and better leadership and organization, but also in part from the extreme vulnerability of complex modern societies to disaster in case of any prolonged interruption of essential services. This vulnerability has been driven home with increasing frequency in many countries, but never more dramatically than by the menace of an epidemic of typhoid and other diseases posed by the sanitation workers' strike in New York City in January 1968.

For these and other reasons, governments are giving more heed than formerly to the demands of their less favored constituents. Frequently, from conviction or expedience, politicians have promised much more than can be delivered at existing or prospective levels of production and within existing frames of priorities and commitments. In some instances, as currently within the United States, such overcommitment has led to cutting back social programs already begun —with results dramatically comparable to the menacing behavior of a dog deprived of a partly eaten bone.

The second complicating dimension is related in various ways to these expanding and intensifying demands from the lowly. This second dimension is the rising cost and widening scope of activities required to keep mature urban societies viable as well as to sustain the processes of modernization in the underdeveloped countries. These expanding activities reach into every sector of society. They include, among many other things, more and better education and social services, ever-increasing outlays for environmental services of all kinds, and, in some countries, enlarged expenses for public order and military defense.

In certain respects the environmental services are becoming the most critically important. Man is the "dirty animal" and destructive beyond any other species.[24] Whether he is so by nature or by culture

24If anyone doubts this statement let him read one or more of the following: Henry Still, *The Dirty Animal* (New York 1967); William L. Thomas and others, *Man's Role in Changing the Face of the Earth* (Chicago 1956); Fairfield Osborn, *Our Plundered Planet* (Boston 1948); William Vogt, *Road to Survival* (New York 1948); Stewart L. Udall, *The Quiet Crisis* (New York 1965); George R. Stewart, *Not So Rich As You Think* (Boston 1967).

may be debatable; in any case it is beside the point at issue here. It is no longer debatable that destructive human activities produce insidious as well as dramatic effects on the physical and social milieu. Nearly every society is accumulating vast and incredibly costly arrears of restoration and maintenance in consequence of the human propensity and ever-enlarging capacity to pollute air and water, to transform verdant landscapes into arid and often noisome wastelands, and otherwise to desecrate and foul the physical habitat.

Varied and costly services are also required to operate and maintain the ever more complex technology of contemporary urban civilization. More costly education is required for adults as well as for children and youth. Greater outlays are required to protect health and maintain mobility, as well as to police congested cities and countrysides. Politicians and civil servants in most of the mature societies, as well as in the modernizing ones, shrink from facing the staggering cost of checking decay, restoring damage, and maintaining a milieu in which people can continue to live a civilized existence. And all this is in addition to the rising cost of military defense and (in the case of numerous states) large nonmilitary as well as military-related external commitments.[25]

Available goods and services in any political community are allocated in accord with more or less discernible patterns and priorities. Allocations are determined in various ways, depending in part on the ideological format, in part on the traditional mores, of the society. But decisions of public authorities (the legitimate rulers) affect in some degree, usually in large degree, who gets what share of what is available; and the role of public authorities tends everywhere to expand.

Public authorities affect allocations *directly*, by their own expenditures from funds derived from taxation, and/or borrowing,

25Failure to give attention to the newer limiting dimensions of domestic politics is widespread among theorists of international politics. Nowhere is this weakness more starkly displayed than in the essay by George Liska, *Imperial America* (Baltimore 1967), sponsored by the Washington Center of Foreign Policy Research and warmly endorsed by its director, Robert E. Osgood. In Liska's recipe for a global American imperialism that would cost incalculable billions for an indefinite future, the author gives no attention whatever to the worsening racial and other conflicts that are tearing American society apart or to the dangerous and accelerating deterioration of our physical habitat. Our query to Liska, Osgood, and others of their persuasion is whether they *really* find it credible that even the United States can pay the astronomical price of the new-style imperialism that they advocate, without eroding, progressively crippling, and perhaps eventually destroying the domestic society from which all power and influence are derived.

and/or profits of state-owned industries, and/or expropriation of private property, and/or subsidies (gifts) received from abroad. In most countries most of the time, taxation in various forms provides the bulk of the funds expended by public authorities; and taxation nearly everywhere serves the additional purpose of redistributing income in accord with some scheme of values and priorities.

Public authorities also affect allocations of goods and services *indirectly*, by taxation, as indicated just above, by rationing of commodities, by wage and price controls, by restrictions on private borrowing, by foreign exchange controls, import and export restrictions, and central bank interest rates, and by still other means.

The allocation of resources in any political community in any statistical period can be represented in various ways, provided, of course, that necessary data are accessible. One graphic device for this purpose is the "pie" diagram, as shown for Britain in Figure 2. This diagram enables one to visualize at a glance the allocations to specified standard categories, or sets of claimants. The area enclosed by the perimeter represents the total value of goods and services distributed in a specified year. The wedge-shaped segments of the "pie" represent the shares allocated to specified categories of claimants.

In general, the dilemma of insufficient resources to cover rising demands and ongoing commitments is managed (when it is effectively managed at all) by changing the relative value of the respective shares or by increasing the total size of the "pie" to be distributed—or usually by some combination thereof. In Britain during the past fifteen years or so, as previously indicated, successive Governments (Labour and Conservative alike) have striven to expand the economy (that is, increase the "pie"), while concomitantly reducing gradually the allocation to military and military-related purposes and increasing proportionately the share of public-financed social services.

The format of national accounting varies slightly from country to country, but in general, as previously indicated with respect to Britain, the categories widely used include (1) *personal consumption*: the goods and services consumed directly by members of the community; (2) formation of *domestic fixed capital*: investments in new equipment or other fixed capital within the community; (3) *exports*: goods and services sent to foreign markets; and (4) the share claimed by *public authorities* and reallocated in part to other sectors of the economy.

In the case of Great Britain, and for the purposes of our model in general, it is desirable to subdivide category (4) into resources allocated by public authorities to *nonmilitary* and *military* purposes.

FIGURE 2. DISTRIBUTION OF RESOURCES (INCLUDING IMPORTS) WITHIN
THE UNITED KINGDOM AND TO FOREIGN CONSUMERS, 1966*

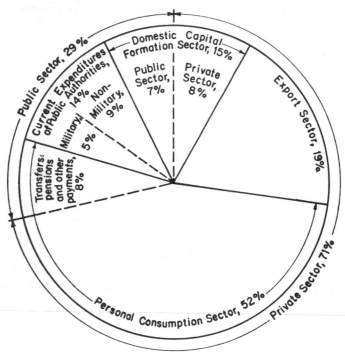

* The enclosed circle (the "pie" as a whole) represents the total of goods and services distributed at home and abroad, including imports. Additional arcs and broken lines indicate overlapping sectors. Several minor overlaps have been omitted, slightly distorting certain sectors but not significantly affecting relative magnitudes. The purpose of this diagram is *not* to depict shares in the GNP, but simply to identify allocations of goods and services distributed. To make the "pie" equivalent to GNP would require substracting taxes on expenditures and value of imports.
SOURCE: *National Income and Expenditure, 1967.*

The reason for doing so is that in Britain, as in many other countries, military and military-related commitments, on the one hand, and demands for education, housing, pensions, and other subsidized social services, on the other hand, pose the dilemma of insufficient resources in one of the more acute and intractable forms. However, one must take care not to focus too exclusively on this particular version of the dilemma.

It must be emphasized that this dilemma exhibits many variations and degrees of severity. It appears in several variants within the modernizing societies; in rather different forms within mature industrial societies, including the former Great Powers that have been or are being "priced out" of the international power market; in still different forms within the Soviet Union and the United States. It is impossible in this limited space to explore these variants in detail. But we do suggest that running through the spectrum of variant forms of the dilemma, two broad types of cases are especially notable: (1) cases in which the primary focus is the conflict between demands for immediate consumption and the need for new capital, complicated in some instances by substantial military and foreign commitments; and (2) cases in which the primary focus is the conflict between domestic demands and external commitments. The first pattern is well exemplified in the cases of India, China, and certain other modernizing societies. The United States is perhaps the foremost exhibit of the second pattern, which is manifested in the many-sided American debate over the priorities of fighting Communist guerrillas in Asia, maintaining a military presence and sustaining client regimes around the world, assisting the processes of modernization, supporting a massive military establishment, landing an American upon the moon, supporting research and development on scores of technological frontiers, *and* getting ahead with alleviating poverty in America, abolishing urban and rural slums, cleaning up and protecting our rapidly and dangerously deteriorating physical habitat, and a host of other pressing and likewise costly tasks at home.

The severity of the dilemma of insufficient resources depends on various conditions—among others, the size of the gap between disposable resources and competing demands and commitments, the nature and intensity of disagreement among competing claimants and between private claimants and public authorities, the ability of various claimants (including those within as well as those outside the structure of government) to exert effective influence on the ultimate determiners of policy, and the state and trend of the economy.

In general, the greater the degree of consensus within the society on goals and priorities, the milder is the political impact of the insufficiency dilemma. A relatively high degree of consensus on goals has kept the struggle in Britain at a relatively low level in recent years. But the reverse is evident in many societies these days. In some instances, probably in more than most students of politics are yet willing to admit, the dilemma reveals starkly a society internally torn and deeply eroded, possibly on the road to large-scale civic disorder and even to anarchy and revolutionary transformation in the image of radical Left or radical Right.

Confronted with grossly insufficient resources and intractable public resistance to the priorities set by the society's rulers, the latter may try to cope with the dilemma in various ways, usually by some combination of the following modes of action.[26]

First, efforts may be made to *expand the economy* sufficiently to narrow the gap between the demands and commitments on the one hand and the disposable resources on the other. Such efforts may include replacement of obsolescent equipment, more efficient use of human skills, and other innovations. This was the strategy followed in the United States with substantial success during the Korean War (1950-1952) and in Britain with very little success during the same period. Optimistic technocrats rise on all sides these days to predict that the continuing stream of technological innovations will enable everyone—at least within the United States—to have plenty of "butter" on top of astronomical outlays for military and military-related commitments. Events may confirm this optimism; but in our view this is an issue to be researched, not an assumption to be uncritically taken for granted.

Second, the rulers may prudentially *revise their order of priorities,* either to bring the commitments and demands and the resources more nearly into balance or to relieve pressure in the domestic political boiler, so to speak. The process of revision may be abrupt and drastic or gradual and moderate. As noted above, gradualness and moderation have characterized the recurrent downward adjustments of British military and foreign commitments and the concomitant gradual rise in allocations to the social services. Change of administration (Government, in British parlance) often expedites revision of priorities. It was manifestly easier for the newly elected President and his Secretary of State to negotiate the truce in Korea in 1953 than it would have been for their predecessors who had invested a lot of "face" in a stern, intransigent posture. In general, short of discontinuity resulting from revolution, military defeat, or other disaster, nations' images of their international role (like most other deeply rooted attitudes) change very slowly and, chronically, lag far behind events in periods of rapid and pervasive change and transformation.

Third, the rulers may resort to ploys of various kinds to *divert public attention* to other values and thereby tacitly increase tolerance

---

[26]Some of the techniques noted in the next few paragraphs have been identified and analyzed by Harry Eckstein in an essay "On the Etiology of Internal War," *History and Theory,* IV, No. 2 (1965), 133 ff.

for official priorities. Such ploys include, for example, public spectacles such as carefully staged appearances by the head of state or government, with or without accompanying ritualistic oratory. There are many kinds of diversionary ploys, summed up in the classic expression "bread and circuses."[27] Diversionary strategems have often proved very effective *for a limited time,* especially when conducted by strongly charismatic leaders. It is relevant, however, to query whether citizens in most countries are any longer as divertable and as malleable as many public relations experts seem to believe.

Fourth, the men in power may try to *change the opinions of dissenters,* and thereby achieve consensus, either by reasoned argument or, more typically, by selection, arrangement, and presentation of alleged facts that the audience is not sufficiently informed to evaluate. A striking example of the latter procedure was the contrived effort of the Johnson Administration in 1967 to convince the divided American public that military and political successes in Vietnam were much greater than these subsequently turned out to be. The more divided the national constituency, the greater usually is the effort devoted to "selling" the government's policies. Such efforts, even in tightly censored societies, tend these days to boomerang, producing rising distrust when official representations fail repeatedly to square with later relevations—a distrust aptly called the "credibility gap" in the United States today.

Fifth, and finally, the rulers may try to *silence dissent and opposition* to their commitments and priorities by threat or exercise of coercion or even of death. Temptation to resort to repression is strong, especially in deeply divided societies, when articulate and potentially powerful dissident groups seem to threaten not only official policies but even public order. The line between maintaining public order and repressing dissent is notoriously flexible and easily shifted toward repression, especially in societies with traditional proneness to violence.

The dilemma of rising demands and insufficient resources evokes many questions for students of comparative and international politics. In the remaining space we can mention only a few of these. For example, does the form of government affect management of the dilemma? Is it plausible, as is often urged, that dictatorships are inherently superior to democratic systems in this respect? Statement of the dilemma also evokes questions regarding the requisites of imperial viability. The British Empire was maintained as long as

[27]"Duas tantum res anxius optat,/Panem et circenses" (Juvenal, *Satires.* X, 80).

lowly folk in the United Kingdom and in the colonies could be controlled and kept working at relatively low cost in money and violence. The British Empire became progressively insupportable as rising demands within Britain and resistance to imperial rule in the colonies coincided with escalating costs of maintaining Britain's historic role in international politics. The British experience also suggests to us the possible utility of thinking about imperialism in terms of viable and unviable types—the former evolving into the latter when erosion of the imperial power's *moral* claims ("civilizing mission," "white man's burden," superior rule, and so on) necessitates progressively heavier reliance on violence to sustain the imperial authority. In other words, do empires—including the new-style imperial patterns exhibited by the Soviet Union and the United States—become increasingly unviable in the face of concurrent peaking of internal and external costs? Under such conditions, imperial rulers may try to repress internal dissent in order to carry external commitments. Alternatively, they may curtail or abandon external commitments in order to cope more effectively with rising domestic demands. Or, what is more likely, they may search for some workable compromise between the two extremes.[28]

The current strategy of the United States, as everyone knows, is to evade the dilemma by the route of economic expansion—to provide "guns" and "butter" simultaneously in unprecedented quantities. At first glance, this strategy seems to have succeeded phenomenally. But the dilemma is becoming painfully evident here too, and in the particularly nasty context of worsening racial conflict. Unless the American *political* economy is qualitatively as well as quantitatively different from all others, continuation of present policies seems likely to reveal still more starkly the conflict between massive foreign and military commitments and escalating domestic demands and requirements.

As our previous writings attest, we do not underrate the past effects and enormous future potentialties of the continuing technological revolution. But to those who preach the optimistic gospel of salvation by technology, we must reply that politics everywhere entails a great deal besides an endless stream of inventions and innovations. Much depends also on what is happening concurrently in other salients of the domestic and international arenas. How many

[28]We are indebted to our colleague, Professor Oran R. Young, for suggesting that we try utilizing the dilemma of rising demands and insufficient resources to establish some of the requisites of viable, conditionally viable, and unviable imperial systems.

scores of billions of dollars will it cost to catch up with environmental arrears and then even minimally maintain our depreciating habitat? How many billions of dollars will it cost to bring depressed segments of the political community to an acceptable level of social usefulness as well as personal comfort?[29] Will military and military-related commitments level off or continue to escalate as the rival holders of superpower strive vainly to outwit and outbuild each other? Will governments spend more, or less, on future probes of outer space and other fantastically expensive projects on the scientific and engineering frontiers? Will the fruits of research be channeled predominantly toward violence and destruction or toward alleviating and improving the human condition? Will growth of population around the world soak up increases in economic productivity? And for how long? Will human demands for material goods and services—in particular, the enormous latent demand in most of the heavily populated modernizing societies—respond temperately or explosively to awakening and spreading visions of plenty?

These are some of the questions evoked by reflection on the British experience and by reconnaissance of a few other societies. These are questions about which, with some notable exceptions, students of comparative and international politics seem to be remarkably reticent. We doubt that any political community, even the most productive and affluent, can evade or avoid these issues that are everywhere implicit in the dilemma of insufficient resources to cover rising and proliferating demands and commitments.

29A recent study of American goals and resources, carried out by Leonard A. Lecht for the National Planning Association of Washington, D.C., presents minimum and maximum estimates of "The Dollar Cost of Our National Goals" (Report No. 1 [May 1965], of the Center for Priority Analysis). A fuller statement of this project and of the data and assumptions upon which the estimates are based is published in Leonard A. Lecht, *Goals. Priorities, and Dollars* (New York 1966). Lecht's estimates rest, in our view, upon overoptimistic assumptions regarding the intensity of domestic social demands exacerbated by worsening racial conflict. But even if Lecht's optimistic assumptions are correct, American society is clearly headed for trouble. This NPA project points to the need for analysis based upon different sets of political assumptions regarding domestic and international conditions and for comparable studies of the Soviet Union, China, Britain, France, India, and other nations.

War as an Investment
The Strange Case of Japan[1]

Kenneth E. Boulding
and Alan H. Gleason

Born in 1910 in Liverpool, England, Kenneth E. Boulding was educated at Oxford University and the University of Chicago. He came to the United States in 1937 and has taught at McGill University, Iowa State University, and the University of Michigan. He is presently professor of economics at the University of Colorado. He is the author of many books which have been translated in several languages. His best known works are: *Economic Analysis* (1941); *A Reconstruction of Economics* (1950); *The Image* (1956); *Conflict and Defence* (1962); *The Meaning of the Twentieth Century* (1964); and *Beyond Economics* (1968).

Alan H. Gleason was educated at Princeton and the Massachusetts Institute of Technology. He has taught at the University of Rochester, International Christian University, Tokyo, and at the University of Pittsburgh. He has conducted extensive research on the Japanese economy and is the author of several articles.

In the case of Japan the war industry was an integral part of imperialism. According to Boulding and Gleason, the consequences have been disastrous. The effect of the war industry on Japan was to produce a "sick nation." The defeat was "shock treatment" which released tremendous amounts of creative vitality and the result was the almost record performance of the economy.

The reader is advised to examine the following: Fritz Sternberg, "Japan's Economic Imperialism," *Social Research*, XII (Sept. 1945) pp. 328-48.

The history of Japan in the last hundred years is perhaps one of the best case studies in the impact of war and military institutions on the whole life of the nation. The main object of this paper is to pursue certain aspects of this history from the standpoint of economics. This means that we look on the war industry as a segment of the economy, just as agriculture might be a segment. The war industry is defined here as that segment of the economy which produces

[1]Reprinted from the *Peace Research Society (International) Papers*, Vol. III, 1965, Walter Isard and J. Wolpert, editors, Philadelphia, pages 1-17. The paper is an interim report arising out of a research project sponsored by Research on the International Economics of Disarmament and Arms Control, directed by Professor Emile Benoit, Columbia University.

what is purchased with the total military expenditure of the government. We inquire about the effects of the war industry on other segments of the economy as it rises and falls, and we ask ourselves why it is as big as it is at any one time. The answers to these questions, of course, go far beyond economics. Nevertheless, there may be economic elements in the answers.

What might be called the crude statistical story is shown in Table 1 and in Figures 1 and 2. We have expressed the data in real per capita terms, eliminating the gross effects of the growth of population and inflation and deflation. The story can be summarized very simply. From the 1880's to the 1930's, real per capita product in Japan grew at a rate of about 2.4 per cent per annum, and with minor fluctuations, grew rather steadily. Consumption kept pace throughout most of the period. Military purchases in real terms were rather low, averaging about 5 per cent of GNP. In the 1930's we see a change. Real per capita consumption declines, even though per capita gross product continues to increase. From 1937 on, military purchases increase remarkably. This process culminates in what the Japanese call dramatically "the valley," which reached bottom in the great disaster of 1945. All the gains of the previous decades were wiped out. The cities were in ruins, the Empire taken away, the merchant marine destroyed, all foreign investments confiscated, three million Japanese had been sent home from overseas; and from this point on the rate of growth is about 8 per cent per annum, which constitutes a world record! We have here what seems like an unusual episode in political mental ill health and recovery. The full study of this, of course, would require all the resources of the social sciences, and here we are concerned as economists with what is actually a fairly minor aspect. It is an aspect, however, which throws a great deal of light on the whole process, partly because economic development and change is a great trend around which many other aspects of social life revolve, and also because in this case there seems to have been a great difference between the *image* of the economic situation as it determined the behavior of the major decision-makers and the realities, at least as revealed by statistics. It is a common picture even outside Japan that the aggressiveness and militarism of the period from about 1880 to 1945 were the result of economic pressures and economic forces. The evidence seems to point quite the other way. Economic difficulties did not cause the military expansion. Indeed, it was economic success that permitted it. A good deal was heard in this period, for instance, of Japan's overpopulation, lack of natural resources, and small area, only a sixth of which is arable. In terms of the economic reality of

TABLE 1*

REAL GROSS NATIONAL PRODUCT AND COMPONENTS PER CAPITA FOR JAPAN, 1887-1960
(1934-36 Prices in Yen)

| | (1) GNP | (2) PCE | (3) PDI | (4) GP | | | | (5) NFI |
				GPnmi	GPnmc	GPmp	Total	
1887	71.7	57.6	6.5	1.4	4.9	2.4	8.6	−1.1
88	73.5	60.9	5.0	1.3	4.9	2.3	8.6	−1.1
89	69.2	55.9	6.2	1.6	4.3	2.3	8.2	−1.0
1890	83.8	68.5	10.4	1.7	4.9	1.8	8.4	−3.5
91	76.7	55.8	12.5	2.4	4.2	2.2	8.8	−0.4
92	78.8	60.0	11.1	1.7	4.9	2.1	8.7	−1.0
93	81.1	62.1	12.5	2.6	3.9	2.1	8.6	−2.1
94	97.7	76.8	6.4	1.9	4.2	10.1	16.1	−1.5
95	92.4	74.2	5.8	1.5	4.3	8.4	14.2	−1.8
96	87.3	74.0	6.9	2.5	4.4	4.5	11.4	−5.0
97	88.0	70.5	9.1	3.0	4.1	6.1	13.2	−4.8
98	113.2	98.7	9.8	2.7	4.7	5.9	13.3	−8.5
99	102.0	84.1	5.3	3.2	6.1	6.4	15.7	−3.1
1900	105.2	82.0	11.5	3.5	6.0	6.6	16.1	−4.3
01	109.1	86.4	7.7	3.8	7.0	5.3	16.1	−1.1
02	93.8	76.1	6.4	3.7	6.9	4.1	14.7	−3.5
03	104.7	86.0	7.4	3.7	6.7	6.4	16.8	−5.5
04	105.6	70.9	10.0	2.4	5.1	25.4	32.8	−8.1
05	95.3	70.6	8.1	2.9	4.4	24.5	31.8	−15.2
06	104.1	79.4	10.2	2.9	5.8	13.7	22.3	−7.9
07	110.6	91.9	8.4	4.4	6.2	7.4	18.0	−7.8
08	117.9	95.8	9.7	5.7	6.7	7.8	20.1	−7.7
09	114.6	88.5	12.8	5.2	7.7	6.5	19.5	−6.2
1910	113.4	87.6	9.4	6.4	8.2	6.7	21.0	−4.6
11	127.3	94.5	14.4	7.4	10.3	6.9	24.6	−6.2
12	135.9	111.2	12.4	6.2	7.1	6.2	19.5	−7.2
13	131.6	100.4	20.5	6.3	6.7	5.7	18.7	−8.0
14	132.1	105.0	11.4	6.0	7.3	7.1	20.4	−4.7
15	132.2	102.8	9.1	4.9	6.7	7.8	19.4	1.1
16	141.2	109.6	9.2	3.9	5.1	7.9	16.9	5.5
17	148.6	114.0	8.1	3.8	5.4	8.8	18.0	8.5
18	173.3	134.3	11.9	4.1	4.3	11.1	19.7	7.4
19	195.8	152.6	24.9	6.3	4.0	13.5	23.8	−5.6
1920	153.9	110.0	24.1	7.5	7.6	11.5	26.7	−7.5
21	157.1	118.8	17.5	8.7	9.8	11.1	29.7	−8.8
22	144.5	117.7	17.1	9.6	11.7	9.0	30.3	−20.7
23	164.0	145.3	13.7	9.3	11.8	7.1	28.3	−23.3
24	180.4	153.0	21.5	10.0	12.6	6.5	29.1	−23.2
25	194.1	161.4	18.9	11.9	11.5	6.0	29.5	−15.6
26	190.2	154.6	22.1	13.6	12.7	6.0	32.4	−18.8
27	183.1	143.6	23.8	14.1	16.4	6.8	37.3	−21.7
28	194.5	150.1	19.0	14.1	20.7	7.2	42.0	−16.6
29	194.1	148.0	22.4	13.9	17.7	7.0	38.6	−15.0

TABLE 1* (Continued)

	(1) GNP	(2) PCE	(3) PDI	(4) GP				(5) NFI
				GPnmi	GPnmc	GPmp	Total	
1930	179.1	141.1	19.1	7.5	18.3	6.9	32.7	−13.7
1930	209.8	169.8	15.5	7.9	18.9	7.1	34.0	−9.4
31	213.1	166.2	17.7	6.5	27.0	8.4	41.9	−12.7
32	212.6	163.2	15.8	8.1	26.0	12.1	46.2	−12.6
33	218.1	161.3	20.9	6.2	25.0	13.9	45.1	−9.2
34	238.7	162.3	35.3	8.4	22.5	14.6	45.5	−4.4
35	241.0	155.4	38.0	7.5	22.9	15.0	45.3	2.2
1936	245.1	157.4	41.1	7.4	22.5	14.8	44.7	1.9
37	299.5	163.7	56.3	8.4	22.9	36.0	67.4	12.2
38	307.7	160.5	57.4	9.5	27.6	48.2	85.3	4.5
39	310.4	152.0	73.1	11.0	17.3	48.8	77.1	8.2
1940	289.1	135.4	70.2	11.4	20.9	48.2	80.6	2.9
41	294.4	131.2	72.3	11.5	23.2	64.1	98.8	−7.8
42	291.1	124.0	72.2	12.0	13.8	76.8	102.6	−7.9
43	292.2	116.4	64.6	12.8	6.5	97.7	117.0	−5.8
44	276.3	95.9	67.8	14.4	−	−	114.4	−1.8
45	−	−	−	−	−	−	−	−
46	148.6	90.1	34.4	13.5	8.7	7.6	29.8	−5.7
47	159.4	94.9	34.5	25.3	3.9	7.5	36.6	−6.5
48	178.9	104.9	41.5	21.6	10.5	6.9	39.1	−6.6
49	178.7	113.7	32.2	18.1	14.6	5.4	38.1	−5.3
1950	194.7	121.1	38.9	9.0	17.1	4.9	31.0	3.7
51	215.1	130.7	42.0	13.8	19.9	3.8	37.5	5.1
52	235.6	150.7	40.3	15.9	24.0	3.7	43.6	1.1
53	249.2	161.6	42.8	20.6	24.7	3.7	49.0	−4.2
54	257.3	166.0	38.9	20.0	24.2	5.4	49.5	2.8
55	279.6	177.4	45.2	23.5	26.1	4.6	54.3	2.7
56	298.8	186.4	66.6	20.4	27.2	4.4	51.9	−6.1
57	320.8	196.7	70.8	23.8	28.3	4.9	57.0	−3.8
58	329.5	205.7	60.3	29.4	30.2	4.9	64.5	−1.0
59	382.5	219.3	100.9	34.2	32.5	5.0	71.7	−9.4
1960	428.0	236.2	128.3	40.3	36.2	5.0	81.5	−18.0

* Notes and sources for Table 1 may be found in the Appendix. All results are tentative and currently under revision.

rising consumption, however, the overpopulation argument for military expansion appears to have been little more than a convenient myth which served to stimulate the laggards at home and to lull the gullible abroad.

Another image which the statistical realities do not confirm is that Japan's military expansion was the result of her difficulties in international trade, in finding, for instance, markets for her exports or sources of supply for her imports. Whatever problems there may have been in this area, however, her attempt to acquire political control of her trading areas contributed very little to their solution. Her principal acquisitions during the pre-1930 period were Korea and Formosa. These and other lesser possessions accounted for about 25 per cent of the external trade of Japan proper in 1928-30.[2] It is difficult to say, however, what the trade with these possessions would have been in the absence of political control. Structurally, at least, it might have been more beneficial to Japan. Lockwood, for example, points out that much of Japan's sugar came from Formosa through tariff preferences, which, if removed, might have permitted cheaper purchases elsewhere.[3]

The period around 1930 is particularly crucial in the rise of the military in Japan, and its economic environment requires particular attention. Japan's trade problem in 1931 was due primarily to the collapse of the United States silk market during the depression and to Finance Minister Inouye's determination to reinstate the gold standard in January 1930, thereby preventing for two years a fall in the value of the yen which would have offset in part the decline in world demand. After the gold standard was abandoned in December 1931, exports increased rapidly and Japan's deficit in her current account was not only reduced, but became a surplus in 1935. This situation continued, with the exception of 1938, until 1941. Her exports, excluding those to Korea and Formosa, showed a steady increase in both monetary and physical terms from 1931 to 1937 when full-scale war began with China.

Much is sometimes made of the restrictions on Japanese exports during the early 1930's.[4] It was, of course, not the first time Japan had been subjected to an increase in tariff rates. The United States, Japan's major trading partner, had already passed the Fordney-McCumber Act in 1922, establishing the highest rates in American history. But Japan's exports to the United States flourished during the 1920's with the bulk of them consisting of raw silk. The Hawley-Smoot Act, in 1930, passed over the futile protests of 1028 economists, provided further increases, but left raw silk, the critical item, on the free list. On the whole, it is likely that the Hawley-Smoot Act had more of a psychological than economic effect on Japan. It came

[2]From data in Bank of Japan, *Historical Statistics of Japanese Economy: 1962.* Tokyo, 1962, p. 90.

[3]William W. Lockwood, *The Economic Development of Japan.* Princeton, 1954, p. 51.

[4]See, for example, Edwin O. Reischauer, *Japan Past and Present* (Second Edition). New York, 1953, pp. 164-65.

at a bad time and added a valuable propaganda weapon to the arsenal of the militant ultra-nationalists. In spite of the act's restrictions and the loud cries of protest from American protectionist groups, Japan's exports to the United States improved after 1931, although they never, during the 1930's, regained the value levels attained during the silk boom of the 1920's. The United States remained Japan's largest single buyer until 1934 when it became a close second to China (including Manchuria and Kwantung province). Until the events of 1937, its purchases remained fairly close to those of China, in spite of the growing hostility toward Japan in the United States. While military conquest and political control may have expanded trade with Manchuria after 1931, these gains may have been more than offset by a retardation in the expansion of trade with other countries as a result of adverse reactions to Japan's military expansionism. If so, the Japanese militarists were responsible for creating one of the very conditions they cited as justification for their activities.

While there was little basis in fact for the overpopulation argument as used by the ultra-nationalists, it could still have provided a primary motivation for aggression as a belief held sincerely even if mistakenly. Evaluation of this possibility requires scrutiny of the many other elements entering into the complex background of the Manchurian Incident and ensuing all-out war. The impact of these elements on the motivations of the decision-makers is frankly a matter largely of inference and conjecture. Even apparently sincere pronouncements of the leaders must be treated with caution, for, as a French philosopher observed, *le coeur a ses raisons que la raison ne connaît pas.* In addition to the problem of the aims of the militarist leaders, we are confronted with the necessity of explaining the widespread popular support they apparently received. The simple answer is always the risky one. All one can do is list plausible contributing causes and give the supporting evidence.

It should be emphasized first that Japan's expansion into Asia was a continuation of a movement dating back many decades, perhaps even centuries.[5] Certainly the desire for military expansion showed itself long before population growth and industrialization created a substantial need for foreign markets and sources of supply.[6] Even before 1600, Japanese ships roamed the Asian seas, colonies were

[5]The following historical sketch is based largely on materials in Hugh Borton, *Japan's Modern Century*, New York, 1955; William L. Neumann, *America Encounters Japan*, Baltimore, 1963; and Reischauer, *op. cit.*

[6]See Lockwood, *op. cit.*, p. 534, for a similar comment.

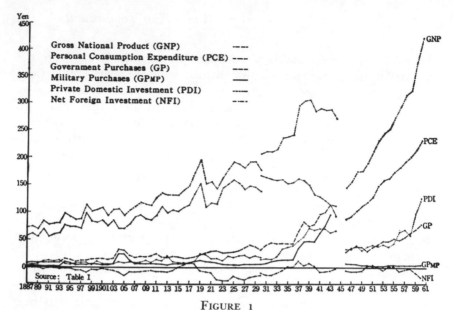

FIGURE 1

Real Gross National Product and Components Per Capita for Japan
1887-1960 (1934-1936 Prices)

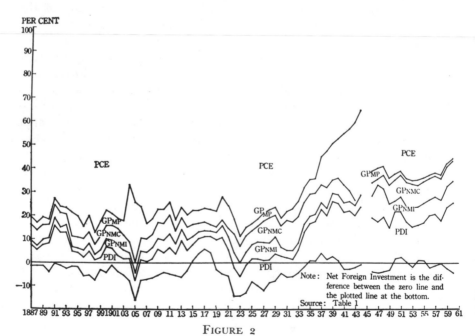

FIGURE 2

Cumulative Percentage Distribution of Components of Real Gross
National Product for Japan 1887-1960

established in areas of Southeast Asia, and in 1592 Korea was invaded in an extraordinary, but abortive, attempt to conquer China. This phase of overseas expansion, paralleling that of Europe during the same period, was interrupted for two and a half centuries by the Pax Tokugawa when Japanese leaders chose isolation rather than conquest as the best defense against expanding European colonialism. But the Meiji government, once isolationism had been abandoned, resumed the imperialistic practices of the earlier era. The policy of expansion was supported by a powerful traditional nationalistic sentiment or pride which rested on the belief that the Japanese were a nation divinely established and favored, a kind of chosen people of the Orient, destined to rule the less favored. Encouragement came from the example of Western nations who had just entered an unusually active period of imperialism of their own. During the 1870's, while the new government was still in the process of consolidating its power at home, it sent military expeditions to both Formosa and Korea, affirmed its claim to the Bonin Islands, obtained possession of the Kurile Islands by treaty with Russia, and formally announced control over the Ryukyu Islands which were claimed by China as tributary vassals.

Efforts to dominate Korea culminated in the successful war with China in 1894-95. Formosa was annexed and influence in Korea extended. In 1897, a clash with the United States over control of the Hawaiian Islands was narrowly averted. The seizure of territory in China and the Pacific by various other countries added further incentive to Japan's expansionist tendencies.

Russia's interference in Korea was met by the Russo-Japanese War in 1904-05.[7] Russia was forced to cede the southern half of Sakhalin, turn over concessions, including her railroads in Southern Manchuria, and recognize Japan's control in Korea. A few years later, Korea was formally annexed by Japan. Japan entered World War I on the side of Great Britain and France and promptly seized Germany's Kiaochow leasehold on the Shantung Peninsula plus certain island possessions in the Pacific area.

In 1915, Japan presented her "Twenty-one Demands" to China. Of these, China accepted the demand for formal approval of Japan's various economic activities in China and the demand for a pledge to refrain from making future coastal area concessions to any third

[7]Japan began the hostilities with a successful surprise attack on the Russian naval forces before formally declaring war. This strategem, while loudly hailed at the time in America for its brilliance, received a quite different reception when used again in 1941.

power. China did not agree, however, to certain requests which were designed to extend Japan's political control over China. The demands aroused protests in the United States as a violation of the so-called "Open Door" policy. Japan's position as an ally in the struggle against the Central Powers, however, prevented the United States from acceding to the clamor for strong action. An accord was reached in 1917 in which the United States publicly recognized that Japan's proximity to China created "special interests" and both powers, in a secret protocol, agreed to refrain from seeking concessions in China which would abridge the rights of other friendly powers. In all this, Japan was only playing a game engaged in by the United States and various European countries over a considerable period of history. In the process, however, her interest in ultimate control over China and certain neighboring areas of Asia became increasingly evident.

During the 1920's, a brief reaction against imperialism set in. A party government, which had little sympathy for the military, restored to China the Kiaochow area and certain other concessions in northern China formerly held by Germany. A pact signed at the Washington Conference in 1922 limited Japan's naval strength. In 1925, the government reduced the standing army from twenty-one to seventeen divisions. The demilitarization process, however, should not be exaggerated. The ministers of the Army and Navy Departments continued to be military officers selected by the armed forces. While military expenditures were reduced, compulsory military training was introduced into the middle schools, higher schools, and universities on a nation-wide basis, staffed in part by the officers who were released by the reduction in the standing army. Here was an extraordinarily economical method of building a powerful war machine using the existing facilities of the nation's educational institutions. And here also was a matchless opportunity simultaneously to indoctrinate the youth on a mass basis in the military tenets of ultranationalism. Certainly while many Japanese during the 1920's may have forgotten or rejected Japan's earlier ambitions, certain members of the military and ultranationalistic groups had not. They made their preparations and they waited for an occasion and adequate popular support. An opportunity first came during the economic crisis of 1927 when Baron Tanaka, army general and leader of the political party called the Seiyukai, formed a cabinet which lasted for two years. He achieved some expansion of military expenditures and used Japanese troops to check the northward advance of the Chinese Nationalist government. Even Baron Tanaka was a moderate compared with extremists in the Kwantung Army, who, on their own initiative, assassinated Chang Tso-lin, an uncooperative Manchurian war lord. Tanaka wished to punish the culprits, but was blocked by the Army Chief of Staff and others on the grounds it would weaken army discipline. Tanaka's government fell in 1929 and the Minseito, an anti-military, business-dominated party, came into power under Prime Minister Hamaguchi. It was not long, however, before a series of political and economic events, combined with other tensions building up during the 1920's, provided the climate for military extremism to become dominant. All that was lacking was an occasion and this had to be created.

We have seen so far that viewed in historical perspective, Japan's militaristic expansion during the 1930's was not something unexpected arising suddenly out of an overpopulation crisis. Rather it was a consistent continuation of a movement which could be traced back for many decades and possibly even centuries. It was supported by a powerful, traditional nationalistic sentiment; it had the sanction of the actual behavior, if not the pronouncements, of other major nations of the world up to that time; and it had enjoyed complete success from the beginning of the Meiji Era to the end of World War I.

Some of the quantitative aspects of this history are reflected in the tables and figures. We see, for instance, that even up to 1936, the proportion of the gross national product taken up by the war industry was relatively small. The Russian war of 1904-1905 was the only one of anything like major proportions. Military purchases rose sharply from about six per cent of GNP in 1903 to about twenty-five per cent in 1904-05. This was accompanied by a moderate decline in consumption and a large import surplus, without much change in private domestic investment. There is some evidence that the war gave a temporary check to Japanese economic development, but in the long run, of course, the effect was small.

The economic history of the first world war in Japan is particularly illuminating. Japan's participation in the war was negligible in terms of actual military involvement, and economically the war was enormously profitable. Japan exported large amounts of supplies to the Allies at inflated prices, and built up a very large foreign balance, mainly in European currencies. In the '20's, Japan proceeded to spend these funds at much lower prices, and even though it has not been possible to calculate the terms of trade on this particular transaction, it must have been very favorable indeed. The first world war is an interesting example of what might be called the deceptiveness of rational appearances. To all appearances Japan behaved with almost complete rationality, following her national interest with extreme skill. Economic behavior seems to be clearly in command; there is very little in the way of military heroics in spite of the fact that this must have seemed like a golden opportunity to the more aggressive militarists to expand, say, into the Russian Maritime Provinces or Manchuria, at a time when Russia was disorganized and the European powers and the United States were busy. Troops were sent to Siberia to join those of other nations, but were eventually withdrawn as a more civilian-minded government came into power during the 1920's. It looked as if Japan was deterred by highly rational considerations, in part perhaps by fear of the rising power of the United States. The line between rational and irrational behavior, however, is a thin one, especially in large and complex social organizations, as the contrast between the first and second world wars shows. Rational considerations of national interest would seem to suggest that Japan should have played exactly the same role in the second world war that she did in the first, and would have done even better out of it. The rapid growth of the ultranationalist influence during the 1930's, however, threw the decision-making process of Japan into the hands of "heroic" hotheads, displacing the careful economic decisionmakers of the previous generation with disastrous results.

Among the psychological factors which have been suggested as leading up to the events of the 1930's we find two major blows to a sensitive national pride. They came at a time when Japan was riding on the crest of a wave of national self-esteem, the culmination of a thirty-year period in which she had defeated in war a major Asian power and a major European power. The first blow was the limiting of Japanese naval power at the Washington Conference in 1921-22, which, in effect, made it clear that Japan was considered a second-rate power and was to be kept that way. The second, and probably more critical event, was the exclusion of Japanese immigrants in the United States Immigration Act of 1924. The exclusion provisions were the culmination of a growing hostility in the United States toward the Japanese, especially in the West where the steady influx of Japanese laborers and farmers into California had led to economic and racial strife. As far back as 1906, San Francisco had attempted to confine Japanese and Chinese to segregated schools, but the uproar in Japan was such that President Theodore Roosevelt personally intervened and the attempt was abandoned in exchange for a "gentlemen's agreement" on the part of Japan to stop voluntarily the flow of migrant labor. This arrangement was no more palatable to the Japanese than her prewar and postwar "voluntary" agreements to limit certain exports to the United States under threat of formal restrictions. Japan had faithfully kept her "gentlemen's agreement" and the exclusion provisions could only be interpreted as a gratuitous slap in the face. Hugh Borton asserts that up to the time of the attack on Pearl Harbor, "This American Law was thrown in the faces of Japanese recruits and subjects alike as proof of the American attitude of disdain and superiority toward Japan."[8] Japan's expansion in the 1930's was probably in part an attempt to restore her international prestige through means of proven historical reliability, and the war with the United States had elements of revenge.

While the population pressure argument was probably little more than a rationalization, though powerful in its psychological effects, economic factors were undeniably involved in the events leading up to the 1930's. We believe that central among those factors was a severe agricultural depression which began as early as 1925 and not in 1929 as some may have assumed. In 1925, the two major sources of farm income were rice and silk cocoons, providing together about two-thirds of the total value of agricultural output. Raw silk prices, after reaching a peak in 1925, began to fall and dropped thirty-two per cent by 1929. The collapse of American demand during the depression brought raw silk prices down to a level in 1931 only one-third of their 1925 peak. They remained low throughout the 1930's, further affected by the growing competition of rayon. In 1926, the price of rice began a steep decline, reaching a trough in 1931 which was fifty-six per cent below its 1925 level.[9] Contributing factors were: growing imports of rice from Korea and Formosa, four large crops in succession beginning in 1927, and a slackening in urban demand during the industrial depression following 1929. The result was an economic disaster for farm cultivators and for those rural workers who depended upon the silk market for employment in reeling and weaving establishments. These people constituted about half of the labor force in 1930 and the decline in their living levels probably accounts for the decline in the national level of consumption after 1925 (see Table 1 and Figure 1).

[8]Borton, *op. cit.*, p. 307.
[9]The statistical data are from G. C. Allen, *A Short Economic History of Modern Japan* (second revised edition), London, 1962, pp. 114-15, 117, 139, and 202; Lockwood, *op. cit.*, pp. 56-7; and R. P. Dore, *Land Reform in Japan*, London, 1959, p. 21.

Strong economic dissatisfaction undoubtedly contributed to rural support of the ultranationalists who promised economic prosperity among other things. The rural situation, in addition, may have contributed to the personal motivation of many members of the military groups. From the early Meiji period, most of the soldiers and sailors were recruited from the rural areas. Many of the officers, especially those trained during the 1920's and 1930's, were sons of rural landlords and occasionally of peasants. It is quite likely that Allen is right in arguing that the intense rural discontent "was communicated to the Army . . . and undoubtedly contributed to the overthrow of the 'liberal' Government and the transference of power to those who favored military aggression."[10] Reischauer also stresses the close relationship between the army and the peasantry and claims that the "younger army officers . . . gradually came to champion the economic interests of the peasantry against the big city groups . . ." while "in return, the peasantry gave the army and its officer corps blind but inarticulate support."[11] It was the younger, rural-oriented officers, rather than the more conservative, urban-oriented, older top-ranking officers, who initiated the militarist period in 1931 and who maintained control when necessary through terrorism. Indeed, one of the major battle grounds for the struggle for power between moderates and extremists was within the armed forces themselves. Mr. Mamoru Shigemitsu, one of the leading participants in the events of the period, claims that three rather than two groups in the army were actually involved: 1) the so-called "young officers"—2nd lieutenants, lieutenants, and captains who were hotheads with assassination their favorite weapon; 2) *chuken* officers—lieutenant colonels and colonels who "connived at the excesses of the young officers because they hoped that the resulting disorders would further their own ends"; and 3) generals, presumably a more moderate group. Majors were split largely between the first and second groups. Naval officers were divided in a similar fashion.[12] It seems plausible to assume that the impact of rural economic distress on the motivations of the officers diminished as their rank became higher. Borton reported that, in 1932, "After agrarian support of the military was assured, General Araki (the War Minister) opposed money grants to the farmers and in the fall suggested that 'mutual aid among the

[10]Allen, *op. cit.* p. 117.
[11]Reischauer, *op. cit.* p. 160.
[12]From notes by Oswald White, translator of Mamoru Shigemitsu, *Japan and Her Destiny: My Struggle for Peace,* London, 1958, pp. 20-1.

peasants and small traders and owners of small enterprises' would
be the best solution."[13] Increased military domination of the government, mainly by the *chuken,* generals, and admirals, brought little help
to the farmers outside of a few measures of a purely "palliative
nature."[14] There is no evidence that the Japanese military was noted
for its sophistication in economics. Their solution to the farm problem,
where they were interested in solving it at all, was apparently
a military one based on the mystical concept that victory solves
all problems.

The role of the great business groups, the Zaibatsu, in the
events of the 1930's is highly controversial. It is natural to assume
that most capitalistic organizations of that era would and did welcome
the profit-making opportunities of war and territorial acquisition. It
was still an age when the techniques of war did not visit mass destruction upon industrial areas. The Sino-Japanese War, the Russo-Japanese
War, and World War I had proved immensely profitable to large
business organizations. Yet there is strong evidence that the Zaibatsu
were considerably less than enthusiastic about the plans of the military
expansionists in the 1930's. Business was very good for the Zaibatsu
and many other concerns in the 1920's. Industrial production doubled
between 1920 and 1929,[15] stimulated partly by the reconstruction necessary after the disaster of the earthquake of 1923. Exports, in yen
terms, increased about seventy per cent from the recession low in
1921 to the peak in 1929.[16] The financial crisis in 1927 afflicted
mainly smaller enterprises, and the Zaibatsu seized the opportunity
to acquire bankrupt concerns and fatten their empires, especially
in the financial fields. Mitsui used its financial power to extend
its control over small producers even in the rural areas.[17] Simultaneously with the growth of economic power, the major Zaibatsu
took advantage of the power vacuum left by the gradual passing
away of the ruling aristocrats who had dominated the Meiji government, and extended their political influence through the major parties
of the period. Their interest apparently lay in avoiding any military
adventurism which would raise taxes and hamper Japan's economic

13See Hugh Borton, *Japan Since 1931: Its Political and Social Development,*
New York, 1940, p. 92.

14*Ibid.,* p. 93.

15Nagoya College index cited in Bank of Japan, *Historical Statistics of Japanese Economy,* Tokyo, 1962, p. 12.

16*Ibid.,* p. 93.

17For details, see Allen, *op. cit.,* Chapter VIII, "Economic Policy and the
Zaibatsu, 1914-1932."

relations with other countries.[18] The industrial depression which followed 1929 was a relatively mild one in Japan and provided little
incentive for Zaibatsu cooperation with the military. The index of
industrial production declined only sixteen per cent between 1929
and its low point in 1931, compared with a thirty-three per cent
drop in the United States during the same period. The real gross
national product per capita dipped only about eight per cent in
1930 and rose slightly in 1931 (see Table 1). Industrial recovery
was well underway by 1932. The real crisis, as we argued previously,
was in the rural areas.

While some of the older, more conservative army officers may
have had sympathy for the viewpoint of big business, there was
apparently no love lost between the Zaibatsu leaders and the younger
military officers. In May 1932, after violent attacks on the Zaibatsu
for allegedly having exploited the peasants and small business concerns,
a young officer group assassinated Baron Dan, the head of Mitsui.
Allen repeatedly refers to the mutual hostility between the Zaibatsu
and the military generally.[19] Much of this arose from the desire
of the military to establish a quasi-wartime economy (Junsenji Keizai)
completely under their control and designed solely to serve their
own strategic purposes. The leaders of the Zaibatsu, now at the
height of their economic and political power, were scarcely eager
to relinquish their hard-won position of eminence, whatever doubtful
economic advantages might accrue. Certain non-Zaibatsu firms, however, with less concern for control and relatively more for profits,
participated eagerly. They formed the nucleus of the "new Zaibatsu"
(Shinko-Zaibatsu) upon whom the military relied heavily in developing the resources of Manchuria and China. Such cooperation as the
Zaibatsu rendered in the military industrial build-up appeared, at
least at the start, the result more of fear of terrorist tactics than of

---

[18]Reischauer says that "The Japanese businessmen of the 1920's influenced
by the philosophies of the victorious Western democracies, tended to look with
disfavor on the high taxes required for large naval and military establishments.
They were also inclined to believe that economic expansion—building up a great
export trade and acquiring economic concessions abroad through diplomacy—was
less costly and more profitable than colonial expansion by war and conquest. This
seemed particularly true in China, the chief field for Japanese expansion. The
Chinese, with a newly awakened sense of nationalism, were beginning to boycott
foreign merchants whose governments were considered to be pursuing an aggressive
policy against China. Consequently, military intervention in China cost the double
price of lost markets and increased military expenditures." *Op. cit.*, p. 149.

[19]Allen, *op. cit.*, pp. 155-56.

mutual interest.[20] Later, after the Manchurian die had been cast, there may have been less reluctance as the opportunities grew for profiting from expanding military expenditures.[21]

On the whole, as far as the period under discussion is concerned, the case for collabortaion between the Zaibatsu and the military extremists in the initiation of the expansionist program is extremely weak. The weight of the evidence supports the view that the Zaibatsu actively opposed the extremists in a struggle for both economic and political power and then reluctantly cooperated when it was obvious popular opinion was against them and there was little more than a shotgun choice.

The industrial depression from 1929 to 1931 is sometimes mentioned as contributing to urban unrest and providing support for those who sought to overthrow the government. As we noted above, the industrial depression was much less severe than in the United States. Real wages of workers actually improved in 1930 and continued high in 1931 primarily because the sharp drop in the price of rice lowered the cost of living faster than money wages fell. Thus the curse of the farmer was the blessing of the urban worker. The number of unemployed in 1930 was only 1.1 per cent of the total gainfully employed population.[22] The export slump affected primarily the silk reeling and cotton textile industries whose labor force consisted largely of farmers' daughters. This added more to the woes of the rural families than to those of the urban proletariat. It is likely that whatever contribution unrest among urban workers made to the revival of militarism, it was small in comparison with the impact of the rural disaster.

The recital of contributing causes leading to the Manchurian Incident in 1931 should include certain inept government economic policies, especially those which related to rural distress. Among these were, first, continued encouragement of rice imports from Korea and Formosa in the face of declining domestic rice prices after 1925. Secondly, there was the re-establishment of the gold standard at just the wrong time, and its continuation even after it was obvious that this was detrimental to exports, especially those of raw silk

[20]See G. C. Allen, *Japanese Industry: Its Recent Development and Present Condition,* New York, 1939, pp. 15-17.

[21]Reischauer implies this, *op. cit.,* pp. 179-80, but it is difficult to know whether he is referring to the "old" Zaibatsu or the Shinko-Zaibatsu.

[22]Lockwood, *op. cit.,* p. 156. Actually unemployment figures are a poor indicator of economic distress in Japan. This is due in large part to the very high proportion of family workers, in urban as well as rural occupations, who are not apt to be observedly unemployed.

on which the rural areas depended so heavily. The unpardonable sin, however, as far as the military was concerned, was the effort to reduce military expenditures. In 1930, the government approved the London Naval Treaty which further limited Japan's naval strength. A few months later, Prime Minister Hamaguchi was wounded by an ultranationalist. In reducing military expenditures, the government was only trying to achieve a balanced budget in accordance with the accepted, pre-Keynesian economic philosophy of the day. Perhaps it was inept only in the context of the situation where popular support required more spending to relieve the agricultural and industrial distress and also where the extremist militarist clique was looking for an excuse to take matters into its own hands. In September 1931, apparently without the approval or knowledge of the government, Japanese army units stationed in Manchuria to protect the South Manchurian Railway began the conquest of all Manchuria on the grounds that the Chinese had tried to blow up the railway. The Minseito government fell, the new Seiyukai government accepted the *fait accompli,* the gold standard was abandoned, the first round of political assassinations took place, Japan withdrew from an unsympathetic League of Nations, and the long march began down the road which led to a nightmare of destruction.

Again, the quantitative aspects of this period are shown in the table and figures. The conquest of Manchuria was almost fantastically cheap, and it involved practically no expansion of the war industry. This in itself is highly significant, because it suggests a process of false learning, and created an impression of high returns to military investment which subsequent events were to prove completely unjustified. The real point of no return seems to have been the advance into China proper in 1937. This led to an expansion of military enterprise and the war industry up to the point where by 1945 it had gobbled up most of the economy, and consumption had been reduced to almost thirty per cent of a greatly diminished national product.

All human activity is in some sense investment, for all activity is undertaken in the light of some image of future costs and benefits. These costs and benefits, of course, may not be measurable in terms of money or even of easily-recognizable goods and services. Nevertheless, they must exist in the mind of the decision-maker. The image of the world on which activity is based is created by a learning process. There is no other way to create it, for it is certainly not given to us genetically. As we stand at any moment of time, the decisions of the decision-makers are based pretty largely on the experiences of their own lifetime, both what they have experienced directly and what they have learned from others or from books. It is tragically easy to learn things which are not so, and to build up an image, especially of the social system, which is unrealistic to the point where decisions become disastrous. The present study clearly points to the need of a much deeper study of this whole period in Japan with a view to finding out exactly how these false images of the world were created, and how there came to be such a fantastic divergence between the image and the reality.

Out of this study also emerges another question of enormous importance. This is the question of how would we estimate in statistical terms the costs and benefits of the war industry to the society which sustains it. War industries are presumably maintained because the societies who decide to do so believe that the benefits exceed the costs. A cost-benefit analysis of the war industry is difficult, not only because of the extreme difficulties of measurement involved, but also because the very concept is repugnant to the "heroic" ideology from which the institution of war draws much of its strength. The most casual inspection of the table and the figures in this paper suggests that while the war industry in Japan may have had a positive rate of return in the early years of the period, taken over the period as a whole the cost has been enormous and the returns very small. The conceptual problem is complicated by what we might call the indirect effects, especially of defeat. The astonishing rate of growth of the Japanese economy since 1945 is unquestionably due in part to the "shock treatment" imposed on Japanese society by the war. We might almost say that the main product of the war industry in Japan was a mentally sick nation, and the defeat not only cured the mental illness but released a flow of creativity and energy which had not been released before. The crucial question here is, what is the contribution of the war industry to the rate of growth of the economy? Unfortunately, this is a question which cannot be answered easily. In the case of Japan, there is a good deal to suggest that in the early days of the period the war industry was an important spearhead of modernization, simply because it was at this point that the motivation was strongest. Even here, however, it is clear that the Russian war created a temporary slowing-down of growth and not enough of a shock to change the rate perceptibly. A rough estimate of the loss due to the industry is the size of the "valley." Suppose, for instance, that Japan had continued her economic development, from say 1930 on, at the rate which she had previously achieved, without military adventure and a major war industry; she would have achieved her actual income as of about 1960, following the line, say, from A to B in Figure

3. The shaded area is then the economic loss due to the war industry. It exceeds by many times the direct damage done to Japan by the American war industry.

It is little wonder that under these experiences Japan has become one of the least aggressive and least militaristic nations of the world, apparently quite content to withdraw from a position as a world power and to live as an American protectorate, quietly getting rich at a fantastic rate. We should beware of projecting this situation with too much confidence too far into the future. Nevertheless, there is evidence to suggest that Japan has made a radical adjustment in her national image in the way, for instance, that the Swedes must have done in the early 19th century, and that if she continues to have economic success, this situation may be quite stable.

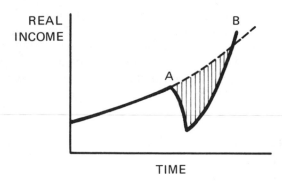

FIGURE 3

APPENDIX

Notes and Sources for Table 1

Notes: Component do not always add to totals because of rounding.

Symbols: GNP=Gross National Product
PDI=Private Domestic Investment
PCE=Personal Consumption Expenditures
GP=Government Purchases
GP_{nmi}=Government Non-Military Investment
GP_{nmc}=Government Non-Military Consumption
GP_{mp}=Government Military Purchases
NFI=Net Foreign Investment

1946-1960 are fiscal years beginning April 1. All other years are calendar years.

Sources and Methods:

a. Column (1) was obtained by adding together the components, each of which was separately deflated.

b. Column (2): for 1887-1930 the series was computed from personal consumption expenditures in current prices in Kazushi Ohkawa and Keiko Akasaka, *Kobetsu Suikei no Sogoka* (Integration of Estimated Components), Working Paper D 21, Hitotsubashi Institute of Economic Research, September 28, 1962 (Addendum of November 15, 1962), pp. 1-3. The deflator is a weighted average of a rural consumer price index (excluding rent) and an urban consumer price index (including rent) given in Ohkawa and Akasaka, *Kobetsu Suikei no Sogoka,* Working Paper D 11, December 18, 1961, pp. 16-17. For 1930-60, the series was computed from personal consumption expenditures given in Economic Planning Agency, *Showa 36 Nendo Kokumin Shotoku Hakusho* (National Income White Paper: 1961), Tokyo, 1963, p. 84. The deflator is a weighted average of the urban and rural price indices obtained from *ibid.,* p. 100 and Economic Planning Agency, *Keizai Yoran* (Economic Abstract), Tokyo, 1963, p. 46.

c. Column (3): For 1887-1930, the series was computed by:
1) subtracting government non-military investment in current prices (given in Koichi Emi, *Government Fiscal Activity and Economic Growth in Japan, 1868-1960,* Tokyo, 1963, pp. 168-70) from gross investment (including government non-military investment) given in Ohkawa and Akasaka *op. cit.,* Working Paper D 21 (Addendum of November 15, 1962), pp. 1-3; and
2) deflating with a producers' goods price index given in Ohkawa and Akasaka, *op. cit.,* Working Paper D 21, pp. 18-20. For 1930-1960, the series was computed from Economic Planning Agency data for gross private domestic capital formation in current prices given in its *Showa 36 Nendo Kokumin Shotoku Hakusho,* p. 84, using as a deflator an index of producers' goods prices from the same sources cited in (b) above.

d. Column (4): Government Military Purchases (GP_{mp}) in current prices for 1887-1936 were obtained from Emi, *op. cit.,* Table A-2(1), col. (6), pp. 145-47; and, for 1937-1960, from *ibid.,* Tables A-2(2) and A-2(3), pp. 148-51, excluding expenses in occupation areas most of which were financed by foreign currencies or army occupation currency (see *ibid.,* p. 150). Payments for pensions, annuities and military "allowances in aid" are excluded as not representing current purchases of goods and services. Other "transfers" may still be present in the data. They are apt to be especially large during war periods. We adjusted for some of them for 1894-98 and 1903-08 by subtracting from Emi's figures such items as gratuities, loans, interest, and subsidies which were listed as war expenditures but which should probably be excluded in estimating purchases of goods and services according to national income concepts. Data for the adjustment were taken from Giichi Ono, *War and Armament Expenditures of Japan,* New York, Oxford University Press, 1922, pp. 273-74; 286-87; and 291-94. The deflator for 1887-1930 is a weighted average of a consumers' goods price index and producers' goods price index given in Ohkawa and Akasaka, *op. cit.*, Working Paper D 21, pp. 18-20, and designed for deflation of the Gross National Product. The combined index was used because military purchases contain both consumption and investment components, though the relative proportions are difficult to determine. The deflator for 1930-1960 is a weighted average of a consumers' goods price index (75% weight) and a producers' goods price index (25% weight) given in Economic Planning Agency, *Keizai Yoran* (Economic Handbook) for 1963, p. 46, and for, 1958, p. 48.

Government Non-Military Consumption (GP_{nmc}) for 1887-1960 was obtained by subtracting the above series of Government Military Purchases (in current prices) from Emi's series of government "current purchases of goods and services" (excluding investment) in current prices, *op. cit.*, Table A-6, col. (1), pp. 168-71. The result was then deflated with the same index used in obtaining real personal consumption expenditures in (b) above.

Government Non-Military Investment (GP_{nmi}) for 1887-1930 was obtained in current prices from *ibid.*, Table A-6, col. (5), pp. 168-70, and for 1930-1960, from Economic Planning Agency, *Showa 36 Nendo Kokumin Shotoku Hakusho*, p. 85. (The EPA data are also given in Emi, *op. cit.*, p. 170.) The deflator was the same used in deflating Private Domestic Investment (PDI) in (c) above.

The data for 1944 did not permit a proper breakdown into government non-military consumption and government military purchases.

e. Column (5): Net Foreign Investment (NFI) in real terms was estimated by subtracting a deflated series of debits (mainly visible and invisible imports) in the current account of the balance of payments from a separately deflated series of credits (mainly visible and invisible exports) in the current account. Figures in current prices, for 1887-1930, were taken from Ohkawa and Akasaka, *op. cit.*, Working Paper D 21, pp. 6-8, and, for 1930-60, came from Economic Planning Agency, *Showa 36 Nendo Kokumin Shotoku Hakusho*, p. 57. The deflator for credits was computed by linking together three indices of export prices and the deflator for debits was computed by linking together three indices of import prices. The indices used came, for 1887-1900, from Kiyoshi Kojima, "Japanese Foreign Trade and Economic Growth: With Special Reference to the Terms of Trade," *Annals of the Hitotsubashi Academy*, Vol. VIII, No. 2, April 1958, pp. 166-7; for 1900-1930 from a preliminary series by K. Yamada, Institute of Economic Research, Hitotsubashi University, cited in Bank of Japan, *Historical Statistics of the Japanese Economy*, Tokyo, 1962, p. 99; and for 1930-1960 from Economic Planning Agency, *Showa 36 Nendo Kokumin Shotoku Hakusho*, p. 100. The EPA series (for import prices and for export prices) were broken at 1953 when the base was changed. We linked them to their post-1953 sections by using Bank of Japan postwar import price and export price indices given in *Economic Statistics of Japan: 1955*, Tokyo, 1956, pp. 289-90.

f. Sources of population data used in computing per capita figures are: for 1887-1920 and 1946 to 1960, Office of the Prime Minister, *Japan Statistical*

Yearbook: 1961, Tokyo, 1962, pp. 10-11; for 1920-1945, Ministry of Welfare, *Vital Statistics: 1960*, Vol. I, Tokyo, 1961, p. 241. Okinawa is included up to 1945 and excluded after 1945 to provide consistency with the gross national product estimates. Figures from 1887 to 1944 are for July 1 in order to correspond to calendar year data. They were obtained by linear interpolation. Figures for 1946 to 1960 are for October 1, as given in the sources, and correspond with fiscal year data.

Russian Imperialism Today[1]

Thomas P. Whitney

Thomas P. Whitney, former chief foreign news analyst of the Associated Press, is widely known for his writings on the Soviet Union economic and political scenes. With ten years' experience in the Soviet Union, three of these as head of the Economic Section of the U.S. Embassy in Moscow and seven as a correspondent for the Associated Press, he early predicted such events as the de-Stalinization campaign of Khrushchev, the dissolution of the Cominform, and the fall of Matyas Rakosi.

Contrary to Marxist assertions that no socialist society can be imperialist, the Soviet Union seems to have clearly demonstrated that it has been perhaps the most imperialistic power in the post-World War Two era. The author discusses the imperialist role of the Soviet Union with respect to the satellite nations. The reader is advised to examine the following in connection with Soviet imperialism:

John Strachey, "New Empires for Old? (II) A Russian Empire," in *The End of Empire*. New York, 1964, pp. 292-306.

J. Hallowell, editor, *Soviet Satellite Nations: A Study of the New Imperialism*. Gainesville, Fla., 1958.

D. B. Shimkin, "The Structure of Soviet Power," *Quarterly Review of Economics & Business*, III, November 1965, pp. 19-24.

If on the one hand since the beginning of World War II the world has seen the very rapid breakup of the old colonial empires built up by Western European powers in modern times, on the other hand it has seen the rapid growth of a new empire, which is simultaneously a new kind of empire, spreading outward from the Soviet Union to the West over much of Central and Eastern Europe and to the East over much of Asia. If on the one hand such populous and rich nations as India, Indonesia, Pakistan, Ghana, Tunisia, and many others have acquired their independence from the swiftly dissolving empires of Britain, France and Holland, on the other hand such populous and rich nations as Poland, China, Czechoslovakia have become parts of what is known to its sponsors as the "socialist camp," but which seems often to outsiders to resemble nothing so much as a nightmare-rebirth of the great empire of Genghis Khan

[1]Reprinted from *The Legacy of Imperialism*, Essays by Barbara Ward, Thomas P. Whitney, R. Strausz-Hupé, and Charles Malik. Pittsburgh, 1960, pp. 23-42.

both in its territorial sway and the spirit of its rulers. For the moment without deciding exactly what kind of a label we should pin on this monstrous growth of communist power—"camp" or "empire"—let us merely chronicle the explicit record of its physical expansion in the last two decades.

First the Soviet Union itself; as a result of the Nazi-Soviet pact of 1939 and of victory in World War II the Soviet Union added to its territory: Bessarabia (formerly part of Romania and before that part of the Russian Empire for a time), the Trans-Carpathian Ukraine (formerly part of Czechoslovakia), the western Ukraine and Western Byelorussia (formerly part of Poland), the Kaliningrad area (formerly Koenigsberg, part of Germany), Lithuania, Latvia, Estonia, parts of Karelia and northern Finland, southern Sakhalin, and the formerly "independent" republic of Tannu Tuva in the heart of Asia. All these additions, though they include territory the size of several populous and powerful European states taken together, added only a little over three per cent to Soviet territory and perhaps up to 15 per cent to Soviet population. Much more important additions to the realms of communism than the mere expansion of the Soviet Union's own territory came as the result of the Soviet irruption into Eastern and Central Europe at the end of World War II and the establishment there, with active Soviet assistance and, in some cases, at the point of Soviet bayonets, of communist regimes in a number of countries: Bulgaria, Albania, Romania, Hungary, Czechoslovakia, Poland, and Eastern Germany. These countries constitute a continuous belt from south to north across Europe along the Soviet Union's western border. Their population amounts to over 100 million—half as much as that of the U.S.S.R. Economically speaking and in terms of technological experience, taking into account East Germany and Czechoslovakia, they are in many respects more advanced than the Soviet Union and have been a source of considerable economic strength to the U.S.S.R.

At the same time that the Soviet Union burst into East Europe at the end of World War II, it also seized a foothold of some importance in the Far East—North Korea. It thus came out of the War with two Asian satellites—North Korea and Outer Mongolia, which had been the original Soviet satellite before World War I. The triumph of communism in China in 1949 brought a new era to the growth of the communist bloc in more ways than one. It added to it some 600 million people—more than twice the number in it previously; and it added a new political-ideological center—Peking—to the world communist movement. With the emergence in the mid-fifties of independent North Vietnam the communist bloc realized its present bounds. It represents an impressive actual and potential strength—a quarter of the world's land surface and probably more than a third of the world's population. The exact number of people under communist rule passes the imagination, but if one estimates some 700 million in East Asia, a little over 200 million in the Soviet Union, and another 100 million in East Europe, one has a fairly good picture of what is involved. More and more, with the upsurge of Soviet and other communist industrial production, the bloc is coming to represent great economic strength.

If the communist bloc has a quarter of the world's land surface under its control, it is of even greater importance what quarter of the world this happens to be. The German geopoliticians used to claim that whoever ruled the world's heartland would rule the world. What they called the heartland is precisely what the Soviet Union and its communist allies cover. One may or may not share the somewhat mystical faith of the geopoliticians, but one cannot neglect, certainly, the strategic value of having a large compact bloc of territory located in the very center of the Eurasian land mass with the possibility of moving outward from it in any direction east, west, or south when opportunity offers. By all accounts or evaluations the communist bloc is a formidable power accumulation.

And perhaps the most interesting thing of all about it is that while it has been building up its realms and strength with almost explosive speed, a large part of the population of the rest of the world has been concerned and worried, not about this expanding bloc, "camp," or "empire," but much more about those dissolving empires of Western European countries which sometimes seem to be disappearing so rapidly that one hesitates to blink lest in the interval another chunk of one of them should fall away and another new country with a new name be born.

To the extent that the peoples of the new Asian-African countries sense danger to their newly-achieved independence, most of them sense it not coming from the direction of Peking or Moscow but instead from London, Paris and, in particular, Washington. If one were to subject to a word association test any miscellaneous group of Arabs, Indians, Indonesians, or Africans and to throw at them the term "imperialist," certainly by far the largest proportion would respond with such words as "Western," "American," "British," "White," and the like, and probably very few if any would respond with "Russian" or "communist." Now, there are a number of very good reasons for this state of affairs, the best of them, of course, being the fact that in most of the Afro-Asian countries it is Western Europeans with whom the people had actual experience as imperial rulers and not Russians or communists. But this is not the whole answer. This is not certainly the reason why Afro-Asians, or for that matter many Latin Americans and Western Europeans, are more likely to associate the term "imperialist" with America than with the Soviet Union and Russians.

Look at the objective facts for a moment. The United States has really engaged in very little empire building in its history and today rules over a culturally homogeneous population of North Americans including literally almost no national minorities except a couple of million self-governing Puerto Ricans and a handful of others. It has no colonies, except for some scattered islands in the Pacific. The President in Washington is unable, sometimes to his great unhappiness, to give orders to the governments of any other states, including nowadays even the so-called "banana republics" of Central America. Contrast this with the situation of the great Russians. They make up according to their own official census figures not much more than one-half of the population of the Soviet Union. They rule over *inside the U.S.S.R.* scores of millions of peoples coming from the most diverse nationalities and cultures, many of whom as a matter of national tradition and temperament, some for the best of reasons, hate Russians with undying bitterness. The Russians occupy whole vast chunks of absolutely alien non-Russian, non-Slavic territory —as in the Trans-Caucasus, on the Baltic, in Central Asia. They are carrying out a campaign of the most intense russification which can be imagined. To some minority nationalities, which they themselves recognize as nationalities, they nevertheless deny—as for example to the Jews—the right to have their own national culture and traditions. Other nationalities they have on occasion, as with the Crimean Tartars, literally uprooted and scattered to the four winds, destroying them as a nationality and a people. At the same time the Russians also exercise rule *outside the U.S.S.R.* over many millions of people, through direct and indirect means, in other countries—in the Eastern European satellite countries, in Outer Mongolia and North Korea. And yet despite this factual situation only very rarely is the term "imperialist" associated in the popular mind in the free world at large with the Soviet Union and yet frequently indeed with the United States. The fact that the Soviet Union has no overseas colonies plays its part in this. Particularly since the end of the First World War and the collapse of the continental empires of Germany, Austro-Hungary, and Tsarist Russia, the terms of "empire" and "imperialism" have become associated for many with the British Empire and the French Empire.

But I would claim that of even greater importance in the failure of peoples in the free world, both in and outside the Afro-Asian countries, to recognize readily Soviet and communist "imperialism" for what it really is, is the fact that the term "imperialism" is one, like many others, which the communists have taken over and endowed with a special meaning which, through the use of intensive propaganda and continual repetition, has come to obscure eventually the basic, obvious, and simple real meaning of the word. The word "imperialism" obviously means a belief in or policy of extension of rule of one state over other states or territories—in an era of universal nationalism obviously the extension of rule of one national state over other nations. This definition, though it is clear and apparent, a communist would not, however, accept. For a Soviet communist "imperialism" is a special term defined by V. I. Lenin in his work *Imperialism, the Highest Stage of Capitalism;* imperialism is "the monopolistic stage of capitalism, its highest and last phase, which is just before the social revolution of the proletariat." According to Soviet Communists imperialism is defined by five specific characteristics: 1) the concentration of production and capital which has proceeded to such a stage that it has created monopolies which play the decisive role in social life; 2) the merging of banking capital with industrial capital and the creation on this basis of "finance capital"—a financial oligarchy; 3) the export of capital in distinction from export of merchandise acquires particular significance; 4) international alliances of capitalists divide up the world; 5) the biggest capitalist powers complete the territorial partition of the world.

One obvious advantage of the Lenin definition of "imperialism" as here set forth is that it obviously can only apply to the "dirty capitalists" and never to communists. Communists can, as they have indeed, set about building themselves an empire in which they exploit various nationalities and even annihilate a few which get in their way. But this is not "imperialism"—not by Lenin's definition. "Imperialism" is the "highest—and last—stage of capitalism." Now, of course, very few people in Russia or outside pay much attention to the strict details of Lenin's definition of "imperialism," but what has stuck from it in the world at large is that it is definitely something to be applied only to capitalists and not to communists and also that it is something basically economic in character. This means that "dollar diplomacy" is a part of it but "ruble diplomacy" hardly, that

Americans who have no empire are imperialists, and Russians who have one are not. And believe it or not this general concept sticks—here in America just as much as elsewhere in the world.

Enough on the question of definitions. Let's look for a while at the actuality of Russian rule over subject peoples inside the Soviet Union from its bad and its good side. The Kazakhs of Central Asia are a people who have come to know the Russians very well—too well, in fact, to suit many of them. A Turkish-speaking people, like most of the rest of the people of Central Asia, they mostly lived before the revolution a nomadic life tending their herds. Many Russians had settled among them even before 1917, particularly in their cities such as Alma Ata. The Kazakhs resisted the Revolution with particular bitterness and their resistance continued long after the Revolution. This was one of the reasons why the population of Kazakhs declined very drastically from the Soviet census of 1926 to that of 1939. If in 1926 there were over 3,700,000 Kazakhs *in the Kazakh Republic alone*, by 1939 the total number in the U.S.S.R., including some in neighboring Soviet Republics, had declined to 3,100,000. This reflected in particular hard treatment given the Kazakhs by the Russians who kept moving in on their lands and into their cities. Furthermore the Russians tried to force the Kazakh nomads to adopt settled forms of existence, an attempt which didn't work well, and since it was done with customary brutality, caused great loss of life. During the war the movement of Russians, Ukrainians, and others onto Kazakh lands continued apace. Many of these "foreigners" sent in were political prisoners and exiles. In 1954 Nikita Khrushchev, on top of everything previously done, decided to inaugurate the so-called "Virgin Lands" campaign to settle the plains of northern Kazakhstan which Kazakh herdsmen had used for grazing their animals. As a result hundreds of thousands more of Russians and Ukrainians poured into Kazakhstan. The non-Kazakhs even before this, through the policy of enforced emigration to Kazakhstan, had become a majority of the population. So by 1954 even the fiction of Kazakh rule over Kazakhstan was abandoned. A succession of tough *Russian* party bosses were sent to rule the Central Asian republic replacing Kazakh puppets. The Kazakhs thus became aliens in their own land. Their situation promises to grow worse in the future, except for those Kazakhs who successfully managed to russify themselves sufficiently in order to get along with the Russians who boss them about.

The reverse side of the Soviet nationalities policy, of which the case of Kazakhstan is admittedly an example of the bad side though by no means the worst, is that participation in the big Soviet

Union alongside Russians has given many members of minority nationalities opportunities for educational and cultural advancement. As
an example one can even take Kazakhstan, despite the severe Russian
oppression of the Kazakhs. In 1955 some 11,000 Kazakh young people
were studying in higher educational institutions including the university in Alma Ata. This is only one illustration of the chances given
under the regime for advancement and self-development. After all,
the Russians do not in general discriminate against members of minority nationality groups on a wholesale basis. Those who are willing
to go along with russification and work with the Soviet Communist
Party can receive favored treatment and even become part of the
Soviet ruling machine only slightly inferior to Russians. Some particular nationalities such as the Georgians and Armenians, more especially the Ukrainians, even get highly favorable treatment. And if the
Kazakhs and some other nationalities have a hard time under the
Russians today, it needs to be remembered that they lived a primitive
and tough life under ruthless rulers even before the Russians showed
up. Nomads have never in any country fared too well when the tillers
of the soil came on the scene and started plowing up their grazing
lands. One could even draw a comparison between the Kazakhs and the
American Indians of the plains. So much for the Russian communist
imperialism at home inside the Soviet Union. What about it outside
the U.S.S.R.?

Under Joseph Stalin after World War II when the Soviet
Union acquired control over the Eastern European satellites, the
Soviet government established at a very rapid pace a vast machinery
for direct imperial rule of all the satellite states straight from the Kremlin. The various revelations and discussions since Stalin's death in
Moscow and the satellite states have disclosed much of what went
on in this dark period. What stands out is that at this time the Russians
were developing on an almost grotesque scale all the characteristics
and forms of ruthless exploitation they condemn most heartily in
Western "imperialist" rule over overseas colonies. For example, economic agreements were negotiated which provided for the direct and
most shameless exploitation of satellite populations including the
workers in particular. Coal, for example, Polish coal, was sold to the
Russians at compulsory very low prices while Soviet goods were
sold the Poles at compulsory very high prices. Billions of zlotys were
thus siphoned out of Polish pockets. In East Germany reparations
were used for the same purpose—ruthless exploitation. In many satellite
countries there functioned a strange organization called the Administration for Soviet Property Abroad which claimed complete extra-

territoriality and exemption from all local laws and norms. This gigantic enterprise took into its fold all the former German-owned properties in Eastern Europe and ran them as Soviet state enterprises, regardless of whose territories they were located on. It was headed by a former Soviet security chief, Vsevolod Merkulov, who was executed with Beria in 1954, which gives some idea of its character, or one aspect of it at any rate. There were also so-called "jointly" owned enterprises in which the Soviet government participated on a nominally equal basis with the Hungarians, the Yugoslavs, the Chinese Communists and others in industrial and transportation enterprises. These were, however, as it appeared, run solely by the Soviet government which used them also as means of exploitation of subject peoples in Eastern Europe and as political weapons with which to expand its controls. Soviet police officers were sent meanwhile to take key spots in the police apparatus of various countries. In the case of Poland, Boleslav Bierut, a Soviet police officer, was made the prime minister of the country, while Marshal Rokossovsky, a Soviet officer and war hero, was sent to take command of the Polish Army. Army officers were sent by the hundreds into satellite armies. Soviet security agents meanwhile recruited substantial espionage networks of their own in the apparatus of their own satellite governments.

Moscow used this control position to make decision on the internal affairs of satellite countries. For instance, in the case of Yugoslavia this was what brought about the break between Moscow and Tito. Stalin tried to tell Tito how to carry out collectivization of Yugoslav agriculture. This was only one phase of widespread effort to decide *all* questions for the satellites in the Soviet government in Moscow and to make of the local heads of government and the communist parties literal marionettes manipulated from the Soviet Union. Materials which have come out on Hungary under Stalin show that the key decisions for Hungary were taken in Moscow in conference between Hungarian communist chiefs and Soviet chiefs. This went on also after Stalin's death. It was considered the normal operating procedure in fact. So taken for granted was it that when Imre Nagy protested against decisions arrived at in Moscow by Matyas Rakosi ·in conference with Malenkov and others he protested, of course, *not* against the fact that the Soviet government was telling the Hungarian government how to run its internal affairs but against what the decisions had been. One could go on in detail summarizing the workings of this system as it was till 1953 and even after. What the whole thing comes down to is that it was a scheme for exploitation of subject nationalities on a scale of which capitalists never even dreamed, and a scheme for direct ruthless rule from one imperial center of a whole group of nations—a scheme which would have made even the Romans gasp for its brazen cynicism and its brutality. Behind the whole apparatus stood the Stalinist method of mass police terror and the vast expanses of Soviet Siberia, with their concentration camps.

Perhaps the most interesting aspect of all this is that it did not work very effectively. True, it did exploit the subject peoples, but since it kept them on an inefficient basis it could not get too much out of them. It did suppress revolt but it pent up vast hate, bitterness, and discontent which was all ready to come out at the least sign of trouble. It was one of the most hated systems of imperialist exploitation ever devised. The Russians were very lucky to escape with nothing worse than the revolt in Hungary as an aftermath. The revolt in Hungary came in fact after some of the worst abuses had been corrected. In the period since Stalin's death the unequal trade agreements have generally been adjusted in favor of the satellite countries, the joint companies dissolved, the reparations ended, the administration for Soviet property abroad dissolved, and its assets turned back to the countries in which they were located. Even the schemes for police and political control have been relaxed considerably. There has been a deliberate attempt to work out a new system and new basis for relations with the Eastern European satellites based on indirect rather than direct methods by and large.

Poland is an example. Since the "revolution" of October 1956 Poland has not been under direct Soviet rule. True, there are Soviet troops on Polish soil and Poland has Soviet-run East Germany on the west and the Soviet Union on the east. But the real sanctions which the Soviet Union possesses against Poland are only in part these so obvious ones. Beyond that there is the question of the Polish western frontiers with Germany and the fact that the Soviet Union is the only country which can offer the Poles security that the Germans will not touch these. So even though Communist Poland has violated several basic tenets of Soviet-type communism—in its attitude toward religious education, for example, and toward collectivization of agriculture—the Kremlin says nothing. And the Poles, generally speaking, go along with the Russians in foreign affairs even when at times it may be in one or another respect distasteful to them. And the Poles pay tribute to the Soviet leadership of the "Socialist camp."

The Poles because of their revolution are an extreme example of indirect controls within the Soviet bloc area. The Chinese Communists are an example of no Soviet control at all. Peking, the evidence shows beyond any doubt, does what it wants when it wants so far as its own internal affairs are concerned without any consultations with Moscow. This even extends into foreign affairs. However, there is a fundamental close relationship between the two great communist powers arising from their mutual dependence on each other to avoid being in an isolated international position and from the dependence of the Chinese Communists on the Soviet Union for material assistance. The two countries function as a result in close cooperation in the field of foreign affairs.

In some other countries, as for instance Hungary, there is no doubt that the Russians themselves exercise the direct rule over the country straight from the Kremlin in Moscow. The same would be true, of course, of East Germany.

Now, enough has been said at this point to make clear one very important fact about the communist bloc or empire: it is not nearly so uniform and homogeneous as is often supposed. Peking does *not* take orders from Moscow in general and as a matter of principle but sometimes goes along with Moscow. North Vietnam is sufficiently far from the Kremlin safely to have good relations with it. North Korea is stuck in between the Russians and the Communist Chinese and the same is even truer of the Soviet satellite state of Outer Mongolia which like North Korea continues to look Moscow-ward for guidance. Poland is independent *but* . . . East Germany not at all. Czechoslovakia *chooses* not to be free despite absence on Czech soil of Soviet troops. Hungary's satellite government must have the Soviet bayonets around to last. Romania is totally surrounded by Soviet influence. Bulgaria doesn't *have* to be a satellite but would just as soon be one so long as Yugoslavs are not. And little Albania is no gift to anyone, not even the Soviet Union, and therefore continues to be the most vociferous of Soviet allies. If enough has been written to show how fearfully disastrous for, say, Poland's economy and body politic Soviet imperial rule under Stalin actually was, it must be kept in mind that this is not the entire picture.

Now, at a time when the world seems to be weeping for Tibet it might be a suitable occasion to recall Outer Mongolia. Mongolia was once a country much like Tibet, devoted to Lamaism—a form of Buddhism which stresses monasticism, with one of every ten able-bodied men in a monastery living off the rest of the poor population. It was a country ridden with superstition, infested with illnesses, and, generally speaking, one of the most backward backwaters of the entire planet. The Russians in a very imperialist way did in Outer Mongolia almost exactly what the Chinese communists are doing to Tibet right now. They moved in on things, threw out the religious oligarchy, and put the country under their ruthless thumbs with local puppets ruling them. Outer Mongolia today is far from being a paradise of culture and joy, but in at least some respects it has come a long way from what it used to be forty years ago. Many of the Mongolians now can read. There are educational institutions. There is some industry. There are even a couple of railways. Some of the people now live in houses instead of tents. There are Mongolian engineers and professors and scientists and teachers, many of whom were trained in Moscow. Probably, if I know my Russians, much local color has been lost in the process of modernization of Outer Mongolia. Probably many Mongolians have lost their heads. But modernization did have to come there as well as everywhere else one way or another, and no matter how it came it would not have been very comfortable. And probably, despite undoubted oppression by Soviet and Russian imperialism there in Outer Mongolia, it is probably now a somewhat better place to live in than it was when it was ruled by the Lamas. This is a reasonable guess. And my advice, incidentally, is not to weep too copiously about the lost freedom of Tibet. Tibet never had any freedom to lose, the Dalai Lama to the contrary notwithstanding.

In short, I wish to point out that "imperialism" may be a bad word in both the Soviet and American vocabulary but that the results of Soviet as of Western imperialism are by no means universally or solely bad. The Soviet Communist bloc or the Soviet Communist empire, whatever one wants to call it, is a real enough force. It is a much closer working arrangement than an alliance like NATO. It has, despite the rather fundamental divergence between Moscow and Peking, a sense of discipline and a community of interest between its members.

But it would be a serious mistake to think that this is a monolithic league, run from one single center with one single unquestioned leader heading it. If under Joseph Stalin the Soviet Union actually was maintaining physical control of a whole series of countries through use of its secret police, intelligence, and armed services as auxiliaries of the Soviet Communist party, this is no longer universally the case among bloc countries. It is still true of some countries that the Kremlin has physical control over them. It is still true of some regimes in the communist bloc as it exists today that their chiefs have to wait to hear from Moscow to undertake to tell the time of day. But these are in a small minority. Most of the communist bloc regimes run their own show. And one aspect of the cohesive force that holds the bloc together consists in common short-run and long-run interests of the regimes making up the bloc in cooperating together under the leadership of Moscow. These regimes are very different kinds of regimes in some respects and in some others very similar. The interests they have in common with each other are military, economic, and political.

But this is not all. The communist bloc of nations is one part of the international communist movement which is worldwide. And like that international communist movement as a whole the communist bloc also is guided by certain common elements, subscribed to by all communists who look to Moscow and Peking. These common elements are a common idea—communism—backed by a universal type of organization—the communist parties—and embodied physically in a generally accepted model—the Soviet Union. Many Americans and Westerners in general have come to think of the international communist movement as solely a vast conspiracy operated by techniques of plot and espionage from a super spy center in Moscow. There is indeed in the international communist movement the element of conspiracy and it plays a very important role. But to see nothing more than this in it is indeed to miss the point, to mistake what it is, and, in fact, to be unable to deal with it effectively for lack of understanding of its essence.

The idea of communism means many things to many different people. To some it stands for revolution to destroy the existing order and erect a new social system. To others it means the hope of an increase in standard of living and education for one's children. To others it means power over other people, a worldwide state perhaps. Indeed, the idea of communism as it is propagated by the Russian communists means all these things and much more. But it is a specific idea or set of concepts set forth in the writings of leaders of the international communist movement and these concepts are far from vague. They constitute both a goal and a program for action. This is particularly true of people in backward countries who are desperately seeking a way out of the social morass in which they all too frequently find themselves and looking for a ray of hope. The organizational expression of these concepts—the communist parties—are unique in that they demand from every member total discipline and total loyalty, in that they never depend on any one person for their development or survival, in that there is a commonly accepted center—Moscow—to which they can look for guidance, in that they are international in the sense that every national party is one part of a much bigger movement.

The model of the Soviet Union is a powerful one, not for the peoples of the highly developed nations of the West, but for the peoples of backward and undeveloped countries of the world, particularly members of the intelligentsia of those countries. Nothing succeeds like success and the Soviet Union has certainly succeeded. From a defeated nation which generally was regarded as backward among European countries, this country has risen to unquestioned second place on the world ladder of power and is contesting the most powerful nation for first place. Here national power and might have been created in an almost incredibly short time on a tremendous scale. Here people have been educated, industries built, and a backward nation modernized. This has been at a terrific cost to those who had to endure it in the Soviet Union, but to many of those looking at this from the outside the accomplishment looks to be worth any cost. Here for many members of the intelligentsia of African and Asian countries there seems to be a formula for modernization of a backward country in a hurry, for a nation to lift itself by its own bootstraps. And this is what many are looking for.

These elements—the idea, the organization and the model—therefore constitute a powerful force of attraction for many in under-developed countries to communism and a powerful cohesive force for the movement itself, including the communist bloc of nations. In these things lies the real difference between Russian or Soviet imperialism and the older imperialisms of the past and present.

Comprehension of this difference, comprehension of the importance of the elements of the idea, the organization and the successful pilot model of their psychological impact on the awakening peoples of Africa and Asia, is not just an academic matter: it constitutes the beginning of understanding of the very practical problem of how to deal with communist imperialism. For the most elementary common sense indicates that what is needed most of all is not more H-bombs, bigger and more effective espionage organizations, tougher internal security laws, but an idea or set of ideas of our own which will have greater appeal to ourselves and to other peoples of the world, including those today inside the communist bloc. It is for the lack of an idea that we may lose the battle, the campaign, and the war.

The Mechanism of Neo-Imperialism[1]

Thomas Balogh

Thomas Balogh is a fellow of Balliol College, Oxford, and since 1964, Economic Advisor to the Cabinet. He has wide experience in the underdeveloped countries; he has been Consultant to the Government of Malta, the Government of Jamaica, and the Government of Greece. He has also served as an economic adviser to the Food & Agricultural Organization of the U.N., the Government of India Planning Commission, the U.N. Economic Commission for Latin America, the U.N. Special Fund, and the Organization for Economic Cooperation and Development. He is the author of numerous publications dealing with the economics of underdeveloped nations.

The author contends that neo-imperialism has inhibited the growth of the ex-colonial countries by preventing the development of infant industries. Neo-imperialism does not depend upon formal political domination. It can be implemented through International organizations such as the International monetary fund which may act as the colonial administration entrusted with the responsibility of enforcing the rules of the game.

The reader is advised to consult the following literature in connection with neo-imperialism and neo-colonialism:

Richard D. Wolff, "Modern Imperialism: The View from the Metropolis," *American Economic Review Papers & Proceedings*, vol. LX, no. 2, May 1970.

J. Woddis, *Introduction to Neo-Colonialism*. N.Y., 1968

Harry Magdoff, "Militarism & Imperialism," *The American Economic Review Papers & Proceedings*, vol. IX, no. 2, May 1970, pp. 237-42.

Harry Magdoff, *The Age of Imperialism*. New York, 1969.

Hugh Seton-Watson, *The New Imperialism*. London, 1961.

Most African territories since their liberation from colonial rule have made accelerated progress. This has happened despite the loss of experienced administrators and technical experts in all fields through the rapid Africanisation of all public services, though in some territories, especially those formerly under French rule, the process has not been as fast as in other territories. The development must be also

---

[1]Reprinted from "The Mechanism of Neo-Imperialism: The Economic Impact of Monetary and Commercial Institutions in Africa," *Bulletin, Institute of Economics and Statistics*, Oxford University, Vol. 24, August 1962, No. 3, pages 331-46.

seen against a background of a systematically damaging impact on the terms of trade of African territories of the development of the world economy in the 1950's. The return to the exclusive use of monetary controls, the trend towards convertibility and nondiscrimination, have undoubtedly retarded growth in important markets of Africa and thus contributed to the depressing effect of monetary policy itself on primary goods prices. While these goods have to be sold in world markets, and therefore are subject to monetary pressures, the price of most of Africa's imports—manufactures—has been administered and showed a continuous upward trend.

The 'record thus seems remarkable and encouraging. In the present paper the view will be put forward that this acceleration of growth is to some extent exceptional and cannot be relied on to continue. It has been the result of the disappearance of the limitations imposed by the monetary and commercial institutions, arrangements and policies on the economic evolution of Africa during the Colonial period. These were dominated by the relations of African territories with their erstwhile metropolitan countries. A historical analysis of the origins and rationale of these relationships is therefore necessary to establish the future requirements of a deliberate acceleration of development.

I believe it can be shown that the automatism which evolved represents by itself a severe limitation on the possibility for the full development of the weaker partner in the 'colonial pact', even if there is no conscious policy which aims at the exploitation for the benefit of the metropolitan area.[2] Beyond this the philosophy of monetary and fiscal soundness itself represents a further handicap to the weaker area. If this analysis is correct two conclusions follow, both unpalatable to current conventional wisdom. The first is that the present upsurge in the ex-colonial areas provides no guarantee of a stable and steady progress in future if special efforts are not made to substitute positive stimuli for the negative ending of colonial limitation. The second is that neo-imperialism does not depend on open political domination. The economic relations of the U.S. to South America are in no way different from those of Britain to her African colonies. The International Monetary Fund fulfils the role of the Colonial Administration of enforcing the rules of the game which bring about the necessary consequences.

[2] I have tried to analyse some of these aspects in a paper written for the Economic Commission for Latin America on 'Economic Policy and the Price Mechanism,' *Economic Bulletin for Latin America,* March 1960.

The theme is fraught with emotional implications. On the one hand strenuous efforts are made to underline the exploitative aspects of the colonial subjection. On the other side the increasing importance of aid, in terms both of technical knowledge and of resources, is stressed, especially contributions to the budgets of African countries, the provision of preferential arrangements in commodity sales, provision of capital.

1. *The Rise of Preferential Systems before the War*

Practically all countries of Africa, both those whose independence dates back a long time and those which have only lately achieved it, belong, or belonged until recently, to monetary and banking systems and commercial areas centred in a highly developed metropolitan country and its institutions.[3] All the modern economic organs in Africa grew up in response to the needs of their creators, these metropolitan countries, whose main interest in Africa lay in the supply of food and raw materials from the tropical zone.[4]

There was, until very recently, no autochthonous demand in these areas for modern monetary or economic institutions, colonial governments were not encouraged to undertake financial operations in the territory for which they were responsible, the large foreign companies operating there had easy access to the capital markets of the metropolis for any financial needs beyond their retained profits. There was thus nothing to deflect the evolution of the monetary and banking institutions of the periphery from responding almost exclusively to the requirements of the centre.

These requirements could best be satisfied by safeguarding the absolute stability of the colonial monetary unit in terms of the metropolitan currency and by encouraging the establishment of banking institutions which would at all times be safe.

(i) *Monetary stability*

The former aim was achieved by the simple expedient of providing for a 100 per cent cover for the colonial currency. It was immaterial whether the institution in charge was a private bank (as in French Africa) or a currency board (as in British Africa), so long as the assets held against the note issue were metropolitan. In this

---

[3]Cf. my articles 'A Note on the Monetary Controversy in Malaya,' *Malayan Economic Review*, 1959; 'Those Sterling Balances,' *Venture*, 1954; 'Britain and the Dependent Commonwealth,' *New Fabian Colonial Essays*, 1959.

[4]Though the immediate reason for their establishing territorial bases in Africa in the nineteenth century was, in many cases, their effort to curb slave trading.

way any increase in the currency circulation in the dependent area resulted in a *de facto* loan by it to the metropolis; on the other hand this arrangement provided an absolute guarantee for the sufficiency of reserves. In a way it reduced the risk of extreme crises. It would incidentally also have prevented conscious policies for economic stabilisation and consciously accelerated development in the dependency, if such policies had (or could have) been conceived in this framework before the war.[5]

(ii) *Banking services*

The second requirement, the provision of reliable banking services was obtained automatically by encouraging the establishment of large (specialised) banking institutions in the metropolis to handle the commerce of the colonial area. These banks became powerful when banking had become stabilised in the metropolitan area and their policies had become impeccably sound and solid. Their freedom of operation, especially the choice of their investments, was not limited by any regulation such as a *minimum reserve* having to be kept *in the colonial or peripheral territory*. There was no other agency for handling the slowly emerging domestic savings of these territories at a time when few, if any, liquid assets of the required quality were available in those areas.

It was then a matter of natural 'evolution' that the colonial banking system to a considerable extent had to find uses for its deposits in the metropolis. Under the canons of sound banking, however, they had to confine their lending to 'self-liquidating' purposes. In practice this meant the finance of the foreign trade of the colonial area, of exports of colonial primary produce and imports of metropolitan manufactures. A large part of total resources was thus necessarily kept in metropolitan 'reserves' *i.e.* in liquid sterling or franc assets. Thus a further and increasing flow of (in effect short-term) lending at low rates of interest originated from the periphery (which was so terribly short of capital) to the Centre.[6] In some dependent areas (such as the British) where savings banks and postal saving institutions were legally bound to invest in the government

---

[5]It did actually impose limitations to the extension of 'Keynesian' policies in the short period after the war before independence was won.

[6]They were used especially before the First War to finance short term credits (acceptances). After 1920 they served increasingly as the basis of British long-term lending first to finance European reconstruction after the First War, and after the Second to prosperous developing areas (South Africa, Australia, etc.). It proved to be an embarrassing change.

securities of the metropolis, there was an additional loss of savings to the dependency.

The export of liquid savings to the metropolitan area and the consequent reliance of the dependency on the metropolis for long-term capital for development secured for the banking system of the latter a useful income, while its control over the financial and economic policy of the dependency (already assured by the hold of the metropolitan administration over the colonial government) was further reinforced and the participation of the ruling financial interests in its administrations obtained. All long-term expenditure for which long-term loans were needed—and the reluctance to increase taxation, and in especial to introduce direct taxation, in practice reduced the possibility of covering capital expenditure out of current budgetary resources—was thus made subject to financial veto.[7] This made any change in policy difficult, for the 'credit-worthiness' of colonial governments became dependent on their strictly abiding by the limitations imposed upon them. If the metropolis offered special facilities for colonial borrowing (*e.g.* the concession by Britain of trustee status to colonial securities) this grant did not by any means fully offset the gains secured to the banking system and the capital market by the special relationship.

The provision of cheap facilities for the finance of foreign trade while domestic activity was unable to obtain capital at comparable terms further distorted the productive structure of the colonial area. It accentuated the unfavourable integration of its economy, in which a subsistence agriculture, tribal or feudal, co-existed with a developed market economy. The differential ease with which the international movement of goods could obtain finance at world rates of interest further enhanced the supremacy of the merchandising, mining and plantation operations of large foreign firms, because long-term capital needed for the diversification of the economy and the rise of domestic industry was either not available at all or only on extortionate conditions.[8]

(iii) *Automatic commercial preference*

Thus the divergence in the tropics between private profitability and real social advantage was widened, and the tropical countries' dependence on primary exports was automatically perpetuated. Diversifica-

---

[7] The history of the establishment of a Central Bank in Ceylon is a good illustration of this veto.

[8] Cf. my article 'Economic Policy and the Price System,' *Economic Bulletin for Latin America*, 1961.

tion would have increased productivity and real income. But it was, in the circumstances, practicable only given *positive* economic intervention, and such positive economic intervention for the conscious acceleration of development of the colonial area was not contemplated so long as the territories were not independent. The role of the State was conceived as limited to assuring law and order.

This so-called *pacte colonial,* the exchange of colonial primary produce against metropolitan manufactures and services was thus in the 19th century (in contrast to the 18th century) not generally based on explicit restrictive or preferential legislation in favour of the metropolis (the monopoly of French shipping to Algeria and Madagascar represented one of the few exceptions). Over a large part of Africa, for example, the Congo basin and Morocco, international treaties or agreements enforced free trade, or at least non-discrimination. The free play of the price mechanism (as in the case of the 'independent' countries of Latin America and the Caribbean) was quite sufficient to restrict the less developed countries to a status of permanent economic inferiority. The implicit preference of the colonial administrations for the metropolitan products did the rest. Their orders on public and private account—and these represented a large portion of the total money demand of the colonial area—in the main flowed toward the metropolis.

As time went on and international industrial competition became more acute these rather informal relationships were increasingly reinforced by preference conceded explicitly in formal legal arrangements. The British Imperial Preference and the French Customs Union, even before the war, brought about a closer integration in those areas in which international treaties did not prescribe free trade or non-discrimination. They were to be reinforced by quantitative restrictions and exchange control. All these arrangements on the whole, secured greater advantages to the metropolitan areas than to the periphery, because the preference granted to the primary produce of the latter was, without quantitative regulation, often ineffectual.[9] The currency disturbances of the inter-war period, during which the dependencies had no option but to share the monetary fate of the dominant country— which meant that the risk of exchange fluctuation was eliminated in the relation of the centre to the periphery—acted as a further bond of some importance. The metropolis continued to secure a large, often overwhelming, share in both the exports and imports of the colonies.

[9]The export capacity of the areas entitled to Imperial Preference was in excess of metropolitan import requirements except in the case of a few products, *e.g.* oil-seeds and tobacco.

2. *The Impact of War Economies: the Rise of Exchange Areas*

The war brought fundamental changes, not merely in the economic relations of the metropolis to the dependencies, but also in the attitude of the colonial administrations to economic problems. This change strengthened the economic relationship between the metropolis and the periphery while the responsibility of the metropolis for fostering political and economic development became more and more recognised. The fact that the emergent political leaders of the dependencies obtained an increasingly influential voice in the administration of the African territories explains to a large extent, though perhaps not wholly, the recognition of the view that the conscious fostering of economic and social development represents one of the most important, if not the most important, functions of the State.

At the same time, the net effect of the change cannot unequivocally be said to have favoured the rapid growth of the dependencies. Even the profound change in the relationship between the prices of primary produce and manufactures which took place during the war and persisted well into the post-war period was insufficient to break the vicious circle of poverty. It is the contrast between the change in Government attitude and the improvement of the resources at the disposal of the African territories and the relatively unsatisfactory degree of progress that asks for an explanation. It is provided by the contrary effects of the interconnection with the metropolitan area on the progress of the dependency.

Already before the war the unrest due to the low prices for colonial primary produce caused by the Great Depression resulted in the appointment of several official committees to inquire into the problem of the marketing of export produce.[10] Their reports question for the first time the adequacy and efficacy of a 'free' market in these commodities. They question the assumption that bargains between weak peasants lacking knowledge and capital, and the indigenous merchants or the agents of the great metropolitan corporations who purchased the produce of the colonies could be said to be between equal partners. They foreshadow the development of government agencies which, by conscious policy, would secure that balance between the two sides which was supposed to be brought about by the free interplay of market forces in perfect markets.[11]

[10]*E.g.* The Cocoa Marketing Enquiry.

[11]The critics of Marketing Boards in their argumentation implicitly and illicitly assume that the peasant obtained a 'perfectly competitive price in the "free" system.' This is nonsense.

The outbreak of the war which disrupted trade in tropical produce merely occasioned a change which would have come about without it. On the one hand, the market for colonial produce was guaranteed by the metropolitan countries. This undoubtedly conferred a great advantage on the colonial area, if only or mainly in the sense that claims on the metropolis were accumulated which could at some point in the future be made effective. It also served to maintain equity in the distribution of incomes within the colonies which would have been gravely disturbed by a collapse of export prices. At the same time it might be and has been argued that this guarantee prevented a partial reorientation of colonial production towards food and other products needed in the home market. It is questionable, however, whether the cost of such readjustment would have been tolerable, or, in the long run, even in the interests of the colonies.

The war brought about another important change on the plane of commercial policy. This was the strong reinforcement of the rudimentary preferential arrangements, the grant of privileged treatment of colonial and metropolitan products respectively in each other's market, by the imposition of *direct controls over imports and over foreign payments, i.e.* payments outside the confines of the group. The *de facto* advantage of a stable currency became consciously and powerfully reinforced by explicit regulation. The loose automatic associations between London and the British dependencies, and Paris and the French ones, were transformed into the powerful groupings of the Sterling and the Franc Zone. The reciprocal possibility of obtaining finance between the metropolis and the dependencies created a unique framework for mutual profitable economic development. During this stage of the monetary and commercial development a series of special connections grew up, which made their interdependence far closer and more purposefully contrived than it had been at any time since the middle of the nineteenth century.

The economic significance of these special relationships is difficult to discern. They must not be evaluated singly because they are to a large extent inter-dependent and their effect on welfare must be judged as a whole. Efforts on either side to show the effectiveness of policy in lessening inequality and promoting development, by pointing to specific measures, *e.g.* the guarantee of purchases of colonial produce well above world price levels, are obviously beside the point. Nor must grants for particular projects, however admirable, by the Metropolis to the periphery be accepted automatically at their face value. It would have to be shown first that a grant was effectively transferred, *i.e.* not offset by the automatic working of the monetary mechanism through increasing the liquid reserves of the colony at the centre. Even if effective transfers took place, the indirect effects of this expenditure might result in a net burden to the periphery. The advantage gained by groups of individuals or firms in the periphery or in the centre might well be more than offset by the disadvantages of others. The net effect either of subsidies or of special privileges might be negatived by the basic mechanism of the system.

The advantages and disadvantages moreover might be in causal relation to one another—in other words, either party might be unable or unwilling to grant advantages or suffer disadvantages without some compensation. For instance, it would seem beside the point to argue in favour of 'untied', convertible, grants when the balance of payments position of the donor countries was such as to make a cut in the grant inevitable if convertibility were insisted upon. The cut might more than offset gains due to the possibility of using 'convertible' money in a third and cheaper market. A detailed evaluation, from the view point of welfare, of the special relationships between the metropolitan areas and their dependencies which have by now emerged into full independence is therefore needed if an adequate policy for the social and economic development of the areas is to be worked out and a suitable international commercial framework is to be established.

To this task we now turn.

3. *The Impact of Preference and Aid*

The preferential treatment accorded to goods and services in intra-group trade may take the form of commercial preferences—commodity purchase agreements, tariff preferences, administrative (quota) preferences—or of a discriminatory application of monetary controls. Of the various types of commercial preferences the first was the most important to the dependent or erstwhile dependent area and the second to the metropolitan areas. The monetary arrangements seems to have worked largely in the interest of the metropolitan areas (or rather certain groups in those countries) and had the result of diminishing the contribution provided, for the periphery in terms of resources and technical knowledge. It should be added, however, that in certain cases the net advantage to the metropolitan area would arise not so much through price relationships as through the fact that the periphery was for one reason or another unable to make full use of the purchasing power which resulted from its sales to the metropolitan area (and *a fortiori,* to third 'hard currency' areas, the proceeds of which accrued to the 'common' pool of reserves) or which was put at its disposal in other ways.

(i) *Commodity agreements*

Commodity agreements provide for the purchase of unlimited or of specified quantities of the African territories' produce. The former type was general during the war. As wartime scarcities lessened and the terms of trade moved against the primary producing areas limitation on quantity became the rule.

(*a*) In the British territories the war-time system was continued in the immediate post-war period of shortages. After 1950—and indeed already under the Labour Government—they were first attentuated and their duration shortened and then—partly because of producers' protests during the Korean boom at being forced to deliver their produce at low prices—purchase at current market price was agreed to. This would have worked against the primary producers after 1953. But in any case after 1951 most bulk purchase was discontinued. Among the exceptions the Imperial Sugar Agreement, the most notable, did not affect Africa substantially.

The post-war bulk purchase agreements seem to have generally worked to the disadvantage of the African colonies inasmuch that in a period of a rising trend of prices long-term purchases in practice proved to be made below current prices on the world markets.[12] Two things need to be said in this context, however. The first is that the relation of prices to the so-called 'world price' is by itself insufficient as a criterion for determining welfare effects of such agreements; 'world prices' are not independent of the existence of the agreement itself. One of the effects of the agreemnt might be a benefit far beyond the direct advantage or disadvantage experienced on the sale to the metropolitan country.[13] Nor must the security of market given by bulk purchases be disregarded.

[12]Cf. the interesting analysis made by the E.C.E. in the *Economic Survey of Europe in 1948,* Geneva, 1949.

[13]This is a significant consideration for the future, *e.g.* when considering the effects of bulk purchase by the Soviet Union on the world price of surpluses and commodities. If Soviet purchases push up 'free' world prices sufficiently for African countries to obtain the same income from sales of smaller quantities to other countries they will represent a net benefit. Thus the fact that the Russians may have bought the commodities at less than the world price ruling *after* the agreement cannot be said to prove that they have exploited the African areas.

It is one of the mysteries of Soviet policy that the Russians did not respond eagerly to the solicitation of Nkrumah to support the cocoa price by purchasing

What might be said to have been really objectionable in British policy from a welfare point of view was the decision to abandon bulk purchase at the precise moment when the world trend of primary prices (and terms of trade with manufacturers) turned and when the countries of Africa would have benefited by, and had a strong case for, the continuation of purchases.

(*b*) In the *French* territories (and to some extent in Somalia) the provision of preferential markets through quota regulation of the metropolitan market and price guarantees still plays a very important part in the marketing of coffee and groundnuts, and also of cocoa, groundnut oil, palm kernels and palm oil. Their impact is to increase the income of the periphery or rather production of the commodities in question relative to the production capacity of the world as a whole. It should be noted, however (and this qualification is habitually omitted in most treatments of this question) that this relative 'distortion' of the productive structure might in fact not be so significant because the innate potentialities of the periphery might be much greater than the actual production, *e.g.* because of ignorance or inertia and that 'artificially' high prices might just achieve what would be achieved automatically by the influence of a better working price mechanism on more knowledgeable producers. This is important because this consideration suggests that it is conceivable that the discontinuance of the provision of preferential markets (because it is not unconnected with the achievement of technical progress) will *not* have a net discouraging effect on production. It is quite likely that such technical progress will be stimulated by the ending or modification of the favourable commodity agreements, especially as this coincides with greater activity by 'Fedom'[14] and other 'European' funds[15] and the international agencies to channel technical knowledge to Africa.

(ii) *Duties and quantitative controls*

The impact of reciprocal *preferential tariffs* (where they existed) seems to have been more effective in securing advantages for the metropolitan country than for the periphery. This follows partly from the fact

---

rather limited amounts of cocoa against industrial output. There seems to be a large unsatisfied demand for chocolate in the Soviet Union and they could have worsened the terms of trade of the West to the benefit of Africa and at relatively little cost to themselves.

[14] The European Fund for the Development of Africa.

[15] On the impact of the new arrangements see my article 'Africa and the Common Market,' *Journal of Common Market Studies*, 1962.

that the tariffs in force for food and raw materials in the metropolitan area (even in France) were rather moderate and partly (especially in the case of the British territories) because in the case of a number of commodities the metropolitan countries were unable to absorb the whole of the export surplus of the periphery. As the exports were homogeneous this meant that the preference became inoperative. The preference granted on manufactures was substantial in a number of areas and it was also effective.

So far as *quantitative regulations are concerned,* their impact worked more evenly in the British zone until the acceptance by Britain of the G.A.T.T. principles of non-discrimination reduced the advantages of the periphery. In the French territories the primary producers continued to enjoy advantages from the discriminatory restriction of imports from outside areas coupled with price guarantees. Their effect on welfare was offset and perhaps more than offset by the discriminatory import controls in the African territories on non-French manufactures. As we shall see[16] the problem resolves itself mainly to one of income re-distribution between the various classes in both the metropolitan and peripheral areas.

(iii) *Monetary and exchange policy*

Discriminatory exchange control reinforced the effect on the pattern of commerce of quantitative import regulations. The ease with which payment could be made and finance secured obviously contributed to the strengthening of intra-group trade even where price relationships were not as favourable as they would have been with other parties. More important than this immediate effect on trade was the impact of exchange restrictions in the financial sphere.

Capital movements: Historically the essence of the functioning of currency areas has been the unlimited freedom of capital movements. This is not necessarily a condition of a functioning of currency areas. Both Australia and India have instituted strict controls on capital, even for transfers within the currency area in which they belong. It certainly has been a feature, until recently, of the relations of both the Franc Zone and the Sterling Area.[17]

It is obvious that a discriminatory ease of capital transfers from the metropolitan area to the periphery would encourage investment there even if this were not as advantageous, or profitable, as investment elsewhere. The assurance of being able to repatriate purchasing power

[16]Cf. below Subsections v. and vi.

[17]Great protests were encountered by the Governments of Ghana and British Guiana when they introduced control on capital flight.

would be an additional incentive. This may well be reinforced by the advantages secured to these investments by the commercial preferences system discussed above. It should be noted, however, that by and large the establishment of new large scale productive units was encouraged more *in the centre*[18] than in the periphery and that it would be impossible to assert that the latter did not suffer a relative disadvantage in consequence.

In recent years with the accelerated movement towards independence it seems likely that the freedom of capital movement on private account predominantly favoured the centre rather than the periphery. The capital flow was dictated not so much by normal profit incentives as by precautionary motives, *i.e.* capital was repatriated to the metropolis. This certainly seems to have been the case in the Franc Zone, but it probably played some part in the Sterling Area too.[19] The resultant weakening of the periphery is obvious. It must not, however, be judged without reference to another feature of the functioning of these economic groupings, the grant of aid in terms of loans or outright contributions from the centre to the periphery.[20]

The monetary and fiscal policy of the colonial areas continued to be dominated by Victorian canons. The plans prepared—especially in the British territories[21]—were little more than a haphazard collection of departmental investment projects unconnected with one another and decided upon without any analysis of their general economic effects. The reserves which were accumulating were kept in separate accounts in the metropolitan centre and thus could not be pooled for an imaginative use for general development. Balanced budgets and conservative finance, the use of long term capital only for long term investment remained the watchword of the administrations. Even when Central Banks were established, against rugged opposition of the metropolis, their powers remained sharply limited. No conscious anti-cyclical policies were conceived of for these areas even after the victory of Keynesian techniques in the metropolis. To some extent this was due to the complete failure to recruit a new type of personnel to devise and execute policy.

[18]Or in other highly developed parts of the currency area. In the case of the Sterling Area it was South Africa and Australia which mainly benefited.

[19]Some of the unexplained credit items of the British balance of payments might well be connected with this capital repatriation.

[20]Cf. below Subsection v.

[21]Planning became respectable at a much earlier date in France as a result of the activity of the *Commissariat du Plan.* Young economists and planners were made available to colonial administrations much sooner and in considerable numbers. The British administrations did not encourage such extravagance.

(iv) *Exchange rates*

The rates of exchange fixed for the African countries and especially those in the Franc Zone had important effects on the relations of Africans to the Metropolitan areas.

So far as the *British Territories* are concerned the problem was dominated and modified by the policy of the marketing boards, which paid less than the world market price to the farmers, thus limiting the incomes in the African territories and until after independence steadily accumulating rather large nest eggs, whose real value has been steadily declining.[22] The fact that the British-African currencies were devalued together with sterling in 1939 and again in 1949 though their balances of payments were showing surpluses may have further slightly worsened the terms of trade of the African countries in comparison to their competitors in, say, Latin America. The policy pursued would have been indefensible had it not happened just before the violent reversal, in 1951, of the postwar improvement in the prices of primary products relative to those of manufactures. Thus the effects of devaluation were completely swamped by the collapse of primary prices. Indeed, the African territories under British control may have benefited by the fact that their currency was at a relatively low level at that critical date, while their price-level was not influenced by the boom owing to its relatively short duration.

In the case of the *French Territories,* the value of the colonial currency was lifted during the postwar monetary vicissitudes of France to a level double that of the metropolitan franc. This decision together with the structure of commercial relations within the franc area resulted in a violent upward thrust of domestic prices in terms of dollars as the price level in the African territory was never revised, when shortages became less acute, and the colonial franc appreciated. The quantitative control imposed on imports from outside and the preferential relationships which French manufacturers enjoyed within the area, prevented the correction of the anomaly and secured exceptional profits to the metropolitan exporters. The producers of those primary products which had preferential markets in France were also shielded from the consequences of the revaluation of the colonial currency on their sale-prices. These included the great tribal-feudal-religious chiefs and the metropolitan corporations interested in plantations and ranches. In a number of areas, *e.g.* Senegal, those who suffered comprised the least

22The Ghana Government complained that the *sterling* value of the assets purchased also declined by £15m. The loss in real terms must have been far greater, perhaps as high as £60m.

privileged part of the population. The policy of high prices (and salaries) also favoured all those whose income and savings accrued in colonial francs but who wanted to spend them in France. Inasmuch as a considerable portion of the money (in contrast to subsistence) incomes in the French area were earned by individuals and firms from France, the high value of the currency had the tendency of enhancing the potential claims against these territories on capital account.

Too much, however, must not be made of this, because most of the money incomes provided in the colonies were strongly influenced either by commodity agreements or by direct subsidies granted by France. To that extent the arrangements meant merely that the French consumer of certain colonial produce and the French taxpayer were burdened with the cost of relatively higher payments to French firms trading in Africa and French citizens in the service of the African territories.

(v) *Taxes, subsidies and welfare contributions*

(a) *Until as late as the last war,* it was a general rule in imperial arrangements, that the colonies had to 'fend for themselves'. This expression was obviously interpreted by the Colonial Powers in a rather flexible manner. In the majority of cases the colonial taxation systems precluded the territory from benefiting from a direct contribution from incomes accruing in the territory to the nationals and firms of the metropolitan area, and this income represented a rather considerable portion of the total monetized and taxable income of the country. Even indirect levies and excise did not discriminate to any extent between essential and non-essential goods and thus accentuated the regressive character of colonial taxation which, as a whole, was biased in favour of the nationals of the metropolitan and other highly developed areas. This was thought to be needed to attract foreign capital. The conventional view is undoubtedly correct that the activities of foreign, or rather, metropolitan, firms represented an overwhelming proportion of total capital investment in the area, and their activity undoubtedly contributed most to such progress in the areas as was made. Whether they would have curtailed their activity if a different taxation policy had been pursued is a different question. The answer is difficult, for a different taxation policy would also have increased the pace of the development of technical knowledge and markets, and increased the attractiveness of investment.

The conclusion that the metropolis exploited the colony cannot be substantiated on the basis alone of the fact that they were able to earn large profits which were not taxed to any extent. It might perhaps be fairer to say that the share of profits and salaries going to the metropolis was substantial and that the latter reaped a greater part of the benefits of the development which it initiated and which would not otherwise have taken place. In the framework of taxation as it was and with a large supply of labour the forces of the 'free' market alone would have strongly favoured the productive factor in shortest supply, *i.e.* capital. These forces were massively supported by the fact that the 'free' market implied a strong *monopoly* economic power buttressed by political influence on the part of the expatriate individuals and firms. The resultant distribution of income was far more unfavourable to Africans than the corresponding one in Europe.

(*b*) The attitude of the metropolitan powers to their dependent territories underwent substantial changes *after the war*. In the British territories the Colonial Development and Welfare Act made available grants for capital expenditure on education and other social services, *e.g.* health and also for substructure investment. In the French Territories F.I.D.E.S., C.C.F.O.M. (now C.C.C.E. and P.A.C.) and lately the European Fund for Social Development, F.E.D.OM., made grants on an impressive scale. In addition the French Government defrayed the cost of the metropolitan military and a large proportion of the civil personnel stationed in former French Territories, but in certain instances granted direct contributions to the regular budgets of the new countries.

It has been claimed[23] that these grants represent a complete break with the past, an application to the relation of the metropolis to the dependent territories (soon to be granted independence) of the principles of the Welfare State.[24] It would be wrong to discount altogether the importance of the change, but its welfare impact can be exaggerated.

In the first place the grant of these subsidies co-determined the policies of the African countries concerned and deflected them from the courses upon which the countries themselves might have decided. To some extent, therefore, they might be thought to be objectionable from the point of view of the self-determination of the territory concerned. This rather constitutional argument is reinforced

[23]*E.g.* Colonial Office White Paper on the U.K. contribution to Development, Cmnd. 1308 of. 1961.

[24]It might be argued of course that the sudden willingness of the Conservative parties to grant independence ('to preside over the liquidation of Empire') is not unconnected with this new relationship. In fact France refused, at first, to make grants, or give technical collaboration to those countries which did not accept a special 'new' political relationship. There was willingness to purchase 'greatness' by continuing grants to the rest.

by the fact that the foreign grants almost always result in increased expenditure which has to be financed from domestic resources. This is clear in the case of capital grants which imply commitments (as in the case of the British-financed Universities) for current and maintenance expenditure outside the scope of the 'welfare' fund. This expenditure might be burdensome and/or for purposes for which otherwise resources would not have been found. In many instances the returns were not commensurate even to the net burden to the country.[25] Moreover such grants may have general repercussions on the Budget and on the distribution of income which might be considered out of keeping with the general situation of the territory.[26]

In the second place, the welfare effects of subsidies or contributions by the metropolitan countries will be strongly influenced if not determined by the geographical distribution of the final expenditure which is undertaken on the basis of these grants. As we have argued above, the very existence of dependent relationships did result in a powerful influence favouring purchases from the metropolitan area, even though they may not have been the most favourable from the economic point of view of the dependency. This preferential system has been perpetuated, if not strengthened, by the impact of the system of subsidies. The grants would have been used in the metropolitan country even if currency regulations and other restrictive measures had not meant a very substantial commercial preference between the metropolitan area and the periphery. In addition capital investment embodied in metropolitan manufactures necessitates purchases for replacement and extension and makes metropolitan goods familiar. Thus, in gauging the net contribution to the recipient countries' welfare of the payments made, the relative terms of trade would also have to be taken into account. These were not favourable to the African countries.

In addition to the assistance or contributions made by the former metropolitan countries, technical and resource contributions

25This has only too often happened in the case of Technical Assistance.

26One blatant example which springs to mind is the foundation of the Oxford and Cambridge type of university colleges in the British territories. These not merely burdened the emergent independent states with heavy expenditure, but, we have argued in a different section, had an unfortunate impact on the social balance and in all probability also influenced and increased the discrepancy between the average income of the population as a whole and of those employed in the Government and other institutions founded by the Metropolitan area, with unfavourable long run implications on the investment capacity of the country. Cf. my article 'Educational Policy for Africa.' *Centennial Review* of the Michigan State University, 1962.

were made by the United States of America on a bilateral basis. These were not large but are increasing rapidly. Soviet contributions to African countries south of the Sahara have been restricted to Guinea, Ethiopia and Ghana. They take the usual form of long-term loans at low rates of interest for capital development purposes, combined in some cases with bulk purchase arrangements. It should be noted, however, that in the case of Africa, large-scale purchases outside the world market have as yet not been undertaken by Russia, despite the favourable conditions which the fall in primary prices has presented in recent years.

International institutions were less active in the 1950's in Africa than in other continents. The relative insignificance of their contribution is explicable by the fact that few countries in Africa were independent before the 1950's and the metropolitan countries did not favour their activity in dependent areas. With expanding independence a very rapid increase in the activity of the international institutions has come about. Thus in calculating the net magnitude of the contribution of the metropolitan to the welfare of the African countries account would have to be taken of the aid which these countries could have obtained from outside sources, from which they were barred while in a dependent status. These must have been very substantial.[27]

(vi) *Conclusion*

In summing up this lenthy discussion of the close interrelationship of the now independent African countries with the erstwhile metropolitan countries, two things need to be noted.

The first is the development of their terms of trade, influenced as these were by the special relationships existing and the balance of payments and, more especially, the changes in their reserves held in the metropolitan centre. The impression one obtains is that the *British* territories on the whole have not been able to use the favourable opportunities presented in the immediate postwar period of rising prices fully, though in certain instances—sugar (which is of no importance for the British territories in Africa) is a conspicuous case— purchases from British territories took place at a relatively higher

---

[27]In the case of the British Territories it can be argued (*ex-post* at any rate) that those contributions would have been rather higher than the aid effectively obtained from Britain: American aid is already a multiple of the British aid in the past and their aid to a large extent was offset by the increase in the assets of the colonies. It is doubtful however, whether, in the absence of the spread of the cold war to Africa, this would have happened. But British claims must be sharply discounted.

level. In the case of the main export commodities of Africa, however, the bulk purchase agreements undertaken by British in the immediate past were relatively (if to some extent fortuitously) unfavourable to the African dependencies. The African territories, moreover, did not benefit from bulk purchase agreements in general after the price trend changed in 1952. The *French*-speaking territories, on the contrary, continued to benefit by such agreements. The impression is unmistakable, however, that the quantitative controls did encourage purchases in the metropolitan area even though the metropolitan area prices were far less favourable to those countries than world prices.

The second criterion is the development of the balance of their payments. In this respect, the *British* territories continuously increased their reserves in the metropolitan country. This meant that the subsidies and loans granted to the dependent areas could not be effectively transferred (even though the areas incurred liability for interest payments in the case of loans.) On the other hand, the combined effect of upward trend in prices and the decline in gilt-edged securities, in which the sterling reserves were partly invested, has severely reduced the real value of the reserves thus acquired. This has necessarily meant a heavy loss to the territories concerned.

So far as the *French-speaking* territories are concerned, a large portion of the public transfers (in some cases nine-tenths) have been offset by private transfers towards the metropolis of which the visible balance of payments only represents a fraction. At times the invisible operations, mainly capital transfers from the colonies towards the metropolis, amounted to double the invisible current balance. Nevertheless, as is shown on the official statistics, the French colonies were at times unable to use the public transfers fully and accumulated unused balances at the Banque de France despite the fact that capital flight from the colonies was very considerable. The effective transfers of capital for use in the colonial area has thus been even smaller.

If account is taken of the opportunities of obtaining capital and aid from sources outside the metropolitan countries the view that the African territories benefited by this special relationship to the metropolis must be sharply discounted. Even in the postwar period the net aid reaching them was more than offset by the concessions or special trading relations granted or obtained for metropolitan firms or individuals. The failure of the administrations dominated by the Metropolis to use taxation and direct controls to speed development consciously further increased the loss of the dependencies. This perhaps explains that it was possible and how it was possible, to accelerate economic progress in a number of areas as soon as independence was gained despite the loss of experienced administrators and the emergence of depressing political complications.

The implications of this analysis are disturbing. The mechanism of what one might call welfare or neo-imperialism seems to have artificially restricted the development of colonial areas by preventing viable infant industries from being established. The present surge of activity might just be the consequence of making up this *artificial backwardness*. Once the obvious manufactured import-substitution has come to an end Africa might be in danger of a Latin American or Middle Eastern frustration. Unless the vast primitive agricultural sector can be energised into a response, the upward surge will not become cumulative, but as in Latin America and the Middle East will peter out. There will remain a vast and increasingly dissatisfied ill-employed class in the primitive subsistence sector confronted with a small privileged class in the cities, unable to provide either supplies or markets for the latter. Only if the rural response were adequate, if productivity and income increased and justified a cumulative increase in industry could a self-sustaining upward spiral be confidently expected. This has not happened yet, and some of the development plans, with their neglect of agriculture and rural technical education seem to be disquietingly[28] inept for the exacting task in hand.

28Cf. my article on African Education *op. cit.*

Burdens and Benefits
of Empire
American Style[1]

Martin Bronfenbrenner

Martin Bronfenbrenner has taught at the University of Wisconsin, Michigan State University and the University of Minnesota. Since 1962 he has been professor of economics at the Carnegie-Mellon University. He is well known for his articles in the area of inflation theory and Marxian Economics. His published writings include *Academic Encounter* (1962) and *Is the Business Cycle Obsolete?* (1969).

Bronfenbrenner attempts to discuss the concepts of neo-imperialism and neo-colonialism in the post world war two world. He suggests that in this era sovereignty is almost non-existent, whereas control still exists in western hands or has slipped into Red China or the Soviet Union. The American empire is cemented largely through American military and economic aid programs. In the following article Bronfenbrenner explores the question—should the American empire cost so much to the taxpayer?

The reader should consult the following: William A. Williams, *The Roots of Modern American Empire.* New York, 1969.

Richard W. Van Alstyne, *The Rising American Empire.* Chicago, 1965.

Ronald Steel, *Pax Americana.* New York, 1967.

Some Preliminary Definitions

Perhaps it seems irresponsible to suggest that America has an empire—any style. However, one question raised in the outline for this symposium was: "Is it America's destiny to have all of the burdens and none of the benefits of empire?" Before answering this question, I want to raise a preliminary question: "What are these concepts called neo-imperialism and neo-colonialism?" Before I finish, I want to think out loud about some alternatives, including getting out of the empire-custodian business altogether, and inquire whether these alternatives would leave us (as taxpayers or otherwise) any better off than we are.

The terms neo-imperialism and neo-colonialism are popular on the other side of the Iron and Bamboo Curtains, but not on this side. However, I think we should look at them anyway, for if there is an American Empire at all, it must be a neo-empire, because there wasn't one before, say, the Spanish-American War of 1898.

[1]Reprinted from *Empire Revisited,* Leland Hazard, ed. Homewood, Ill, 1965, pages 45-66.

I do not have a universal definition of imperialism (or colonialism) valid for all times and places. (Neither did Lenin, who wrote the standard Marxist text on the subject; his definition involved capitalism, and so did not fit, for example, the Roman Empire.) To be perfectly frank, I don't know whether Canada is part of the American Empire today, or Albania is a part of the Chinese Empire, although I can guess how Lenin would classify these cases if he were alive. What I want to present, in lieu of a leak-proof definition, is a list of symptoms of imperialism, half economic and half political, valid for the present generation.

Country B is more completely a part of the empire of Country A, according to this list, if:

On the economic side:

Country B does not restrict movement of Country A's capital in and out of B, or Country A's earnings of interest, profits, and dividends in Country B. If there are any restrictions, they apply with at least equal severity to the domestic capital of Country B.

A's capital invested in B is in fact concentrated in low-wage or pre-modern industries like agriculture and mining. When A's capital is invested in B's modern industry, it is concentrated in A-owned firms or branch plants. In these firms or branch plants, the higher positions are in the hands of A's citizens, or of a special group of B's citizens educated in A, speaking A's language, professing A's religion, and often supporting A's government, even in disagreements with B's government.[2]

With regard to the products of skilled labor or modern technology, A's products have free entry into B's market; B has no significant protective duties against them. Any reciprocal concessions given B in A's home market will be confined to agricultural products and industrial raw materials.

On the political-military side:

A provides substantial assistance to B's military budget, often supplemented by free, or below-cost, military hardware and training services.

---

[2]In the special jargon of contemporary Marxism, these people are called *compradores,* and a system of private ownership in which they play important roles is called *compradore capitalism.*

In exchange, A is permitted bases in B for its military, naval, and air forces, sometimes including atomic weapons and guided missiles.

A also provides aid to B's civilian budget, or carries on civilian functions and projects in B which B's government cannot afford. Whether or not political "strings" are attached formally to A-B aid agreements in advance, aid from A to B is often cut off unilaterally by A for political reasons.

A has sufficient power within B to embarrass, and perhaps to subvert or overthrow, any B government unfriendly to A.
And finally, on both counts:

If more than one country plays in B the role we have assigned to A, country A', A", . . . , are allied with A and subordinate to A, at least within B.

The feature which is *neo-* about all this is that *sovereignty,* which is the political counterpart of *ownership,* ordinarily is no longer involved.[3] In neo-imperialism, it is not customary to decorate the map to show B in A's color; B ordinarily has its own flag, diplomatic corps, United Nations membership, national anthem, and so on. Neither are formal "protectorates" set up any more, nor is a nominally independent country like China divided into "spheres of influence" (Shantung to the Germans, Manchuria to the Japanese, the Yangtze Valley to the British, for examples).[4]

As for neo-colonialism, if I understand the term realistically, this is a type of neo-imperialism where B is usually a former colony of A, in which A has abandoned its political sovereignty more or less willingly, like the United States in the Philippines. Another type of neo-colonialism arises when B recovers complete sovereignty after having been occupied by the military forces of A, but A retains substantial political and economic influence in B. Japan after 1952 and South Korea after 1953 are spoken of in anti-American circles as seats of neo-colonial as well as neo-imperialist American policies.

Neo-imperialism and neo-colonialism, as practiced after World War II, represent, I suggest, at least as great a separation of ownership

[3]Of course, "sovereignty," like "ownership," is itself a difficult notion in concrete cases, as witness American disagreements with foreign powers over the division of sovereignty in Okinawa and in the Panama Canal Zone.

[4]The modern replacement of the "sphere of influence" appears to be the *divided* country, with regional governments each claiming sovereignty over the whole. Korea and Viet Nam are examples.

from controls as Berle and Means claimed to find in the corporation in their book, *The Modern Corporation and Private Property,* in 1933. Ownership (sovereignty) has reverted to Kipling's "lesser breeds without the law," but control has either stayed put in some Western power or migrated through the Curtains to China or to the Soviet Union.

This split between ownership (sovereignty) and control, in the less advanced pro-Western and neutral countries at least, has been seized upon and exaggerated by Marxists (and semi-Marxists) throughout the world, and so we hear a great deal about neo-imperialism and neo-colonialism today. An interesting paradox (in Marxian terms, contradiction) seems to arise between their recognition of the separation of ownership from control in these developing countries and their refusal to recognize it within Western business. This "contradiction" comes about, I think, because the Berle-Means thesis in its original form can lead to dangerous thoughts, including thoughts about *Managerial Revolution* (Burnham) and a *New Class* (Djilas). The neo-imperialist separation of ownership from control, however, seems to provoke no such heresies. Quite the contrary, Lenin hints at it himself, when he mentions the China of his day as an example of imperialism at its worst.

What I have done thus far is to give you a (hopefully) clear checklist of symptoms of neo-imperialism, in lieu of a definition which might have been equally long. I hope we can agree that some of the American government's relations around the world approximate neo-imperialism to a significant extent, without obligating ourselves to sing the *Internationale,* start a "Yankee Go Home" riot, or burn down the nearest office of the U.S. Information Service. The next question is, is neo-imperialism worth its cost?

Empires Old and New: Cost-Benefit Analysis
I do not propose to prove to you that empire in B costs A taxpayers money, because you know that. You may, like most of us, overestimate the direct cost; for example, if A's troops and planes are pulled out of B and stationed at home in A, some costs now assigned to A's military aid program in B will be "domesticated" rather than extinguished, but that is a secondary issue. Neither must I prove to you that, at one time, empire in B would have been a source of substantial gross and net income to A's treasury, both in tribute and in loot. You know that, too. Rather we need to concentrate on two points less generally known: (1) the negative contribution of empire to the imperialist country's public treasury is nothing new, and (2) the

balance on fiscal account is not all that matters, even on the strictly economic side.

It was probably the French and Indian War, followed by the American Revolution, which aroused in modern Europe the suspicion that colonial empire did not pay in the long run. You remember that the French and Indian War was the last and costliest of a series of three conflicts in which Great Britain defended and expanded her North American empire at French expense, while the American Revolution was the colonists' response to British efforts to shift a substantial part of the cost to them. ("Taxation without representation" was a thin smoke screen, given the relative populations of the Mother Country and the Colonies at the time.) Within fifty years after Paul Revere's Ride and the Glorious Fourth, a Haitian slave revolt against France and a series of Latin-American revolutions against Spain (and Portugal) emphasized the point. In fact, when Karl Marx was writing *Das Kapital* in London, "Little-Englandism" was riding high, so that Marx's own structures against imperialism were mainly historical. That is to say, Marx denounced past colonial oppression as one of the main sources of primitive capital accumulation. (The conventional economists of his day talked about saving and abstinence.) Detailed analysis of imperialism in the Marxian tradition was left to Nikolai Lenin; this is one of the reasons why modern Communists refer to themselves as Marxist-Leninists and not simply Marxists.

Jumping over the years from Marx's time (1818-1883) to the period of my own graduate training immediately before World War II, our generation learned that only one of the colonial empires was currently paying for itself. (This was the Dutch Empire, concentrated in what is now Indonesia.) The other colonial empires, we were assured, cost their home governments more to administer and defend than they paid in taxes to the imperial treasury. The implication of these teachings is that imperialism was a losing proposition well before the alleged foreign-aid giveaways. You will notice that the evidence relates only to *colonial* empires, rather than those which grew by continental expansion of contiguous territory like the Russian or American (or, for that matter, the ancient Egyptian, Persian, Macedonian, or Roman) Empires.

In those writings of Lenin which I have read, he never took this cost-benefit line of argument seriously enough to refute it. Neither did "the reformist Englishman, John A. Hobson," from whom Lenin obtained much of his evidence and some of his ideas. Neither did the Left Wing in my own classes. To all these people, what really mattered for the "balance sheet of imperialism" was not the impact on the governmental budget but the impact on the national one. The gains and losses to be considered were not only in the public sector (taxes *versus* expenditures) but also in the private sector (sales *versus* purchases). And on this larger and more comprehensive account it is not at all certain that the present American Empire costs the country any positive amount, either absolutely or relative to its alternatives.

But of that, more later. Let us return to Lenin. What he, as distinguished now from Marx, had in mind as the gains of imperialism were chiefly three items. They accrued primarily to the business class, the *bourgeoisie,* the recipients of surplus value, and secondarily to their "pampered palace slaves," the skilled craftsmen organized into trade unions, but not to imperialist treasuries. The three gains of imperialism were: (*a*) purchase of raw materials, embodying the man-hours of labor used to grow or extract them, more cheaply than they could be had at home or from other advanced industrial countries; (*b*) sale of "surplus" finished goods in "happy dumping grounds" abroad, reducing pressure on domestic prices as output rose in excess of "mass purchasing power"; and (*c*) outlets for capital invested in protected foreign operations at higher returns than prevailed domestically. At the same time, this capital export helped hold wages down at home by reducing the demand for domestic labor.

Such were the gains to raw-material-importing, finished-goods-exporting, capital-investing elements of the business class. Offsetting these, of course, were losses to domestic suppliers of raw materials, domestic purchasers of export-type goods, and borrowers of domestic capital, including other members of the capitalist class. The assumption-plus-observation of Lenin and Hobson was that the gaining group is characteristically the larger, better-financed, more powerful, and generally more important in framing international economic policy in most advanced countries.

Could imperialism save the capitalist system indefinitely? The reformist socialists of the German Social Democratic Party were afraid it might, if it led to a peaceful division of the entire world into empires, including spheres of influence. Lenin, however, thought otherwise. Rather, the process of imperialism would give rise to two additional conflicts or "contradictions" in capitalism, in addition to the one between workers and capitalists. One set of conflicts was between rival imperialist powers over valuable or strategic areas like China, the Middle East, and the Balkans. (Because these powers were growing in wealth and power at different rates, it would be impossible for any world division or world settlement to be realistic for very long.)

The second major conflict Lenin foresaw was between individual colonial powers and their exploited "native" subjects in search of higher living standards. Even when imperialist war, colonial war, or revolutionary "war of liberation" resulted, however, the cost might for a time be borne by taxpayers and the loss of life by the masses, while the gains went to business firms, their stockholders, and their employees.

Let us apply the Leninist argument to an American Empire tied together loosely, as empires go, by programs of economic and military aid. Taxpayers are assessed for the costs, and complain. The benefits go to exporters of civil and military finished goods, consumers and users of imported raw materials, and lenders of capital in the international market. Additional indirect costs are borne by the American agriculture and mining industries, by segments of American labor, and by American consumers of export goods. It is hard to make these gains and losses commensurable; each individual must decide for himself whether his gains in one capacity do or do not balance his losses in another. I shall not try to go further, beyond reminding you for the third time that fiscal effects upon taxes and the national debt are by no means the whole story of the economics of empire building.

Three Alternatives to Empire

If we agree that there is something we might call an American Empire in being, cemented largely by the American military and economic aid programs, let us inquire what might happen if these programs were cut sharply, as recommended, for example, by Congressman Passman on the Democratic side and Senator Goldwater on the Republican side of the political spectrum. Let us consider separately in extreme forms three alternatives which would probably be combined in some proportion. One of these is the "Trade, Not Aid" approach. This opens the American market to foreign competition and maintains the essentials of empire at reduced taxpayer expense. Another approach is the "Chinese Wall," which maintains or heightens our protectionism and abandons the empire almost entirely. The third and last approach is a peculiar compromise I have christened "Capital, Not Aid." It amounts to private lending to Countries B and C to expand export industries for trade with each other (as well as for purely domestic industries in both countries), while both B and C remain largely excluded from the American market and must repay their loans mainly from the proceeds of new ones.

This third alternative sounds impractical, and perhaps it is. But both the others—repeating the argument of a controversial piece on

"The Appeal of Confiscation in Economic Development" which I wrote in 1955—sacrifice American firms in developing countries to substantial risk of expropriation. Our aid expenditures have been for many countries periodic ransom payments, warding off nationalization or "nativization" on confiscatory terms. My third alternative of "Capital, Not Aid" shifts this burden to the private sector of our own economy. (I don't propose to guess in what countries confiscatory nationalization is a likely reprisal for dropping aid; in 1955 I mentioned Cuba as an *exception,* where this would *not* happen, and learned my lesson five years later.)

Trade, Not Aid
Of the three alternatives I have mentioned, "Trade, Not Aid" is the least unpopular in Washington, perhaps because its consequences are not realized. It would mean, at the very least, the sacrifice of a large fraction of American agriculture, extractive industry (including both mining and petroleum), and light industry (textiles) to developing-country competition, if these countries are to win by exports the dollar exchange they now receive by aid. The direct burden on the U.S. taxpayer would be less, and the U.S. consumer would benefit by lower prices. It is possible, but by no means certain, that expansive monetary and fiscal policies could permit the transition toward free trade to occur without much cost to employment and growth. Even so, the blow to some segments of the existing labor aristocracy would be hard to withstand. There would be a substantial, if indirect, tax burden, however, in the financing of partial compensation to farmers, ranchers, miners, and factory owners for their losses in income and property values, unless these were financed entirely by additions to the money stock and national debt. American exporters would gain, but less than one might anticipate, since the developing countries B and C would probably retain their infant industry protective duties, and exports now monopolized to some degree by Americans under "tied aid" would be subject to renewed international competition.

I should not anticipate any great reduction in the U.S. gold drain or balance-of-payments deficit. The gold drain might indeed accelerate, at least temporarily, if our trade balance became less positive and returns on developing-country investments were cut off under this freer-trade alternative. In terms of empire, however, opening up the American market to developing countries would certainly weld some of these countries closer to the United States than the present aid program does.

Some developing-country spokesmen seem to doubt that even these concessions to present developing-country industries would permit many such countries to develop modern high-wage industry rapidly enough to reduce the gap separating their incomes per head from advanced-country standards. Dr. Raul Prebisch of Argentina, long-time framer of policy for the U.N. Economic Commission for Latin America (ECLA), would, for example, like to see additional special concessions for developing-country heavy-industry exports, such as steel products, in the American market, in addition to the "package" just outlined. This step would, in his view, accelerate the development of "modern" industrial skills in developing countries, especially Latin-American ones. He also favors, for much the same reasons, strengthening trade preferences within the present South and Central American Common Market areas, and he looks with disfavor on the repatriation of interest and dividends earned in Latin America to their home countries. Should his views prevail, the supplementary effects in this country would be more unfavorable than I have indicated.

The Chinese Wall

The conservative alternative is to cut off aid, just like that. No trade concessions to developing countries should sweeten the blow. American protectionism should remain unchanged, if not restored to its level under the Smoot-Hawley Tariff. A variant of the same alternative would involve the imposition of unacceptable restrictions on aid recipients, such as limitations to the private sectors of receiving countries or more liberal treatment of American private investors as a condition on actual transfer of funds.

These are what I have coupled together as a "Chinese Wall" policy. (This term is probably too strong, since it implies American isolation from other advanced countries as well as from the developing ones, whereas the cessation of aid would actually isolate us only from part of the developing world.) Support for "Chinese Wall" isolation comes not only from Midwestern Republicans within the United States, but from foreigners of internationalist and Socialist bent. Impressed with our capacity for what seems to them error in international economic relations, and impressed with our low growth rate and periodic recessions, foreigners sometimes feel the world would be better off were we indeed quarantined behind a Chinese Wall. An extreme example of this position was the request of Prince Norodom Sihanouk of Cambodia, in the autumn of 1963, that U.S. aid to his country be cut off and the aid mission withdrawn, because aid and the aid mission served (he felt) as covers for political subversion to his government.

The immediate effects of a "Chinese Wall" policy have their attractions. Lower government expenditure is one of these attractions; reduced international pressure on the dollar is another. It may not take long, however, for the disadvantages to appear, as they did in Cuba after aid was suspended in 1959. Anticipated first steps in retaliation are cuts, often discriminatory, in imports from the United States and restrictions on repatriation of American capital and its earnings. Next may come confiscatory nationalization of U.S. properties, followed by a frankly hostile political posture if the U.S. government backs the companies concerned. From membership in the American Empire, Co-Prosperity Sphere, or the like, to downright anti-Americanism required—in Cuba—only two years (1959-1961). Elsewhere, of course, it may take longer or be avoided altogether.

Capital, Not Aid

Come to think of it, how odd it is that we no longer take long-term capital transfer seriously as an alternative, or even a major supplement, to trade and aid in holding empires together! It is odd because so many of the ties binding America to Great Britain in the last century, or Latin America and Canada to the United States in the present one, have been based on "Capital, Not Aid." The contemporary revulsion of feeling against private international capital transfers on any large scale is affecting both potential borrowing and potential lending countries. Perhaps I might remind you of four reasons for the revulsion.

In the first place, the foreign investor in the developing country has sometimes shown a "get-rich-quick" bias. He has extracted quick monopoly returns, and gotten out on a hit-and-run basis after the oil is pumped or the metals mined, leaving the country in worse shape than before. More commonly, he has abused his position, or so it seems to the borrower, to set up foreign enclaves in the borrowing country, to exclude "natives" from skilled labor and administrative jobs, and to evade the economic plans, controls, and unwritten laws of Countries B and C. Examples of "unwritten law" trouble have been the driving of "inefficient" native competitors out of business, and refusing to provide "guaranteed lifetime employment" for native employees. I made a speech to Carnegie Tech alumni in 1963 about some of these problems, to which someone appended the title, "The Corporate Ugly American."

The second reason is historical. In the nineteenth century, capital, and returns on capital, could cross most international boundaries most of the time freely and easily at constant exchange rates between national currencies. The present world is a jungle of transfer controls and exchange devaluations. Foreign capital, therefore, cannot be relied on steadily at low interest rates by developing countries for development purposes.

Thirdly, developing countries as a group have chronic balance-of-payments problems. They often cannot meet service charges on outstanding private capital indebtedness, unless these are financed by a larger volume of new loans. To put it differently, private capital transfers are only palliatives for the payments problems of developing countries and must be repeated in increasing doses. (If lending countries are growing too, these doses, while growing absolutely, may not be increasing relative to the national incomes of the countries concerned.)

Professor Evsey Domar has worked out, under simplifying assumptions, a condition under which a borrowing country can avoid a net return flow of investment income. In words, Domar's condition is:

(AMORTIZATION RATE + INTEREST RATE) *less than*
(GROWTH RATE OF INTERNATIONAL LENDING).

Domar's condition can be simplied further. If private lending and investment are to replace aid as a solution of the balance-of-payments problems of developing countries in the American Empire, the annual rate of increase of such lending must be greater than the average rate of interest earned by these loans or investments. If loans, and particularly investments, are profitable, and if profits are repatriated to the United States, this will be a difficult condition to satisfy.

Lastly, of course, potential lenders here and elsewhere can seldom forget for very long the risk of confiscatory nationalization of capital investment in developing countries, especially if ransom is not paid by periodic additions to gross investment. This sort of confiscation was, of course, known long before the Russian Revolution, but only in conjunction with "national bankruptcy." It is more common now and does not need bankruptcy as an excuse. As insurance against it, lenders demand "unreasonable" interest and profit rates. The higher the interest and profit rates, the greater the appeal of confiscation, and a vicious circle gets under way.

If foreign aid were, nevertheless, by some miracle to be replaced by increased private lending to the developing countries, what can we say about the resulting redistribution of costs? A gain to Americans as taxpayers goes without saying, although if interest rates rise (as one would expect), this would affect the cost of carrying our national and local debts. More important costs would affect us as borrowers and workers. The rise in interest rates would affect, for example, home financing charges and business loan rates; money would be generally tighter. With less capital to work with domestically, workers would face a declining growth rate of productivity, and some combination of lower rates of wage increase with emigration of job opportunities in private industry. So much for "Capital, Not Aid."

Suggestions for Aid Programs
In answer to the original question, "Must the American Empire always cost so much?" (to the taxpayers, that is), my first answer would therefore be, "Yes, unless we decide to abandon imperialism as a bad job, or transfer its cost to Americans in other than their taxpaying capacities." But I should certainly add another more palatable but also unlikely qualification, with an eye to the Marshall Plan in Western Europe, "unless the developing countries of the American Empire begin rapidly to 'take off' and close the widening gap separating their living standards from our own."

From a conventional economist, tainted with professional orthodoxy, you can expect to hear a preference for the "Trade, Not Aid" alternative, shifting the cost of empire from Americans-as-taxpayers to Americans-as-producers in such industries as agriculture, fishing, shipping, and textiles. As a matter of fact, this position is even harder to accept than is "free trade," because (like the Swedish economist Gunnar Myrdal) I look with more leniency on "infant industry" protection in developing countries than on "senile industry" protection here at home. You also know that this alternative is not promising politically in the here-and-now, when something called "vote-fare" prevails so often over what we think of as "welfare." Let us therefore return to some discussion of foreign aid in itself, and consider whether, to the extent we cannot cut its cost without risk, we can at least get a "bigger bang for a buck."

A number of plausible ideas have been turned out on this subject, some by Americans and more by people in the receiving countries. I have myself sought to contribute to this discussion, in some congressional testimony in 1957. (Joint Economic Committee, U.S. Congress, *Federal Expenditure Policy*).

Perhaps the most telling improvement we might make would be to stop giving aid in the form of surplus agricultural commodities, which neither we nor the importer need particularly. What the representative receiving country wants is capital goods, bought with dollars but from the cheapest source, which often will not be the United States. With the aid of these capital goods, meaning machinery, they can set up viable industries as Western Europe did, and they are willing to postpone increases in consumer living standards. In South Korea, for example, it has been the United States which insisted on a 70-30 mix in favor of consumer goods, to maintain the South Korean living standard above the North Korean one. The Republic of Korea preferred a 70-30 mix in favor of capital goods, and used to argue, "You can't starve a Korean." What is more, our rivals across the Curtains seem to get better long-term results by exporting capital goods than we do by raising living standards to "showcase" levels—which receiving countries then have difficulty in maintaining.

If we recall Marshall Aid to Western Europe, it took the capital form in increasing amounts in its later years, and the Europeans could use their own best judgment as to where they would buy the machinery they wanted. I am aware, as who is not, that aid in capital goods means later "unfair" competition for both our exports abroad and our import-competing industries at home. As a consumer, however, I say, "What of it?"

We are told, however, by people who should know, that developing countries' capacity to absorb machinery imports is limited by lack of those labor skills which, in the United States, we call "human capital." The answer is to send "complete factories" as the Soviets do, meaning to be sure that all necessary components are included in the "package," including, in most cases, the skilled men to supervise their assembly and teach the tricks of operation.

On the other hand, I have heard the constant complaint against aid funds diverted to the support of too many unwanted and expensive specialists, supervisors, administrators, and general checker-uppers. These people are usually too young or too old, too sickly or lazy or incompetent for their jobs, and yet Country B must pay and house them as a condition of receiving aid.

I should much prefer to eliminate these "warm bodies," and let the aid recipient hire any foreigners it pleases from wherever it pleases. As for ascertaining the use or misuse of aid, it can be done, on what journalists call a "post-censorship" basis, by fewer people. If progress is unsatisfactory, if graft is rampant and reform promises unfulfilled, cut next year's aid appropriations, nothing more.

Along these same lines, I suggested to Congress in 1957 that countries might compete for a budgeted volume of economic aid in the same way scholars and universities in America compete for foundation grants. Little or nothing would be earmarked for individual countries. All, or nearly all, would be allocated on the basis of rival proposals or "projects" submitted by or for the various applicants, with costs and benefits estimated as carefully as possible and American specialists making decisions on the basis of each country's past "performance" as well as the *ex ante* "intrinsic merit" of its proposals. My friends in the International Bank for Reconstruction and Development criticize this as impractical and unrealistic. Too few developing countries have specialists who can make the necessary supporting estimates intelligently, and they hesitate to employ foreigners, influence peddlers excepted, until the loans or grants are already signed, sealed and delivered. I expect these World Bank criticisms to be correct in the first year or two, but not thereafter.

You need very few words from a non-psychologist on "making friends and influencing people." Given the fact of an American Empire and the emotions it engenders, I can accept one of Milton Friedman's generalizations that pro-American sentiment seems to correlate negatively (both within and without the American Empire) with American aid received per head of population. Resentment is usually phrased in terms of "strings attached," or of "meddling" by outsiders, or of the drain in funds to the support of American advisers and the purchase of American goods. Probably a more important fact is simple jealousy of America, directed at "happy, undeserving A" by "wretched, meritorious B."

Post-censorship, staff reduction, and shifts to capital good exports are all parts of the answer to this problem, but the major part is probably a lowering of our own sights—from positive friendship to benevolent neutrality. To quote Premier Kadar of Hungary, "He who is not against us is for us." As for anything warmer and more appreciative, let me quote the contemporary poet, Richard Armour:

> In foreign lands they do not love us,
> Instead of hugging us they shove us.
> But one with even slight acumen
> Can see that this is only human.
> For being host and guest soon ends
> The friendship of the best of friends.

A Single Case—South Korea

Thus far I have been quite general and abstract. Now I want to be more concrete and specific, and end with a few words about the situation in South Korea, one of the more "expensive" bits of the American Empire. In Korea we are trying to shift to a third country, namely Japan, most of our aid costs, via a "normalization" treaty between Japan and Korea, under which the Japanese will pay the Koreans reparations and make them loans. Korean students, who overthrew one pro-American government there in 1960, have been rioting against the proposed normalization treaty. I have a correspondent in Korea, a Fulbright visiting professor in one of the national universities. I asked him whether the student demonstrations were anti-American or anti-Japanese, and he replied (early in April, 1964):

> The demonstrations... reflect (1) suspicion of the Japanese, of course. (2) Lack of confidence in their own Government. Even [with] a perfectly satisfactory agreement, the students feel that the reparations and loans would be used badly. (3) Lack of confidence in the Opposition parties.... (4) Frustrated anti-Americanism. My students tell me they considered, but voted down, extending the demonstration to express their anger against the delay in a Status of Forces Agreement with regard to the U.S. Army. They did include placards... warning the U.S. not to interfere in the Korean-Japanese talks.
>
> The anti-Americanism is only thinly restrained, and in any real break-out of student revolution, might emerge full force. [The students] are furious at the continued dependence of their economy on American "generosity" (which they distrust), but at the same time their awareness of dependence inhibits them (momentarily) from attacking the Americans.... Although increasingly, you hear talk of foregoing aid.
>
> A student, presumably on his own, has been distributing leaflets calling for the unification of Korea through joint negotiation. He was jailed, of course. The relatives and friends of the jailed Progressives (Socialists) have been increasingly calling for their release. The Opposition parties... have just begun to press for this.

Very well, what is the answer? Here are the burdens of empire in a nutshell—a historically and strategically important nutshell called South Korea, inhabited by some 25 million Koreans. Where do we go from here? Keep on as we have for the past twelve years, or transfer the cost to the Japanese taxpayer, and take our chances (either way) of another Korean War? Let the products of cheap Korean labor into our textile and agricultural markets? Give the Koreans the machinery and equipment and training they need to displace our exports in Korea, and compete with us elsewhere in Asia? Ask American companies, as business propositions, to replace our aid in Korea with their private investment? When you find the least worst answer or combination of answers, don't just write your Congressman. Write me as well.

Bibliography

Compiled by
TAPAN MUKERJEE

Abbott, C. C. "Economic Defense of the United States," in *Harvard Business Review*, XXVI (September 1948), 613-26.
—————. "Economic Penetration and Power Politics," in *Harvard Business Review*, XXVL (July 1948), 410-24.
Aderibigbe, A. B. "Trade and British Expansion in the Lagos Area in the Second Half of the Nineteenth Century," in *Nigerian Journal of Economics and Social Sciences*, IV (July 1962), 188-95.
Ady, P. "Colonial Industrialization and British Employment," in *Review of Economic Studies*, XI, 1 (1943), 42-51.
Ambirajan, S. "McCulloch on India," in *Manchester School of Economics and Social Studies*, XXXIII (May 1965), 125-40.
Andrus, J. R. *Burmese Economic Life*. Palo Alto, 1957.
Angell, J. W. "Financial Foreign Policy of the United States," in *The Council on Foreign Relations*, New York, 1933.
Angell, N. *The Great Illusion*. (4th ed.). New York, 1913.
Arendt, H. *The Origins of Totalitarianism*. New York, 1966.
—————. *The Origins of Totalitarianism* (2nd ed.). New York, 1958.
Arnault, J. *Procès du Colonialisme*. Paris, 1958.
Aron, R. *War and Industrial Society*. Oxford, 1958.
—————. *The Century of Total War*. Garden City, 1954.
—————. "The Leninist Myth of Imperialism," in *Partisan Review*, XVIII, 6 (1951), 646-62.
Ashworth, W. *An Economic History of England, 1870-1939*. New York, 1960.
Balogh, T. "The Mechanism of Neo-Imperialism: The Economic Impact of Monetary and Commercial Institutions in Africa," in *Oxford University Institute of Economics and Statistics Bulletin*, XXIV (August 1962), 331-46.
—————. *Unequal Partners*. Oxford, 1963.
Baran, P. A. *The Political Economy of Growth*. New York, 1957.
Baran, P. A., and Sweezy, P. M. *Monopoly Capitalism*. New York, 1967.
Barnes, H. E. *World Politics in Modern Civilization: The Contributions of Nationalism, Capitalism, Imperialism and Militarism to Human Culture and International Anarchy*. New York, 1930.
Barraclough, G. "Guide to Imperialism," in *The New York Review* (December 18, 1969), 3-6.
Bastin, J. *The Native Policies of Stamford Raffles in Java and Sumatra*. Oxford, 1957.

Bauer, O. *Der Kampf um Wald und Weide*. Vienna, 1925.
————. "Die Akkumulation des Kapitals," *Die Neue Zeit*, XXI (1913), 831-38; 862-74.
————. *Die Nationalitätenfrage und die Sozialdemokratie* (2nd ed.). Vienna, 1907, 1924.
————. *Zwischen zwei Weltkriegen*. Bratislava, 1936.
Benham, F. *Great Britain Under Protection*. New York, 1941.
Benson, A. C., and Esher, V. (eds.). *The Letters of Queen Victoria*. Ser. 1, London, 1908.
Betts, R. F. *Assimilation and Association in French Colonial Theory, 1890-1914*. New York, 1961.
Bhattacharya, S. *The East India Company*. London, 1954.
Blaisdell, D. C. *European Financial Control in the Ottoman Empire*. New York, 1929.
Blakeslee, G. H. Review of Thomas Parker Moon's *Imperialism and World Politics,* in *American Historical Review*, XXXII (April 1927), 597-99.
Blaug, M. "Economic Imperialism Revisited," in *The Yale Review*, L (March 1961).
Blumberg, A. "The Second French Empire, Eugene Rouber and the Italian Railroads: Documents, Illustrative of Economic Imperialism," in *Economy and History*, VII (1965), 78-82.
Bodelsen, C. A. G. *Studies in Mid-Victorian Imperialism* (2nd ed.). London, 1960.
Boeke, J. H. *Indische Ekonomie*. Harlem, 1940.
Bonn, M. J. *The Crumbling of Empire: The Disintegration of World Economy*. London, 1938.
Boulding, K. E., and Gleason, A. H. "War as an Investment: The Strange Case of Japan." Peace Research Society (International), Papers, III (1965), 1-17.
Brailsford, H. N. "Can the League Cope with Imperialism?" Stenographic report of the 104th New York luncheon discussion of the Foreign Policy Association, February 4, 1928.
————. *The War of Steel and Gold*. London, 1917.
British Labour Party. *The Colonial Problem*. Brussels, 1928.
Brougham, H. *An Inquiry into the Colonial Policy of the European Powers*. 2 vols. Edinburgh, 1803.
Brown, M. B. *After Imperialism*. London, 1963.
Brunschwig, H. *French Colonialism, 1871-1914: Myth and Realities*. New York, 1966.
Bryce, J. B. *Sudies in History and Jurisprudence*. New York, 1901.
Buchanan, D. H. *The Development of Capitalist Enterprise*. New York, 1934.
Bukharin, N. I. *Der Imperialismus und die Akkumulation des Kapitals*. Vienna-Berlin, 1926.
————. *Imperialism and the World Economy*. New York, 1966. (First published in 1929).

Cady, J. F. *The Roots of French Imperialism in Eastern Asia.* Ithaca, 1958.
————. *A History of Modern Burma.* Ithaca, 1958.
Cairncross, A. K. *Home and Foreign Investment, 1870-1913: Studies in Capital Accumulation.* Cambridge, Mass., 1953.
Calwer, R. "Kolonialpolitik und Sozialdemokratie," in *Sozialistische Monatshefte,* XIII (March 1907), 192-200.
Casanova, P. G. *Sociología de la explotación.* XXI (1696), Siglo, Mexico.
Charle, E. G., Jr. "An Appraisal of British Imperial Policy with Respect to the Extraction of Mineral Resources in Nigeria," in *Nigerian Journal of Economic and Social Studies,* VI (March 1964), 37-42.
Chesson, F. W. *The Political Writings of Richard Cobden* (4th ed.). London, 1903.
Church, F. "Gunboat Diplomacy and Colonialist Economics," in *Transaction,* VII, 8 (June 1970), 25-32.
Clapham, J. H. "Imperial Economics," in *Economic History Review,* XIV (1944), 84-88.
Clark, G. *The Balance Sheets of Imperialism: Facts and Figures on Colonies.* New York, 1936.
————. *A Place in the Sun.* New York, 1936.
Cole, C. W. *Colbert and a Century of French Mercantilism.* Hamden, Conn., 1964.
Colis, M. *Last and First in Burma.* London, 1956.
Conant, C. A. *The United States in the Orient.* Boston and New York, 1900.
Condiliffe, J. B. "Economic Power as an Instrument of National Policy," in *American Economic Association Papers and Proceedings,* XXXIV (March 1944), 305-14.
Conquest, R. *The Last Empire.* London, 1962.
Court, W. H. B. *British Economic History, 1870-1914.* Cambridge, 1965.
Cowie, D. "How the British Acquired Their Empire," *Great Britain and the East* (January 18, 1940), 37.
Cram, R. A. *The Sins of the Fathers.* Boston, 1919.
Cramb, J. A. *The Origins and Destiny of Imperial Britain.* New York, 1915.
Cromer, E. B. *Ancient and Modern Imperialism.* London, 1910.
Cross, C. *The Fall of the British Empire, 1918-1968.* New York, 1969.
Crozier, W. P. "France and Her Black Empire," in *The New Republic* (January 23, 1924).
Cunow, H. "Handelsvertrags- und imperialistische Expansions-Politik," *Die Neue Zeit,* XVIII (1900), 207-15; 234-42.
Daalder, H. "Capitalism, Colonialism and the Underdeveloped Areas: The Political Economy of Anti-Imperialism," in Egbert Devries (ed), *Essays on Unbalanced Growth: A Century of Disparity and Convergence.* The Hague, 1962.
————. *Imperialism.* David L. Sills (ed.), *International Encyclopedia of the Social Sciences,* VII (1968), 101-9.

Dalton, J. H. "Colony and Metropolis: Some Aspects of British Rule in Gold Coast and Their Implications for an Understanding of Ghana Today," in *Journal of Economic History,* XXI (December 1961), 552-65.

Dampierre, J. de. *German Imperialism and International Law.* New York, 1917.

Davidson, J. W. "The History of Empire," in *Economic History Review,* XVI, 1 (1946), 69-73.

Davies, K. G. "Empire and Capital (in the Writing of R. Pares)," in *Economic History Review,* Ser. 2, XII (August 1960), 105-10.

Davis, H. B. "Imperialism and Labor: An Analysis of Marxian View," in *Science and Society,* XXVI, 1 (1962), 26-45.

Day, C. *The Dutch in Java.* London, 1904.

Dehio, L. *Precarious Balance: Four Centuries of the European Struggle.* New York, 1962.

Del Mar, A. *The Middle Ages Revisited.* New York, 1900.

Desai, T. B. *Economic History of India Under the British.* Bombay, 1968.

Deschamps, L. *Histoire de la question coloniale en France.* Paris, 1891.

Deutsch, H. C. *The Genesis of Napoleonic Imperialism.* Cambridge, Mass., 1938.

Digby, W. *Prosperous British India: A Revelation from Official Records.* London, 1901.

Dilke, C. W. *Greater Britain.* London, 1868.

Dobb, M. *Political Economy and Capitalism: Some Essays in Economic Tradition* (rev. ed.). New York, 1940.

Dos Santos, T. "El nuevo carácter de la dependencia," *CESO* (1968), Santiago de Chile.

————. "La crisis de la teoría del desarrollo y las relaciones de dependencia en America Latina," *Boletín del CESO,* 3 (1968), Santiago, Chile.

————. "The Structure of Dependence," in *The American Economic Reviews: Papers and Proceedings,* LX, 2 (May 1970), 231-36.

Dulles, F. R., and Ridinger, G. E. "The Anti-Colonialist Policies of Franklin D. Roosevelt," in *Political Science Quarterly,* LXX (March 1955).

Dutt, R. C. *Economic History of India Under British Rule.* 2 vols. London, 1903.

Eckert, C. *Alter und neuer Imperialismus.* Jena, 1932.

Edwardes, M. *British India, 1772-1947: A Survey of the Nature and Effect of Alien Rule.* New York, 1968.

Edwards, G. W. *The Evolution of Finance Capitalism.* New York, 1938.

Egerton, H. E. *British Colonial Policy in the 20th Century.* London, 1922.

Emerson, R. *From Empire to Nation: The Rise to Self-Assertion of Asian and African Peoples.* Cambridge, Mass., 1960.

Emery, S. E. V. *Imperialism in America: Its Rise and Progress.* Lansing, 1892.

Emmanuel, A. *L'Echange inégal.* Paris, 1969.

Faber, R. *Vision and the Need: Late Victorian Imperialist Aims.* New York, 1966.

Faucher, A. "Some Aspects of the Financial Difficulties of the Province of Canada," in *Canadian Journal of Economics,* XXVI (November 1960), 617-24.

Fawcett, C. *The English Factories in India.* New York, 1952.

Fay, C. R. "The Growth of the New Empire, 1783-1870," in *Economic Journal,* LI (April 1941), 80-91.

Feierabend, I. K. "Expansionist and Isolationist Tendencies of Totalitarian Political Systems: A Theoretical Note," in *Journal of Politics,* XXIV (1962), 733-42.

Feis, H. *Europe: The World's Banker, 1870-1914.* New Haven, 1930.

Ferguson, W. S. *Greek Imperialism.* Boston and New York, 1913.

Fieldhouse, D. K. *The Colonial Empires: A Comparative Survey from the 18th Century.* London, 1966.

—————. "Imperialism: An Historiographical Revision," in *Economic History Review,* Ser. 2, XIV (December 1961), 187-209.

—————. *Theory of Capitalist Imperialism.* New York, 1967.

Fisher, L. *Empire.* New York, 1943.

Flux, A. W. "The Flag and Trade: A Summary Review of the Trade of the Chief Colonial Empires," in *Journal of Royal Statistical Society,* Ser. A, LXII (September 1899), 489-533.

Foust, C. M. "Russian Expansion to the East through the Eighteenth Century," in *Journal of Economic History,* XXI (December 1961), 469-82.

Frank, T. *Roman Imperialism.* New York, 1914.

Frankel, S. H. "Agenda for the Study of British Imperial Economy: Note," followed by W. K. Hancock's reply, in *Journal of Economic History,* XIV, 1 (1954).

—————. "Some Observations on the Rhodesia-Nyasaland Royal Commission Report," in *South African Journal of Economics,* VII (June 1939), 198-206.

Freymond, J. *Lénine et l'impérialisme.* Lausanne, 1951.

Furber, H. *John Company at Work.* Cambridge, Mass., 1948.

Furnivall, J. S. *Colonial Policy and Practice: A Comparative Study of Burma and Netherlands India.* New York, 1956.

—————. *An Introduction to the Political Economy of Burma.* Rangoon, 1957.

—————. *Netherlands India: A Study of Plural Economy.* Cambridge, 1944.

Gallagher, J., and Robinson, R. "The Imperialism of Free Trade," in *The Economic History Review,* Ser. 2, VI, 1 (1953).

Ganguli, B. N. "Dadabhai Naoroji and the Mechanism of 'External Drain,'" in *Indian Economic and Social History,* II (April 1965), 85-102.

Garrett, G. *People's Pottage.* Caldwell, 1953.

Garson, N. G. "British Imperialism and the Coming of the Anglo-Boer War," in *South African Journal of Economics,* XXX (June 1962), 140-53.

Ghosh, R. N. "The Colonization Controversy: R. J. Wilmot-Horton and the Classical Economists," in *Economica,* New Series, XXXI (November 1964), 385-400.

Giddings, F. H. *Democracy and Empire.* New York, 1900.

Gollwitzer, H. *Europe in the Age of Imperialism, 1880-1914.* New York, 1969.

Gooch, G. P. *Imperialism: The Heart of the Empire* (2nd ed.). London, 1907.

Gordon, W. E. "Imperial Policy Decisions in the Economic History of Jamaica, 1664-1934," in *Social Economic Studies,* VI (March 1957), 1-28.

Grant, W. J. *The New Burma.* London, 1942.

Greaves, I. "The Character of British Colonial Trade," in *Journal of Political Economics,* LXII (February 1954), 1-12.

Greene, M. "Schumpeter's Imperialism: A Critical Note," in *Social Research,* XIX (December 1952), 453-63.

Greene, T. P. *American Imperialism in 1898.* Boston, 1955.

Gretton, G. (ed.). *Communism and Colonialism: Essays.* New York, 1964.

Gretton, R. H. *Imperialism and Mr. Gladstone.* London, 1913.

Grossmann, H. "Eine neue Theorie über Imperialismus und die soziale Revolution," in *Archiv für die Geschichte des Sozialismus und der Arbeiterbewegung,* XIII (1928), 141-92.

————. *Das Akkumulations- und Zusammenbruchsgesetz des kapitalistischen Systems.* Leipzig, 1929.

Gruchman, L. *Nationalsozialistische Grossraumordnung: die Konstruktion einer 'Deutschen Monroe Doktrine.'* Stuttgart, 1962.

Hagen, E. E. *The Economic Development of Burma.* NAPA Planning Pamphlet No. 1, 96, 1956.

Halgren, M. A. *The Tragic Fallacy: A Study of America's War Policies.* New York, 1937.

Hall, W. P. *Empire to Commonwealth: 30 Years of British Imperial History.* New York, 1928.

Hallgarten, G. W. F. *Imperialismus vor 1914* (2nd ed.). 2 vols. Munich, 1963.

Hallowell, J. (ed.). *Soviet Satellite Nations: A Study of the New Imperialism.* Gainesville, 1958.

Hamilton, E. J. "The Role of Monopoly in the Overseas Expansion and Colonial Trade of Europe Before 1800," in *American Economic Association, Papers and Proceedings,* XXXVIII (May 1948), 33-53.

Hammond, R. J. "Economic Imperialism: Sidelights on a Stereotype," in *Journal of Economic History,* XXI (December 1961), 582-98.

Hancock, W. K. "Agenda for the Study of British Imperial Economy, 1850-1950," in *Journal of Economic History,* XIII, 3 (1953), 257-73.

————. *Wealth of Colonies.* Cambridge, 1950.

Harnetty, P. "The Imperialism of Free Trade: Lancashire and the Indian Cotton Duties, 1859-62," in *Economic History Review,* Ser. 2, XVIII (August 1965), 333-49.

Harper-Smith, J. W. "The Colonial Stock Acts and the British Guiana Constitution of 1891," in *Social and Economic Studies*, XIV (September 1965), 252-63.

Harvey, G. E. *British Rule in Burma, 1824-1942*. London, 1946.

Hashagen, J. "Marxismus und Imperialismus," in *Jahrbücher für Nationalökonomie und Statistik*, CXIII (July 1919), 193-216.

Hawtrey, R. G. *Economic Aspects of Sovereignty*. New York and London, 1930.

Hazard, L. *Empire Revisited*. Homewood, 1965.

Heckscher, E. F. *Mercantilism*. (rev. ed). London and New York, 1955.

Heimann, E. "Schumpeter and the Problems of Imperialism," in *Social Research*, XIX (June 1952), 177-97.

Henderson, W. O. "British Economic Activity in the German Colonies, 1884-1914," in *Economic History Review*, XV (1945), 56-66.

————. "German Economic Penetration in the Middle East, 1870-1914," in *Economic History Review*, XVIII, 1-2 (1948), 54-64.

————. "Germany's Trade with Her Colonies, 1884-1914," in *Economic History Review*, IX (November 1938), 1-16.

Hilferding, R. "Boehm-Bawerk's Criticism of Marx," in P. M. Sweezy (ed.), *Karl Marx and the Close of His System.* New York, 1959.

————. *Das Finanzkapital*. Vienna, 1910.

Hill, D. J., *The Rebuilding of Europe*. New York, 1917.

Hobsbawm, E. J. *Industry and Empire*. London, 1968.

Hobson, J. A. "Capitalism and Imperialism in South Africa," in *Contemporary Review*, 1900.

————. *Confessions of an Economic Heretic* (3rd rev. ed.). London, 1938.

————. *The Economics of Distribution*. New York, 1900.

————. "An Economic Interpretation of Investment," in *The Financial Review of Reviews*, London, 1911.

————. *The Evolution of Modern Capitalism*. London, 1894.

————. *Imperialism: A Study*. New York, 1902.

————. *Imperialism: A Study* (3rd ed.). London, 1948.

————. *The Industrial System.* London, 1909.

————. *Problems of Poverty*. New York, 1889.

————. *The Psychology of Jingoism*. London, 1901.

Hobson, K. C. *The Export of Capital*. London, 1914.

Holbik, K. "West German Development Aid—The Means and Ends," in *Quarterly Review of Economics and Business*, V (Winter 1965), 5-19.

Hook, S. *Towards the Understanding of Karl Marx: A Revolutionary Interpretation*. New York, 1933.

Horrabin, J. F. *An Atlas of Empire*. New York, 1937.

Hoskins, H. L. *European Imperialism in Africa*. New York, 1930.

Hovde, B. J. "Socialistic Theories of Imperialism Prior to the Great War," in *Journal of Political Economy*, XXXVI (October 1928), 569-91.

Hoxie, R. F. "The American Colonial Policy and the Tariff," in *Journal of Political Economy*, XI (March 1930), 198-219.

Hu, S. *Imperialism and Chinese Politics*. Peking, 1955.

Hussey, W. D. *The British Empire and Commonwealth, 1500-1961*. Cambridge, 1963.

Hutchins, F. G. *The Illusion of Permanence*. Princeton, 1967.

Hutchins, J. G. B., *et al.* "The Role of Monopoly in the Colonial Trade and Expansion of Europe: Discussion," in *American Economic Association, Papers and Proceedings*, XXXVIII (May 1948), 63-71.

Huttenback, R. A. *British Imperial Experience*. New York, 1966.

Imlah, A. H. "The Crisis of Trade of the U. K., 1798-1913," in *Journal of Economic History* (November 1950).

————. *Economic Elements in the Pax Britannica*. Cambridge, Mass., 1958.

"Imperialism and Truth," in *Great Britain and the East*, 54 (April 11, 1940), 256.

Innis, H. A. "The Penetrative Powers of the Price System," in *The Canadian Journal of Economics and Political Science*, IV (August 1938), 299-319.

Issa, M. K. "The Economic Factor Behind the British Occupation of Egypt in 1882," in *L'Egypte Contemporaine*, LV (October 1964), 43-57.

Iyengar, S. K. "British and Indian Finance," in *Indian Journal of Economics*, XXI (April 1941), 830-37.

Jaffe, P. J. "Economic Provincialism and American Far Eastern Policy," in *Science and Society*, V, 4, 289-309.

Jalee, P. *The Pillage of the Third World*. New York, 1968.

Jenkins, E. C. "Economic Equality and the Mandates Commission," in *Journal of Political Economy*, XXXVII (October 1929), 604-16.

Jenks, L. H. *Our Cuban Colony*. H. E. Barnes (ed.). New York, 1928.

————. *The Migration of British Capital to 1875*. New York, 1927.

Jouget, P. *Macedonian Imperialism and the Hellenization of the East*. London, 1928.

Karwal, G. D. "The Political Factor in Indian Economic Depression," in *Indian Journal of Economics*, XIII (January 1933), 377-92.

————. "Buy Swadeshi (Indian)," in *Indian Journal of Economics*, XIII (July 1932), 89-91.

Kat Angelino, A. D. A. de. *Colonial Policy*. Abridged translation from the Dutch by G. J. Renier in collaboration with the author. 2 vols. Chicago, 1931.

Kaufman, K., and Stalson, H. "U.S. Assistance to less Developed Countries," in *Foreign Affairs* (July 1967).

Kautsky, K. "Aeltere und neuere Kolonialpolitik," in *Die Neue Zeit*, XVI, 769-81, 801-16.

————. "Der Imperialismus," in *Die Neue Zeit*, XXXII (1914), 908-22.

————. *Die Internationalität und der Krieg*. Berlin, 1915.

————. "Finanzkapital und Krisen," in *Die Neue Zeit*, XXIX (1911), 764-72; 797-804; 838-46; 874-83.

————. "Krisentheorien," in *Die Neue Zeit,* XX (1901-1902), 37-47; 76-81; 110-18; 133-43.

————. *Nationalstaat, Imperialistischer Staat und Staatenbund.* Nürnberg, 1915.

Keller, A. *Colonization.* New York, 1908.

Kemp, T. *Theories of Imperialism.* London, 1967.

Kepner, C. D., Jr. *Banana Empire: A Case Study of Economic Imperialism.* New York, 1935.

Keynes, J. M. *Indian Currency and Finance.* London, 1924.

Khaled, A. H. "The Colonial Problem: Economic and Political Aspects," in *L'Egypte Contemporaine,* XLVI (January 1955), 1-34.

Kidd, B. *The Control of the Tropics.* London, 1898.

Kidron, M. *Foreign Investments in India.* London, 1965.

Kiernan, V. G. *The Lords of Human Kind. Black Man, Yellow Man and White Man in an Age of Empire.* Boston, 1969.

Kindersley, R. "British Overseas Investment, 1938," *Economic Journal* (December 1939).

Kittrell, E. R. "The Development of the Theory of Colonization in English Classical Political Economy," in *Southern Economic Journal,* XXXI (January 1965), 189-206.

Knorr, K. E. *British Colonial Theories, 1570-1850.* Toronto, 1963.

Knowles, L. C. A. *The Economic Development of the British Overseas Empire.* London, 1924.

Koebner, R. *Empire.* Cambridge, 1961.

————. "The Concept of Economic Imperialism," in *Economic History Review,* Ser. 2, II, 1 (1949), 1-29.

Koebner, R., and Schmidt, H. D. *Imperialism: The Story and Significance of a Political Word, 1840-1960.* Cambridge, 1964.

Kohn, H. *Nationalism and Imperialism in the Hither East.* London, 1932.

————. "Reflections on Colonialism," in Robert Strausz-Hupé and Harry Hazard (eds.), *The Idea of Colonialism.* New York, 1958.

————. *World Order in Historical Perspective.* Cambridge, Mass., 1942.

Kojima, K. "Japan's Foreign Trade Policy," in *Hitotsubashi Journal of Economics,* VI· (February 1966), 45-60.

Kolarz, W. *Russia and Her Colonies.* New York, 1955.

Kulp, B. "The Influence of Foreign Trade on Income Distribution," in *Weltwirtschaftliches Archiv,* XCVII (September 1966), 116-38.

LaFeber, W. *The New Empire: An Interpretation of American Expansion, 1860-1898.* Ithaca, 1963.

Laidler, H. W. (ed.). *New Tactics in Social Conflict.* New York, 1958.

Landes, D. S. *Bankers and Pashas.* Cambridge, Mass., 1958.

————. "Some Thoughts on the Nature of Economic Imperialism," in *Journal of Economic History,* XXI (December 1961), 496-521.

Langer, W. L. "A Critique of Imperialism," in *Foreign Affairs*, XIV (October 1935), 102-119.

――――. *The Diplomacy of Imperialism, 1890-1902*. New York, 1935.

Lannoy, de C., and Linden, H. V. *Histoire de l'expansion coloniale des peuples européens*. 3 vols. Brussels, 1907-1921. Vol. 1 *Portugal et Espagne*. Vol 2 *Néerlande et Danemark*. Vol. 3 *Suède*.

Lehman, F. "Great Britain and the Supply of Railway Locomotives of India: A Case Study of Economic Imperialism," *Indian Economic and Social History Review*, II (October 1965), 297-306.

Lenin, V. I. *Imperialism, the Highest Stage of Capitalism*. New York, 1933.

LeRoy, J. A. "Laissez-Faire in the Philippine Islands," in *Journal of Political Economy*, XII (March 1904), 191-207.

Lewis, M. D. *British in India: Imperialism or Trusteeship*. New York, 1942.

Liska, G. *Imperial America: The International Politics of Primacy*. Baltimore, 1967.

Lubell, H. "The Soviet Oil Offensive," in *Quarterly Review of Economics and Business*, I (November 1961), 7-18.

Lugard, F. J. D. *The Dual Mandate in British Tropical Africa*. (5th ed.). London, 1965.

Luxemburg, R. *The Accumulation of Capital*. New York, 1964.

――――. *Die Akkumulation des Kapitals: ein Beitrag zur ökonomischen Erklärung des Imperialismus*. Berlin, 1921.

――――. *Die Akkumulation des Kapitals oder was die Epigonen aus der Marxschen Theorie gemacht haben: eine Antikritik*. Leipzig, 1921.

MacDonagh, O. "The Anti-Imperialism of Free Trade," in *Economic History Review*, Ser. 2, XLV (April 1962), 489-501.

Magdoff, H. "Militarism and Imperialism," in *The American Economic Review, Papers and Proceedings*, LX, 2 (May 1970), 237-42.

――――. *The Age of Imperialism*. New York, 1969.

Mandel, E. *Marxist Economic Theory*. 2 vols. London, 1968.

Marwick, A. *Britain in the Century of Total War*. Boston, 1968.

Marx, K. *Capital*, translated by Ernest Untermann. Chicago, 1906, 1909.

――――. *Capital, the Communist Manifesto and Other Writings*, ed. with an introduction by Max Eastman, with an unpublished essay on Marxism by Lenin. New York, 1932.

――――. *Der Bürgerkrieg in Frankreich*. Leipzig, 1876.

Masani, R. P. *Britain in India*. London, 1960.

Masselman, G. "Dutch Colonial Policy in the Seventeenth Century," in *Journal of Economic History*, XXI (December 1961), 455-68.

――――. *The Cradle of Colonialism*. New Haven, 1963.

Mauro, F. "Towards an 'Intercontinental Model': European Overseas Expansion Between 1500 and 1800," in *Economic History Review*, Ser. 2, XIV (August 1961), 1-17.

May, R. S. "Direct Overseas Investment in Nigeria, 1953-63," in *Scottish Journal of Political Economy*, XII (November 1965), 243-66.

May, R. S., and Plaza, G. *The United Fruit Company in Latin America.* Washington, D. C., 1958.

Merk, F. *Manifest Destiny and Mission in American History: A Reinterpretation.* New York, 1963.

Miliband, R, and Saville, J. (eds.). *Socialist Register.* New York, 1964.

Miyamoto, M., Sakudo, Y., and Yasuba, Y. "Economic Development in Pre-industrial Japan, 1859-1894," in *Journal of Economic History,* XXV (December 1965), 541-64.

Mizuno, F. "Trends in East-West Trade and the Position of Asia," in *Asian Affairs,* III (March 1958), 56-70.

Model, L. "The Politics of Private Foreign Assistance," in *Foreign Affairs* (July 1967).

Moon, P. T. *Imperialism and World Politics.* New York, 1926.

Moore, R. J. "Imperialism and 'Free Trade' Policy in India, 1953-54," in *Economic History Review,* Ser. 2, XVII (August 1964), 135-45.

Morgan, H. W. *America's Road to Empire: The War with Spain and Overseas Expansion.* New York, 1965.

Morgan, T. "The Pattern of Commodity Trade," in *Economics and the Idea of Mankind,* Bert F. Hoselitz (ed.). New York, 1965.

Muir, R. *The Expansion of Europe: The Culmination of Modern History.* Boston and New York, 1923.

Mukerjee, T. "The Theory of Economic Drain: Britain in India in the Nineteenth Century." Paper presented at the Western Economic Association Conference, Long Beach, California, August 1969. Abstract published in *Western Economic Journal,* VII (September 1969).

Mukherjee, R. *The Rise and Fall of the East India Company* (2nd ed.). Berlin, 1952.

Mullett, C. F. "English Imperial Thinking, 1764-1783," in *Political Science Quarterly,* XLV (December 1930), 548-79.

Mummery, A. F., and Hobson, J. A. *The Physiology of Industry: Being an Exposure of Certain Fallacies in Existing Theories of Economics.* London, 1889.

Mun, T. *A Discourse of Trade from England into the East Indies.* London, 1621.

Murray, G. *Liberalism and the Empire.* London, 1900.

Myint, H. *The Economies of the Developing Countries.* London, 1964.

Myrdal, G. *Asian Drama.* 3 vols. New York, 1968.

Nadel, G. H., and Curtis, P. (eds.). *Imperialism and Colonialism.* New York, 1964.

Nagaoka, S. "A Study on the Formation of Colonies Under Mercantilism," in *Rekuski Kyoiku,* II (December 1954), 29-34.

Nearing, S. *Tragedy of Empire.* Harborside, 1945.

————. *The Twilight of Empire.* New York, 1930.

Nearing, S., and Freeman, J. *Dollar Diplomacy: A Study in American Imperialism.* New York, 1925.

Neisser, H. "Economic Imperialism Reconsidered," in *Social Research,* XXVII (April 1960), 63-82.

Nettels, C. P. "British Mercantilism and the Economic Development of the Thirteen Colonies," in *Journal of Economic History,* XII (Spring 1952), 105-14.

Nichols, J. P. "The United States Congress and Imperialism, 1861-1897," in *Journal of Economic History,* XXI (December 1961), 526-38.

Nicholson, J. S. "The Economies of Imperialism," in *Economic Journal,* XX (June 1910), 155-71.

————. *A Project of Empire: A Critical Study of the Economics of Imperialism.* London, 1910.

Niebuhr, R. *The Structure of Nations and Empires.* New York, 1959.

Nkrumah, K. *Neocolonialismo, última etapa del imperialismo.* Mexico City, 1966.

————. *Neo-colonialism: The Last Stage of Imperialism.* New York, 1966.

O'Brien, D. P. "McCulloch and India," in *Manchester School of Economics and Social Studies,* XXXIII (September 1965), 313-17.

Orth, S. *The Imperial Impulse: Background Studies of Belgium, England, Germany and Russia.* New York, 1916.

Oser, J. "Private Enterprise, Government Intervention, and Economic Development," in *Quarterly Review of Economics and Business,* IV, 2 (1964), 31-41.

Owen, D. W. *Imperialism and Nationalism.* New York, 1920.

Padmore, G. *Africa, Britain's Third Empire.* London, 1948.

————. *How Britain Rules Africa.* London, 1936.

Page, H. W. "Profit Sharing Between Producing Countries and Oil Companies in the Middle East: A Reply," (followed by E. Penrose's Rejoinder), in *Economic Journal,* LXX (September 1960), 622-30.

Paish, G. "Great Britain's Capital Investments in Individual Colonies and Foreign Countries," in *Journal of Royal Statistical Society,* LXXIV (1910-11).

Palloix, C. *Problèmes de la croissance en Economie Ouverte.* Paris, 1969.

Pannikar, K. M. *Asia and Western Dominance.* London, 1953.

Pares, R. "The Economic Factors in the History of the Empire," in *Economic History Review,* VII (May 1937), 119-44.

Parrish, J. B. "Iron and Steel in the Balance of World Power," in *Journal of Political Economy,* LXIV (October 1956), 369-88.

Parry, J. H. *The Age of Reconnaissance.* Cleveland, 1963.

————. *The Spanish Theory of Empire in the Sixteenth Century.* Cambridge, 1940.

Patel, S. J. "British Economic Thought and the Treatment of India as a Colony," in *Indian Economic Journal,* XXVII (April 1947), 367-71.

Pavlovitch, Michel (Mikhail Lazarevich Weltmann). *The Foundations of Imperialist Policy.* London, 1922.

Peffer, N. *The White Man's Dilemma.* New York, 1927.

Penner, R. G. "The Benefits of Foreign Investment in Canada, 1950-1956," in *Canadian Journal of Economics and Political Science,* XXXII (May 1966), 172-83.

Penrose, E. "Middle East Oil: The International Distribution of Profits and Income Taxes," in *Economica,* New Series, XXVII (August 1960), 203-13.

————. "Profit-Sharing Between Producing Countries and Oil Companies in the Middle East," in *Economic Journal,* LXIX (June 1959), 238-54.

Phillips, C. H. *The East India Company, 1784-1834.* Birmingham, 1940.

Pigou, A. C. *The Political Economy of War.* New York, 1941.

Pope, A. B. "Imperialism and Colonialism: Origins and Early Development," in *United Asia,* X (April 1958), 146-53.

Porter, B. *Critics of Empire.* New York, 1969.

Power, T. F., Jr. *Jules Ferry and the Renaissance of French Imperialism.* New York, 1966.

Pratt, J. W. *America's Colonial Experiment.* New York, 1950.

Price, J. M. "Origins of Modern Economic Life: (Comparative Illustrations) Discussion of papers by R. P. Thomas and A. C. Land," in *Journal of Economic History,* XXV (December 1965), 655-59.

Priestly, H. I. *France Overseas: A Study of Modern Imperialism.* New York and London, 1938.

Primus (pseud). *L'Impérialisme et la décadence capitaliste.* Paris, 1928.

Pruden, D., and Steinberg, S. *Colonialism, Yesterday, Today and Tomorrow.* New York, 1956.

Rabb, T. K. *Enterprise and Empire.* Cambridge, Mass., 1967.

Rai, L. *England's Debt to India.* New York, 1917.

Rangnekar, D. K. *Poverty and Capital Development in India.* London, 1958.

Reich, E. *Success Among Nations.* London, 1904.

————. *Imperialism.* London, 1905.

Reid, A. G. "General Trade Between Quebec and France During the French Regime," in *Canadian History Review,* XXXIV (March 1953), 18-32.

Reimann, G. *The Myth of the Total State.* New York, 1941.

Reinsch, P. S. *World Politics at the End of the Nineteenth Century, As Influenced by the Oriental Situation.* New York, 1900.

Renner, K. *Marxismus, Krieg und Internationale.* Stuttgart, 1918.

Ricardo, D. *The Principles of Political Economy and Taxation.* Everyman's Library.

Richards, C. S. "Africa and the World Economy," in *South African Journal of Economics,* VII (September 1939), 305-9.

Robbins, L. *The Economic Causes of War.* London, 1939.

————. *The Economic Causes of War.* New York, 1967.

Roberts, S. H. *History of French Colonial Policy: 1870-1925.* Hamden, Conn., 1963.

Robinson, H. *The Development of the British Empire.* Boston, 1922.

Robinson, J. *Economics: An Awkward Corner.* New York, 1967.

Robinson, R. *Africa and the Victorians.* New York, 1961.
————. "The Partition of Africa," in *The New Cambridge Modern History,* Vol. 2, Cambridge, 1962.
Robinson, R., and Gallagher, J. *Africa and the Victorians: The Official Mind of Imperialism.* New York, 1961.
Romilly J. de. *Thucydides and Athenian Imperialism,* translated by P. Thody. Oxford, 1963.
Rose, J. H. (ed.). *The Cambridge History of the British Empire.* 8 vols. Cambridge, 1929-1963.
Salera, V. "A Note on Profit-Sharing in Middle East Oil," in *Economic Journal,* LXIX (December 1959), 812-13.
Salz, A. "Die Zukunft des Imperialismus," in *Weltwirtschaftliches Archiv,* XXXII (October 1930), 317-48.
Saul, S. B. "The Economic Significance of 'Constructive Imperialism,' " in *Journal of Economic History,* XVII (June 1957), 173-92.
————. *Studies in British Overseas Trade, 1870-1914.* Liverpool, 1960.
Schatz, S. P. "Economic Imperialism Again" (Comment, followed by H. Neisser's Rejoinder), in *Social Research,* XXVIII (October 1961), 355-58.
Schippel, M. "Kolonialpolitik," in *Sozialistische Monatshefte,* XIV (January 9, 1908), 3-10.
Schuman, F. L. *International Politics.* New York, 1958.
Schumpeter, J. A. *Capitalism, Socialism, and Democracy.* (3rd ed.). New York, 1943.
————. *Imperialism and Social Classes.* New York, 1951.
————. "Zur Soziologie der Imperialismen," in *Archiv für Sozialwissenschaft und Sozialpolitik,* XLVI (December 1918), 1-39; (June 1919), 275-310.
Schurman, J. G. *Philippine Affairs.* New York, 1902.
Schuyler, R. L. "The Climax of Anti-Imperialism in England," in *Political Science Quarterly,* XXXVI (December 1921), 537-60.
————. *The Fall of the Old Colonial System: A Study in British Free Trade, 1770-1870.* New York, 1945.
————. "The Rise of Anti-Imperialism in England," in *Political Science Quarterly,* XXXVII (September 1922), 440-471.
Schwadron, B. *The Middle East, Oil and The Great Powers.* London, 1955.
Seeley, J. R. *The Expansion of England.* London, 1883.
Seers, D. "Big Companies and Small Countries: A Practical 'Proposal,' " in *Kyklos,* XVI, 4 (1963), 599-607.
Seillière, E. *Introduction à la philosophie de l'impérialisme.* Paris, 1911.
————. *La Philosophie de l'impérialisme.* Paris, 1903-1908.
Semmel, B. *Imperialism and Social Reform: English Social-Imperial Thought, 1895-1914.* Cambridge, Mass., 1960.
————. "On the Economics of Imperialism," in B. F. Hoselitz (ed.) *Economics and the Ideas of Mankind.* New York, 1965.
Seton-Watson, H. *The New Imperialism.* London, 1961.
Shimkin, D. B. "The Structure of Soviet Power," in *Quarterly Review of Economics and Business,* III (November 1963), 19-24.

Shizuta, H. "Imperialism as a Concept," in *Kyoto University Economic Review*, XXXI (April 1961), 1-13.

Singh, V. B. (ed.). *Economic History of India, 1857-1956*. Bombay, 1962.

Sklar, M. J. "The N. A. M. and Foreign Markets on the Eve of the Spanish-American War," in *Science and Society*, XXIII, 2 (1959), 133-62.

Smith, A. *An Inquiry Into the Nature and Causes of the Wealth of Nations*. Chicago, 1952. Available in a 2 vol. paperback edition.

Smith, D. T. "Financial Variables in International Business," in *Harvard Business Review*, XLIV (January-February 1966), 93-104.

Smith, G. *Commonwealth or Empire*. New York, 1962.

Snape, R. H. *Britain and the Empire, 1867-1945*. Cambridge, 1952.

Snyder, L. L. (ed.). *The Imperialism Reader*. Princeton, 1962.

Southworth, C. *The French Colonial Venture*. London, 1931.

Sovani, N. V. "British Impact on India After 1857," in *Cahiers d'histoire mondiale* (July 1954).

—————. "British Impact on India Before 1850-1857," in *Cahiers d'histoire mondiale* (April 1954).

Speers, P. C. "Colonial Policy of the British Labor Party," in *Social Research*, XV (September 1948), 304-26.

Sprout, H., and Margaret. "Dilemma of Rising Demands and Insufficient Resources," in *World Politics*, XX, 4 (July 1968).

Staley, E. "The Economic Side of Stable Peace," in *Annals of the American Academy of Political and Social Science*, CCXL (July 1945), 27-36.

—————. "Mannesmann Mining Interests and the Franco-German Conflict Over Morocco," in *Journal of Political Economy*, XL (February 1932), 52-72.

—————. "Private Investments and International Politics in the Saar, 1919-1920: A Study of Politico-Economic 'Penetration' in a Post-War Plebiscite Area," in *Journal of Political Economy*, XLI (October 1933), 577-601.

—————. *War and the Private Investor: A Study in the Relations of International Politics and International Private Investment*. New York, 1935.

Steel, R. *Pax Americana*. New York, 1967.

Sternberg, F. *Der Imperialismus*. Berlin, 1926.

—————. *Der Imperialismus und seine Kritiker*. Berlin, 1929.

—————. "Japan's Economic Imperialism," in *Social Research*, XII (September 1945), 328-48.

Stokes, E. *The Politial Ideas of English Imperialism*. Oxford, 1960.

Strachey, J. *The End of Empire*. New York, 1956.

Strauss, W. L. "Joseph Chamberlain and the Theory of Imperialism," in *American Council on Public Affairs*. Washington, D.C., 1942.

Sutherland, L. S. *The East India Company in Eighteenth Century Politics*. New York, 1952.

Sweezy, P. M. *The Theory of Capitalist Development: Principles of Marxian Political Economy.* New York, 1956.

————. "Three Works on Imperialism (Arctic and Antarctica)," in *Journal of Economic History,* XIII, 2 (1953), 193-201.

Sweezy, P. M., and Baran, A. *Monopoly Capital: An Essay on the American Economic and Social Order.* New York, 1966.

Taira, K. "Ryukyu Islands Today: Political Economy of a U. S. Colony," in *Science and Society,* XXII, 2 (1958), 113-28.

Taniguchi, K. "The Theory of Wider Territory Economy," in *Kyoto University Economic Review,* XVI (October 1941), 20-41.

Taylor, A. J. P. *The Rise and Fall of Diplomatic History.* London, 1956.

————. *A History of Economic Thought.* New York, 1960.

Thomas, R. P. "A Quantitative Approach to the Study of the Effects of British Imperial Policy upon Colonial Welfare: Some Preliminary Findings," in *Journal of Economic History,* XXV (December 1965), 615-38.

Thompson, A. H. "British Imperialism and the Autonomous Rights of Races," in *Kansas City Review of Science and Industry,* III (1879), 229-34.

Thorner, D. *Investment in Empire.* Philadelphia, 1950.

Thornton, A. P. *The Imperial Idea and Its Enemies: A Study in British Power.* New York, 1959.

————. *Doctrines of Imperialism.* New York, 1965.

Thurow, L. C. *Poverty and Discrimination.* Washington, D.C., 1969.

Tinbergen, J. *Shaping the World Economy.* New York, 1962.

Tinkes, H. *The Union of Burma.* London, 1957.

Townsend, M. E. "The Economic Impact of Imperial Germany: Commercial and Colonial Policies," in *Economic History Association, The Tasks of Economic History,* III (December 1943), 124-34.

————. *The Rise and Fall of Germany's Colonial Empire: 1884-1918.* New York, 1930.

Tucker, R. S. "A Balance Sheet of the Philippines," in *Harvard Business Review,* VIII (October 1929), 10-23.

Usher, A. P. "The Role of Monopoly in Colonial Trade and in the Expansion of Europe Subsequent to 1800," in *American Economic Association, Papers and Proceedings,* XXXVIII (May 1948), 54-62.

Van Alstyne, R. W. *Rising American Empire.* New York, 1960.

Vanderbosch, A. "The Netherlands Colonial Balance Sheet," in *Southern Economic Journal,* IV (January 1938), 328-38.

Varga, E., and Mendelsohn, L. *New Data for Lenin's "Imperialism."* New York, 1940.

Viallate, A. *Economic Imperialism and International Relations During the Last Fifty Years.* New York, 1923.

Viekke, B. H. M. *Nusantara: A History of Indonesia* (rev. ed.). Chicago, 1960.

Villari, L. *The Expansion of Italy.* London, 1930.

Vindex (ed.). *Cecil Rhodes: His Political Life and Speeches, 1881-1900*. London, 1900.

Viner, J. "International Finance and Balance of Power Diplomacy, 1880-1914," in *The Southwestern Political and Social Science Quarterly*, IX (March 1929), 407-51.

—————. "Political Aspects of International Finance, Part I-II," in *Journal of Business*, I (April-July 1928), 141-73; 324-63.

Volkov, A., and Grebennikov, B. "Soviet-Chinese Economic Collaboration," in *Problems of Economics*, I (March 1959), 66-69.

Wagner, D. O. "British Economists and the Empire," in *Political Science Quarterly*, XLVI (June 1931), 248-76; XLVII (March 1932), 57-74.

Wells, S. *Trade Policies for Britain*. London, 1966.

Wesson, R. G. *The Imperial Order*. Berkeley, 1967.

Weyl, W. E. *American World Policies*. New York, 1917.

Williams, W. A. *The Roots of Modern American Empire*. New York, 1969.

Winch, D. N. *Classical Political Economy and Colonies*. London and Cambridge, Mass., 1965.

—————. "Edward Gibbon Wakefield and American Development," in *Explorations in Entrepreneurial History*, II, 1, 3 (1964), 263-75.

Winks, R. W. *British Imperialism: Gold, God, Glory: European Problem Studies*. New York, 1963.

Winslow, E. *The Anti-Imperialist League: Apologia pro vita sua*. Boston, 1898.

—————. "Marxian, Liberal and Sociological Theories of Imperialism," in *Journal of Political Economy*, XXXIX (December 1931), 713-58.

—————. *The Pattern of Imperialism: A Study in the Theories of Power*. New York, 1948.

Woddis, J. *Introduction to Neo-Colonialism*. New York, 1968.

Wolff, R. D. "Modern Imperialism: The View from the Metropolis," in *The American Economic Review, Papers and Proceedings*, LX, 2 (May 1970), 225-30.

Woodruff, W. *Impact of Western Man*. New York, 1966.

Woolf, L. S. *Economic Imperialism*. London, 1921.

—————. *Empire and Commerce in Africa*. London, 1920.

Wright, A. *East Indian Economic Problems*. London, 1961.

Wright, H. M. (ed.). *The "New Imperialism": Analysis of Late Nineteenth Century Expansion*. Boston, 1961.

Wright, H. R. C. "The Anglo-Dutch Dispute in the East, 1814-1824," in *Economic History Review*, Ser. 2, III, 2 (1950), 229-39.

Yagi, Y. "The Agricultural Interrelation of Japan, Manchukuo and China," in *Kyoto University Economic Review*, XIV (July 1939), 23-44.

Young, A. A. *Economic Problems New and Old*. Boston, 1927.

Zimmerman, L., and Grumbach, F. "Saving, Investment, and Imperialism: A Reconsideration of the Theory of Imperialism," in *Weltwirtschaftliches Archiv*, LXXI, 1 (1953), 1-19.

Index